ROOTS AND SHOOTS

A Guide to Counselling and Psychotherapy

ROOTS AND SHOOTS

A Guide to Counselling and Psychotherapy

ROGER HURDING

HODDER AND STOUGHTON
LONDON   SYDNEY   AUCKLAND   TORONTO

ACKNOWLEDGMENTS

T. S. Eliot Extract from 'Fragment of an Agon' in *Collected Poems 1909–1962* (London: Faber and Faber Ltd. 1963). Reprinted by permission of the publishers.

B. A. Farrell *The Standing of Psychoanalysis* (Oxford University Press 1981). Used with permission.

Frank Lake *Tight Corners in Pastoral Counselling* (London: Darton, Longman and Todd Ltd. Published and copyright 1981) and *Clinical Theology* (DLT 1961). Used by permission of the publishers.

B. F. Skinner *Beyond Freedom and Dignity* (Harmondsworth: Penguin Books Ltd. 1973). Used with permission of Jonathan Cape Ltd., London.

Steve Turner 'History Lesson' in *Up To Date* (London: Hodder and Stoughton 1983). Reprinted by permission of the publishers.

Ken Wilber *No Boundary: Eastern and Western approaches to personal growth* (Boulder, Colorado: Shambhala Publications 1981).

Unless stated to the contrary, all Bible references are from the New International Version (Hodder and Stoughton 1979).

British Library Cataloguing in Publication Data

Hurding, Roger
   Roots and shoots: a guide to counselling and
   psychotherapy.
   1. Pastoral counselling
   I. Title
   253.5   BV4012.2

   ISBN 0 340 38327 5

To friends and colleagues

at

CARE & COUNSEL

CONTENTS

Preface

PART I   THE RISE OF THE SECULAR PSYCHOLOGIES

PART II   CHRISTIAN REACTION AND RESPONSE

DIAGRAMS

PREFACE

At the 1980 Christian Booksellers' Convention in London, on the occasion of the publication of my first book *Restoring the Image*, a young man I had never met before accosted me with the words, 'Do you follow Jay Adams, or Narramore?' As far as I can remember, I replied, 'Neither!' I was astounded that, in at least some Christian circles, there were seen to be only two possible schools of thought in the area of counselling. Gradually, over the next few years, I resolved to sort out my own thinking with respect to the bewildering range of approaches to counselling and psychotherapy held by believers and non-believers on both sides of the Atlantic. Why were there, for example, so many different methodologies within the burgeoning movement of the so-called 'new therapies'? Were they all valid in one way or another? On the other hand, did their essential humanism rule them all out of court for the Christian? Or, were some of the approaches acceptable to the believer? If so, which and on what grounds? Was it right to 'baptise the therapies'? And what about those types of counselling that were claimed to be Christian: 'biblical', 'discipleship', 'growth', 'nouthetic', 'dialogue', 'spiritual' and 'prayer' counselling methods, the concept of the 'inner journey' and a number of attempts to heal the past – including inner healing, primal integration and the healing of the family tree? Were all these emphases authentic in their different ways? Were some more Christian, more biblical or more orthodox than the others? Was there only *one* method that could claim to be Christian counselling?

In trying to answer these and similar questions I have written a book which seeks to trace the development of today's counselling and psychotherapeutic practice from the soil of the Enlightenment and the ensuing growth of the secular psychologies. It is argued that the rise of these 'listening arts' has, to a large extent, rivalled and, at times, taken over the caring ministry of traditional

Christianity. And yet, the tree of pastoral care is still there – crowded but not choked, hemmed in but not stifled.

I have sought to show, further, that the Church has not been passive towards the contrary growths of behaviourism, psychoanalysis, personalism and transpersonalism. In Part II I explore Christian reaction, assimilation and dialogue in relation to secular modes of caring for the needy. In delineating the terrain of the Church's response I aim to give, particularly in chapter eleven, both a map and a compass to help you and me in our assessment of this or that approach to counselling. On meeting a 'new' system of helping others, whether secular or Christian, my hope is that we will be better able to answer such questions as 'Is this type of counselling or therapy right?', 'What are its assumptions and how do they square up to biblical insight?', 'How do its aims compare with God's revelation for our lives?' and 'Are the techniques it puts forward ones that respect the value of our createdness and humanity?'.

Like so many contemporary writers, I have been much exercised on the issue of sexist language. I find myself caught between my sympathies for feminism and for the living language. I have thus sometimes compromised radicalism for the sake of style. For example, the generic word 'man' is used where it seems required by the balance of a phrase and the cumbersome 'humankind' is occasionally sacrificed for the simpler 'mankind'.

In writing a book which examines the methodologies of different protagonists, I put myself on the line. I realise the danger of misrepresenting others. We all, of course, have ideas that change and develop. What we argued in 1975 we may have left behind in 1985 – and may even have returned to in 1995. It is those ideas, even if outdated from the originator's point of view, that may still be worth exploring. In doing this, I have done my best to be fair and accurate but, at the same time, I apologise to any I have inadvertently offended. My aim has been, where possible, to find a common bond with the views of others. I have tried to avoid a partisan approach which polarises too readily into 'either-or' positions. I am increasingly aware that God's thoughts are far above ours and that his truth cannot be held captive by one party or another. Jesus himself is the Truth and it is in relationship with him that we can move humbly towards greater understanding. Such caution is as appropriate in the complex area of the human sciences as in any other. Nonetheless, I trust there is some cutting edge in my observations on counselling and psychotherapy which will stimulate further thought, prayer and action in the service of the Lord.

I am indebted to many people for the compilation of this book: to Joy and our family – Sarah, Simon and Rachel – for their love and patience during nearly three years of writing; to the secretarial help of Penny Tuohy and Pam Lapraik in the earlier chapters; to the meticulous care of Janet Croysdale in helping me sift the text to make the Index; and to the staff at the libraries of Trinity College, Wesley College, the Medical Faculty of the University of Bristol, Barrow Hospital and Avon County Council. Behind all the practicalities, I would like to express my gratitude to colleagues in the caring professions who have stimulated thinking and discussion at the interface between theology and psychology. These comprise, in particular, members of an association of Christian psychiatrists and other professionals, who have met informally in Bristol since the early 1970s, and of the study group held under the auspices of Care and Counsel, a Christian counselling service based in London. There are many names that could be included but I would prefer to make special mention of Monty Barker, Michael Clarke, Finn Cosgrove, Glyn Harrison, Tim and Anne Hockridge, Glenn Roberts, Alison Sankey and Jan Smith amongst the former, and David Atkinson, Myra Chave-Jones, Jenny Francis, Joy Guy, Sonia Hall, Harold Harland, Julie Holborn, Denzil Jarvis, Elizabeth Shedden and Ian Williams of the latter; my good friends Roger Moss and Richard Winter have links with both groups. Finally, I would like to thank David Atkinson, Joy Guy, Nick Isbister, Peter van de Kasteele, John Wesson and Peter Williams for their perceptive comments on different aspects of the text. I am particularly grateful to Joy Guy and Nick Isbister for their discerning views on the manuscript, and to Nick for his helpful suggestions on references, especially on Freud and Laing.

Some Christians despair of any good coming from the counselling movement and urge us to return to the Bible, the Church Fathers or Christian tradition for all our perspectives on caring for others. I sympathise with these views but would rather argue that, for those with eyes to see, there is much within secular therapy that is an expression of God's common grace and harmonises with his revealed word. There is a great need for those of us with Christian convictions to sift the methodologies on offer so that we may discern evidences of the kingdom. In doing this we aim at an integration of valid psychological and theological insight. Such an enterprise should not be a mere academic exercise but an attempt to bring the love of the Father, the fellowship of the Son and the healing power of the Spirit into every part of the lives we seek to help.

Roger F. Hurding, Trinity 1985

PART I

THE RISE OF THE SECULAR PSYCHOLOGIES

1

INTRODUCTION: THE TREE OF PASTORAL CARE

History repeats itself.
Has to.
No-one listens.
                Steve Turner

In a book which examines the rise of the secular psychologies and the range of Christian adjustments to that rise, it is important to put the discussion into historical context. In today's debate on the validity of counselling and psychotherapy and the relation between these often highly professionalised activities and the day-to-day pastoral concerns of the Church, there are many questions to be asked. Is 'counselling' a purely twentieth century phenomenon – exported to Western Europe from the United States along with Levi jeans, McDonalds restaurants, 'Dallas' and Cruise missiles? Or, is it an elaboration of an age-old caring of one human being for another? Whatever the origins of the counselling movement, how should Christian people view its blandishments? Should the insights of counsellors and psychotherapists be welcomed or rejected by the Church? If welcomed, should these 'new' perceptions simply enhance traditional pastoral care – or be allowed to usurp it? If rejected, what is the basis for our dismissal?

However we understand the place of counselling and psychotherapy today (and it is the aim of this book to wrestle with that issue), we should recall that God's people have always had a commitment to love one another and to care for neighbour and 'enemy' alike. This burden of compassion has a track record of at least two thousand years' duration and has issued in countless 'acts of mercy', restitutions and reforms. We can, perhaps, see

the history of this 'love in action' as a great tree – the tree of
pastoral care – with its roots deep in the soil of God's calling, its
trunk and branches growing in obedience to Christ and its life
vitalised by the Spirit.

The story of the growth of this tree has been variously
assessed.[1] Amongst these appraisals, Clebsch and Jaekle's
Pastoral Care in Historical Perspective describes four essential
functions in effective pastoral care:

> The ministry of the cure of souls, or pastoral care, consists of helping
> acts, done by *representative Christian persons*, directed toward the
> *healing, sustaining, guiding*, and *reconciling* of *troubled persons* whose
> troubles arise *in the context of ultimate meanings and concerns*.[2]

This book gives numerous examples of the way 'representative
Christian persons' – from the Western and Eastern Church,
Roman Catholics and Protestants, mystics and activists, sac-
ramentalists and evangelicals – have reached out to others to
bring healing, sustaining, guiding and reconciling. Clebsch and
Jaekle point to the immensely rich heritage of literature which
can inspire and encourage the pastor today – including John
Chrysostom's *Letter to a Young Widow* (*c.*380), Gregory the
Great's *Book of Pastoral Care* (late sixth century), Thomas à
Kempis's *The Imitation of Christ* (early fifteenth century), Martin
Luther's letter, 'Fourteen Comforts for the Weary and Heavy
Laden' (1520), Ignatius Loyola's *Spiritual Exercises* (mid-sixteenth
century) and Richard Baxter's *The Reformed Pastor* (1656). The
value of the re-discovery of traditional pastoral writings by caring
Christians in the twentieth century is also emphasised by Thomas
Oden, the American theologian.[3]

In spite of the stimulus to growth given by such historical
works, the life of the tree of pastoral care has not always been
strong. Apart from inner weakness due to distortions of biblical
perspectives and quenchings of the Spirit, outside influences
have at certain periods threatened to sap the vitality from
Christian caring. At times, it is as if rival trees have grown
stiflingly close at hand in the field of human need so that a
veritable thicket of alternative systems has grown up. At other
times, there has been more space in our imaginary forest and the
effect of neighbouring trees has been less intrusive. Whether the
influence is baleful, neutral or even companionable, it is perhaps

inevitable that the nature and quality of the Church's pastoral care is affected to some extent by surrounding ideologies. Clebsch and Jaekle put the point more positively when they declare that 'pastoral care has always utilised current psychologies'.[4] We can see this borrowing of ideas, for instance, in the influence of Stoicism on John Chrysostom[5], of Aristotelian thinking on Thomas Aquinas in the thirteenth century[6] and in the powerful emphasis on the primacy of reason and will on post-Enlightenment pastors like John Keble.[7]

It was during the seventeenth and eighteenth centuries that the ancient root systems, reaching down to early Greek thought on the nature of humanity, began to push up fresh growth which, in time, produced some especially formidable neighbours for the tree of pastoral care. These impressive giants – the trees of behaviourism, psychoanalysis, personalism and transpersonalism – will be looked at in detail in the coming chapters. Their precursors, in the soil of the Enlightenment, offered competing understandings of human life so that 'Reason' became the final arbiter in matters of belief and morality. As a result, a great deal of pastoral supervision began to centre on the need to sustain the faithful in the face of the perplexities of the age. Against this background, the concept of 'pastoral theology', or pastoralia, was elaborated, influenced by English-speaking Puritanism, German Pietism and classical Reformed Christianity, as well as by Catholicism with its continuing rites and ceremonies. At the same time, great strides were being made outside the boundaries of the Church in the realms of psychological and physical healing.[8] A belief in the prime importance of demonology and witchcraft started to wane and other explanations for the needs and sicknesses of people were sought. As these contending anthropologies established, they threatened to crowd and weaken the tree of traditional Christian pastoral concern. Clebsch and Jaekle write, 'it was during the Englightenment that pastoral healing lapsed into a desuetude from which it has as yet not fully recovered'. Sadly, pastors became 'professional religionists' as they steered people towards 'personal religious virtuosity'.[9]

From the end of the eighteenth century, there was a tendency for devotional practice to become more and more individualistic and private. This stress on 'personal religious virtuosity' led to an increasing receptivity to the psychological insights that were to come. Amongst these insights, the perspectives of the 'psychology of religion' were an almost inevitable by-product of the rise of the psychological sciences. William James (1842–1910), the brother of the novelist Henry James, was a virtually unique influence in the early days of this new study. The son of a Swedenborgian theologian, he held the chair at Harvard University, successively, in medicine, psychology and philosophy. Following the publication of *The Principles of Psychology* in 1890, he was asked to give the Gifford Lectures on Natural Religion at the University of Edinburgh in 1901–1902. The resulting book, *The Varieties of Religious Experience*, is still a best-seller. In it James considered two main categories of people: the 'healthy-minded', or 'once-born'; and the 'sick souls', or 'twice-born'. Under the term 'healthy-minded' he encompassed those optimists who have little or no concept of human sin – and he blamed liberal Christianity as at least partly contributing to this attitude.[10] Although 'healthy-mindedness', with its insatiable quest for happiness, can be an attractive stance, James conceded that the reality of evil and sin will not permit success at the hedonistic level for most of us. He argued that it is the 'sick soul', with his or her sin-consciousness and awareness of suffering, who lives life on a deeper plane and may, through a conversion experience, join the ranks of the 'twice-born'.[11]

In spite of these perceptions about human nature, James was no orthodox Christian. Unable to accept 'either popular Christianity or scholastic theism', he saw his position as that of 'piecemeal supernaturalism'.[12] His approach was essentially that of a pragmatist who found that the idea of a deity makes sense for everyday living; he declared:

> . . . the practical needs and experiences of religion seem to me sufficiently met by the belief that beyond each man and in a fashion continuous with him there exists a larger power which is friendly to him and to his ideals.[13]

William James' pragmatism has been taken as representative of the trends that were threatening to undermine traditional pastoral care at the turn of the century. The more openly antagonistic systems of Darwinism and Freudianism were thriving and the world views of biological determinism and optimistic humanism were more and more to prove dangerous rivals to the

Church's perspectives on humankind. The tree of pastoral care, as we have seen, is used to having other anthropologies in the vicinity. Furthermore, Clebsch and Jaekle argue that pastoral care 'has always utilized current psychologies'. How would Christianity fare in the face of such pressing alternatives as behaviourism, psychoanalysis and secular personalism, as well as the less aggressive questionings of American pragmatism and the psychology of religion? Would it absorb – perhaps uncritically – the insights of its non-Christian counterparts; would it turn inwards – repelled by alien ideas; or would it somehow learn to live alongside its neighbours, spreading out its branches of compassion?

When Clebsch and Jaekle write that 'pastoral care has always utilized current psychologies', they add that it 'produces no unique psychology of its own'.[14] We have conceded that, historically, the Church has for ever stood within the world and thus has been prone to outside influence – in matters of human psychology as in all other areas. However, do we need to conclude that Christian pastoral care 'produces no unique psychology of its own'? It is perhaps self-evident that, with the rise of the secularisation of our understanding of humankind, 'current psychologies' have appeared to be especially oppressive towards the tree of pastoral care. At times its life-giving influence has seemed to be stifled out of recognition by its exuberant neighbours. It is my contention that, behind Christianity's struggles with the human condition, pastoral care does have a 'unique psychology of its own'. This is no obscure or fanciful system of thought but is a psychology that is rooted deeply in the way God has made us. Rival theories, hammered out within the realms of the Creator's 'common grace' as well as under the baleful influence of the Enemy, have often stumbled on the gold nuggets of divine revelation about human nature. My hope and prayer is that this book will help us recover something of this 'unique psychology' as we seek to reach out to others in need. We cannot put the clock back. History is still busy repeating itself. The present alternative systems that seem to rival the Church's ministry are, on the whole, flourishing. Let us aim to understand them, to reject what is false, to discern where God speaks through them and to grasp once more the wonder and distinctiveness of his call to us to give ourselves gladly in caring for our fellow human beings.

2

WHAT IS COUNSELLING?

Good Counsellors lacke no Clients.
Shakespeare *Measure for Measure*

*Anyone with a modicum of human warmth, common sense,
some sensitivity to human problems, and a desire to help can
benefit many candidates for psychotherapy.*
Jerome D. Frank

Having traced certain strands in the history of pastoral care and
noted the emergence of a pastoral theology, or pastoralia, in the
age of Enlightenment, let us begin to define some terms in order
to help our thinking as we discuss the rise of counselling, both
pastoral and secular, during the twentieth century.

What exactly *is* counselling? Is pastoral counselling the same
animal harnessed with a dog collar?[1] Is there such a thing as
Christian counselling? If there is, is it simply the phenomenon of
committed Christians exercising a counselling ministry; or is it
something more specific, with uniquely Christian assumptions,
aims and, possibly, methods? And what of biblical counselling? Is
that an entity more 'Christian' than Christian counselling? Is
there a sequence of increasingly sharp theological understanding
and commitment from 'pastoral' to 'biblical' counselling via
'Christian' counselling? Or, are all three, in their essentials, the
same?

Once we have defined 'counselling' in a reasonable and hopefully acceptable way, we face another fusillade of questions. Can
latter-day counselling be seen in historical continuity with pastoral care? If not in a broad sense, can its 'pastoral', 'Christian'
and/or 'biblical' components be seen as entirely within this
legacy? Moreover, what is the relationship between counselling
done by Christians and evangelism? Are they synonymous?

Are they separate? Do they overlap? And what of psychotherapy? Many talk of psychotherapy and counselling as if they are one and the same. Are they? Or, are there clear-cut distinctions between them?

Let us, before attempting answers in this and the coming chapters, acknowledge that we are trying to pick our way through a particularly tangled forest of complex issues. These issues, because they involve questions of the essence of our humanity, the substance of our difficulties and how they are best resolved, can be examined from so many different vantage points that they may, by their very nature, defy satisfactory analysis. However, it is my conviction that the labyrinth is made more tortuous by a great deal of misunderstanding, muddled thinking and even professional rivalry in the areas of pastoral care, evangelism, counselling, psychotherapy and general psychiatry. It is sometimes difficult to see the complete wood of a common care for humankind for the individual trees of professional and lay concern.

Firstly, it may be useful to look at some recent definitions in which various theorists and practitioners have tried to delineate the essentials of counselling. In doing this, we will find ourselves spending some time considering those qualities that make up the effective counsellor. Although the relations between counselling and psychotherapy, and counselling and evangelism will be considered briefly in this chapter, I shall reserve an attempt to examine biblical insights for counselling in a comprehensive way until later chapters.

Definitions

Mention the word 'counselling' today in certain professional and quasi-professional circles and the reaction will be very mixed. Some will accept the term readily and without question, others, desirous of precise definitions, will be uneasy with using the word in a general way, while yet others will scorn this particular noun as covering such a rag-bag of phenomena that its use is virtually obsolete. This diversity of response is understandable in the light of the multifaceted nature of the so-called 'counselling movement'. We will study the ascendancy of this movement in the coming chapters. In the meantime, it seems to me that many of the concepts under the umbrella term 'counselling' are so useful in the matter of helping one another that it is wisest to do our best in rescuing some sort of workable definition. This is preferable, I suggest, to hunting for alternative terms which are just as open to generalisation and misunderstanding, such as 'pastoring', with its connotations of shepherding care within the body of Christ, and the rather clumsy, and too vague 'people-helping'.

Immediately we seek a clear definition of counselling we are taken into the question of the relationship between counselling and psychotherapy. The link between the two terms has been forged from the 1950s and 1960s onwards and, for many, they are synonymous. For example, Truax and Carkhuff in their book *Towards Effective Counselling and Psychotherapy* use the words interchangeably.[2] Thomas Szasz, arguing against the idea that psychotherapy is a *medical* activity, indicates the difficulty of delineament in this area when he writes:

> . . . psychotherapy is the name we give to a particular kind of personal influence: by means of communication, one person identified as the psychotherapist exerts an ostensibly therapeutic influence on another person identified as the patient. This process is, of course, but a special member of a much larger class – indeed, a class so vast that virtually all human interactions fall within it. In countless other situations people influence one another.[3]

From my own personal experience, working within a medical framework as a general practitioner from 1961 to 1969, with a particular interest in Michael Balint's adaptations of psychotherapy[4], as a Student Health doctor specialising in counselling and psychotherapy from 1969 to 1979 and then in the capacity of counsellor and psychotherapist functioning both privately and as part of a pastoral team from 1980 onwards, I like to argue that there is a continuum from the simplest form of counselling through to the deepest levels of psychotherapy.[5]

This gradation is seen in the vast army of people involved in Western society as counsellors or psychotherapists: general practitioners, social workers, nurses, occupational, speech and art therapists, clinical and educational psychologists, psychiatrists, marriage guidance counsellors, sex therapists, family therapists, hospital chaplains, other clergy and ministers, and a wide range of voluntary workers in every conceivable area of human need. Behind the great variety of caring activities of these professionals and laypersons lie a number of different ways of viewing the human condition. Although the remit of this book is to consider psychological, sociological and theological perspectives primarily, it is essential that we note the importance of the 'medical' model behind a great deal of counselling and psychotherapy – particularly in the context of psychiatry.[6]

Psychiatry, which has been defined as 'that field of study which comprises everything contributing to the recognition, elucidation, prevention, and treatment of mental abnormalities', is regarded as a medical discipline.[7] However, the psychiatrists Eliot Slater and Martin Roth point out psychiatry's 'peculiar position' between medicine and neurology on the one hand and philosophy and psychology on the other. It is this linkage between the natural sciences and the human sciences that is sometimes under strain so that the psychiatrist can feel threatened or misunderstood from both sides. Nonetheless, Slater and Roth declare a prior connection between the general physician, neurologist and psychiatrist and state that the regard by the first two specialties for 'physical manifestations as a prime focus of interest' is the only distinction from the latter.[8]

The view that psychiatry is a branch of medicine has led to the systematisation of mental disorder. This is not the place to give a detailed account of the classification of psychiatric conditions, although it is important that we clarify a few of the commoner terms. The widely used word *neurosis* is extremely difficult to define – as we shall see throughout this book in the variety of ways the term is employed. Most definitions emphasise the presence of faulty responses to inner conflicts. These responses are essentially irrational in the sense that no immediate explanation for them is satisfactory. We find this often irksome lack of logic in, for example, people with a morbid fear of the unknown, intensely obsessive behaviour, an unconsolable degree of depression, persistent physical symptoms that are unrelated to organic disease, or a deeply ingrained anxiety towards every eventuality. However, these apparent irrationalities do begin to make sense as the patient's thoughts, feelings and experiences are explored.[9] Thus the neuroses can, by and large, be helped by counselling and psychotherapy, although, in their more severe forms, hospital admission and the prolonged use of prescribed drugs may be necessary.

Although the boundaries between neurosis and psychosis are far from watertight, there are some fundamental distinctions between these two broad categories of psychological disturbance. Whereas neurosis is a reaction that affects aspects of a person, a *psychosis* involves disruption of the whole personality. As part of this total transformation, the individual undergoing a psychotic breakdown experiences a change in the quality of reality and a disorganisation of the thought processes. Consequently, the subject may believe that she or he is the Virgin Mary or Napoleon and be convinced that every thought is controlled by an outside force. Such disorders, including manic-depressive psychosis, various paranoid states and schizophrenia, are considered by traditional psychiatry to be largely inaccessible to psychotherapy and will, therefore, be outside the range of this book. Psychoses require admission to hospital in their more acute forms as well as long-term medication and supervision. We will return briefly to the question of schizophrenia and its management in chapter seven when we consider R. D. Laing and 'antipsychiatry'.[10]

The continuum of therapeutic help for the non-psychotic person has been portrayed by R. H. Cawley who describes four types of psychotherapy[11], in which the term counselling can be used of the first level[12]. Cawley's classification is based on the experience, training and aims of the counsellor or psychotherapist:

Psychotherapy 1   This includes what any good doctor (and, for that matter, any caring person of some experience, lay or professional) does in terms of support and encouragement towards his patient. This level contains a great deal of what is described as *counselling*.

Psychotherapy 2   Here the person being helped is taken to a deeper level in terms of the causes of his personal problems. Furthermore, those psychological masks behind which people hide, called *defences*, may be challenged.

Psychotherapy 3   This *dynamic psychotherapy* probes unconscious processes and uses the phenomenon of *transference* (in which the client or patient transfers past experiences of a key person or persons on to the therapist) to help the one seeking counsel to move beyond old unhelpful patterns of relating to others. This is the province of the experienced professional which, by and large, lies at a deeper level than that usually reached by counselling, as the latter term is ordinarily understood.

Psychotherapy 4 This is the level designated for *behavioural psychotherapy*, in which the patient's dilemmas are seen to relate to 'bad habits'. The aim is to help him re-learn behaviour patterns within which he can adapt socially. Certain phobias, such as a fear of spiders or of open spaces, may be specially relieved by this 'level'.

In this model, counselling can be seen as subsumed under level 1 and the initial part of level 2, while psychotherapy 'proper' occupies the remaining levels; as the descriptive elements are not sharply defined, there is bound to be overlap in level 2 between counselling and psychotherapy. Dennis Brown and Jonathan Pedder in their *Introduction to Psychotherapy* include these features under the 'counselling layer' of Cawley's levels:

1 unburdening of problems to a sympathetic listener;
2 ventilation of feelings within a supportive relationship;
3 discussion of current problems with a non-judgmental helper. [13]

Although these ingredients move us into the area of methods (which we will explore thoughout the rest of the book), they also demonstrate that the essence of counselling and psychotherapy includes the idea of *helping another through a caring relationship*.

Here, then, we have two elements in the function of counselling: helping another (or others), and a relationship (or relationships). The first of these ingredients is emphasised in the definition by Truax and Carkhuff: *Counselling of Psychotherapy is aimed at producing constructive behavioural and personality change.*[14] Both aspects are included in Anthony Storr's description of psychotherapy: *Psychotherapy is the art of alleviating personal difficulties through the agency of words and a personal, professional relationship.*[15] As we have seen in Cawley's classification, the degree of professional expertise is a variable in the art of counselling and psychotherapy, although both Cawley and Storr agree on the intrinsic need for the 'professional relationship' at the deeper levels of psychotherapy. Conversely, we can argue that, at its more basic levels, counselling can be undertaken by the non-professional with good effect. Jerome D. Frank, emeritus professor of psychiatry at Johns Hopkins Hospital in Baltimore and a doyen in the realm of research into the efficacy of psychotherapy, writes of the value of the lay person helping others, including that of 'even strangers, especially if they occupy roles like that of the bartender, for example, which create the expectation that they will be good listeners'.[16]

Keeping these important strands in mind, we can define counselling as: *That activity which aims to help others in any or all aspects of their being within a caring relationship.*

Let me comment on each of the three parts of this definition:

Helping others. This phrase puts counselling on to a broad canvas, although the other elements in the definition narrow the framework somewhat. It would be too vague to use the word counselling to cover every eventuality of comradely aid to another. The ethos of the Beatles' song 'I get by with a little help from my friends' is about everyday relationships rather than the planned encounter we call counselling, with its agreed aims and carefully preserved confidentialities.

Lawrence J. Crabb in his *Effective Biblical Counselling* argues that, within a church situation, we can help others at any of three levels:[17]

Level 1 – by ENCOURAGEMENT, in which every Christian is called to help others with *problem feelings*;
Level 2 – by EXHORTATION, in which those Christians called and trained as lay or ordained leaders are to help their fellow believers with *problem behaviour*;
Level 3 – by ENLIGHTENMENT, in which a few who are specially gifted and experienced are trained further to help others with *problem thinking*.

The aim under Crabb's schema is to enable others to move towards feelings, behaviour and thinking which accord with scriptural principles.

Although I will reserve a closer look at the methodology of Lawrence Crabb's counselling till later, we can, at this stage, take his three descriptive levels of counselling and use them on a wider conceptual basis. Encouraging, exhorting and enlightening are all important functions of counselling, even outside a

Christian setting. We can combine these categories with Cawley's classification of 'psychotherapies' to give this plan:

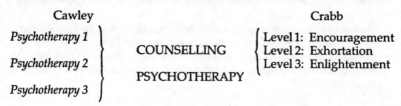

Figure 1   Counselling and psychotherapy

The parallels in this table cannot be drawn too closely as Cawley's conceptual framework is essentially psychoanalytic (involving the examination of unconscious processes and the use of transference – see page 24) and Crabb's is biblical in a sense that we shall discuss later. However, in utilising Crabb's three levels more widely, they accord well with Cawley's Psychotherapy 1 and the initial part of Psychotherapy 2.

Later, we will tackle more fully the key question of what are appropriate *aims* for helping others through counselling.

In any or all aspects of their being.   However we understand the complexity of human nature, counselling, I would argue, can help people in any or all aspects of their inner being – emotional, volitional, attitudinal, rational, psychological or spiritual. Moreover, this constructive change will have behavioural components as well as the possibility of increased health in physical, relational and social areas.

As the book unfolds we will see that there are many counselling approaches which major on one particular aspect of a person's life, often reasoning that where there is progress in one area, for example the rational, then other changes, such as attitudinal and behavioural, should follow. One of the particular strengths of the L'Abri Fellowship, the worldwide Christian association founded by Francis and Edith Schaeffer, is to state that right thinking has a pervasive and wholesome effect on the rest of the personality. This view is bolstered by Paul's injunction in Romans 12:2 (RSV), 'Do not be conformed to this world but be transformed by the renewal of your mind, that you may prove what is the will of God, what is good and acceptable and perfect.' Many lives have been profoundly changed as they have been opened up to the influence of the Holy Spirit speaking to the mind through the scriptures. Ranald Macaulay and Jerram Barrs, both from L'Abri, make the point well in their book *Christianity with a Human Face*:

> As we seek to understand the Bible with our minds and to see more clearly our privileged position as believers, the Spirit helps us grow. Because the work of Christ is actual, because he died and rose again in history, this is not just positive thinking or a psychological technique. It is reality.[18]

Other methodologies are reductionist, seeming to encapsulate men and women in the confines of one main mode. We shall see this restrictive view *par excellence* when we consider behaviourism in the next chapter. Yet other approaches seek to be holistic in the sense of aiming to help in any or all aspects of the client's being, depending where his or her most pressing needs lie at the time of counselling.

Within a caring relationship. The listening and talking aspects of counselling (see, for example Anthony Storr's definition on page 25) inevitably lead to some level of relating between counsellor and client. As in all relationships this means a certain measure of commitment from both parties.[19]

In the 1950s and 1960s there was something of a crisis point in counselling and psychotherapy because a great deal of research suggested most strongly that they did not work! H. J. Eysenck, the British psychologist, led the spearhead in 1952 with his paper 'The effects of psychotherapy: an evaluation', in which he declared that many neurotic patients got better without professional help and that the results of psychotherapy did not improve on this pattern. A powerful controversy within the ranks of counsellors and psychotherapists was thereby launched, ensuing in papers both attacking and defending the efficacy of what Freud had called the 'talking cure'.[20] In 1961 Jerome Frank in the United States substantiated the main thrust of Eysenck's argument when he reported that two-thirds of neurotic patients improved immediately after treatment regardless of the type of psychotherapy used and, further, that a similar proportion of comparable patients, who had no psychotherapy, improved over an equivalent span of time. The year before Frank's findings were published, Eysenck stated that psychotherapy was like the 'wondrous cure' of the second century physician Galen in that:

All who drink this remedy recover in a short time, except for those whom it does not help, who all die and have no relief from any other medicine. Therefore, it is obvious that it fails only in incurable cases.[21]

Intensive research continued through the 1960s spurred by the provocative suggestion that psychotherapy was ineffective.[22] While different aspects of the counselling engagement were being studied it emerged that some counsellors and psychotherapists appeared to facilitate improvement, others did not affect the therapeutic outcome and a third category actually seemed to make the clients and patients worse! The focus of enquiry then shifted to questions of the personality and character of the therapist in order to ascertain those qualities that helped the client get better. At least one could begin to argue that psychotherapy was effective as long as the psychotherapist was effective, and so some members of the profession started to breathe again.

In 1957 Carl Rogers pointed out the need for certain characteristics in the therapeutic personality, but it was not until a decade later that Charles Truax (a colleague of Rogers) and Robert Carkhuff published a careful appraisal of the relevant literature in their *Towards Effective Counselling and Psychotherapy*, showing that the essential triad of qualities for effective counselling is:

1 Genuineness;
2 Non-possessive warmth;
3 Accurate empathy.

As we define and examine these dispositions, we shall see that there is a natural progression in the order they are considered. The counsellor who is genuine will the more readily show non-possessive warmth and that warmth, in turn, can fuel accurate empathy.

Genuineness. Synonyms used by the theorists have included the words 'authenticity' and 'self congruence'. These terms are descriptive of the counsellor who is essentially consistent as a person, has enough self-awareness to see his or her own weaknesses and has a degree of transparency in relationships. In other words, the counsellor needs to be sufficiently secure in personality to weather the potential storms of helping someone in difficulty. This means that he or she is less effective if there is undue concern about status or role. Where this is the case, it is as if the counsellor is saying, 'You must be aware of my position and so be careful how you handle me!' This is an imposition on the counselling relationship which may be too onerous for the client to bear.

Further, where the would-be therapist is seriously inconsistent as a person, lacks a sense of integrity or is especially vulnerable due to blind spots about the sort of man or woman he or she really is, then genuineness cannot be 'conjured up' or worn as a convincing 'mask'. Truax and Carkhuff make this point eloquently:

> There is no real alternative to genuineness in the psychotherapeutic relationship. Even if he were a skilled, polished actor, it is doubtful that a therapist could hide his real feelings from the client. When the therapist pretends to care, pretends to respect, or pretends to understand, he is fooling only himself. The patient may not know why the therapist is 'phoney', but he can easily detect true warmth from phoney and insincere 'professional warmth'.[23]

These observations about the subversive effects on counselling of the counsellor who has an undue concern about status or who attempts to masquerade as a more genuine person apply to both the professional and the lay therapist. In fact a consideration of Truax and Carkhuff's triad of desirable qualities is a great leveller in this respect. Good or bad therapy hinges strongly on the personality of the counsellor regardless of degrees and diplomas achieved, courses attended or positions held. This conclusion has been well supported by research carried out from the mid-1960s onwards. For example, in 1964 Truax, Carkhuff and Douds devised a training programme for both professional and lay counsellors, seeking to engender qualities of genuineness, non-possessive warmth and accurate empathy. After rather less than one hundred hours of training they tested out the therapeutic effectiveness of the lay participants, of a group of clinical psychologists and of a section of experienced therapists. Interestingly, the lay counsellors scored less well with respect to genuineness, assumedly because of less exposure to the need for self-awareness. However, they achieved similar levels to the professionals in demonstrating warmth and empathy in their counselling. Truax *et al.* concluded that 'these data suggest that these ingredients can be learned, by both professional and non-professional persons'.[24]

The valuable work carried out by bodies like the National Marriage Guidance Council, the Samaritans and a host of other voluntary agencies demonstrates the undoubted effectiveness of lay counselling and that such success can be enhanced through training programmes.

Non-possessive warmth. This term has the same sense as the phrase used by Carl Rogers in describing the attributes of the successful counsellor: 'unconditional positive regard'. The effective helper needs not only to feel concerned and respectful towards the client but should be able to show that 'positive regard' both verbally and through facial expressions, eye contact, gestures and silences. A person in difficulty is often desperate for someone *who really cares* and that warmth needs to be communicated to set the stage for worthwhile counselling.

This also means that the counsellor should be at home in the world of feelings and emotions, both his own and those of the client. The helper needs to be in touch with and understand his or her own reactions to the person being helped and to what is being said. This awareness should prevent the counsellor from being caught on the wrong foot and thereby causing the client to withdraw. If, for example, a counsellor drops the corner of his mouth or narrows his eyes as a client is sharing something painful, then the one in need may conclude, 'I won't go any further; he can't cope with it!' This circumspection does not mean that one is condoning all that is declared so much as that the story needs to be fairly and fully heard before the issues can be discussed with a measure of helpful objectivity. When the counsellor is 'safe' in the realm of emotions then he or she will be able to cope with hostility, criticism, misunderstanding or rejection from the client.

With respect to the 'non-possessive' element in the counsellor's warmth there can be some confusion if this adjective is equated with Rogers' word 'unconditional'. We see the seeds of this double meaning in this quotation from Truax and Carkhuff's *Towards Effective Counselling and Psychotherapy*:

> The non-possessive, or unconditional, aspect of this warmth has been heavily underscored by Rogers *et al.* . . . in speaking of warmth and prizing for the client being without 'if's, and's, or but's'.[25]

From Freud onwards the value of being 'non-judgmental', or

'unconditional', has been stressed. If we see this disposition as one which countenances all that we meet in counselling then I would dispute its value. To be 'unshockable', a quality in a counsellor which can be seen as useful, does not mean we should be undiscerning.

To underscore the point, being non-judgmental does not require us to be undiscriminating. I suggest that this attribute, particularly from a scriptural perspective,[26] includes avoiding 'summing up' other people in a dismissive way. To say to someone, 'Oh, she's just a neurotic' or, 'He's nothing but a lazy good-for-nothing' is judgmental if the object of the comment is seen as without hope of being otherwise. The statements are given as 'final judgments'. If then we are non-judgmental or unconditional in this discerning, yet charitable sense we will use our critical faculties in counselling, keeping an open mind as long as possible in order to achieve a fair assessment of the client's frailties and difficulties.

We have seen that non-possessiveness needs to be non-judgmental. It also should be non-manipulative – and this raises the thorny question of one's motives as a counsellor. We ought to ask, 'Do I have an interest in counselling for wrong reasons? Is it because I enjoy confidences? Does it give me a sense of power over people's lives? Or do I counsel because I need to be needed?' Even for the experienced counsellor, the temptations to wrong motivation can be powerful. We need to ask constantly, 'Is my handling of this counselling situation in the best interests of the person I am trying to help?' If we cannot answer 'Yes' with confidence, then we need to do some heart searching.

If our warmth has any degree of possessiveness, then our prime concern for the client's welfare is being eroded and *both* parties are vulnerable. The counsellor is in danger of developing clouded judgments as he may become too emotionally attached to the client; the client may respond to the counsellor's vulnerability by moving towards dependency ('Ah, here at last is someone I can lean on!') or manipulation ('Aha, if I play my cards right I can lead this one quite a song and dance!').

There will of course be times when it seems impossible for us to find adequate warmth towards certain needy individuals. Such people may be beyond our experience, our understanding or our sympathy; however we try, we feel little but antipathy towards them. We may even get dangerously near reflecting, 'People who want by the yard but try by the inch should be kicked by the foot!' Whether our reaction is one of irritation or one of bewilderment, it can be unrealistic to persist and we may need to declare to the client, 'We have tried to work together but somehow the "chemistry" between us does not seem to help. I think you may be better helped by someone else. What do you think? . . . If you agree, I can suggest someone else you might see . . .' Such a declaration may of course lead to a breakthrough in the relationship, the difficulties are identified and a more open encounter begins, within which non-possessive warmth may start to glow flickeringly.

So we can see that, where possible, non-possessive warmth is an integral part of the counsellor's approach to the client. This level of uncontaminated caring encourages the one in need towards personal responsibility and healthy independence.

Accurate empathy. In almost any discussion between counsellors or psychotherapists on how to help others, sooner or later the word 'empathy' will be heard. It has become, perhaps, *the* vogue word of the counselling world. The danger of any fashionable term is that its sense and value can easily be lost by repetition. Familiarity breeds contempt. Let us try therefore to be as precise as possible as to its meaning.

The word 'empathy' derives from the Greek words 'suffering (or feeling) in (or into)'. The *Shorter Oxford English Dictionary* definition is a useful one: empathy is 'the power of projecting one's personality into, and so fully understanding, the object of contemplation'. The key word in the counselling context is *understanding* so that counselling includes understanding the client on a 'moment by moment' basis, and that understanding needs to be 'accurate' to be effective. At a simple level this means getting the story right. It does little for the counselling relationship if the counsellor is 'feeling into' the client's situation and yet calls her 'Jane' instead of 'Janet' or cannot remember whether John is an only child or not. On a deeper plane, accurate empathy comprises identifying with the client enough to feel something of his or her anguish or despair. Metaphorically, it involves stepping into someone else's shoes. Rogers coined the phrase 'as if' to emphasise this identification and Truax and Carkhuff echoed this when they wrote that with empathy 'we begin to perceive the events and experience of his life "as if" they were parts of our own life'.[27]

Sometimes the counsellor is readily empathetic because he too has suffered and has learnt through his suffering. Such an attribute can be seen in Paul's second letter to the Corinthians where he wrote:

> Blessed be the God and Father of our Lord Jesus Christ, the Father of mercies and God of all comfort, who comforts us in all our affliction, so that we may be able to comfort those who are in any affliction, with the comfort with which we ourselves are comforted by God.[28]

Such caring counsellors have been called 'missionaries of comfort'. In August 1980 I listened to a recording on Radio Wales of a lady called Sarah Parry who was dying of multiple sclerosis and who had been in hospital with this condition for twenty-five years. She was almost completely paralysed from the neck down and, quite literally, could not lift a finger. She spoke of her suffering in a soft, Welsh accent and as she did so her vital Christian faith shone through: 'It's an awful illness; it's a cruel illness . . . I listen to the radio . . . to keep up with current affairs. I'm blessed with a sense of humour . . . it's a funny thing but I still enjoy life . . . I have a religious background . . . I don't want to sound sanctimonious but I believe in prayer.'

There is no doubt in my mind that this good lady, who had died between making the recording and its broadcast, had been comforted by 'the God and Father of our Lord Jesus Christ' and was a 'missionary of comfort' to any who came in contact with her. I suspect she showed 'accurate empathy' in her dealing with others and, most importantly, could communicate that identification. Truax and Carkhuff stress this twin perspective which accurate empathy requires:

> *Accurate empathy* involves more than just the ability of the therapist to sense the client or patient's 'private world' as if it were his own. It also involves more than just his ability to know what the patient means. Accurate empathy involves both the therapist's *sensitivity to current feelings* and his *verbal facility to communicate this understanding* in a language attuned to the client's current feelings.[29]

Inevitably, there are different levels of empathy. Someone of Sarah Parry's experience and compassion will probably have a strong sense of solidarity with the sufferer and a great ability to verbalise that understanding. As Truax and Carkhuff express it:

'At a *high* level of accurate empathy the message "I am *with* you" is unmistakably clear – the therapist's remarks fit perfectly with the client's mood and content.' Others, whose self-knowledge, experience, imagination and sense of caring are more limited, may exhibit lower levels of empathy: 'At a *low* level of accurate empathy the therapist may go off on a tangent of his own or may misinterpret what the patient is feeling.'[30] However, as has already been alluded to (see note 24), research has confirmed that greater degrees of empathy can be *learnt* – by paying careful attention to the client's story, working hard at remembering important details, using imagination, as well as experience of other people's lives, to enter into the client's suffering, and growing in the ability to speak accurately and appropriately.

We have seen that psychological research has concluded that the attributes of genuineness, non-possessive warmth and accurate empathy, rightly understood, are essential for the effective counsellor. Others have commented more generally on the quality needed in the therapist. Sandor Ferenczi, for example, the Hungarian psychoanalyst who died in 1933, stated towards the end of his life that the 'indispensable healing power in the therapeutic gift is love'.[31] Although insights like these pale in comparison to the blazing light of biblical revelation concerning right relationships, it is, I suggest, a useful exercise to compare such ideas on the potentially successful counsellor with the picture portrayed in Galatians 5:22–23 of the fruit of the Spirit. Here is a description of the life of the believer who is allowing the Holy Spirit's transforming power its full sway. By the same token, we can see that these nine characteristics are those of the person of Christ, who was designated prophetically the 'Wonderful Counsellor' (Isaiah 9:6). It is interesting to reflect that the qualities of love, joy, peace, patience, kindness, goodness, faithfulness, gentleness and self-control not only supersede but encompass some of the attributes we have considered under Truax and Carkhuff's triad. The Spirit-filled, fruit-bearing Christian is likely to be endowed with a genuineness that arises from goodness and faithfulness, a non-possessive warmth that is fostered by kindness, gentleness and self-control, and an accurate empathy sustained by patience, all undergirded by peace and joy, and motivated by love. This linkage may seem rather contrived, but we should not be surprised if research has demonstrated that the attributes of an effective counsellor have some overlap, at least, with Christian qualities, or, more comprehensively, with the character of our Lord. Jesus, supremely, was the one who was the most genuine of human beings, who had boundless compassion which never infringed another's right to choose and who gauged people accurately, communicating his understanding, when appropriate, in a perfect way.

We have discussed in some detail those qualities needed by the counsellor in the therapeutic encounter. Moreover, as we mentioned earlier, there are two sides to a relationship and, however gifted and experienced the counsellor may be, there will be little progress unless there is commitment to change in the client. Where the needy person strongly desires to find help the outcome of counselling is more likely to be successful. It is then that the compassionate counsellor can be most effective. As Jerome Frank has written:

> . . . many receivers of psychotherapy can be greatly helped by anyone who is able to combat their demoralization, mobilize their expectations of help, and shore up or restore their self-confidence.[32]

In 1965 he reported his investigations as to whether there are any characteristics in the counsellor that encourage the client to be hopeful. We have come full circle, since Frank found that the three-fold qualities that we have studied in this chapter are those that engender most hope in the person seeking help.[33]

However, to achieve progress through the counselling relationship, it is important that the counsellor and client share similar expectations and realistic aims. If the counsellor's overriding goal is that the client should become a Christian before proceeding to look at his situation, and the client is equally determined that all he wants is help with a problematic marriage, then the chances of a relationship developing between counsellor and client that is constructive for the recipient is remote. Such issues will be picked up more fully as we consider different methods of counselling later in the book.

Research and simple observation of counselling practice have suggested that many counsellors get trapped into offering most help to what Schofield has described as the YAVIS client – young, attractive, verbal, intelligent and successful.[34] This, again, points up a particular temptation in counselling which is, in effect, to offer the most help to those who, perhaps, are in the least need.[35] This is not to deny that there are many YAVIS people who are needful but to state that, sadly, older, unattractive, tongue-tied, less intelligent, and unsuccessful people may have less appeal to the counsellor at the human level. Once more, the counsellor's motivation is strongly challenged and the need for something of our Lord's compassion for everyone is stressed.

Counselling and evangelism

We have considered, then, some crucial definitions and, in doing so, have tried to demonstrate the relationship between counselling and psychotherapy. In turn, we have examined the nature of counselling in terms of 'helping others in any or all aspects of their being within the context of a caring relationship'. In doing so, we have touched briefly on another area of controversy for the Christian, that is the relationship between counselling and evangelism. Are they the same thing? Is one more important than the other? Is one the handmaiden of the other? Do we need to evangelise *before* we can counsel effectively? Should we only see evangelism in the context of counselling? Or, are they two separate, distinct activities with little or no overlap?

Christian counsellors hold a range of views on the links between counselling and evangelism (by evangelism I simply mean the declaration of the Good News in Christ). Some, for example Jay Adams, reason that the unbeliever should not be counselled; his need is for the Lord and until he is regenerate he cannot respond in the midst of his problems in a God-given way. In fact, Adams argues, the counsellor does the non-Christian a disservice in seeking to unravel his problems before conversion because the client may then feel all the more that he can manage his affairs without God (see chapter twelve). Some, like Lawrence Crabb, seem less stringent in this respect while others, for example Frank Lake (see chapter fifteen) and Paul Tournier (see chapter thirteen), exercise an openness towards both believer and unbeliever in their counselling. The latter position, which is my own, argues that God is concerned about responsibility and justice in people's lives[36] as well as about their reception or rejection of the gospel. Where the claims of the Lord are presented in the context of counselling the non-believer, I suggest that our evangelism should take place in the spirit of this extract from Richard Lovelace's *Dynamics of Spiritual Life*:

> Our task as evangelists is therefore that of midwives, and not that of parents. It is not our responsibility to get people regenerated but simply to present a consistent witness in life and word, and to appeal for commitment to Christ secure in the inward recognition that his sheep will hear his voice and follow him because his Spirit will open their hearts to do so.[37]

Although the context is that of the life of the church, Ephesians 4:11 (RSV) indicates the complementary nature of certain ministries: 'And his gifts were that some should be apostles, some prophets, some evangelists, some pastors and teachers'. Whether we conclude that counselling today is an important facet of pastoral care and nothing more, whether we see it as distinct from the realm of pastoralia, or whether we view its legitimate exercise as being *both* within the body of Christ and in the community at large, this passage does at least show that the call of the evangelist and the pastor-teacher are not identical.

We can, I believe, argue at least two basic points from biblical revelation in this area of evangelism and counselling. Firstly, just as all believers are called to be witnesses to the Lord and only a certain number are endowed with the gift of evangelism, so, as Crabb argues, all believers are required to be part of a mutual ministry of 'encouragement', many are singled out for the exercise of 'exhortation' while a few are called to counselling by 'enlightenment'.

Secondly, the doctrine of God's common grace, under which all men experience something of his generosity and mercy, and the teaching on God's concern for righteousness and justice throughout all humankind point to the need to see the availability of appropriate counselling for all, both Christian and non-Christian. As far as our counselling is Christ-centred, then our reaching out to others in the counselling relationship will always be a vehicle of God's love for people. The unbelieving client may respond quite specifically to Christ's invitation to receive forgiveness and new life, and to his challenge to live for him. He or she may take faltering steps towards this commitment within the counselling process. He may become a more loving husband and a more just employer, or she a more caring mother and a less selfish colleague, even though the claims of Christ may not be seen as relevant to the person seeking help. In other words, our counselling may lead to successful evangelism, it may not. Either way, we aim to go the second mile in helping our needy friend at the level of his or her difficulties.

And so we can return to our allegorical woodland scene having visualised something of the relationships between the outgrowths of counselling and psychotherapy and the distinctive tree of evangelism. Pursuing the representation further we might see the tree of evangelism as standing in holy ground, alongside our tree of pastoral care, in the centre of the wood and reaching out its probing branches in all directions, interlacing them with the growing systems of all the other trees. The situation with counselling and psychotherapy is more complex as they have grown from a variety of stocks with roots running down through the centuries. In coming chapters we will consider how much, or how little, they are in some respects outgrowths from the tree of pastoral care. Further we will examine four forest giants of psychological theory and practice which have sprung up in alien soil during the last one hundred years or so, producing countless ramifications of growth within the twentieth century.[38] I will seek to argue that their relationship with the tree of pastoral care has sometimes been beneficial and at other times undermining. The tree of pastoral care has found their influence in some respects malignant and parasitic, and in others helpfully symbiotic.

3

BEHAVIOURISM: MAN AS MACHINE

To man qua man we readily say good riddance. Only by dispossessing him can we turn to the real causes of human behaviour. Only then can we turn from the inferred to the observed, from the miraculous to the natural, from the inaccessible to the manipulable.

B. F. Skinner

Of course, Behaviourism 'works'. So does torture. Give me a no-nonsense, down-to-earth behaviourist, a few drugs, and simple electrical appliances, and in six months I will have him reciting the Athanasian creed in public.

W. H. Auden

The four impressive neighbours of our tree of pastoral care have their roots in the common soil of metaphysics, that branch of philosophy which seeks to analyse the existing universe and resolve problems concerning matter and spirit.[1] This soil has an enormous depth extending down to the foundational theories of the ancient world, from which the influences of Plato and Aristotle, in particular, have worked up through the soil levels to be tapped not only by our four neighbours but by the tree of pastoral care itself.

By the beginning of the nineteenth century this soil of metaphysics was breaking down into two components: 'mental philosophy', which sought to explain the functioning of men and women in terms of the 'mental faculties' of memory, reason, will and emotion; and the 'empirical sciences', which argued the supreme validity of conclusions about matter reached solely by observation and experiment. Here was the age-old dilemma of the nature of man in its latest guise. If man is a duality of body and spirit, as the ancient Greeks had reasoned and as philosophers like the Frenchman, Descartes (1596–1650) had tended to underline, then how could those aspects be reconciled? Were the mental philosophers right as they tried to study man's conscious life, or were the experimental scientists at least pursuing the more convincing course by majoring on the external and material?

Initially, attempts were made to hold both fields of enquiry by studying man's inner being using the scientific method.[2] In 1879 Wilhelm Wundt (1832–1920) set up the first psychological laboratory in Leipzig. He decided to dispense with the complicated debate on mental faculties and the soul of man, and concentrate his attention on *experience* as the appropriate subject of psychology. As a result he conducted experiments with human subjects in which they would declare their impressions of the type of colour, the brightness of light, the pitch of sound and of other sensory messages so that he could check out their experiences of these sensations against their actual value. This method of evaluating subjective assessments is known as *introspection* and the philosophy behind it, with its examination of the elements of conscious experience, has been called *structuralism*.

Wundt's work was taken up and continued by Edward Bradford Titchener (1867–1927) who, although an English scientist, emigrated to the United States because British psychology was not yet ready for the new experimental approach. During his research at Cornell University, he declared that psychology is 'experience dependent on an experiencing person';[3] he studied that experience through investigating people by the empirical method, that is through observation, measurement and experiment. However, introspectionism did not resolve the classic body-soul dichotomy and its methodology was strongly criticised by animal psychologists from Charles Darwin onwards, who argued from their discipline that introspection was not needed in order to study behaviour, and by psychiatrists with a neurological bias like Jean-Martin Charcot (1825–1893) in Paris, who were unhappy with the new emphasis on inner processes that was appearing in the writings and lectures of Josef Breuer and Sigmund Freud. An impasse had been reached.[4] What possible routes could psychology now take through the seemingly impregnable wall of the nature of man and its study?

At the turn of the century three main attempts to resolve the dilemma were emerging. To return to our forest floor, these three ways forward can be seen as the first three of our formidable neighbouring trees: the psychologies of behaviourism, psychoanalysis and personalism. Somewhat later a fourth tree shot up, sharing much of its root system with the tree of personalistic psychology: the tree of transpersonal psychology.

Let us, in this chapter, examine the growth of the tree of behaviourism from its roots in the mixed soil of mental philosophy and the empirical sciences through to its latter-day branches.

The roots of behaviourism

Benjamin Wolman and Susan Knapp in their *Contemporary Theories and Systems in Psychology* describe three primary roots that encouraged the rise of behaviourism in the early years of the twentieth century: functionalism, instrumentalism and associationism. These rather grand terms have closely allied concepts behind them.

The *functionalists* sought to answer the question 'What is this or that fact we have observed actually *for*; what is its function?' Charles Darwin (1809–1882) in his famous book *On the Origin of Species* (1859) summed up the functionalist position when he wrote 'Human behaviour is *goal directed*. Those who adjust better to outer conditions have better chances for survival. Psychology has to study the ways of human adjustment.'[5]

William James, whom we met in chapter one, was a functionalist as well as a pragmatist and saw human life as one long process of adjustment, emphasising 'usefulness and pleasure as motives of behaviour'. His position, between the world of pastoral care and that of ascendant behaviourism, was a bridging one. Although, as we have seen (page 18), he had some notion of a spiritual self, he saw all aspects of the inner life in a pragmatic and somewhat behaviouristic way: 'I am often confronted by the necessity of standing by one of my empirical selves and relinquishing the next . . .'[6]

John Dewey (1859–1952), the American social philosopher, strongly influenced by the theories of evolution, argued that in all forms of life, including the human, units of organisation could be used as means (or instruments) for experimentation so achieving progress towards more complex and more useful systems. Habits, opinions, morals and human institutions could all be utilised as building blocks in this philosophy of *instrumentalism*.

Although functionalism and its variant, instrumentalism, were forerunners of behaviourism, it was the *associationism* of Thorndike and Pavlov that was the most overt influence on this first of our neighbouring trees. Ivan Petrovitch Pavlov (1849–1936), the Soviet pharmacologist and physiologist, who as a clergyman's son had once prepared for the priesthood, felt that the position of psychology as a true science was 'completely hopeless'. Wolman and Knapp write: 'Pavlov's way was clear, simple and safe. He did not deny psychology; he simply did not care much for it.'[7]

Pavlov's views were *monistic* in that he saw nature as a totality of matter and energy, *materialistic* in that he regarded man as simply a higher animal, and *deterministic* in that all behaviour was perceived as inflexibly bound to causation. He saw the fundamental element of interaction between man (as with all the animals) and the environment as the *reflex arc*, within which basic instincts lead to predictable responses to certain stimuli. His experiments on the food reflex in the dog are well known. He described the salivation which took place as soon as the dog was fed as an *unconditioned reflex*. On examining the effect of sounding a tuning fork at, for example, eight seconds before giving the food, he found that, in time, the dog salivated solely on hearing the sound; a *conditioned reflex* had been formed. The food given after the short interval acted as a *reinforcer* to this conditioning. Further, he discovered that, if food was withheld following each initial stimulus of sound, eventually the conditioned reflex was *extinguished*.

Associationism in one form or another had existed since the time of Aristotle. This theory of remembering, which is implicit in an understanding of Pavlov's research, stated that the association between one item which prompts the memory of another and that other can be one of *similarity*, *contrast* or *contiguity*. Thus, if I meet someone called John, he may remind me of Bill because of their striking resemblance, of George because they could not be more different, or of Harry simply because I saw them together last week. Edward Lee Thorndike (1874–1949) was one of the new breed of associationists and worked at Columbia University in the United States quite independently of Pavlov, establishing by 'trial-and-error' experiments with animals his *law of effect*. In this law he stated that 'any act which in a given situation produces satisfaction becomes associated with that situation, so that when the situation recurs the act is more likely than before to recur also'.[8] Conversely, acts producing discomfort become dissociated from the appropriate situation. In everyday terms, if my helping a certain lady friend with her coat produces a flashing smile from her I will tend to repeat my performance as further opportunity arises. On the other hand, if the same act with another acquaintance results in a slapped face then in a similar situation I am likely to let her struggle!

The beginnings of behaviourism

During the second and third decades of this century there was a great deal of controversy between the different schools of psychology and, within this combative state of affairs, the methodology of behaviourism began to assert itself.

John Broadus Watson (1878–1958), professor at Johns Hopkins University from 1908, was the founding father of this movement. He dismissed introspection as hopelessly subjective in the evaluation of human life and wrote, in 1913, 'The time seems to have come when psychology must discard all reference to consciousness.' A year later, in his book *Behaviour: an Introduction to Comparative Psychology*, he declared:

> It is possible to write a psychology, to define it . . . as the 'science of behaviour', and never go back on the definition: never to use the terms consciousness, mental states, mind, content, will, imagery, and the like . . . It can be done in terms of stimulus and response, in terms of habit formation, habit integration, and the like . . . The reason for this is to learn general and particular methods by which behaviour may be controlled. . . . Those who have occasion to apply psychological principles practically would find no need to complain as they do at the present time . . . If this is done, work . . . on the human being will be directly comparable with the work on animals.[9]

This Watsonian behaviourism, with its rigorous insistence that psychology is only concerned with animal and human behaviour and excludes all that cannot be proved by observation, has been called 'a psychology of everybody but me'.

In the mid-1920s Watson carried his thinking into crusading perspectives. He postulated that man's behaviour could be controlled scientifically and that the place of traditional religious mores could be replaced by experimental ethics. This inflated ambition to direct the destiny of others can be seen in the following quotation from his book *Behaviourism*, written in 1925: 'Give me a dozen healthy infants, well formed . . . and I'll guarantee you to take any one at random and train him to become any type of specialist I might select.'[10]

Perhaps the most fundamental flaw in Watson's behaviouristic approach is revealed when the question is asked 'How can he use his own consciousness in a methodology which, by definition, dismisses consciousness?' The inevitable inconsistency in his position is glimpsed in his autobiography where 'he includes many personal introspections of this type: "I enjoyed . . .", "I hated to leave," "The thought presented itself," "I honestly think . . . ," "I still believe . . ."'[11]

The growth of behaviourism

Watson's position of reductionism, a view of man that reduces the individual to one aspect or function, for example 'man is nothing but a higher animal' or 'man is nothing but a machine', was perpetuated with a variety of refinements by the neo-behaviourists.

Burrhus Frederic Skinner (born in 1904) has been described by Anthony Storr in the *Sunday Times* as 'the most influential experimental psychologist of our time'. The son of a lawyer and his beautiful wife, he was brought up in Susquehanna, Pennsylvania. In the first volume of his autobiography, *Particulars of My Life*, he describes how in his teen years he rebelled against his Presbyterian background:

An important part of my religious training was the novel *Quo Vadis* . . . Sienkiewicz no doubt intended it to be a convincing statement of Christian principles, and the description of Peter's appearance at Ostianus covers a great deal of ethical self-management with which I was familiar and which I continued to practice, but the book miscarried, because I admired and agreed with Petronius. After Ursus saves Lygia from the aurochs in the Colosseum and the populace insists that Caesar spare the girl, Petronius comments, 'Possibly Christ saved Lygia, but Ursus and the populace had a good deal to do with it.' . . . Petronius's point impressed me . . . In any event, when I began to see that my new testament was to go no further, I told Miss Graves, when I met her one day in the hallway of the high school, that I no longer believed in God. 'I have been through that, too,' she said.[12]

Later, while at college, a friend recounted to him a supposedly humorous tale about Peter the apostle and Jesus Christ which had a decidedly blasphemous flavour. Skinner comments, 'I found that story a new and refreshing kind of religious freedom.'[13]

With his agnostic, and even atheistic, frame of mind he continued his studies, hoping to become a successful writer. This plan failed and, in his early twenties, he suddenly realised: 'I was interested in human behaviour, but I had been investigating it in the wrong way.' Another friend had said to him, 'Science is the art of the twentieth century'; Skinner continues, 'and I believed him. Literature as an art form was dead; I would turn to science.'[14] In 1927, impressed by the writings of Bertrand Russell, John B. Watson and Ivan Pavlov, he decided to read psychology at Harvard University.

As with Pavlov and Watson, Skinner carried out innumerable experiments on animals to establish his behaviouristic psychology. In 1932 he introduced what is now known as the Skinner box, with which he studied the learning habits of pigeons and rats. He observed two basic forms of behaviour: *respondent*, which results from environmental stimuli; and *operant*, where no stimulus is detected at the time. In one experiment, whenever the pigeon raised its head food was given. He regarded this *operant conditioning* as improving the efficiency of the bird's behaviour. The head-raising was initially fortuitous but in time the pigeon learnt that this manoeuvre was productive.

Skinner went on to argue that all behaviour is essentially a product of operant conditioning: 'When a bit of behaviour is followed by a certain kind of consequence, it is more likely to occur again, and a consequence having this effect is called a reinforcer.'[15] He declared that *reinforcers* may either be positive, as when arriving home punctually results in a freshly cooked meal, or negative, as when a mother's nagging leads to a child's obedience; in the second case, the ready compliance reinforces the nagging because the latter is seen by the mother as effective.[16] Where the consequence of behaviour is unproductive, in time the original activity will be lost. We might take as an example, from the world of tennis, the famous McEnroe service 'grunt'. Researchers at Nottingham University have found that McEnroe's silent serves win him more points than his noisy ones. The champion needs to see that his 'grunt' deliveries are not being 'reinforced' by higher scoring. Skinner would, I think, argue that a lack of 'reward' will eventually 'extinguish' the distinctive McEnroe grunt.

In his book *Beyond Freedom and Dignity*, in which he seeks 'a technology of behaviour' to meet the world's needs, Skinner reasons that the so-called freedom and dignity of 'autonomous man' are simply the products of reinforcement. Of freedom he writes:

> Man's struggle for freedom is not due to a will to be free, but to certain behavioural processes characteristic of the human organism, the chief effect of which is the avoidance of or escape from so-called 'aversive' features of the environment.[17]

The quest for freedom, then, is seen as a response to *negative* reinforcement. For instance, the strictures of an oppressive government may lead a family to desire to emigrate; the more oppressive the régime, the more the family translates their inclination into an attempt to escape. In contrast, Skinner argues, the experience of a sense of dignity arises from *positive* reinforcement. A concert pianist who receives a standing ovation and a powerful feeling of her worth as a virtuoso will almost certainly repeat her applauded behaviour by playing an encore. More generally, Skinner regards the behaviour of people as a product of evolution. He writes that 'things are good (positively reinforcing) or bad (negatively reinforcing) presumably because of the contingencies of survival under which the species evolved'.[18]

In his search for a technology of behaviour, Skinner dismisses a number of society's ways of dealing with people, including punishment, permissiveness, guidance, and building dependence on such aids to living as motor cars and wrist-watches, as inadequate in terms of a desirable control of the lives of men and women. He places religion in the same comprehensive framework of behaviourism when he writes:

> A religious agency is a special form of government under which 'good' and 'bad' become 'pious' and 'sinful'. Contingencies involving positive and negative reinforcement, often of the most extreme sort, are codified – for example, as commandments – and maintained by specialists, usually with the support of ceremonies, rituals, and stories.[19]

The idea of control is central to Skinnerian thinking, whether it is the operant conditioning of a hungry pigeon in a 'puzzle box' or the re-shaping of an entire culture: 'The intentional design of a culture and the control of human behaviour it implies are essential if the human species is to continue to develop.'[20] He sees culture as 'a set of contingencies of reinforcement!'[21]

In the final chapter of *Beyond Freedom and Dignity*, he seeks to answer the question 'What is man?' To some extent we find Skinner a little less reductionist than John B. Watson in that he does at least accept that human consciousness should not be ignored: 'Rather than ignore consciousness, an experimental analysis of behaviour has stressed certain crucial issues. The question is not whether a man can know himself but what he knows when he does so.'[22] However, he does not permit that inner life an autonomy:

> The problem arises in part from the indisputable fact of privacy: a small part of the universe is enclosed within a human skin. It would be foolish to deny the existence of that private world, but it is also foolish to assert that because it is private it is of a different nature from the world outside. The difference is not in the stuff of which the private world is composed but its accessibility.[23]

He devalues consciousness further by arguing that it is merely a result of verbal interchange, implying that a person isolated on a desert island lacks not only conversation but, thereby, self-awareness too: 'Without the help of a verbal community all behaviour would be unconscious. Consciousness is a social product. It is not only *not* the special field of autonomous man, it is not within the range of solitary man.'[24] All in all, Skinner allows consciousness a very limited place in the lives of men and women. Human behaviour rules the roost: 'The picture which emerges from a scientific analysis is not of a body with a person inside, but of a body which *is* a person in the sense that it displays a complex repertoire of behaviour.'[25]

These conclusions are reached by thinking that is undergirded by two reductionist assumptions: that man is simply a higher animal, and that man is a machine. In this final chapter Skinner writes with a certain degree of black humour:

Krutch has argued that whereas the traditional view supports Hamlet's exclamation, 'How like a god!', Pavlov, the behavioural scientist, emphasized, 'How like a dog!' But that was a step forward. A god is the archetypal pattern of an explanatory fiction, of a miracle-working mind, of the metaphysical. Man is much more than a dog, but like a dog he is within range of a scientific analysis.[26]

Having underlined man's creatureliness, he declares in what way he sees man as a machine: 'Man is a machine in the sense that he is a complex system behaving in lawful ways, but the complexity is extraordinary.'[27]

The overall thesis that emerges from *Beyond Freedom and Dignity* is that 'a scientific analysis of behaviour dispossesses autonomous man and turns the control he has been said to exert over to the environment'.[28] Skinner reasons that man has developed through 'the biological evolution responsible for the human species and the cultural evolution carried out by that species'[29] and urges that these evolutionary processes should be encouraged through a balance of control and countercontrol.[30] Somewhat optimistically, amidst the powerfully reductionist nature of his view of man, he concludes his book with: 'A scientific view of man offers exciting possibilities. We have not yet seen what man can make of man.'[31]

A critique of behaviourism

Time magazine has described Skinner as 'the most influential of living American psychologists and the most controversial figure in the science of human behaviour'. Let us look briefly at both the appealing and the disputatious nature of his theories.

The popularity of the Skinnerian approach amongst certain experimental psychologists may relate to the attractiveness of a methodology which pares man down to the fundamental dimension of behaviour. The rise of behaviourism took place in a climate of frustration with the endless theorising of those psychologists who sought to hold on to mental, and even spiritual, aspects of the men and women they studied. The god of a restricted form of science beckoned: 'Follow me. Draw conclusions only from what you can observe, measure and experiment with. Better still, see that man is simply a part of the whole of nature and therefore waits to be examined and understood according to the same principles used in the study of the rest of the animal kingdom. Ignore all concepts of thinking, feeling, willing, and experiencing; behaviour is *all*.' This position of *scientism*, described by C. Stephen Evans as 'the thesis that all truth is derivable by scientific method',[32] has the attraction of potential omniscience and omnipotence for its adherents. In order to worship science as the key to the whole of life's mystery, life itself has to be reduced to what is measurable by the scientific method. The follower of scientism bows before a puny god who reveals the limited secrets of a diminished world. Joel Kovel in his *A Complete Guide to Therapy* seeks to rescue science from this belittling stance: 'Happily science has more to it than the puppetry of behaviourism. Science is the application of creative reason and the rules of evidence to phenomena.'[33]

Many Christian writers have levelled criticism at B. F. Skinner's psychology because of its reductionist nature.[34] Amongst these, Malcolm Jeeves is careful to distinguish between the value of Skinner's theories in the areas of shaping and controlling appropriate human behaviour in certain circumstances and the dehumanising flavour of his conjectures about the nature of man, society and culture.[35] Other critics, of a variety of different persuasions, have made similar distinctions to Jeeves', pointing out Skinner's methodological integrity and the thoroughness of his empirical scientific approach. Benjamin Wolman and Susan Knapp in *Contemporary Theories and Systems in Psychology*, for example, comment on the way that he restricted what he would study to the 'externally observable' and then proceeded to observe 'very carefully'. However, these writers also criticise his speculative side when they add, 'If a prize were offered for sober generalization and parsimonious use of concepts, it would be surely given to Skinner.'[36]

It would be quite wrong to give the impression that the school of behaviourism is peopled by psychologists who hold identical views. We have already seen that Skinner is somewhat less reductionist than Watson, the father of the movement. Other experimental psychologists of a behaviouristic persuasion seem to be more open to the developmental aspects of man. For example, H. J. Eysenck (b 1916), the well known British psychologist, has described human personality as 'the more or less stable and enduring organization of a person's character, temperament, intellect, and physique, which determines his unique adjustment to the environment'.[37] Although his emphasis on 'organization' in this definition is, to some extent, reductionist, Eysenck also acknowledges at least the existence of certain features of man's inner life. Elsewhere, he gives credence to the more 'dynamic' approach in which human development is studied but, at the same time, states that our present lack of knowledge precludes that particular tack.[38]

By and large, behaviourism, especially in its Watsonian and Skinnerian forms, suffers from a lack of reality in its assessment of people. Because the complex and rich variety of the inner lives of men and women, including creativity, imagination, aspiration, faith in God and love for others, cannot be measured and scrutinised narrowly, they are either dismissed or explained simply in terms of the conditioning of behaviour. Further, as has already been said (page 45), the more rigorous behaviourists are inconsistent, as well as unrealistic, in that they use their own awareness to dispel the self-awareness of those they study. Either way, human nature is diminished to suit the experimenter's assumptions. Arthur Koestler has criticised this dehumanising tendency most powerfully:

> Behaviourism is indeed a kind of flat-earth view of the mind. Or, to change the metaphor: it has replaced the anthropomorphic fallacy – ascribing to animals human faculties and sentiments – with the opposite fallacy: denying man faculties not found in lower animals; it has substituted for the erstwhile anthropomorphic view of the rat, a ratomorphic view of man.[39]

This 'ratomorphic' view is a far cry from the psalmist's rhetorical question in the face of the Lord's majesty and the glory of the creation:

> What is man that thou art mindful of him, and the son of man that thou dost care for him? Yet thou hast made him little less than God, and dost crown him with glory and honour. Thou hast given him dominion over the works of thy hands; thou hast put all things under his feet, all sheep and oxen, and also the beasts of the field, the birds of the air, and the fish of the sea, whatever passes along the paths of the sea.
> O Lord, our Lord, how majestic is thy name in all the earth! (Psalm 8:4–9 RSV).

Behaviour therapy

It is important to distinguish between the methodology of behaviourism with its commitment to empirical scientific research, the philosophy of behaviourism with its reductionist view of man and society, and the practice of behaviour therapy with its aims of helping people in a prescribed way.

V. Meyer and Edward S. Chesser in their *Behaviour Therapy in Clinical Psychiatry* contrast the more dynamic psychotherapies with behaviour therapy:

> . . . we would emphasize the predominantly verbal method of psychodynamic treatments, their aim to give understanding of present behaviour and their specific exploration of attitudes and feelings. Behaviour treatments make more use of non-verbal methods and have as their primary aim the modification of behaviour rather than the understanding of it.[40]

More explicitly, they write:

> Behaviour therapy does not refer to any specific theory or method. It is more an approach which attempts to apply the findings of experimental psychology to the modification of abnormal and undesirable behaviour.[41]

The behaviour therapist generally tries to help the person in need by narrowing down his or her difficulties into a *target* symptom. This key problem may be, for example, bed-wetting, stuttering or the fear of open spaces, and it is with these rather specific disturbances that behaviour therapy is at its most successful.

One technique used for such target symptoms is that of systematic *desensitisation*, pioneered by Joseph Wolpe in 1958, in which a particularly troublesome phobia is gradually overcome by progressive exposure to the dreaded object. First of all a hierarchy is worked out between the therapist and the patient as to which features of the thing feared are the most unsettling. In the case of a fear of spiders, the appropriate elements might include the size, colour, movement and proximity of the spider. Following instruction in relaxation by the therapist, the person with the phobia is then exposed, either in imagination or reality, to a range of encounters starting with a small, pale, stationary spider some yards away through to a large, black, mobile one in contact with the patient's skin.

Other behaviour therapists apply their craft to behavioural aspects of neurosis and depression, while others adopt Skinnerian insights for helping couples who are in difficulty within their relationship, as indicated by Joel Kovel: 'Each partner can be shown what he or she does to reinforce the other's negative response, and that the other's response reinforces his or her reinforcement, etc.'[42] It may help a marriage greatly, for example, if the wife can be helped to see that her sullen silence in response to her husband's tetchiness is counter-productive, and if the husband can realise that his further irritability with her seeming obtuseness continues the vicious circle.

With respect to counselling, a moment's reflection will help us understand that a great deal of traditional care for others involves advice with behavioural components. If we look right back to the biblical record we see, for example, in the sermon on the mount a considerable amount of exhortation which is essentially about the way we behave; '. . . if any one strikes you on the right cheek, turn to him the other also; and if any one would sue you and take your coat, let him have your cloak as well; and if any one forces you to go one mile, go with him two miles' (Matthew 5:39–41 RSV).

Whenever we try to help an individual, a couple or a family with their ways of acting we are bound to be using, to some extent at least, behaviouristic techniques, whether we are encouraging what Skinner would call negative reinforcement in advising someone to 'turn the other cheek' or positive reinforcement when we urge a client to respond to his wife's cooking with genuine compliments instead of the usual studied silence.

Summary

In this chapter we have traced the growth of the formidable tree of behaviourism in the forest of the care for humanity. We have examined its roots of functionalism, instrumentalism and associationism, growing in the mixed soil of metaphysics and the empirical sciences. We have looked at the way the tree broke surface in the rigid reductionism of Watson and continued its branching growth through the work of theorists like Skinner and

Eysenck. Last of all, we have considered the application of some of these insights in the area of behaviour therapy, observing both its limits and its usefulness.

On the whole, the tree of pastoral care has not been unduly crowded by this important neighbour. The overt reductionism of the tree of behaviourism has ensured a fair distance between the two, although the practical nature of the behavioural elements in counselling has allowed an intertwining of their branches.

PSYCHOANALYSIS: MAN AND HIS INSTINCTS

His claim to greatness . . . lies largely in the honesty and courage with which he struggled and overcame his own inner difficulties and emotional conflicts by means which have been of inestimable value to others.

Ernest Jones on Freud

. . . we cannot at this point in time, regard his total effort as anything but a failure.

O. Hobart Mowrer on Freud

From the ferment of nineteenth-century opinion in the realms of psychology and the empirical sciences another solution to the age-old dilemma posed by the nature of humanity (see pages 40–41) began to emerge. We have considered the origins and growth of the tree of behaviourism. Concurrently, another, more complex system started to take root, a system whose main trunk, in spite of numerous splittings and branchings, is represented in the theories and practice of Sigmund Freud.

The roots of this tree of psychoanalysis reach down to metaphysical psychology, especially to the writings of Johann Friedrich Herbart (1776–1841).[1] This German thinker's views, akin to those of the associationists described in chapter three (pages 43–44), were a formative influence on both general and educational psychology for much of the nineteenth century. Herbart understood the mind's attention as continually seeking to fuse opposing lines of thought into a congruous whole. He argued that where material does not contribute towards this integration of thinking then it is set aside. The mind is too finite, he said, to hold completely disparate elements in consciousness at one and the same time. Initially dismissed matters could reappear for consideration when the issues turned to at a later time were relevant. This reasoning of Herbart's bestowed a great deal to the idea of repressing information or experiences into what was later called the unconscious, a concept that was central to the development of Freud's view of man.

This practical way of understanding the mind's workings is all too familiar to us today. My wife Joy frequently accuses me of being unable to attend to two matters at once; she is right! I find it next to impossible to listen attentively to a Radio 3 discourse on Mahler and my son's account of the contents of his most recent biology lesson at school. Herbart would have understood!

Freud's ideas took shape, not only by way of linkage with such metaphysical psychologists as Herbart, but also within the soil of Darwinism and the empirical scientific method. He was con-vinced, according to Frank J. Sulloway, that 'psychoanalysis, with its insight into conscious and unconscious psychical adap-tation, was itself a culminatory achievement in evolutionary theory'.[2]

Sigmund Freud (1856–1939) was born in the town of Freiberg in Moravia, the central part of what is now called Czechoslovakia.[3] He was the first child of his father's second marriage and, being born in a caul, was acclaimed by the superstitious of the time to be destined for happiness and fame. There was much in his support-ive family and his own emerging self-confidence and ambition to justify the possibilities of that prediction. His father, a Jewish wool merchant, is described by Ernest Jones, perhaps the best known of Freud's many biographers, as 'of a gentle disposition, well loved by all in his family'; his mother, of a 'lively personal-ity', is said to have adored her firstborn. Anti-Semitism was amongst the factors which led to the uprooting of the Freuds from Freiberg in 1859 when Sigmund was three years of age. After a spell in Leipzig, the family settled in Vienna a year later.[4]

Another cardinal influence in his early years was a severe and elderly nannie, whom Freud later referred to as 'that prehistoric old woman'. As a Catholic, she would take the young Sigmund to church services regularly. When considering the paucity of in-formation on Freud's religious background, Jones writes: 'There was, of course, the Catholic nannie, and perhaps her terrifying influence contributed to his later dislike of Christian beliefs and ceremonies.'[5] Although his Jewish origins meant a great deal to him, Freud 'grew up devoid of any belief in a God or immortality, and does not appear ever to have felt the need of it. The emotional needs that usually manifest themselves in adolescence found expression first in rather vague philosophical cogitations and, soon after, in an earnest adherence to the principles of science.'[6]

It was these 'principles of science' that seem to have fired Freud as he moved from adolescence into early adulthood. He was in good company for, whereas religion, politics and philosophy were seen by many nineteenth-century thinkers to have failed, science was widely hailed as the panacea for the world's ills.

As a Viennese Jew, it was appropriate for him to seek a career in one of the principal professions. It appears to have been an investigative curiosity about the human condition that prompted him towards medicine, a discipline that he was never completely at home in.[7] Within his studies as a medical student, it was the biological sciences to which he gave the priority, the subjects of zoology and physiology, in particular, fuelling his achievements in research. While studying at the University of Vienna he came under the far-reaching influence of Ernst Brücke (1819–1892), the renowned physiologist who belonged to the so-called Helmholtz 'school of medicine', named after its most famous member. The scientific philosophy behind this school stressed both an evolutionary view, in which the higher animals, including man, have developed over millions of years from simple one-cell organisms, and a dynamic concept, within which life is subject to no other forces than the chemico-physical ones of attraction and repulsion. This biological stance became integral to Freud's understanding of human personality and its psychological conflicts.[8]

Another crucial influence on Freud's thinking was the rise of sexology as a science in the 1870s and 1880s. Amongst the earlier sexologists, the work of Richard von Krafft-Ebing (1840–1902) of Vienna and Havelock Ellis (1859–1939) of England can be seen as especially relevant to Freud's understanding of human development, with its emphasis on the pervasive importance of sexuality.[9]

Once qualified, Freud continued to work at the Brücke Institute pursuing his research in physiology. However, after a year or so, facing the prospect of dwindling financial resources, he moved out into hospital medicine. Even so, his interest in the biological sciences persisted and he spent most of the next fifteen years following investigations in neuranatomy and neurology. It was not until the age of thirty-nine or so that he began to develop the essentials of his psychoanalytic theory.

Whereas Pavlov and the associationists (see pages 43–44) pursued the apparently straightforward path of investigating animal and human behaviour, Freud carried the enquiry into the largely unknown, and perhaps unknowable, field of man's inner life by asking what is going on below the surface. In order to follow this venturesome course, he would postulate a theory first and then proceed with his probings on the basis of its validity in order to see whether it could be confirmed. If observable facts did not fit with his conjectures, the hypothesis was rejected. In this way he built up his elaborate and complex perspectives on the psychological understanding of human nature. His theories were so far-reaching and, to many minds, subversive that he received criticism from all sides. His medical colleagues accused him of neglecting the organic, academic psychologists found him un-scientific and philosophers regarded him as unethical.[10] In spite of this censure, as Wolman writes: 'Nothing could stop him in the ardent pursuit of the truth; neither his personal biases nor even his own former statements were spared by his critical mind.'[11]

It is impossible in the space of one chapter to do justice to the comprehensiveness of Freudian theory, but it is important to describe some of the salient pillars of the system he initiated if we are going to comprehend something of the growth in psychoanalysis and attempt to measure its relation to Christian thinking. His general approach was *deterministic*; of this he once said, 'no causes without effects, no effects without causes'.[12] Although, like the behaviourists, he was *monistic*, believing in the unity of humankind and nature, he was less reductionist than the 'man is only an animal' or 'man is only a machine' theorists. It is part of his integrity as a scientist that he was prepared to modify his views as new evidence came his way. Let us consider four main areas of his understanding of human nature: the uncon-scious, the theory of instincts, the notion of developmental stages and his theory of personality.[13]

The unconscious

Although earlier psychologists had largely ignored all aspects of the mind except those conscious areas of reason, memory and the will, there were a few enquirers who tapped the deeper layers of the 'unconscious'. The idiosyncratic Franz Anton Mesmer (1734–1815), whose treatment of nervous conditions by 'animal magnetism' has brought the word 'mesmerism' into the language, was one of these. This Austrian physician induced a drowsy state in his subjects through, so he declared, a mysterious fluid which passed from the 'magnetising' doctor to bring its healing properties to the patient. This trance-like condition was, in the middle of the nineteenth century, investigated by the Scottish surgeon, James Braid (1795–1861), who first coined the word 'hypnotism' to cover its induction by means of urging the client to stare fixedly at a bright light.

In the early 1880s, the neurologist, Jean-Martin Charcot (1825–1893), working at the Salpêtrière in Paris, revived the interest in hypnosis still further by using this method to elucidate the condition of hysteria. In 1885 the newly qualified Dr Sigmund Freud began a period of four and a half months at the Salpêtrière, attending Charcot's intriguing demonstrations and, thereby, learning how hitherto hidden mechanisms of the mind can operate to produce hysterical paralysis under hypnosis. Freud wrote of the impact of these experiences in his *Autobiography*: 'I received the profoundest impression of the possibility that there could be powerful mental processes which nevertheless remained hidden from the consciousness of men.'[14]

On his return to Vienna, Freud started to work with Josef Breuer (1842–1925) the physiologist, thus establishing, in time, their combined understanding of hysteria and its cure. Finding that the patients' past experiences, although apparently inaccessible to conscious memory, could be recalled under hypnosis, Freud began to formulate his appraisal of the 'mental provinces': the *conscious*; the *preconscious*, that level which can readily become conscious as when slips of the tongue, the mislaying of significant objects or the forgetting of well known names come into awareness; and the *unconscious*, the deeper layers of which may never reach consciousness.

Freud argued that an infant gradually builds up a conscious mind through experiencing persistent stimuli such as noise or hunger. In the older person, access to the unconscious may be achieved through an understanding of dreams. When we dream, Freud stated, we go back, or *regress*, into a state of mind that has been present since the womb. In this inner world our more hidden desires may be given expression unwittingly, a phenomenon alluded to by Freud as *wish-fulfilment*.

When certain mental processes are prevented from rising into consciousness *repression* is taking place. Where that repression is steadfastly held even in the face of therapy, Freud calls this *resistance*. By the same token, he argued that many neurotic symptoms arise as a compromise between unconscious demands and their conscious monitoring. For example, if I, having lied to someone, insist on repressing the memory of that falsehood because its recall makes me feel uncomfortable, then I may well develop a tension headache every time I meet the person I have deceived.

Theory of instincts

Within the psychological structure of a person, Freud believed there is a *principle of constancy* that tends to restore inner equilibrium. He also postulated psychic *energy* which is involved in achieving that stability. This energy can be used unproductively in trying to resolve inner conflicts so that the man or woman who battles with submerged dilemmas can become very tired physically. Those 'forces' that release this mental energy Freud described as *instincts*. In his *Beyond the Pleasure Principle* he said that instincts are:

> the representatives of all the forces originating in the interior of the
> body and transmitted to the mental apparatus – at once the most
> important and the most obscure element of psychological research.[15]

Freud frequently modified his understanding of these powerful forces. Initially he argued that there are two basic instincts: the *ego* (or self-preserving) and the *sexual* (or self-reproducing) instincts. The self-preserving instinct was seen to comprise the *pleasure principle* and the *reality principle*. The former leads to the avoidance of pain by an unrealistic 'wishing' of the 'satisfaction necessary to reduce the tension'. This 'wish-fulfilment' can be replaced by the adaptive behaviour of the reality principle which helps the person to adjust to the external world.[16] If I long profoundly for a particular pleasure, say a sailing holiday with a special friend, then the reality principle will need to apply in terms of discovering whether the friend shares my enthusiasm for the venture and, if so, arranging mutually suitable dates, booking the boat and planning practicalities in some detail. Without this circumspection, the pleasure principle will try to relieve frustration through unrealistic day-dreaming and may end up running blindly ahead in a self-defeating way. The desired holiday will either never take place or will be an unqualified disaster.

Later in the development of his thinking, Freud subsumed both these instincts under the one force of *eros* whose energy he called *libido*. He saw the dual aim of eros as being to establish 'ever greater unities and to preserve them, thus – in short, to bind together'.[17]

In 1920 Freud revised his theory of instincts once more as he faced up to the destructive aspects of man's nature. Here he postulated *thanatos*, the death instinct. He contrasted the sexual instincts, with their bid for life, with those instincts that tend towards destruction:

> They (the sexual instincts) are the true life instincts. They operate against the purpose of the other instincts, which leads, by reason of their function, to death; and this fact indicates that there is an opposition between them and the other instincts . . .[18]

Developmental stages

Like Darwin did with respect to other animals, Freud argued for a series of stages of development in the human species. The concept of a number of fairly clear-cut phases and the fact that Freud based these stages on strongly sexual themes lead to a fair amount of difficulty for minds with more fluid ideas of development and for thinking that baulks at any notion of sexuality within childhood. We will consider some objections to both this area of Freud's reasoning and other aspects of his theory later in this chapter. Each developmental stage is characterised by the part of the body which is thought to give the most pleasure during that phase.

The neonatal phase.   Freud said that the newborn infant is pre-occupied with sleep and a self-preservation which he dubbed *narcissism*. The neonate is seen as at one with the foetal state in his or her experience of *oceanic feelings* where there is an 'unconscious craving for unification with the outer world'. We shall pick up this perspective once more when we look at the methodology of Frank Lake in a later chapter.

The oral phase.   According to Freud, the newly born infant is 'polymorphously perverse' in that all areas of his or her body may 'strive for pleasure'. However, the oral pleasure of sucking is paramount and the mother's breast becomes the first *object* of sexual desire. A refinement of Freud's argument, put forward by his associate, Karl Abraham, is that the infant moves from an early stage of dependency, called *oral-passive*, through to the time of teething when there may be frustration with the breast in the *oral-aggressive* stage. Many nursing mothers will find some agreement with this second descriptive term!

The anal phase.   This phase is the hallmark of the second and third years of the child's life, within which satisfaction may be found from both the excretion and the retention of faeces. Again, Abraham distinguished an early *anal-expulsive* phase followed by an *anal-retentive* period. The latter is seen as linked with the child's pleasurable involvement with possessing and preserving such objects as certain toys and small pets.

The urethral phase.   Freud saw this as an autoerotic phase within which there might be fantasies of urinating on others and being urinated on. He argued that this stage may lead small girls into wanting the unique possession of their brothers, so-called *penis envy*.

The phallic phase.   At the age of four the phallic phase is entered wherein the life instinct, or libido, becomes 'located' in the child's genital organs.

For the four or five-year-old boy the phallic phase is the stage of the *Oedipus complex*, a period of inner conflict that Freud compared with the tragic Greek story by Sophocles of the young Oedipus who slew a man and, later, married the man's wife, not realising that in so doing he murdered his father and committed incest with his own mother. Freud postulated that during this phase a boy desires his mother and longs to take his father's place. This longing may lead to a powerful psychic struggle between wanting to do away with the father and loving him.

Freud reasoned that various irresolutions of this complex can lead to conflicts which continue into adult life. For example, where a boy's love for his father is particularly strong then his desire for his mother may be persistently repressed; this 'negative' Oedipus complex can develop, Freud said, into homosexual tendencies later. Conversely, fear of the father and undue dependency on the mother can, in turn, result in a predominantly submissive attitude towards women.

In girls of this age, Freud argued for a continuing 'penis envy' which leads a child, initially, to reject her mother. In time, with normal development, she begins to identify increasingly with the mother, seeing her father as her main 'love object'.

The latency phase.   From the age of six up to puberty both boys and girls experience a decline in sexual desire and tend to identify strongly with both friends and the parent of the same sex. This is the period in which boys group into warring tribes and girls cluster together to enter a collective fantasy world. It is also during this time that parental prohibitions and strictures are taken into the child's mind, or *internalised*. In this way, Freud believed, a conscience is established.

Puberty.   At this stage of renewed sexual awareness the libido begins to detach from the parents and becomes focused increasingly on to the opposite sex. If this process of disengaging from childhood's dependence on mother and father advances normally, the emergent adolescent feels tenderness towards his girlfriends or her boyfriends.

Although Freud regarded these phases of development as universal, he also conceded a degree of variation due to environmental factors. A family with an only child, one with a son or daughter who is seriously ill, or one in which a parent has died are obvious examples where circumstances will modify the dynamics of Freud's stages.

Further, Freud saw *neurosis* as a going back, or *regression*, to an earlier phase. As an example of this point, I know of an eighteen-year-old young man who is extremely isolated by a series of circumstances and has responded to these by neurotic behaviour. His parents' marriage has split up, he lives alone with his father, he is gauche and shy with his contemporaries, he has no job and he has regressed to playing 'cowboys and Indians' with seven and eight-year-olds. Freud might have said that this adolescent's 'libido has returned to earlier love objects'. Alternatively, such inappropriate ways of behaving may be seen as the result of a *fixation* of the libido, in which the person is held up at one or other of the developmental stages, in this instance at the latency phase.

Theory of personality

Freud's hypotheses led him to declare two instinctual forces, eros and thanatos, as 'the economy of the mind'; three mental provinces, the conscious, preconscious and unconscious, as the 'topography of the mind'; and, later in his thinking, three mechanisms of personality, the *id*, *ego* and *superego*, as the 'dynamics of the mind'.

The id.   The aspect of the personality called the id dwells entirely in the unconscious and its energy is almost completely at the disposal of the two basic instincts. Within this framework, the id 'blindly obeys the pleasure principle'. This concept is seen most clearly in the newborn child who, Freud maintained, has only this one mechanism within his or her mind. The neonate's id expresses 'the immediate satisfaction of its innate needs'. That pressing immediacy is known by every mother as she offers her breast to her complaining newly born baby.

The ego.   As the tiny infant develops, the outside stimuli of human voices, doors opening and closing, the switching on of a light, the smell and taste of the mother's milk, the warmth and softness of her breast, the feel of a changed nappy, all help to build up an awareness that is part of the emerging ego. At first, Freud conjectured, the baby, satiated by milk, has an essentially narcissistic love. In time, with increasing response to the external world, this self-love merges into elements of object love – love for the mother's breast initially and, later, love for other aspects of the parents, for brothers and sisters, for a cuddly toy, a particular piece of blanket, and so on.

The main goal of the ego is the 'self-preservation of the organism'. Although it may obey the pleasure principle most readily, as the years pass the ego, if developing healthily, learns to abide by the reality principle to a large degree. The perception of the ego becomes progressively refined through reasoning, memory and learning by testing out the environment. Most of us use a different language to that of psychoanalysis in the everyday situation. If an eight-year-old boy invariably snatches the one remaining cream bun without asking and wolfs it down, we see him as selfish and spoiled. Here the pleasure principle operates unabated. If the same child one day offers his aunt the cream bun, we may regard him as being altruistic. However, it may simply be that he believes this move will still bring the coveted bun his way.

Better still from the boy's point of view, he may be able to devour his prize with his aunt's approval sounding in his ears. Here the reality principle has been found to augment the pleasure principle and the boy's ego is a shade wiser, if not less selfish.

The superego. As the child's ego continues to develop, parental prohibitions: 'Don't you dare do that!', 'Come away from there!', 'Put that down!', 'If you say that again, I'll smack you!' are taken into the child's mind as the forerunners of the superego. This mechanism is further built up by the five-year-old child's tendency to idealise his or her parents, producing an internal picture of human perfection that Freud called the *ego-ideal*. In these ways the superego becomes gradually separate from the ego and forms a monitoring device which is the source of moral and behavioural strictures, an inner 'parental voice'. Freud described the superego's functions in powerfully autocratic terms:

> The superego has the ego at its mercy and applies the most severe moral standards to it; indeed it represents the whole demands of morality and we see all at once that our moral sense of guilt is the expression of the tension between the ego and superego.[19]

As the child grows into adolescence and adulthood the superego commonly becomes a less strident censor, acquiring a greater sense of objectivity related to the moral stance of the society within which the person lives.

The relation between id, ego and superego has been helpfully likened to driving a motor-car.[20] The id longs to put the foot down on the accelerator and be completely governed by the sheer thrill of driving at breakneck speed to leave a trail of havoc glimpsed in the wing mirror. The superego is the back seat driver, urging slower speeds and excessive circumspection, and repeatedly quoting the Highway Code, anticipating police intervention at every corner. The ego strives to contain and utilise these opposing energies by driving in a realistic but enjoyable way commensurate with road conditions, time available and choice of route.

Before considering the application of Freud's theories to therapy and an appraisal of his views and their practical implications, it may be useful to look briefly at some of his comments in the realms of religion and philosophy.

Freud and religion

Although from quite early on in his psychoanalytic career (e.g. in the 1907 paper 'Obsessional Actions and Religious Practices' and in his 1912–13 book *Totem and Taboo*) Freud declared an interest in religious matters, it was not till after 1920 that he turned his attention more fully to an assessment of such general themes as civilisation, the nature of religion and issues of war and peace.[21] This thinking led to the publication of *The Future of an Illusion* in 1927, *Civilization and its Discontents* in 1930 and *Moses and Monotheism* in 1939.

In *Totem and Taboo*, Freud had argued that the longing for a father is at the root of man's need for a religion. As a result of this atavistic desire, mankind invented God as the 'exalted father' to give protection against adversity and the unknown. Freud continued this thesis in *The Future of an Illusion*: 'a man makes the forces of nature not simply into persons with whom he can associate as he would with his equals . . . but he gives them the character of a father. He turns them into gods . . .'[22] Freud saw religion as an illusion, that is 'derived from human wishes', although, he went on, such illusions 'need not necessarily be false – that is to say, unrealizable or in contradiction with reality'. However, he underlined, '. . . we call a belief an illusion when a wish-fulfilment is a prominent factor in its motivation'. He declared his own hand by writing: 'But scientific work is the only road which can lead us to a knowledge of reality outside ourselves.'[23]

Later on in *The Future of an Illusion*, he was even more forcible when he wrote that religion is 'the universal obsessional neurosis of humanity' which civilisation needs to grow out of.[24] Interestingly, he explained the lack of neurosis that he observed in religious believers as due to 'their acceptance of the universal neurosis' which 'spares them the task of constructing a personal one'.[25]

As has already been suggested in our consideration of Freud's theory of the personality, he saw a person's moral sense as developing in childhood through the child's views of his or her parents. Within adult life, the superego is the seat of a man's or woman's belief in a superior 'Father' who punishes wrong and rewards right.[26] Freud was particularly astringent about this growth of a conscience when he wrote in 1933:

The philosopher Kant once declared that nothing proved to him the greatness of God more convincingly than the starry heavens and the moral conscience within us. The stars are unquestionably superb but, where conscience is concerned, God has been guilty of an uneven and careless piece of work, for a great many men have only a limited share of it or scarcely enough to be worth mentioning.[27]

The practice of psychoanalysis

As we have seen earlier in the chapter, Freud's psychoanalytic view of human nature began to take its clearest shape following his period of study under Charcot in the winter of 1885–86. His profoundly awakened awareness of the unconscious was reinforced during his subsequent work with Breuer in Vienna. These men, using hypnotherapy, cured many hysterics through the recall of their subjects' past experiences; the discharge of repressed 'energy' achieved under hypnosis was labelled the method of *catharsis*.

In time, Freud moved beyond the technique of hypnosis into the world of dream interpretation. Here he used the method of *free association*, within which, using a part of a patient's dream as a starting point, he encouraged the client to declare whatever sprang to mind regardless of apparent relevance and considerations of social nicety. Sometimes, if a proper name or a number surfaced in the patient's account, Freud would encourage the client to focus his attention on that specific item or numeral and then verbalise any associations that occurred. He said of what came to mind on such occasions 'that it is always strictly determined by important internal attitudes of mind which are not known to us at the moment at which they operate . . .'[28] With this technique Freud was able to plumb the depths of the unconscious and help his patients to understand some of the more hidden forces in their lives.

Free association became the primary method of psychoanalysis in which the patient, reclining on a couch and with the therapist out of sight, was invited to declare quite freely whatever came to mind, whether the starting point was part of a dream or some other notion in his consciousness. There had been a shift from a very active role for the therapist in hypnosis through to a much more passive one using the technique of free association.

In the initial period in the psychoanalysis of a client, the therapist often finds that his or her explanations of what the patient is saying are at their most effective. However, this 'analytic honeymoon' often leads into a stage of resistance on the part of the patient when all insights seem to be lost and any interpretation is useless. Beyond this frustrating phase, a period follows in which the analysand's neurotic thoughts and words are caught up in the developing relationship with the analyst. The person in need may, for example, be a young woman harbouring a great deal of subconscious fear towards a powerful father. This fear is neurotic in so far as it stems from her childhood impressions of him although, by all accounts, he is now an amicable old man. She may transfer this largely irrational fear on to her therapist. This phenomenon, the *transference neurosis*, is the turning point in Freudian analysis. The deeper layers of the patient's repressions have been tapped and their released force channelled towards the therapist. At this stage, there is a real danger of the client becoming dependent on, in our example, her therapist as she begins to discover she need not fear *him*, at least.

With these emerging insights, the analyst seeks again and again to interpret this transference to the analysand, relating the source of her neurotic fear back to childhood. As she understands the origin of her anxiety the process helps release her from the fear of her father, and its transference to the therapist, through to a loss of a crippling apprehension with older men generally.

The analyst's role in this classical Freudian therapy is both to keep in the background while the analysand struggles to declare *all* that comes to mind and also to help the client in that struggle by three main techniques: confrontation, interpretation and reconstruction. In *confrontation*, the patient is challenged by the therapist in this manner: 'You are clearly afraid and yet you will not admit it'; in *interpretation* the analyst offers some explanation to the analysand, for example: 'You are afraid of me because I remind you of your father, and you deny your fear because you want to be thought well of'; and in *reconstruction*, there is an attempt to explain the present in terms of the past, as in: 'Your fear of older men arises from your intense anxiety as a child whenever your father threatened violence.'[29]

The aim of all this clarification is to help the patient face up to his or her true self by allowing repressed memories, desires, thoughts and attitudes to surface into consciousness.[30] For most people this is a daunting prospect, both in terms of the painful nature of a surfeit of self-revelation and the commitment of time and money required in the relationship with the analyst. In traditional Freudian analysis, the analysand would be expected to attend for therapy four or five days a week for three or more years. Some of the early analysts, notably Ferenczi and Rank in the 1920s, sought a briefer involvement to help the patient although, in time, there was a tendency for treatment to lengthen once more.

In recent years, there have been some laudable further attempts to shorten the period of time needed to help someone substantially by analytic methods. D. H. Malan in his book *A Study of Brief Psychotherapy* wrote up evaluations of a therapy which centred on one key area of need (so-called 'focal therapy') and occupied ten to forty one-hour weekly sessions. This research established that the best outlook for this particular approach was found where:

> The patient has a high motivation; the therapist has a high enthusiasm; transference arises early and becomes a major feature of therapy; and grief and anger at termination (of treatment) are important issues.[31]

More succinctly, and in accordance with our discussion in chapter two (see pages 28–36), Malan concludes:

> That the prognosis is best when there is a willingness on the part of both patient and therapist to become *deeply involved*, and . . . to bear the tension that inevitably ensues.[32]

A critique of Freudianism

The theoretical framework of Freud's thinking on the psychology of man is so comprehensive and far-reaching that, inevitably, he has gathered many critics and even enemies through the years, as well as being the inspiration of a sometimes adulatory following. In the next chapter we will examine some of the ways his views have been venerated, modified, refuted and superseded in the years since his hey-day by various other therapists; here our assessment will consider the implications of Freud's thought for a Christian view-point.

First of all, let it be said that we owe a great deal of our understanding of the complexity of men and women in the psychological area to Freud. The extent of the infiltration of his ideas into our everyday language is remarkable. Such concepts as the ego, libido, repression, slips of the tongue, the significance of dreams and the Oedipus complex are well embedded in Western culture. Moreover, his relentless exploration of the realm of the unconscious was innovative and, in fact, courageous in the face of the reductionist and materialist views of his time. He was quite extraordinary in the earnestness of his application of psycho-analytic thinking and it is extremely impressive that, with all the imperfections of his theories, one man's lifetime could see the initiation, development and virtual completion of a whole methodological system.

Given that Freud has been under fire from the academic psychologists for being unscientific, from humanistic and theistic psychologists for being too reductionist and from the behaviour-ists for not being reductionist enough, let us try to evaluate some of the cardinal points of his psychological theory and his more philosophical writings.

Psychological theory

Freud's theory of instincts, which he repeatedly revised, has always been open to strong criticism. The extreme pervasiveness of the sexual instinct that he postulated is a source of continuing controversy. Is the mother's breast primarily an object of sexual desire to the infant? Is not the baby's drive to suckle more likely to relate to hunger and the need for warmth and security? Is the fondling of the genitals in a four-year-old inevitably 'autoerotic'? May this manipulation of organs not be a natural part of a child's curiosity about his or her own body? Similarly, Freud's view of the generality of the 'pleasure principle' is questionable. How, for example, does this striving for self-gratification (and, for that matter, its modification by the 'reality principle') operate where a refugee mother gives her last morsel of rice to her dying child or when an internee of a concentration camp steps forward to face execution on behalf of his fellow-victim?

Many in the psychoanalytic tradition have also criticised Freud's idea of developmental stages along with the powerfully sexual connotations of his theory. Included under this criticism is the question of the Oedipus complex and its universality. Are the conflicts within the five-year-old boy, in relation to his longing for his mother and his ambivalence towards his father, as inevitable as Freud said? Conversely, is 'penis-envy' an intrinsic preoccupation for a girl of a similar age? This questioning is not to say that these mechanisms never operate in the life of a growing family, but simply to ask what evidence there is for them being integral to the development of all individuals.

Freud's theory of personality has also come under cross-fire with respect to both the emergence of the ego and the growth of the superego. Whether the ego, with its perceptions of the inner and outer worlds, is already present at birth is one of the imponderables of life, although the methodology which includes the reliving of foetal and neonatal experiences (see chapter fifteen) suggests that it might be. But where many readers of this book will part company with Freud is with regard to his belief that the conscience is primarily a harsh parental voice that is instilled into the psyche during childhood.[33] Without denying that a parent's strictures are internalised in this way and that a moral stance develops in the context of society while a person matures, the Christian would want to add that God is at work too, seeking to challenge and educate conscience through his Spirit and according to his word.

Freud's theories on the nature of guilt have been another source of dispute. He spent a great deal of his time elaborating a theory of *neurosis*, that psychological state in which mental conflicts, whose origins are often hidden in the unconscious, disrupt a person's life. The commonest symptom of the neuroses is *anxiety*, in which the sufferer may be continually preoccupied by fearful and apprehensive feelings; for some these fears relate to specific situations and for others there is a general unease, or 'free-floating' anxiety. Freud saw anxiety as comprising: *moral anxiety*, which arises from dilemmas posed by the superego; *reality anxiety*, which preoccupies the ego and is engendered by objective danger and difficulty; and *neurotic anxiety*, which is the result of submerged conflicts within the id. An integral part of anxiety is commonly a sense of guilt and Freud pursued his own thinking on this widespread phenomenon. In *Totem and Taboo*, he related mankind's awareness of guilt to the twin taboos of incest and parricide. In turn, these forbidden activities of sexual intercourse with a mother and the murdering of a father were linked by Freud to the Oedipus complex (see page 62). We pick up the far-reaching implications of his view that much guilt relates to the repression of these proscribed desires in this extract from his *Introductory Lectures on Psychoanalysis*:

> There can be no doubt that the Oedipus complex may be looked upon as one of the most important sources of the sense of guilt by which neurotics are so often tormented. But more than this: in . . . *Totem and Taboo* . . . I put forward a suggestion that mankind as a whole may have acquired its sense of guilt, the ultimate source of religion and morality, at the beginning of its history, in connection with the Oedipus complex.[34]

Here again, a Christian mind will find much to disagree with. Allowing for the concept that a great deal of guilty feeling is neurotic in that the sense of conviction bears little or no relation to reality (and even this concession is disputed in some Christian circles), we cannot permit so comprehensive a view on humankind's guilt to go unchallenged. As Harold Darling writes: 'Because Freud reasons from naturalistic presuppositions, he does not accept the roles of freedom, autonomy and responsibility in personality. Nor does he postulate a sense of sin that can be remedied by repentance.'[35] The Bible, of course, is crystal-clear about the universality of man's sin and his objective guilt before a holy and righteous God. We see this declared uncompromisingly in, for example, Psalm 14:2,3:

> The Lord looks down from heaven upon the children of men, to see if there are any that act wisely, that seek after God. They have all gone astray, they are all alike corrupt; there is none that does good, no, not one.[36]

We will pick up the important discussion on true and false guilt at a number of points in the coming chapters.

Philosophical ideas

As we have looked at Freud's views on religion (pages 66–67) and attempted a critique of some of his psychological conclusions, we have seen the wide-ranging implications of his assumptions with respect to man's conscience, his sense of guilt and his aspirations for a heavenly Father. Freud argued, as we have also seen, that belief in God is a wish-fulfilment in countless people who feel the need for that sort of security. He regarded this 'illusion' as essentially neurotic, that is to say as appropriate to an earlier stage in mankind's evolutionary progress. Modern, civilised man should dispense with such props.

Freud also said that religion lacked integrity because:

1 It argues that we should believe because our primal ancestors did;
2 We have handed down to us so-called 'proofs' which 'bear every mark of untrustworthiness';
3 We are *not* allowed to challenge the authenticity of these 'proofs'.[37]

This position of Freud's is, not surprisingly, a dated one, fitting the scepticism towards religion and the adulation of the scientific method of his day. His view that belief in God developed simply to meet man's needs and his dismissal of 'untrustworthy proofs' are strongly opposed by the traditional Jewish and Christian faiths, backed by God's revelation of himself through both the Old and New Testaments within the framework of history.[38]

Of Freud's presuppositions, Wolman has written:

Freud's starting point was the natural sciences. He adhered strictly to the principles of determinism, monism, conservation of energy, and empiricism. . . . His theory was deeply rooted in the biological sciences and their methods of research.[39]

In other words, he operated within a 'closed system' of 'cause and effect' in which the biological and physical laws of nature determined every aspect of man's existence. In essence, he argued that man's evolution from the lower animals, the emergence of religious belief and civilisation, and the development of each individual personality were subject to inexorable natural laws.

Perhaps it is here that Christian thinking takes greatest issue with the founder of psychoanalysis. The Christian believes in a creator God who brought all that exists into being and who sustains the universe by his power and love; he also declares a redeemer God who has intervened in history in countless ways but supremely in the incarnation, life, death and resurrection of his Son, and in the sending of the Holy Spirit. This is a God who calls man, both individually and corporately, to *choose* good rather than evil, life rather than death, the Lord's way rather than the Enemy's. This blend of divine determinism ('I will have mercy on whom I have mercy') and man's freedom to choose ('choose this day whom you will serve') is at the heart of biblical revelation and is a far cry from Freud's naturalistic world view.

Summary

We have taken pains to trace the rise and initial growth of the tree of psychoanalysis from its roots in the generative soil of Darwinism, the empirical sciences and the metaphysical psychology of Herbart. We have both honoured and censured the theory and practice of the man whose inquiring mind started and sustained the impressive main trunk of the psychoanalytic system.

This tree, some of whose roots interlace with those of the tree of behaviourism, especially in the soil of the scientific method, is a formidable neighbour for the tree of pastoral care. Although the Freudian tree's predominant growth is away from the rigorous externality of behaviourism and towards the enticing obscurities of man's inner nature, its very involvement with the deeper needs of humankind has entangled its branches with its other, more saintly neighbour. As we shall see in the coming chapters, this tree of pastoral care has found the proximity and apparent omniscience of its secular companion seductively attractive. At times the commingling of the two systems has led to hybridisation, the resultant progeny including saplings which bear a much stronger resemblance to the analytic tree than the pastoral one.

In the next chapter we will explore the continuing growth, branching and splitting of the endlessly ramifying tree of psychoanalysis.

5

PSYCHOANALYSIS: MAN AND SOCIETY

I consider my contribution to psychology to be my subjective confession. It is my personal psychology, my prejudice that I see psychological facts as I do . . . But I expect Freud and Adler to do the same and confess that their ideas are their subjective point of view. So far as we admit our personal prejudice, we are really contributing towards an objective psychology.

C. G. Jung

In the last chapter we traced the burgeoning growth of our second tree of secular psychology, the system of orthodox Freudian psychoanalysis. In this chapter we will attempt to disentangle some of the major branchings of this main trunk. The bifurcations have led to a bewildering picture and so we will try to discern the primary elements that distinguish the tree's essential framework.

We have seen that Freud's classical position contains the important strands of a scientific determinism, an emphasis on the unconscious, an understanding that human behaviour is directed towards certain ends by powerful instincts and a developmental approach to personality. Broadly speaking, these four ingredients are continued in one form or another in the methodologies of most post-Freudian psychoanalytical theorists. However, it is with respect to Freud's rigorously biological orientation and his insistence on the primacy of his libido theory that the tree of psychoanalysis has experienced the strongest split in its main trunk. As a generalisation, orthodox Freudians have embraced these last two perspectives whereas the so-called neo-Freudians have, to a varying extent, questioned, revised and rejected them.[1]

J. A. C. Brown, in his *Freud and the Post-Freudians*, illustrates the divergence of these views when he postulates the different ways a Freudian and a neo-Freudian might regard an enthusiastic stamp-collector.[2] The strict Freudian will see his obsession as 'satisfying his libidinous needs at the anal level', whereas the neo-Freudian, with an emphasis on social and cultural factors, will admit that this *may* be the right perspective though not necessarily so; the latter's view will permit a motive of making money, an appreciation of the aesthetics of philately, the thrill of hunting for rare stamps in competition with others or other considerations as possible explanations for the stamp-collector's single-mindedness.

In assessing the predominant branchings of psychoanalysis, I propose to look at these subdivisions on a broadly chronological basis, starting with the early schismatics and then proceeding from the disruption and dispersal of the Austrian, German and Hungarian schools with the rise of Nazism to the continuing development of analytic insights on both sides of the Atlantic. This purview cannot do justice to the complexity of growth of this particular system but, hopefully, it will supply a skeleton of the outer structure of the tree of psychoanalysis which will be useful in our appraisal of Christian methodologies later in the book.

Early dissension

In the first decade of this century there grew up an increasing commitment to psychoanalysis around the figure of Sigmund Freud in Vienna. *Alfred Adler* (1870–1937), the son of a Hungarian Jewish family that had settled near the Austrian capital, was a part of this inner circle, although from 1907 onwards his formulation of his own psychological theory challenged certain of Freud's conclusions. In 1911 he gave a series of lectures criticising Freud's emphasis on the primacy of sexuality and advancing his own view of the importance of an innate aggressive drive (the *masculine protest*), which urges a person to strive to be adequate, thus expressing the *inferiority complex*. His papers met an apparently concerted opposition from Freud and his followers with the consequence that Adler severed his links with psychoanalysis later that year. In 1912, the publication of his book *The Neurotic Constitution* marked the founding of his individual psychology.

This so-called Second School of Viennese Psychotherapy rejected many Freudian features, including the theory of developmental stages and the universality of the Oedipus complex. Adler eschewed determinism and held a purposive view of human-kind, arguing that men and women are motivated by a striving towards goals. He also emphasised the importance of sociability and held a generally optimistic view of human nature. His humanistic tendency can be seen in what he wrote, in 1935:

> Whether one names the highest ideal as God or as Socialism or, like ourselves, as pure community feeling . . . we always see mirrored the powerful goal of human overcoming, with its promises of fulfilment and grace.[3]

In 1907, the year that Adler began to establish his views through his first published monograph, Carl Gustav Jung (1875–1961) was invited from Zurich in his native Switzerland to meet Freud, twenty years his senior, in Vienna. Jung had grown up in a Swiss village – the son of a clergyman, whose faith was often racked by doubt, and an outgoing and loving mother. His parents' marriage was far from happy and the inner turmoil of his father's Christian commitment did little to help Jung to resolve his own thinking about God. He studied medicine at Basel University and his doctoral thesis, based on observations of a young female medium known to some relatives of his, indicated a lifelong interest in the occult.[4]

Initially, Freud and Jung were a strong mutual stimulus and found a great deal of accord together. Jung became deeply involved with the psychoanalytic movement and was advanced by Freud as a prospective president of the International Psychoanalytical Association. However, like Adler's, Jung's thinking increasingly diverged from that of Freud. He rebelled against Freud's theory of libido with its strong sexual connotations and, while the founder of psychoanalysis was preoccupied with infantile sexuality, Jung turned his attention to the barely charted depths of the unconscious. The rift between these two men came in 1914.[5] We pick up something of the width and depth of this break in this extract from Jung's The Practice of Psychotherapy:

> . . . there is no denying the fact that Freud's theories have come up against certain rooted prejudices. It was to no purpose that he modified the worst aspects of his theories in later years. In the public eye he is branded by his first statements . . . they are backed by a

philosophy that is falling more and more out of favour with the public: a thoroughly materialistic point of view which has been generally abandoned since the turn of the century. Freud's exclusive standpoint . . . misinterprets the natural facts of the human psyche . . . Common sense does not tolerate the Freudian tendency to derive everything from sexuality and other moral incompatibilities. Such a view is too destructive.[6]

In his analytic psychology, Jung rejected the rule of the conscious in his elaboration of the unconscious. He saw libido as a primal and undifferentiated energy that can be expressed in a host of ways for man's self-preservation, for example through creativity, sensuality and superiority. He held that a principle of opposites, or *dialectic*, operated within man to maintain stability: 'all life is energy, and therefore depends on forces held in opposition'.[7]

Jung's view of personality is complex in that he paid a great deal of attention to the depths within man below the conscious level. He argued that all people have a *persona*, a 'mask' that signifies the different roles we play in our various functions and relationships. My persona may include my activity as husband, father, son, brother, doctor, counsellor, writer, church leader, bird-watcher, and so on. Behind and beneath the persona is the *shadow*, that darker side of ourselves which Jung placed in the *personal unconscious*, that realm beneath consciousness which is unique to the individual. He once said of this aspect of our human nature: 'the shadow is a moral problem which challenges the whole ego personality'.[8]

Deeper still within man's inner life, Jung postulated the *collective unconscious* which contains the memories of a whole race of people. He argued that within the collective unconscious there are hidden primordial images, or *archetypes*, which represent these memories. The archetypes include such concepts as the 'old wise man', the 'great mother' and the 'child-hero'. Of special significance amongst these images are the archetypes of the *anima* and the *animus*. Within each man, according to Jung, there is an anima, an image of woman that has been built up through the experience of men with women down through the ages. This archetype, which may have, for example, the guise of a *femme fatale* or a goddess of perfection, may surface into consciousness as part of a man's fantasy, dreams or hopes. Conversely, each woman has the image of the animus deep within her – an image that is often centred on the figure of her own father. Both the anima and the animus can be projected (the psychological mechanism whereby we ascribe to someone else images, qualities or conflicts that really belong within) on to another woman or man – sometimes with disastrous consequences. For example, a young woman, who has an image within her of a strong, decisive and resolute father, may see her new boyfriend in the same light, perhaps because he looks rather like her father did as a younger man. She may be blinded by this 'projection of the archetype' to the fact that, deep down, her man is weak, indecisive and irresolute. Blinkered to his faults, she may marry him and then spend the rest of her days discovering her mistake and, hopefully, adjusting accordingly.

With respect to his technique of psychotherapy, Jung has written in a diffident vein:

> My contribution to psychotherapy is confined to those cases in which rational treatment yields no satisfactory results. The clinical material at my disposal is of a special nature: new cases are decidedly in the minority. Most of my patients have already gone through some form of psychotherapeutic treatment, usually with partial or negative results. About a third of my cases are suffering from no clinically definable neurosis, but from the senselessness and emptiness of their lives. It seems to me, however, that this can well be described as the general neurosis of our time. Fully two-thirds of my patients have passed middle age.[9]

He goes on, not surprisingly with his emphasis on the unconscious, to consider dream analysis as at least one way of unlocking the door to a patient's real needs and difficulties, writing: 'I know that if we meditate on a dream sufficiently long and thoroughly – if we take it about with us and turn it over and over – something almost always comes of it.' Unlike Freud, who saw the stuff of dreams as repressed wishes, Jung seemed to regard the dream-world as having an anticipatory or even prophetic function. Of that 'something' which might come out of a dream, he wrote: 'It is a practical and important hint which shows the patient in what direction the unconscious is leading him.'[10]

With Jung's clerical background, his interest in the supernatural and his emphasis on the darker side of man's nature, it is not surprising that Christians, both Catholic and Protestant, have taken an interest in analytic psychology from time to time. In recent years, the erudite writings of Morton Kelsey are a case in point. In his book *Encounter with God* he evaluates the work of Carl Jung in some detail, demonstrating a great deal of compatibility between the thinking of the Swiss professor and some aspects of traditional Christianity. Describing a personal conversation with Jung, Kelsey writes:

> Yet many Jews, Protestants, and now present-day Catholics, have been torn from the systematic fabric of religion and so are forced to make their own adaptation to the spiritual world or flounder. Jung discovered that many of his patients came to him simply because their lack of religious framework had made them neurotic. In talking with him I learned that he did not get into the area of meaning and religious direction because he wanted to, but because he could find no clergy who knew this realm to whom he could refer patients who needed help along these lines, and therefore he had to enter this area himself.[11]

Jung, perhaps unduly influenced by his father's rather cerebral, and even arid approach to Christian doctrine, seems to have majored on the experiential aspect of religion. Kelsey quotes the famous statement by Jung when interviewed by the BBC in 1961, shortly before his death: 'Suddenly I understood that God was, for me at least, one of the most certain and immediate experiences . . . I do not believe; I know. I *know*.'[12] Christopher Bryant, a member of the Anglican community known as the Cowley Fathers, draws out Jung's abhorrence of Church dogma and his insistence on the need for a personal experience of God in his book *Jung and the Christian Way*:

> All his life Jung was concerned with knowing God, with the immediate intuitive awareness of God. He believed that the religion of many Christians who, like his father, relied on an intellectual faith, divorced from any experience of the realities believed in, was seriously defective. In a letter written in 1945 at the age of seventy he affirms, '*It is of the highest importance* that the educated and "enlightened" should know religious truth as a thing living in the human soul and not as an abstruse and unreasonable relic of the past.'[13]

It is clear from the writings of Christian protagonists like Kelsey and Bryant that Jung's position with regard to orthodox Christianity is an elusive one. His rejection of the credal dimensions of the Church is perhaps understandable in terms of his reaction to the effete clericalism he saw within his own family and in society. His quest for an understanding of the unconscious has proved attractive to certain Christians of a meditative and even mystical cast of mind. Believers who are perhaps more intellectualising and activist have been more wary of Jung's supernaturalism. I suspect that a wise approach to Jung is one of cautious open-mindedness, where his theories are tested out in the light of scripture and where his often intriguing insights are given due credence if compatible with divine revelation. We shall return to Jung and his ideas in chapter fourteen.

Perhaps the key to Jung's 'religious' position lies in his emphasis on *individuation*, that process through which a man becomes a 'whole' individual tempered by the conflict between his conscious and unconscious. This perspective, with its Christian connotations, is seen here in his essay 'Psychotherapists or the Clergy':

> We Protestants must sooner or later face this question: Are we to understand the 'imitation of Christ' in the sense that we should copy his life and, if I may use the expression, ape his stigmata; or in the deeper sense that we are to live our own proper lives as truly as he lived his in all its implications? It is no easy matter to live a life that is modelled on Christ's, but it is unspeakably harder to live one's own life as truly as Christ lived his.[14]

Since both Adler and Jung broke with Freud, the history of psychoanalysis has continued in a similar pattern, comprising a stream of Freudian adherents and a series of divergent channels which represent the thinking of the innovators. This formation is not surprising because any movement as comprehensive as Freud's system of psychology is bound to be followed by those who idolise and idealise the founder, as well as those variously described as amplifiers, modifiers or rebels.

Amongst the early 'modifiers', *Sandor Ferenczi* (1873–1933) was noteworthy in that he moved away from Freud's impassive stance in therapy, in which the psychoanalyst must never reveal anything of himself to the patient. Ferenczi cultivated a real two-way relationship between the therapist and client in which both transference (see pages 24, 68) and *counter transference* (in which the analyst may find his or her own feelings for a significant person transferred to the patient) were permitted and worked with. Ferenczi also sought to cut down the excessive length of Freudian analysis to save both time and, for the patient, money (see page 69).

Another 'modifier', *Otto Rank* (1884–1939), who was originally an orthodox Freudian, moved into open rebellion against Freud. He denied that the Oedipus complex is a primary source of neurosis and argued that the trauma of birth is the origin of all neurosis. He declared that the birth experience leads to a *separation anxiety* which, in turn, can be triggered by later 'separation' events, such as weaning, going to school and leaving home. We shall be reminded of Otto Rank's theories when we consider the work of Frank Lake later in the book.

The British school

The use of psychoanalytic theory extended dramatically during and after the First World War as conventional methods of dealing with the 'shell-shocked' proved inadequate. In Britain in the 1920s and 1930s the main analytical schools – Freudian, Adlerian and Jungian – were modestly represented. As on the Continent, there were two primary factions amongst the Freudians: an orthodox party, centred on Ernest Jones, the doyen of British psychoanalysis; and a more disparate group which held more individualistic and eclectic views.

Some members of the latter focused their work in and through the Tavistock Clinic, founded by Dr Crichton Miller in London in 1920. Amongst the more influential analysts working at the clinic was *Ian D. Suttie* (1889–1935) whose *The Origins of Love and Hate* was published in the year of his death. His position has been succinctly described by Dr J. A. C. Brown in his *Freud and the Post-Freudians*. He writes that to Suttie the 'child's basic need is for mother-love, his basic fear is loss of such love, and all his later cultural and social attitudes depend upon the nature of this relationship'.[15] Later, he declares: 'Suttie saw religion as performing the function of a psychosocial therapy, since both religion and psychotherapy exercise their influence in maintaining or regaining mental health by love.'[16] In these two perspectives we see a wide divergence from Freud's views with the latter's insistence on the primacy of the sex instinct and his assessment of religion as a compulsive neurosis.

Both the United States and Britain profited enormously from the mass exodus of talented Jews from Europe during the rise of Nazism. The psychoanalytic schools in Austria and Germany were disrupted as gifted émigrés headed westwards. Amongst those who came to England were Freud himself, his daughter Anna and Melanie Klein.

Melanie Klein (1882–1960) was born in Vienna of a Jewish family. Her father was from a strictly orthodox background and had been destined to become a rabbi. However, he rebelled against this eventuality and chose to read medicine instead. Dr Reizes divorced his first wife and later married a woman fifteen years his junior. He was over fifty when Melanie, the fourth and youngest child of this match, was born. Although his daughter respected his intellect, he seems to have been an impatient and somewhat distant figure. Melanie had a much closer relationship with her enterprising mother and the middle two of her siblings. Her upbringing was a liberal one, her father being rather anti-clerical. Although, at the tender age of nine or so, she was attracted to Catholicism through the influence of a French governess, beyond this early period of her life she regarded herself as an atheist, albeit one who respected her Jewish roots.[17]

Despite wanting to become a doctor, her engagement to her brother's friend, Arthur Klein, led to the frustration of these plans. This lack of a medical qualification was a continuing embarrassment to her during the controversies of her later career in psychoanalysis.

In 1910 she first encountered Freud's work while in Budapest with her husband but it was not until seven years later that she met the famous Viennese doctor. In the meantime she had sought her own analysis with Ferenczi who, in turn, encouraged her towards an interest in analysing children. In 1920 she met Freud's associate from Berlin, Karl Abraham, with whom she was very impressed. Dissatisfied with the results of her analysis with Ferenczi, she persuaded Abraham to continue her treatment. Subsequently, she saw her growing work in psychoanalysis as following the footsteps of both Freud and Abraham.[18]

Melanie Klein's marriage was an unhappy one and there was a divorce in 1922. Following an invitation by Ernest Jones to lecture in England in 1925, she emigrated to this country the next year, regarding the British as more supportive of her innovative ideas than the analysts of Vienna and Berlin.

In the late 1920s and 1930s an increasing amount of work was carried out which looked at the possibility of the psychoanalysis of children. On the Continent, Freud's daughter Anna pioneered this assessment amongst older children, stressing the importance of the ego and the many *defence mechanisms* that begin to operate within the developing child to enable him or her to cope with inner fears; one psychological reaction in this category that she outlined is that of *denial* when, for example, a toddler handles the unpleasantness of taking a bitter-tasting medicine by declaring, 'I love taking the medicine Mummy gives me' or a small boy deals with the everyday stress aroused by a harsh father by retreating into a fantasy: 'Teddy loves me and will chase Daddy away.' *Anna Freud* (1895–1982) was true to the Freudian tradition in that she emphasised the importance of the sexual drive; we can describe her as an 'amplifier' of her father's theories.[19]

In Britain, Melanie Klein argued that 'talking therapy' does not work with younger children and so developed her *play technique* of analysis. In this method she encouraged and observed the child's free play together with any verbal communication that emerged. She used the professional setting of a particular room, letting the child play with a special box of toys, including, for example, very small, indeterminate human figures where the two sizes could be used to represent adults and children. Hanna Segal, one of Melanie Klein's co-workers, in her book *Klein* points out the way this technique analyses 'the play exactly as one analyses dreams and free associations, interpreting phantasies, conflicts and defences'.[20] Klein herself spells out this extension of Freud's methods in her 1955 paper 'The Psychoanalytic Play Technique':

> . . . the brick, the little figure, the car, not only represent things which interest the child in themselves, but in his play with them they always have a variety of symbolical meanings as well which are bound up with his phantasies, wishes, and experiences. This archaic mode of expression is also the language with which we are familiar in dreams, and it was by approaching the play of the child in a way similar to Freud's interpretation of dreams that I found I could get access to the child's unconscious.[21]

Controversy between Anna Freud and Melanie Klein over Klein's use of transference in her work with young children, and other points of issue, flared up in 1927 at a symposium of child analysis. In spite of this interchange the British Psychoanalytical Society continued to thrive up to 1935, when dissent broke out in a fresh wave. This new outbreak followed the presentation of Melanie Klein's paper, entitled 'A Contribution to the Psychogenesis of Manic-Depressive States', in which she pursued her *object-relations theory* with respect to the inner life of the child within his or her first year of life. In this theory of personality development, 'objects' are internalised by the infant: this process of assimilating an outside influence into one's inner world is known as *introjection* (the opposite of *projection* in which aspects of the self are imagined as coming from external sources). These objects may be 'part objects', Klein argued, such as the mother's breast or they may, in time, be 'whole objects' such as the mother or father. Melanie Klein reasoned that there is a degree of conflict within the child relating to unadulterated pleasure on the one hand ('the good breast') and to feelings of frustration on the other ('the bad breast').

Controversy in the British Psychoanalytical Society was aggravated in the late 1930s by the advent of the Freud family who arrived in London in 1938. The dispute between Anna Freud and Melanie Klein became the 'focus of the scientific life of the Society'.[22] Ironically, the beginnings of the Second World War led to a truce between the warring parties for a while, although the debate was picked up in earnest in 1943 and 1944 through a series of papers which sought to clarify the Kleinian position. Both sides quoted Freud – the orthodox Freudians 'early Freud', and the Kleinians 'late Freud'.[23] Out of this melting pot three streams of thought and commitment emerged: those who followed Anna Freud; Melanie Klein's protagonists; and the majority, who accepted a limited amount of Kleinian theory.

It is interesting to reflect on the extreme intensity with which these pioneers of analytic thought attacked one another. It seems that the corpus of theory built up under Freud's name was viewed as some sort of inviolable temple in the minds of its adherents. As a result those who sought to examine the stonework or reassess some sections of the architecture were virtually accused of sacrilege, particularly if they were brave enough, or foolish enough, to inspect the foundations. Segal writes of Melanie Klein's reaction to this debate, which seemed at times to polarise between iconoclasm and adulation: 'She understood it intellectually, but she found it hard to accept that Freud would naturally be more disposed to support his own daughter.'[24]

In spite of her disappointment at Freud's coolness towards her, Melanie Klein has been a strong influence on many key figures in British psychoanalytical circles. Although she has been criticised for the complexity with which she endows the psyche of the infant and for the fact that her theories are basically unproven, her object-relations theory has become the starting-point for some very useful understandings of the development of human personality and its breakdown into mental illness.

This British school of Kleinian influence includes such analysts as Fairbairn, Winnicott, the Balints and Bowlby.[25]

W. *Ronald Fairbairn* (1890–1964), from Edinburgh, developed a purist approach to the object-relations theory in which he discarded Freud's libido theory completely. His thinking has been widely acclaimed in the United States, possibly because his dismissal of a biologically deterministic view and his espousal of a 'genuinely psychological psychology' accords with American sensibilities.[26]

Donald W. Winnicott (1896–1971) was less dominated in his thinking by the baby's orality and basic need for food than Melanie Klein. He coined the phrase 'good-enough mothering' for the quality of care shown by the mother, or mother-substitute, who offers the warmth and security needed by the infant to develop healthily as a person.[27] In 1948, he wrote of such a mother: 'she exists, continues to exist . . . is *there* to be sensed in all possible ways . . . she loves in a physical way, provides contact, a body temperature, movement and quiet according to the baby's needs'.[28] His comment at a medical society meeting in 1952 gives the flavour of his perceptive and humanising approach: 'By good-enough child-care, technique, holding and general management the shell becomes gradually taken over and the kernel (which had looked all the time like a human baby to us) can begin to be an individual.'[29]

Michael (1896–1970) *and Alice Balint*, from the Hungarian school of psychoanalysis, developed their views in the 1930s, departing from those of their fellow-countryman Sandor Ferenczi by arguing for an *active* concept of the 'object' relationship between the infant and the mother. The Balints regarded the baby's 'loving' of the mother as essentially egotistical, lacking any appreciation of the mother's interests. It was Michael Balint and his third wife Enid who, based at the Tavistock Clinic in London, later did so much to make psychoanalytic concepts available to the general practitioner in his or her busy surgery.[30]

Melanie Klein and these fellow-theorists each saw a different part of the child's early life as the most crucial and vulnerable period for the development of personality.[31] These distinctions can be shown as follows:

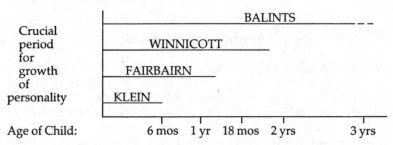

Figure 2   Growth of personality in childhood

Let us conclude our consideration of the British school of psychoanalysis by looking briefly at the important work of *John Bowlby* (b 1907) on 'attachment' and 'loss'. His research in the 1950s and 1960s was stimulated by a request from the World Health Organisation that sought advice on the mental health of homeless children. Working at the Tavistock Clinic and the Tavistock Institute of Human Relations and using a psychoanalytic frame of reference, he shaped his theory of the growth of personality in the child. Although acknowledging a debt to the 'object-relations' theorists, he also sees his thinking as essentially dovetailing with Freudian theory.

In volume one of his monumental *Attachment and Loss* Bowlby declares the reasoning behind his own instinct theory. He looks to ethology, the study of animal behaviour in near-natural conditions, and the behavioural sciences generally to argue that human instinct, as with other animals, has been adapted through the evolutionary process. He sees the attachment behaviour of the infant, including sucking, clinging, crying, and head movements, as a result of this adaptation. He contrasts the *dependence* of the child on the mother, with its decline in intensity through the years, with *attachment*, a bond which develops increasingly from the child's side from the age of six months and then decreases more gradually later.[32] Bowlby points out that many behaviour patterns of the adolescent and the adult can be related to this early attachment. One example is the close emotional tie often seen between a mother and her adult daughter; another is seen in the way an adolescent, when first away from home, may attach readily to a group or institution that formerly would not have interested him.

Beyond Freudianism

There is insufficient space to do justice to the great variety of valuable developments in psychoanalysis that have diverged to a varying degree from the main trunk of orthodox Freudianism over the last thirty to fifty years. Nonetheless, I would like to write a little about two important branches that have exercised considerable influence in psychotherapeutic circles: psycho-analysts who have majored on the study of certain cultures, namely Wilhelm Reich and Erik Erikson; and the so-called neo-Freudians – Karen Horney, Erich Fromm and Harry Stack Sullivan. I propose to concentrate mainly on Erikson, Horney and Fromm.

Psychoanalysis and culture

Wilhelm Reich (1897–1957) was originally a traditional Freudian whom Wolman describes as 'more Freudian than Freud himself in regard to the importance of libido'. He continues: 'To Reich, sexual potency was a criterion of mental health, and sexuality was the main factor in personality structure.'[33] Reich became particu-larly interested in the links between psychoanalysis and Marxism and is renowned for emphasising the way that certain types of personality are fostered by different socioeconomic systems. He also pointed out the link between many inner tensions and bodily postures and expressions, such as facial grimaces, tightly held abdominal muscles or a rigid stance. He advocated educating the patient to observe and find release from these strains before proceeding with analysis. This approach to mental health through a concentration on bodily aspects of stress is the main-spring of *bioenergetic therapy*.[34] Reich's later writings moved way beyond orthodoxy in, for example, his advocacy that the sexual orgasm is of 'fundamental importance in understanding the problems of the individual and society'.[35]

Erik H. Erikson (b 1902), the son of Danish parents, was born near Frankfurt in Germany. His parents separated before his birth and his mother, a few years later, married the German Jewish paediatrician who had been attending her son. Erik grew up to be a young man of artistic ability who spent a great deal of his time wandering the mountains of Western Europe. While teaching art in a school in Vienna from 1927 onwards, he came under the influence of the Freuds and, in due course, was analysed by Anna. Like many others during the ominous rise of Nazism, Erik Erikson was caught up in the view that

> . . . the study of psychoanalysis seemed to offer an urgent and valuable answer to such irrationality – if only enough people could understand themselves in a way never before possible. Then, and only then, said many of Freud's students, the madness that was gaining dominance over the market-places and parliaments of the West might be stopped.[36]

He completed his analytical training in 1933 to become a member of the Vienna Psychoanalytic Society, having married a visiting American a little before. That same year he and his wife emigrated to the United States where he took up the post of child analyst in Boston, also receiving an official position at the Harvard Medical School. Later, at Yale, and then in California from 1939 onwards, he spent a great deal of his time studying the children of the Sioux Indians and the fish-hunting Yurok people respectively. This interest in the links between cultural influences and the growth of the individual has been an abiding passion.

Although Erikson sought to build on and extend Freudian thinking, he was critical of the psychoanalytic tendency to relate the human condition inexorably back to infancy; he dismissed 'a habit of thinking which reduces every human situation to an analogy with an earlier one, and most of all to that earliest, simplest and most infantile precursor which is assumed to be its "origin"'.[37] He aimed to move away from the over-use of terms like 'oral' and 'anal' in an analytical context and put forward a theory of the development of 'infantile sexuality' to demonstrate the naturalness of the process. In time, he postulated a complete step-like advance from birth to adult maturity which is character-ised by an inner struggle between opposing forces at each stage.[38] This growth towards the 'wholeness' of the individual is based on an *epigenetic principle*, that is to say that out of a 'ground plan the parts arise, each part having its time of special ascendancy, until all parts have arisen to form a functioning whole'.[39] This model of psychological development is not a rigid one and allows for both overlap and regression of the stages. For example, a toddler at Erikson's second stage may, from time to time, slip back from a newly acquired autonomy ('I'm a big girl now!') to the first stage of dependency and the need to re-establish trust ('Mummy, I want you to stay with me!'). Erikson's successive steps of growth are depicted in figure 3 (below).[40]

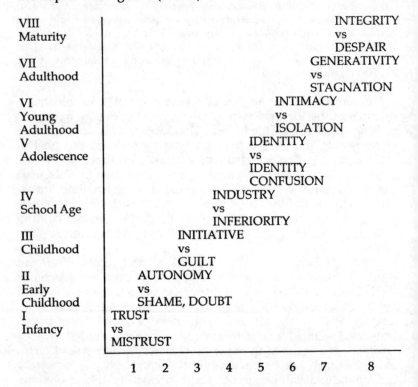

Figure 3　Steps to human maturity (after Erikson)

It is a feature of Erikson's sensitivity on behalf of others that he resisted the unhappy practice of so many psychoanalysts of using analytical terms pejoratively. He would refuse to dismiss a young man as showing 'marked passivity' or a middle-aged woman as 'sick' mentally or a 'typical sociopath'. Much of his work was amongst groups in society so easily overlooked or taken for granted, including Indian tribes, the children of American blacks, adolescents and war veterans.

In his work amongst young people, he pioneered the key concept of 'identity' (see figure 3), a perspective that is now deeply woven into the language of English-speaking people. Described by Robert Coles in his *Erik H. Erikson: the growth of his work* as 'a pragmatic clinician who developed concepts as a response to real-life experiences'[41], Erikson does not seem to have been too concerned to define his idea of 'identity' clearly.[42] However, Coles writes of Erikson 'that through his writings on the subject of "identity" he accomplished the single most important shift in direction that psychoanalysis required if it was to become at all useful for other disciplines'. On this concept, Coles adds:

> The concept of identity is in essence a statement about the past, the present and the future, all three of them abstractions that try to encompass every hour ever spent. A sense of 'ego identity' emerges; it is an 'accrued confidence' that starts from the very first moment of life but in the second or third decades reaches a point of decisive substance, or indeed fails to do so. Confidence about what? Confidence that somehow in the midst of change one *is*; that is, one has an 'inner sameness and continuity' which others can recognize and which is so certain that it can unselfconsciously be taken for granted.[43]

All those who have teenage children, who work amongst adolescents or can think back to their own 'in-between' years, will appreciate the relevance of Erikson's pioneer thinking on the subject of identity. Towards the end of the second decade or in the first part of the third decade of life the struggle to 'know myself', 'be myself' and 'be at peace with myself' can be profound. Happily, most of us emerge at some stage in our late teens, early twenties or later with a sense of identity, an awareness of at least some degree of 'inner sameness and continuity'.

Heinz Hartmann, a fellow-analyst, once said: 'Erikson has

really helped *integrate* psychoanalysis with history and anthropology, and that's a very hard job and an important achievement.'[44] Erikson's interest in certain key historic figures involved him in studies on Francis of Assisi, Martin Luther, Hitler and Gandhi. In his consideration of the self-giving lives of Francis and the Mahatma, he sought to reformulate the Golden Rule, emphasising a mutuality between the doer and the recipient. He wrote: '. . . it is best to do to another what will strengthen you even as it will strengthen him – that is, what will develop his best potentials even as it develops your own'.[45]

In 1962 Erikson visited Gandhi's India in order to research his work on the great leader. Before landing in India he had spent some time in Israel. His reflections on both Jesus and Gandhi led him to write:

> Now I sensed again what I had known as a youth, namely, the affinity of that Galilean and the skinny Indian leader enshrined in Delhi. There is a word for what they seem to have had in common: presence – as pervasive a presence as only silence has when you listen.[46]

The neo-Freudians

The neo-Freudians, Horney, Fromm and Sullivan, essentially form a sociological school which sees interpersonal relations as the key to interpreting human nature. These analysts, although rooted in Freudian theory, differ profoundly from Freud in their rejection of his view that personality is based on biological drives which are mainly sexual in nature and that it develops through a series of inevitable stages during the first five years of life. Accentuating the prime influence of the environment, the neo-Freudians are more optimistic about humankind than the biologically deterministic Freudians.

Karen Horney (1885–1952) was born near Hamburg in Germany and was the daughter of a God-fearing Nordic sea-captain. Her parents had a turbulent relationship which was so marked by the father's predictable responses that the children nicknamed him 'Bible-thrower'. The discrepancy between the Christian beliefs taught within the family and her father's behaviour caused a great deal of heart-searching in the young Karen. At the time of her confirmation at fourteen she wrote in her diary: 'My religion is in a desperately sad state. Questions and doubts bother me, which no one can solve for me. What is God? Is God personal? Is he a God of love?'[47] At the age of seventeen, she asked this of herself: 'to know what I am in the religious, moral sense. Christian, deist, pantheist, monist, atheist? Berndt (her brother) says that developing larvae like me describe themselves best as "skeptics"'. Her biographer, Jack Rubins, adds that Karen remained agnostic 'throughout most of her life, at least until her sixties'.[48]

Like so many of the psychoanalysts mentioned thus far, Karen Horney fled Germany during the emergence of the Third Reich. In the United States she enjoyed a valuable fellowship with the theologian Paul Tillich, another German émigré. She was also influenced by Albert Schweitzer in her later years and had a developed sense of the moral and the immoral in the lives of men and women.

Initially a classical psychoanalyst, her book *New Ways in Psychoanalysis* brought a storm of protest from the orthodox. In this work, she challenged Freud's insistence that sexuality is the dominant factor in a child's development:

> Freud points out that a baby's expression of satisfaction after being nursed is similar to that of a person after intercourse. Certainly he did not mean to present this analogy as conclusive evidence. But one cannot help wondering why it is presented at all, because no one has ever doubted that pleasure can be derived from sucking, eating, walking and the like; the analogy, therefore, omits the dubitable point as to whether the baby's pleasure is sexual.[49]

Whereas Freud saw the unchangeable sex instinct as striving to love another, Horney argued that the main human drive is for social acceptance and the need to be loved. She disputed the pervasiveness of Freud's 'pleasure principle', declaring that the requirement of both satisfaction *and* security is the basis for much of man's activity.

Horney has stressed the importance in the lives of many of *basic anxiety* which is the result of a lack of acceptance by others. Neurosis, according to her, is the outcome of conflicts between the individual and the environment. Within a family, neurosis may arise if a child does not feel loved; within society, a man or woman may become neurotic if overcome by the competitiveness of others.

Generally, Karen Horney's theories have come under fire

because they are often incomplete and not substantiated. However, her many fine insights and clear thinking have been valuable contributions to analytic understanding.

The last of the Freudian revisionists whom we shall consider is *Erich Fromm* (1900–1980), who practised psychoanalysis in Berlin but left Nazi Germany to settle in New York in 1934. Calling his approach 'humanistic psychoanalysis', he has established a reputation on both sides of the Atlantic as a social historian as well as an analyst. Of Fromm's emphasis on the way the environment influences people, Wolman writes: 'Freud regarded history as man-made, while Fromm regards man as history-made.'[50]

Fromm's view of humanity is both optimistic and, to some extent, realistic. He sees man as faced with 'existential dichotomies' which are insoluble. Nevertheless, he argues that men and women can achieve happiness and productivity by unfolding their own powers.[51] He desires a 'sane society which gives man "the possibility of transcending nature by creating rather than by conformity, in which a system of orientation and devotion exists without man's needing to distort reality and to worship idols"'.[52]

In his book *Psychoanalysis and Religion* Erich Fromm explores the aims of psychoanalysis and asks whether its function is a threat to religious belief and practice. In its early days, he points out, Freudian analysis aimed essentially to assuage neurotic symptoms. If an hysterical woman was relieved of persistent vomiting or an obsessional man eased of his compulsive habits then psychoanalysis was considered successful. However, in time, the analyst's enquiring mind responded to the challenge of a different type of patient that began to come his way. Increasingly, people presented with deeper problems of personality and character, seeking an improvement in the quality of the lives they lived. Fromm sees this shift in the challenge offered to psychoanalysis as a move from the analyst needing to be simply an 'adjustment counsellor' to being, using Plato's expression, a 'physician of the soul' as well.[53]

Fromm argues the need to help the patient towards a *religious* attitude, which he seeks to distil as a 'core of ideas and norms' common to a wide range of teachings, including those of Buddha, Socrates and Jesus. In this 'common core':

. . . man must strive to recognize the truth and can be fully human only to the extent to which he succeeds in his task. He must be independent and free, an end in himself and not the means for any other person's purposes. He must relate himself to his fellow men lovingly. If he has no love, he is an empty shell even if his were all power, wealth, and intelligence. Man must know the difference between good and evil, he must learn to listen to the voice of his conscience and to be able to follow it.[54]

As is shown here, Fromm's position is essentially humanistic with overtones of moralism. Later in *Psychoanalysis and Religion* he argues explicitly for a 'humanistic religion' within which: 'sin is not primarily sin against God but sin against ourselves'.[55] In the final chapter he expresses a difficulty in the concept of God. He rightly inveighs against idolatry and religious intolerance and yet, although quoting the scriptures persuasively, he seems to step aside from God's self-revelation to pursue man's destiny in terms of man:

> Even from a strictly monotheistic standpoint the use of the word God constitutes a problem. The Bible insists that man must not attempt to make an image of God in any form. Undoubtedly one aspect of this injunction is that of a tabu, guarding the awesomeness of God. Another aspect however is the idea that God is a symbol of all that which is in man and yet which man is not, a symbol of a spiritual reality which we can strive to realize in ourselves and yet can never describe or define.[56]

Discussion of post-Freudian psychoanalysis

World views

A world view, as defined by James Sire, is 'a set of presuppositions (or assumptions) which we hold (consciously or subconsciously) about the basic make-up of our world'.[57] It would be unreasonable to expect all purveyors of psychological theory to have a carefully worked out philosophy of life, and yet, as we have already seen to some extent, the views that, for example, an analyst holds on the nature of humanity, the existence of God and the purpose, if any, of the universe are bound to mould his or her hypotheses. Any ideas postulated will, in turn, have powerful effects on the nature of any treatment offered.

We have noted, in chapter three, the profound reductionism of

the behaviourists. Further, in the last chapter, we have examined
the somewhat less materialistic but nonetheless strongly deterministic views of Freud. Nikolai Berdyaev, the Russian writer,
has said, 'Where there is no God, there is no man' and we see
something of this equation in the atheistic stance and powerfully
biological assumptions of the founder of psychoanalysis and
some of his protagonists.

Generally speaking, the rifts that came about between the
Freudians and the dissenters at least partly hinged on the emergence of world views which, though often only tentatively thought
out, moved away from seeing people as completely at the mercy
of their instincts towards perspectives which argued greater
complexity, autonomy and morality for humankind. This trend
has been an uneven one; we see, for example, amongst the earlier
schismatics a wide range of presuppositions including such
extremes as the questing supernaturalism of Jung and the bizarre
orgastic emphasis of Wilhelm Reich.

It is in the United States, amongst European immigrants with
Judaeo-Christian backgrounds, that we observe the appearance
of psychologies which look more to historical, cultural and social
aspects of humanity in a way that engenders more hope for
individual and corporate freedom and responsibility. Erik Erikson, with his compassionate work amongst neglected minority
groups and his incisive studies of certain spiritual leaders, brings
an importantly caring dimension into the appraisal of a complex
and needy mankind. Similarly, neo-Freudians like Karen Horney
and Erich Fromm, with their sociological priorities, spread the
discussion on human psychology away from an undue concentration on the inner and early life of the individual to interpersonal considerations. It is interesting that both these
analysts give due weight to the moral aspects of people's lives –
Karen Horney seemingly from a formerly sceptical position
modified by liberal theology and Erich Fromm from a world
view that appears to have some similarity to the deism of the
Enlightenment, in that God is seen, at best, as an 'absentee
landlord'.

Overall, in theological and anthropological terms, in the post-
Freudians we have a general trend in the right direction. It is
surely a truer picture of a person to see him or her in the context of
society and in relationship with others rather than as 'just a
machine', as 'simply an animal' or as essentially a 'prey to

powerful inner drives'. Sadly though, there is a danger in viewing men and women as basically designed to meet their own needs, both individual and social. If a creator-redeemer God who reveals himself to humankind is left out of the picture then there are a limited number of alternative routes to take; they all, sooner or later, finish in a dead end. When people, including analysts, seek to turn their backs on God, however politely, they tend to move into the blind alleys of an optimistic humanism, existential despair or a quest for other supernatural gods. Man is obliged to bow down at one temple or another; these cul-de-sacs offer him the limited choice of worshipping himself, his own nihilism or a host of deceiving spirits who serve a common Enemy. We shall look at the first two of these perils in the next chapter and see something of the third in chapter eight.

Aims

Before attempting an overall critique of psychoanalytic theory and practice, let us ask what the aims and methods of analysis are. Melanie Klein has written, 'as we all know, the ultimate aim of psychoanalysis is the integration of the patient's personality'.[58] Certainly, given the premises of Freudian theory, including the idea that the repression of childhood experiences leads to the persistence of neurotic conflicts, the goal of integration, in which the patient finds some measure of inner harmony, is most desirable. The path to this better sense of cohesion is, of course, often fraught with the pain of facing up to strong negative emotions like envy and resentment as the analyst seeks to uncover the deeper layers of the personality. However, as Klein points out: 'When the analysis can be carried to these depths, envy and the fear of envy diminish, leading to a greater trust in constructive and reparative forces, actually in the capacity for love.'[59]

Similar aims are found amongst neo-Freudians like Karen Horney where the emphasis is on both the discovery of inner strength and the improvement in the patient's relations with others.

Thomas Szasz, who has been a practising psychoanalyst in the United States since 1950 and has challenged certain aspects of traditional psychiatry in his many books, has summed up the aims of analysis under the banner of education rather than the medical arts. In his *The Ethics of Psychoanalysis* he writes:

In my view, the basic operation of psychoanalysis is the sharing of information between the participants. This is, of course, true of all types of psychotherapy. What distinguishes psychoanalysis is that it places special emphasis on learning about learning (metaeducation).[60]

The aim of this educative process, Szasz declares, is 'to give patients constrained by their habitual patterns of action greater freedom in their personal conduct'.[61] He sees that this personal liberation includes 'freedom to endure, modify, or sever any given relationship'[62] and that it can only have meaning 'for persons who enjoy a large measure of economic, political, and social freedom'.[63]

So, in the writings of Klein, Horney and Szasz, we see some common ground amongst analysts that the goals of psychoanalysis include the movement of the patient towards a greater sense of integration or (to use Erikson's term) identity as a person, together with an increased experience of freedom within the self and within relationships with others. Like Szasz,[64] the Christian will want to see that that freedom is tempered by unselfishness and the exercise of responsibility. We shall observe later in the book the way concepts of integration, identity and maturity can be variously understood in both psychological and spiritual terms.

Methods

We have already examined (pages 67–69) the main features of the practice of classical Freudian psychoanalysis in terms of free association, the interpretation of dreams and the use of transference. Within these therapeutic approaches, we described the three techniques of confrontation, interpretation and reconstruction. We noted too some more recent attempts to shorten the inordinate length of orthodox psychoanalysis. Not surprisingly, we see the essential retention of these practices in analysts who have tried to keep to the mainstream of Freudian thought. We have previously remarked that, for example, Melanie Klein's play technique makes use of free association as well as utilising (controversially) the phenomenon of transference with young children.

Inevitably, the primary breaks with Freudian theory we have traced have, in turn, led to different emphases in therapy.

Amongst the early schismatics, Jung's pursuit of the unconscious led him to stress the priority of dream analysis, whereas Otto Rank's increasing interest in the 'trauma of birth' persuaded him to major on the re-enactment of the birth experience.

Interestingly, just as Jung stressed the hidden world of the unconscious more than the founder of psychoanalysis, so Wilhelm Reich insisted on the overarching primacy of sex in an even more vigorous way than Sigmund Freud. In fact, Reich crusaded for the libido so vehemently that he became completely absorbed in his own idiosyncratic theory of the presence of the 'orgone' – a flow of physical energy that needed to be released in a therapy that, with its powerful emphasis on breaking bodily tensions and its resistance to the use of transference, was a far cry from psychoanalysis. His preoccupation with the therapeutic goal of sexual orgasm led him 'to remorselessly criticize all existing moral restrictions on sexuality'; in this criticism, however, he was against promiscuity and perversion although serial monogamy was advocated in the quest for sexual fulfilment.[65]

The most cohesive branching away from Freud has been the school of the neo-Freudians with its origins in the sociological concepts embraced by Adler. As we have seen, this outgrowth includes a number of important theoreticians, each making a distinctive contribution to the field of analysis as well as sharing some common ground in the shift from Freudianism. It is the move from an emphasis on infantile sexuality and the unconscious to one on the importance of self-esteem and relationships with others that has led to certain trends in neo-Freudian therapy. Generally, these trends mark a stepping away from Freud's stress on childhood experiences to a greater preoccupation with the 'here and now' – in other words with how the traumata of the early years are affecting life *now* and why any neurotic maladjustment still persists. These considerations are viewed in the context of personal relationships. Karen Horney in her *New Ways in Psychoanalysis* typifies these points when she writes:

My contention is that by working through the consequences the patient's anxiety is so much lessened, and his relation to self and others so much improved, that he can dispense with the neurotic trends. Their development was necessitated by the child's hostile and apprehensive attitude toward the world. If analysis of the consequences, that is, analysis of the actual neurotic structure, helps the individual to become discriminately friendly toward others instead of indiscriminately hostile, if his anxieties are considerably diminished, if he gains in inner strength and inner activity, he no longer needs his safety devices, but can deal with the difficulties of life according to his judgment.[66]

As a result, neo-Freudian therapy tends to be less protracted than classical psychoanalysis, the therapist is inclined to intervene more readily and the thrust of treatment is towards adaptation within the patient's view of himself and in his everyday contact with others.[67]

As Kovel points out, the Freudians have edged towards the neo-Freudians with respect to the concept of 'self'. Analysts like Horney and Fromm have stressed the value of the individual and his or her responsibility to strive for achievable goals in life whereas the movement of *ego psychology* amongst Freudians like Anna Freud, without relinquishing its interest in the unconscious and the sexuality of childhood, has accentuated the supremacy of the central ego in the person's struggle to adapt to both inner and environmental factors.[68]

Critique of psychological theory & practice

Theory

In this chapter we have looked primarily at the theoretical framework of a selected number of post-Freudians. Again, we have seen a wide diversity of conceptual thinking on the psychological nature of man and the growth of personality. The uniquely Freudian tenets of a pervasive theory of libido and of the prime importance of fixed developmental stages in infancy and childhood have been largely rejected by the neo-Freudians and analysts of similar persuasions, like Erik Erikson. What of the theories that have been worked out either to modify Freud's conjectures or to replace them? Is the object-relations theory of the Kleinian school any more valid than the ideas it was meant to supersede? Does the epigenetic nature of Erikson's view of human inner growth fit the observable facts? How do Karen

Horney's concepts of the roots of 'basic anxiety' square up with what actually happens in peoples' lives?

Here we are in the difficult area of testing the validity of psychological theory. It is reasonable for us to want to establish whether this or that thesis on the human psyche is true or not. With this aim in mind, is it even possible to prove, or disprove, the authenticity of such theorising?

The philosopher B. A. Farrell, in his book *The Standing of Psychoanalysis*, addresses himself to thorny questions like these. Quoting Karl Popper's comment that psychoanalysis contains 'most interesting . . . suggestions, but not in a testable form',[69] he nonetheless seeks to establish in what limited senses this form of therapy can be assessed. He shows that psychoanalysis is too complex to be evaluated by the empirical scientific method, which lays down stringent rules for what is verifiable. This approach requires that a concept must be ascertainable in an observable way in particular instances and, further, that a theory must lead to reliable predictions of outcome if a certain set of circumstances apply.[70] In everyday life we rely on this scientific method of observability and predictability in innumerable ways. At the simplest level, the hypothesis that water boils at a certain temperature, and the evidence for that is seen in the rise of water vapour, has been established beyond all reasonable doubt. We can say, with confidence, that, if I fill the kettle with water and ensure that the electricity makes connection, then the contents will boil in a few minutes – confirmed by the sight of rising vapour and the sound of bubbling water; the tea we then promptly make will at least be hot and, if we stick to the rules, well infused. These consequences would not be susceptible to scientific proof if we could only say, 'If I fill the kettle and switch on a reliable source of electricity, the water *tends* to boil.' A lot of us would give up trying to make cups of tea if the outcome was so unpredictable! In fact, most of the tenets of psychoanalysis come into this latter category. At the most, we can say, 'If people are frustrated they *tend* to regress'; we cannot declare with conviction, 'If people are frustrated they *will* regress.'

On this view of scientific method, Farrell argues that the credibility of psychoanalysis cannot be established experiment-ally although – and this is an important point – analytic theories form rational propositions. However, he persists in the enquiry by asking, 'Yes, it may be intelligable, but is it *true*?'[71] He rightly says that intelligibility does not necessarily validate a hypothesis. Tolkein's proposition that small creatures called hobbits lived in a land known as Middle Earth is intelligible but its historical veracity is not thereby proven.

Farrell goes further by showing how analysts, believing profoundly in the rationality of their craft, bolster their convictions by certain non-rational considerations. He writes: 'Analysts are unlikely to be much disturbed by the acids of scepticism we have been pouring on their theory and practice. Their chief reaction is likely to be one of mild boredom. The reason for this response is of fundamental importance'.[72] He shows that the most powerful reason for this imagined reaction is the 'non-rational' one that arises because the analyst has also been an analysand. The psychoanalyst himself has been helped, through analysis, towards a perhaps painful self-knowledge that makes sense of his life and situation. He has experienced a 'valid method of personal discovery'[73] and is therefore committed personally, as well as professionally, to the validity of psychoanalysis as a means of aiding others along a similar road. Farrell describes the circular argument that the analyst may be caught in as follows:

. . . it is not merely that the analyst views the patient through the spectacles of a certain theoretical perspective . . . It is *also* the case that, by using these spectacles in analysis, the analyst changes the patient so as to fit in with his perspective, and so support it.[74]

Nonetheless, Farrell is not completely dismissive of psychoanalytic theory. He does concede that there is some degree of truth in what he describes as the 'Low Level theories', in which more hesitant predictions of psychological mechanisms are made; these conjectures are, he argues, confirmed to some extent by case material:

However, in spite of its defects, the material does seem to point to a large core of something authentic about human nature – about patterns of connections between past and present, of ways we deal with our difficulties, and of psychological make up with related motives and functioning.[75]

Hence, it seems, we can cautiously accept certain aspects of psychoanalytic theory where the concepts make sense in the interaction between analyst and analysand – as long as we realise that they may be beyond scientific proof and, from a Christian standpoint, we assess their compatibility with a biblical view of human nature.

Practice

We face similar difficulties in assessing whether the practice of psychoanalysis actually works. Here, we are hamstrung by the impracticality of examining the efficacy of such a complex process as the interplay between an analyst and an analysand. Normally, in evaluating a method of treatment, we need to compare the group being assessed with a 'control' group, comprising individuals who have been matched, for age, sex, nature of disturbance and other circumstances, as closely as possible. In assessing the value of any form of psychotherapy or counselling, there are considerable problems in attempting this matching – partly because the simple procedure of interviewing the candidates can have a therapeutic effect, partly because of the ethical issues in ascribing a section of needy people to 'no treatment' and partly because the person who does the appraisal is usually either the therapist or the patient, and not a 'third party'.[76]

Farrell examines three studies which are as satisfactorily staged as can be expected.[77] Even so, their claims for a degree of success for psychoanalytic method are open to question. Farrell concludes perceptively, in a way that will be valuable to us later as we look at methodologies used by Christians:

> In view of the poor state of our knowledge in this field, it is clear that the chief desideratum is more knowledge. It is fortunate that a great deal of continuous research is going on about it. Some of this may fail, for one reason or another, to throw much light on the effectiveness of psychotherapy and analysis. But it is worth noting that interest in the scientific world is moving away from the *general* question of effectiveness to questions about what specific treatment, offered by whom, will be most effective for this specific type of disorder with this type of patient, under these particular circumstances, and why. This move safeguards us to a large extent from the danger – to which some have succumbed in the past – of using science as propaganda for or against analysis, or any other method of treatment. As such, this move is to be welcomed.[78]

It is this shaping of method to a person's needs and circumstances that is the hallmark of innumerable counselling approaches today.

Conclusion & summary

However we understand the need for and the value of psychoanalysis in society we have to conclude, even though the trend amongst the neo-Freudians and ego psychologists has been to offer therapy of a briefer duration, that its availability is something of a luxury for most of us – both in terms of time and money. In the face of the interest in the United States in expensive and prolonged forms of therapy, together with a general flight from 'common sense' in everyday Western life, Farrell finishes his book with these trenchant words:

> For much of ordinary life, it is quite unnecessary to bother ourselves about psychoanalysis, or any of the other psychodynamic psychologies that are on sale in the market-place. The path of wisdom – for most of us most of the time – is to forget about them.[79]

Farrell's assessment may appear iconoclastic to the professional but 'for much of ordinary life' (and this is Farrell's point) the offers of psychoanalysis are superfluous. This is not to deny the enormous value of many Freudian and post-Freudian insights but, 'for most of us most of the time', the time- and money-consuming elements of analytical methods can pass us by. The 'path of wisdom' in forgetting about them does not argue that we are already whole so much as that the task of daily living requires our fullest attention. Where that attention falters in the face of crying needs and unresolved conflicts, psychoanalysis will be one of many 'methodologies of help' vying for our healing. It is one of the intentions of this book to encourage discernment as we seek aid at crisis points along Farrell's 'path of wisdom'.

We have now completed our survey of the tree of psychoanalysis, from its roots in the soil of evolutionary biology and metaphysical psychology to its rise, centred on the sturdy and often unyielding figure of Sigmund Freud, through its multiple branching away from the main trunk of Freudianism in the dissensions of Adler, Jung, Rank and Reich, the development of the Kleinian school, the culturally-based work of Erikson and the emergence of the neo-Freudians with their emphasis on sociological factors. The tree is a massive and complex one with its base not far from the tree of behaviourism, sharing the common ground of the empirical sciences, but with some of its branchlets fanning out from the branch of 'humanistic psychoanalysis' and the work of Erich Fromm to mingle with the canopy of our third woodland giant, the tree of the personalistic psychologies – to which we now turn.

PERSONALISM: MAN AND SELF
(1) HUMANISTIC PSYCHOLOGY

*Only on paper has humanity yet achieved glory, beauty,
truth, knowledge, virtue, and abiding love.*
George Bernard Shaw

In Germany, in the late nineteenth century, a number of psychologists cried out against the increasing trend within their profession of looking primarily to the natural sciences in order to evaluate humankind. Wilhelm Dilthey (1833–1911) was particularly outspoken in urging the need for an 'understanding' psychology that seeks to appreciate individuals as living unities capable of personal integration.[1] In contrast, he bemoaned the trends within 'explanatory' psychology with its scientific techniques and inability to comprehend the motives and achievements of the people it studied.

This emphasis on the whole person was reflected in the thinking of other German psychologists and philosophers in the early part of this century, including: Wilhelm Stern (1871–1938), Kurt Goldstein (1878–1965) and Edward Spranger (1882–1963). Such holistic views were also contributive towards the rise of Gestalt psychology, which branch of 'understanding' psychology we will look at in chapter nine.

Spranger implemented Dilthey's ideas from the 1920s onwards; Wolman has expressed this trend clearly:

> Dilthey said that psychology should describe rather than analyze; understand rather than interpret; deal with the totality of human actions rather than with their fragments; turn to the humanities rather than to social science.[2]

Spranger, as Dilthey's disciple, strongly opposed the reductionism of, for example, the behaviourists with their attempts to
explain human behaviour in purely biological terms. He argued
that the subject matter of psychology is *human experience* and its
method is the understanding of the *meaning* of that experience in
terms of an individual's goals in life and basic values. In order to
evaluate a person he postulated six 'ideal' types of people, each
type representing a different philosophy of life: the *theoretical*
type who faces the world with careful reasoning and relentless
logic; the *economic* type who is intensely practical and is concerned with personal and material security; the *aesthetic* type who
is individualistic and preoccupied with beauty, harmony and
diversity in the world around; the *sociable* type who is friendly,
unselfish, considerate and values what is moral; the *power-politics*
type whose main goal is to outwit others and gain control over
them; the *religious* type who prizes inner peace and ultimate
truth, and seeks a sense of unity with the universe.

We can all, of course, see something of ourselves within these
brief descriptions. Spranger's types form a useful framework for
understanding people but, more importantly, they have been a
great influence on the thinking of many other psychologists and
psychotherapists, including the analysts Adler, Horney and
Fromm, and the psychologists Kurt Lewin and Gordon W.
Allport, both working in the United States. Allport's theories on
motivation, personal traits and temperament have widened
the horizons of psychological enquiry greatly so that we now
have a viable psychology of personality, alongside the more biological and reductionist psychologies of behaviourism and
Freudianism.[3]

In terms of methodologies of counselling and psychotherapy,
we can divide personalism into two main categories: humanistic
and existential psychology. We will devote the whole of this
chapter to the first of these and deal with existential psychology
in chapter seven.

Humanism, a view of life that centres its focus on humanity, its
potential and achievements, has had its adherents throughout
history. However, it was through the exaltation of human skill
and creativity in the arts and sciences during the Renaissance,
followed by the elevation of reason from the Enlightenment
onwards, that modern humanism was conceived and born. In
this century humanism has grown into a body of great complexity

within which a wide range of views are held. Even so, at its heart, humanism sees reason as the final arbiter, regards humankind as a peak in the evolutionary process and dismisses the reality or the relevance of the supernatural.

In 1961, *The Humanist Frame*, under the editorship of Sir Julian Huxley, attempted to 'present Humanism as a comprehensive system of ideas'. Other distinguished contributors included Sir Russell Brain, J. Bronowski, Baroness Wootton, Sir Robert Platt and Aldous Huxley. Julian Huxley, in the opening essay, makes a plea for a 'satisfactory idea-system' to revive people in the face of post-war disillusionment and the failure of materialism. This proposed 'idea-system' is, in effect, a new religion. On behalf of 'evolutionary man' Huxley rejects traditional belief in a personal God in these powerful but subversive words:

> Evolutionary man can no longer take refuge from his loneliness by creeping for shelter into the arms of a divinized father-figure whom he has himself created, nor escape from the responsibility of making decisions by sheltering under the umbrella of Divine Authority, nor absolve himself from the hard task of meeting his present problems and planning his future by relying on the will of an omniscient but unfortunately inscrutable Providence.[4]

In the place of theism, he puts forward 'the new ideology' of modern humanism:

> The emergent religion of the near future could be a good thing . . . Instead of worshipping supernatural rulers, it will sanctify the higher manifestations of human nature, in art and love, in intellectual comprehension and aspiring adoration . . .[5]

Huxley's words evoke a vision of the vast stage of the natural order on which humankind holds the centre, dazzlingly lit up by powerful spotlights and heralded by an exultant fanfare of trumpets. In fairness to the movement, many humanists in more recent years have become less optimistic about humanity and less fulsome in their praise of 'the higher manifestations of human nature'.

Keeping in mind both the diversity and the central tenets of humanism, let us now look at one of the best-known proponents of a humanistic psychology, Carl Rogers.

Carl Rogers

Carl Ransom Rogers (b 1902), the fourth of six children, grew up in the suburbs of Chicago. He was part of a family that had a strong sense of solidarity and yet lacked the desire and the ability to communicate personal feelings and private thoughts.[6] His parents, although loving, controlled their family through a set of prohibitions that arose out of their Protestant faith and fundamentalistic outlook. They appear to have fostered a beleaguered atmosphere in the home within which the family felt itself to be different from the lesser mortals around them. Rogers describes the parental injunctions in these words:

> Other persons behave in dubious ways which we do not approve in our family. Many of these play cards, go to movies, smoke, dance, drink, and engage in other activities, some unmentionable. So the best thing to do is to be tolerant of them, since they may not know better, but to keep away from any close communication with them and to live your life within the family.[7]

It seems that Carl Rogers' mother was most sharply aware of the apparent dangers of taking on board the attitudes and habits of their neighbours. One of her two favourite sayings was 'Come out from among them and be ye separate.' The other emphasised her sense of the universality of sin: 'All our righteousness is as filthy rags in thy sight, O Lord.' It is intriguing to observe that Rogers' views on the importance of communicating with everyone and on the intrinsic worth of each individual could not be further removed from his mother's twin maxims.

Not surprisingly, Carl grew up with an attitude to outsiders 'characterized by the distance and the aloofness' that he had taken over from his parents. He writes, 'I was socially incompetent in any but superficial contacts. My fantasies during this period were definitely bizarre . . .' and adds, somewhat wryly, 'but fortunately I never came in contact with a psychologist'![8]

When Rogers was twelve, the family moved from Chicago to his father's hobby farm thirty miles west of the city. Ostensibly, the move enabled Mr Rogers, a prosperous business man, to indulge his enthusiasm for farming, but Carl Rogers suspects that the uprooting was also linked with his parents' desire to remove their adolescent offspring from the 'temptations' of suburban life.

Life for Rogers expanded in this new rural setting. Already something of a loner, and a studious one at that, he became fascinated by the variety and order within the natural world around him. His main passions were the study of the great night-flying moths and, later, an increasing interest in the scientific aspects of agriculture. His lifelong commitment to experimental methods within the new science of psychology grew out of these years on the farm.

In 1919 Rogers went to the University of Wisconsin to study agriculture. Staying at a hostel of the Young Men's Christian Association, he began to identify strongly with the attitudes and activities of a group of new friends with Christian convictions. The YMCA had been very influential in the United States since the middle of the nineteenth century under its aim of 'evangelization through social service'. By the time Rogers was at college, the thrust of this movement was essentially humanitarian and its support was mainly from the liberal wing of Protestantism. He became a leader of a boys' club and, in due course, was one of ten student delegates from the United States who attended a conference of the World Student Christian Federation in Peking. During his six months in China both his thinking and his feelings became increasingly independent of his parents' world view. Growing more liberal in both political and religious understanding, his new departure from parental values was sealed by a conversation on the return journey from which he reached the conclusion that 'Jesus was a man like other men – not divine!'

In spite of these liberalising influences Rogers gave up the study of agriculture and began to read history to prepare for a life of 'religious work'. Van Belle points out that, within these new studies, Rogers wrote a paper on Luther which concluded that 'man's ultimate reliance is upon his own experience'.[9] This *credo* became the heart of Rogers' lifelong perspective.

Graduating in history in 1924 and marrying Helen, a friend from childhood days, Carl Rogers proceeded to New York to train for the ministry. Although his father offered to cover his expenses if he studied at Princeton Seminary, the centre for conservative Protestant studies at that time, Rogers marked his newly found independence from his parents and their views by choosing the Union Theological Seminary as 'the most liberal in the country and an intellectual leader in religious work'. Although he sees this move towards the ministry 'as the result of some emotionally charged student religious conferences', he nonetheless values his time at the seminary for extending and widening his understanding of life. In time, he sought a discipline that was more compatible with his 'free thinking' – and found psychology.

Taking courses at Teachers College, Columbia University, just across the road from the seminary, Rogers became aware of the 'two completely different worlds' of Freudianism and the scientific method. On qualifying, he began twelve years in Rochester, New York, where he worked as a psychologist in the Child Study Department of the Society for the Prevention of Cruelty to Children. During this period he started to move away from the more coercive approaches of his training because he found such techniques less effective than a method which learned 'to rely upon the client for the direction of movement in the process' of counselling.

In 1940, he became a professor at Ohio State University and began to shape his own distinctive approach to helping others, a way that offered a revolutionary alternative to the controlling techniques of behaviourism and the protracted questing of Freudianism. This new dimension in psychology has been broadly labelled the 'Third Force' by Abraham Maslow (see chapter eight). Rogers' particular brand has been described successively as non-directive, client-centred and person-centred therapy. Let us look at the assumptions, aims and methods of Rogerian counselling.

Assumptions

Rogers was a man of his time. He grew up in an America which, through its Protestant roots, protested the right of the individual to *choose*. This democratic fervour was accompanied by a tide of pragmatism which sought to solve the dilemma posed by a spirit of pioneering 'self-help' and the desire to conform to 'the tyranny of the majority'. John Dewey, the educational philosopher, grappled particularly with this issue, arguing that every view and institution of the establishment should be continually renewed through the voice of the individual. In marked contrast to the heavy determinism of the behaviourists and Freudians, Dewey saw reality as dynamic rather than static. As Van Belle has remarked, 'life for Dewey is perpetually experimental'.[10] This open-ended approach, which sought to free the individual from the 'stranglehold of tradition', has found an echo in Consciousness III, Charles Reich's collective term for the liberalising and hedonistic mentality of the late 1960s, described in his best-seller *The Greening of America* (1970). Here the moralistic thinking of the purveyors of the 'American Dream' (Consciousness I) and the monolithic control over people's lives of the technological society (Consciousness II) were challenged – at least for a decade – by an individualistic philosophy which said, 'I'm glad I'm me.'

Carl Rogers' view of humankind was (as is true, to some extent, of all of us) influenced generally by the prevailing cultural climate of his day, that is to say by a rising tide of optimism in the power of individual men and women to change both self and society for the better. More specifically, Van Belle has argued that Rogers' later thinking on the importance of *process* and *growth* in people's lives is traceable to the influence of some of John Dewey's followers at Teachers College, where Rogers studied psychology.

It has been said of Rogers that he 'expressed an idea whose time had come' and there is no doubt that his phenomenal popularity relates to the timing of his emphasis on the 'primacy of the individual in human life, now not as an ideal but as a programme, first as a therapeutic programme and finally as a social programme'.[11]

We can see in Rogers' beliefs, that society ought to free the individual and that all men and women have the resources within them for constructive change, a strongly humanistic vein. He has been particularly suspicious of the sort of view his mother held, that all are essentially sinful by nature; for example, in *On Becoming a Person*, he criticises 'Religion, especially the Protestant Christian tradition' which 'has permeated our culture with the concept that man is basically sinful, and only by something approaching a miracle can his sinful nature be negated'.[12] He sees the core of human personality as something positive 'which is essentially both self-preserving and social'. Although he concedes that there are 'hostile and anti-social feelings' within people, he declares that these do not exist at the deepest and strongest levels of human nature. (Other aspects of Rogers' anthropology will emerge as we consider the aims and the methods of his approach to counselling.)

Aims

It should not surprise us that, because of the strongly pragmatic nature of Rogers' understanding of life, there should be change and development in his theory and practice through the years. We can trace his fluidity of ideas from his non-directive counselling of the 1940s, with its emphasis on non-interference by the counsellor, through the client-centred therapy of the 1950s, with its stress on the therapeutic relationship, to the person-centred approach of the 1960s with its increasingly transpersonal perspectives in the 1970s and 1980s. Within Rogers' progression of thought we can discern both shifts of focus and a widening vision of both the aims of counselling and the goals of being human.

In order to simplify the complexity of Rogerian concepts in this area, I propose to consider four aspects of the change in the client desired in therapy; these are catharsis, insight, experience-centredness and growth.

Catharsis. The word 'catharsis' contains the idea of purgation and purification, and has been used in a psychological sense since the earliest days of psychiatry. This 'cleansing' of the client's inner life through the release of previously stifled emotions is an important initial aim in Rogerian therapy. By means of the unhindered expression of buried feelings, the client, it is argued, becomes more relaxed and is better able to look at his or her life objectively.

For most of us this aim of 'letting it all hang out' is threatening; we are much more comfortable as we hide behind the sort of impression we want others to have of us. This front of respectability is summed up well by Noël Coward, that quintessential Englishman, in *Bitter Sweet* when he wrote:

> Though we all disguise our feelings pretty well
> What we mean by 'Very good' is 'Go to hell'.[13]

Insight. From early in his career, Rogers has stressed that people can only change for the better if they achieve a level of true insight into their condition. Following the undamming of trapped emotions, the way is cleared for new perceptions within the client. Once again Rogers emphasised the importance of subjectivity, for the person in need must *feel* differently about his or herself in order to achieve greater understanding. In turn, he argued, where emotional and perceptual insight are found then choices are made and altered behaviour will follow.

If, in the course of therapy, I find myself flooded with pent-up anger against a friend whom I feel betrayed by, and express that resentment without let or hindrance, then, according to Rogers, I am likely to feel less cluttered within myself and so more ready to perceive reality. I may begin to appreciate deep down that my bitterness is largely unwarranted and that my own nature is too sensitive to a friend's apparent vagaries. This increasingly held conviction will free me to be a more circumspect, but less vulnerable friend in present and future relationships.

Experience-centredness.   If we were to ask Rogers what authority he looks to in his methodology, the answer would be illuminating. In *On Becoming a Person* he has written: '*Experience is, for me, the highest authority*' and 'No other person's ideas, and none of my own ideas, are as authoritative as my experience.'[14] In that he declares that his own 'direct experience' acts as a monitor for his life, we are not surprised to find that 'experience-centredness' in the client is a crucial goal for Rogerian therapy. He writes that one of the marks of successful counselling is an openness to all personal experience. The client

> comes to realize that his own inner reactions and experiences, the messages of his senses and his viscera, are friendly. He comes to want to be close to his inner sources of information rather than closing them off.[15]

However, Rogers goes further in his exaltation of experience. It is not simply that you or I should gain greater insight and so be more open to what happens to us day by day. We are to *become* the experience that we *are*. This means that we are to give up the control over experience and allow experience to be our sole teacher. Van Belle has put this well: 'The self is now no longer the watchman over experience but rather an inhabitant of experience. Experience has its own meaning and the self must let it tell it its own meaning.'[16]

Rogers has likened this relinquishment of the self to the higher wisdom of what we experience to the handling of a car on an icy road; if we steer with the slide we survive, whereas if we turn the wheel against it we may perish.

Growth.   Of all the concepts that build up Rogers' methodology, that of *growth* is paramount. Van Belle shows its pervasiveness when he writes: 'For Rogers, growth is in the final analysis the origin, pathway and destiny of man, alone and together.'[17]

What does Rogers mean by this somewhat nebulous word 'growth'? He seems to be describing human life as a continuous process that moves forward by differentiating and assimilating new insights and ways of feeling in the direction of increasing complexity. Because, in his view, human nature is essentially good there is an intrinsic momentum about this growth. As has been said: 'There is no beast in man. Human nature is inherently "good" and moves in a forward, constructive direction.'[18]

Rogers argues that this process of growth (or process of 'actualization') occurs naturally as an individual's personality develops. There is a progression from the fulfilment of the simple physiological needs of food, warmth and sleep in the infant, through the assimilation of actual experiences, an increasing level of conscious awareness, an emergence of a concept of self and so to a regard for both oneself and others. This last level in turn leads to the development of a sense of community.

This natural growth can be blocked at any stage, leading to a greater rigidity at and dominance by the level of arrest. For example, if an adolescent has a clear concept of who he is and yet nurses a marked degree of self-loathing, his whole view of life may become contaminated by his denigration of himself. He has not achieved (or has lost) a reasonable regard for himself and for others, and so becomes trapped in a cycle of self-absorption. Rogerian therapy would aim to help this young man express his negative emotions and so begin to move into new insight and more constructive behaviour. His process of growth would be unblocked as he moves forward into accepting his day-to-day experience and learns to relate better to himself and others. He will no longer declare 'this is who I am' but rather 'this is who I am becoming'.

In Rogers' *A Way of Being*, his aim for growth within the individual and in relationships extends into transpersonal realms when he argues for the existence of an evolutionary force that moves humanity towards cosmic consciousness. He conjectures that there is 'a formative directional tendency in the universe . . . This is an evolutionary tendency toward greater order, greater complexity, greater interrelatedness.' This tendency is exhibited in humankind as the individual moves from 'a single-cell origin . . . to a transcendent awareness of the harmony and unity of the cosmic system, including humankind'.[19]

Methods

As has already been mentioned, Rogers, influenced by Dewey's pragmatism, has, since the 1940s, continually reshaped his methodology of counselling. This moulding and modification is seen in the development of his methods and techniques in therapy.

Non-directive counselling.   In 1942 the publication of his *Counselling and Psychotherapy* introduced the public to Rogers' non-directive counselling. In this approach the therapist adopted a position of non-interference, arguing that all the client needs is a *facilitator* who will allow the person in need to achieve insight into his or her condition. For this reason, all giving of advice, cajoling, suggesting, interpreting, directing, challenging, confronting, persuading are ruled out of court. Such interference is seen as obstructive of the client's path towards new insight and new action. (Much of our present-day jargon about being 'laid back' and 'keeping a low profile' may reflect the pervasiveness of Rogerian thinking.)

Through this non-directiveness, Rogers stated, the client is given the space to recognise and express emotions and, as we have already seen, move into more valid concepts about himself. This therapeutic process is essentially a movement towards personal autonomy, in which the client is freed for 'self-directed integration and personal growth'.[20]

Client-centred therapy.   During the following decade Rogers moved from a primary emphasis on *technique* in his non-directive approach to see the crucial nature of the therapist's *attitude* in effective counselling. Thus, in 1951, his book *Client-Centred Therapy* was published and the enriching concept of 'client-centredness' was introduced to the therapeutic scene.

The linchpin of Rogers' new position is the basic *trust* that the therapist must genuinely have in the client. In non-directive counselling, those things that the counsellor must not do were stressed; in client-centred therapy the role of the therapist is seen in a more positive light. He or she is to have an attitude which trusts the client's capacity to change at every level, and this attitude needs to be mediated to the person in difficulty by the therapist's genuineness, unconditional positive regard and empathic understanding (see pp. 29–36 in chapter two). Here Rogers is beginning to stress the therapeutic value of the *relationship* between therapist and client. He is shifting from the intrapersonal towards the interpersonal.

In Rogerian terms, an individual is ripe for counselling when his or her concept of self is at variance with daily experience. Supposing a married woman in her thirties called Mary sees herself as of little or no personal worth and yet meets a barrage of reassurance from her family and workmates that she is valued; the discrepancy between her deep conviction of unworthiness and the apparently strongly held belief of others that she is special will fan the flames of continuing inner conflict. She may, in time, become so desperately unsure of herself that she seeks therapy.

If the help she is offered is 'client-centred' then Mary is likely to experience a therapeutic process during the coming months which amounts to a restructuring of her sense of who she is. At first she will be encouraged by the counsellor to recognise and give vent to her feelings as they arise. She may find the possibility of emotional outlet threatening to start with but the therapist's trusting and reassuring mien will create a safe climate for her. During this period of 'disorganization of the self', Mary will become disturbed by a bewildering array of inner discords and inconsistencies. However, she finds that even her emotional pain is valued by the therapist and she gradually achieves a sense of progress. In time, she realises that the worst is known about her and yet she is still prized as a person of worth. There is now a 'reorganization of the self' in which a more peaceful, realistic and confident Mary is emerging.

On becoming a person.   Rogers' book *On Becoming a Person* was first published in 1961 and takes us into the theme of 'person-centredness'. We have seen the development of his view on therapy shifting from the primacy of the client's intrapersonal life to a more symmetrical emphasis in which factors within the therapist are also deemed important; we now have a therapeutic approach which majors on the *inter*personal. This progression is well illustrated by Rogers when he writes:

. . . in my early professional years I was asking the question, How can I treat, or cure, or change this person? Now I would phrase the question in this way: How can I provide a relationship which this person may use for his own personal growth?[21]

In 'person-centred' therapy, Rogers rates very highly his concept of genuineness, or *congruence*. A congruent therapist is one whose feelings 'are available to him, available to his awareness' and who 'is able to live these feelings, be them, and able to communicate them if appropriate'.[22] In another place, Rogers puts this genuineness on a wider footing when he writes: 'Being genuine . . . involves the willingness to be and to express, in my words and my behaviour, the various feelings and attitudes which exist in me.' This transparency, Rogers argues, is catching! He continues: 'It is only by providing the genuine reality which is in me, that the other person can successfully seek for the reality in him.'[23]

It is in his 'person-centredness' that Rogers extends his thinking beyond the therapeutic encounter to embrace *all* relationships. The qualities of trust, understanding and transparent genuineness that mark the counselling relationship, and in which *both* the therapist and client change for the better, become a paradigm for the relations between parent and child, teacher and student, leader and led.[24]

Rogers' shift to the interpersonal in therapy is, of course, extended further in his development of encounter groups, in which individuals learn to express more freely how they think and feel as trust and genuineness are engendered. In his *Encounter Groups*, he writes that in such a group a person 'becomes deeply acquainted with the other members and with his own inner self, the self that otherwise tends to be hidden behind his façade. Hence he relates better to others, both in the group and later in the everyday situation.'[25]

A way of being. In his 'person-centredness', Rogers seems to continue his thesis that human becoming is more important than human being. Van Belle describes Rogers' emphasis on personal growth as *monistic dynamism*, because the inner process of change is 'totalitarian' in that it will not tolerate any reality outside itself.[26] In Rogers' thinking, if a client is experiencing new insight and a reorganisation of self, then this unifying process of change will tend to discard any 'alien' influences, such as the contrary demands of a close friend or the disturbing dictates of an awakened conscience. Van Belle senses a tendency to remove not only inner barriers in this monism but also the legitimate boundaries between one person and another. In Rogers' *A Way of Being*, we see this trend continuing into a philosophy which is moving beyond personhood to something transcendent and mystical. He alludes to this advance beyond ordinary levels of consciousness when, at times in therapy, he acknowledges that 'his *presence* is releasing and helpful to the other . . . it seems that my inner self has reached out and touched the inner spirit of the other. Our relationship transcends itself and becomes a part of something larger. Profound growth and healing and energy are present.'[27] In the next chapter we will pick up a little more of Rogers' 'monistic dynamism' when we consider transpersonal psychology.

A critique of Rogers' methodology

As we have considered Carl Rogers' presuppositions, aims and methods, many of us will have had mixed feelings. We may have warmed to a number of his shrewd insights and caring practice, and have been repelled by some aspects of his assumptive basis and by the direction in which his changing theories have carried him. As with Skinner and Freud, Rogers' critics have been numerous.[28]

It is important, first, to acknowledge the vast influence of Carl Rogers on both sides of the Atlantic.[29] His theories on therapy have contributed enormously to the rise of the counselling movement from the 1940s onwards, not least in his emphasis on the vital nature of the therapist's qualities and attitudes in the therapeutic relationship.

More fundamentally, the Christian will want to assess Rogers' view of humankind in order to evaluate the validity of his methodology. In counselling, as in all walks of life, what is believed about human nature is likely to filter through to practical considerations. If there is to be any consistency between theory and practice this needs to be so. As Van Belle has said: 'Anthropological viewpoints are not just viewpoints. They need to have concrete implications for the practice of living.'[30]

As we have already seen, one of Rogers' basic tenets is that human nature is essentially 'good' in the sense of being constructive and trustworthy.[31] Although individuals 'can and do behave in ways which are incredibly cruel, horribly destructive, immature, regressive, anti-social, hurtful', Rogers has discovered 'the strongly positive directional tendencies which exist in them, as in all of us, at the deepest levels'.[32]

We can contrast this optimistic note with Jesus's realistic reaction to unredeemed humanity. For example, in the face of the speedy response of many people to his miraculous signs, we read, 'But Jesus would not entrust himself to them, for he knew all men. He did not need man's testimony about man, for he knew what was in a man' (John 2:24,25).

Rogers' conviction that individuals are, at heart, desirous of positive inner change led to his exaltation of the concept of growth, or process. He wrote that, within psychotherapy, this process is 'a unique and dynamic experience, different for each individual, yet exhibiting a lawfulness and order which is astonishing in its generality'.[33] For Rogers, the outcome of successful therapy seems to be the process itself. Of clients profoundly helped by counselling, he writes: 'They are in flux, and seem more content to continue in this flowing current. The striving for conclusions and end states seems to diminish.'[34]

This inexorable process of 'lawfulness and order' has led to various interpretations of Rogers' thought. On the one hand, he has been widely criticised as a 'self-theorist' in that he is said to aggrandise the concept of 'self' in his methodology. Paul Vitz, for example, in his *Psychology as Religion*, although conceding the value of Rogerian therapy for young people 'reared by overly moralistic, overly critical, rigidly authoritarian parents', argues that client-centredness can allow, or even encourage, 'the patient to slide into a self-gratifying narcissistic world'.[35]

On the other hand, Van Belle, in his painstaking survey *Basic Intent and Therapeutic Approach of Carl R. Rogers*, declares the view that Rogers does not see the 'fully functioning *person*' as 'the self but the organismic actualization process'. In other words, the individual self cannot control the dynamic change which moves inexorably in the direction of the unifying experience of being fully human. Van Belle sees Rogers' approach as a 'developmental-psychological psychotherapy' and not a 'self-theory'.[36]

Whether Vitz, Van Belle or other critics are right, we can argue that Rogers' affirmation of either self or process parts company with God's self-disclosure about human nature. Behind these Rogerian concepts is the baleful idea of autonomy, that men and women can be, and should be, completely self-governing with respect to their destiny. Paul, in Romans 1 paints a terrifying picture of the extremes of autonomy, where human wilfulness, by dishonouring and rejecting the creator, leads to abandonment by God and the ultimate loss of true humanity. Jesus, the perfect man, resisted the invitation to autonomy in each of the three wilderness temptations and showed us for all time that we are the people we should be when we are most dependent on our Father. His example is clear: 'Jesus gave them this answer: "I tell you the truth, the Son can do nothing by himself; he can do only what he sees his Father doing, because whatever the Father does the Son also does. For the Father loves the Son and shows him all he does"' (John 5:19,20a).

With respect to Rogers' anthropology, we have raised questions about his views that people are intrinsically good, that the process of growth, or self-motivation, is *the* driving force towards maturity and that autonomy is the path and goal of life. It is also relevant to comment on one more aspect of his thought, this time in the areas of both aims and techniques – the issue of the ventilation of feelings.

Once more, from a Christian perspective, we can see both value and danger in Rogers' teaching. It is undeniable that many of us, particularly in the Protestant and Western traditions, are very diffident about feelings. We often ignore them, deny them and find them disturbing, untidy things. It is salutary for us to make a study of the emotions felt and sometimes expressed in the life of Jesus in terms of his anger, indignation, longings, sorrow, compassion, grief, agony and experiences of betrayal, desertion and dereliction.[37]

However, we also need to appreciate that the Bible urges upon us the lordship of Christ over our feelings as with all aspects of our being. There are certain negative feelings, like jealousy and resentment, that should be repented of and many positive feelings that need to be cultivated. For example, our anger needs to be harnessed so that we can learn to be angry in a Christlike way, vehement against injustice, oppression, hypocrisy and blasphemy.

I vividly remember a series of events on an autumnal day a few years ago when I was caught out on both these counts: I tried to deny my feelings and failed; and, furthermore, eventually expressed them in an un-Christlike manner. The sun was shining, my wife Joy was busy in the house and the possibility of an hour's gardening beckoned invitingly. First, I opened the door to the front garden to retrieve my wellington boots from the doorstep. I plunged an eager foot into one, only to experience a soaked sock; it had rained overnight and each boot had collected a puddle! Nothing daunted, I found the alternative of a pair of old shoes. The season was right for pruning and so I strode out to the garage to collect my secateurs. They were not there! Never mind, I'll borrow Joy's. Returning to the kitchen, I asked Joy for her secateurs only to find that they too were missing from their customary place. No matter, I assured myself, there are plenty of other garden jobs to be done. And so, armed with a fork, I began to tackle an unkempt border at the back of the house. As I did so, I saw the blue grip of my freshly rusting secateurs gleaming beneath a climbing rose. Of course – silly me – I had been pruning before the rains started and, untypically I felt, had left them to fend for themselves for a few days. Top marks so far. I fairly glowed with satisfaction as, smilingly, I brandished the rose-cutters at Joy, whose head had just emerged from an upper window. 'Here they are, dear! I found them in the border', I said breezily. Her face seemed to lack sympathy as she replied accusingly, '*So* – you've found them have you?' Lightning thoughts that Joy herself had felt accused by my earlier search for both pairs of secateurs flitted through my mind. As I rounded the corner of the house, out of sight of the windows, it started to rain. Half an hour of suppressed frustration erupted and I hurled the miscreant cutters into the lawn. In many ways, this example is a trivial one but behind it lay deeper tensions and conflicts which were barely being acknowledged. Rogers was right – we do need to be able to recognise and express our feelings. We need even more to allow the lordship of Christ to reign over our emotional lives, giving us insight, humbling us and encouraging our sensitivity, honesty, self-control and ability to laugh at ourselves.

Summary

As we have traced Rogers' story from childhood to his latest theories we have to concede that, following his rejection of his parents' brand of Christianity as a young man, once more we have a methodology within which God is declared redundant. Nonetheless, the deterministic basis of behaviourism and Freudianism has been seen to be a more fully atheistic concept than the pragmatism of Rogers' thought. And further, along with Adler and the neo-Freudians, we see in Rogers' humanism a loftier vision of human worth and potential. What is strikingly lacking though, as in all these approaches, is an adequate admission of the extent of personal and collective sin. Francis Schaeffer has described humanity not only as a ruin, but as a glorious ruin. Rogers' optimistic views, although compatible with the 'glory', do not accord with the 'ruin' of mankind. Schaeffer's 'glorious ruin' has become a 'do-it-yourself' structure where men and women do not bear the divine image but are made in the image of themselves. Sadly, such an edifice is built on the shaky ground of human autonomy and is doomed to ultimate collapse.

PERSONALISM: MAN AND SELF
(2) EXISTENTIAL PSYCHOLOGY

I know that there is . . . something that has meaning, that is man, for he is the only being who demands to have it.
Albert Camus

Existentialism, even more than humanism, is a way of looking at human nature and the natural order that embraces a wide range of different emphases. Its protagonists include strange bed-fellows, a number of whom have been averse to being called existentialist: Søren Kierkegaard (1813–1855), the scholastic and theistic Danish philosopher; Friedrich Nietzsche (1844–1900), the 'prophetic German-born Swiss moralist' with his anti-Christian views; the German existentialists Karl Jaspers (1883–1969), the Protestant psychiatrist somewhat given to sermonising about his brand of philosophy, and Martin Heidegger (1889–1976), an academic who had a particular concern for the concept of 'Being' and was preoccupied by the roots of words; and Jean-Paul Sartre (1905–1980), the atheistic French writer. Other literary figures like Dostoevsky, Kafka and Camus, and religious thinkers like Buber, Bultmann and Tillich are sometimes listed under the umbrella title of existentialism. What do all these luminaries have in common? What do we mean by existentialism?

Kaufmann writes: 'Existentialism is not a philosophy but a label for several widely different revolts against traditional philosophy.' Of the different existentialists mentioned above, he adds that 'the one essential feature shared by all these men is their perfervid individualism'.[1]

Sartre, in his lecture 'L'existentialisme est un humanisme' given in 1946, is more specific; he writes of existentialists:

What they have in common is simply the fact that they believe that *existence* comes before *essence* – or, if you will, that we must begin from the subjective. What exactly do we mean by that?[2]

In answer to this question, Sartre goes on to compare the manufacture by an artisan of an article like a paper-knife to the creation of humanity by God and concedes that, in both these examples, essence comes before existence. The raw materials and intrinsic qualities of both a paper-knife and a man or woman (their essence) are handled and understood in advance by the artisan and Creator respectively; for this reason, in these instances, essence precedes existence. However, Sartre does not believe in God, and he is therefore consistent in arguing that, at least in atheistic existentialism,

> . . . if God does not exist there is at least one being whose existence comes before its essence, a being which exists before it can be defined by any conception of it. That being is man . . . Man simply is. Not that he is simply what he conceives himself to be, but he is what he wills, and as he conceives himself after already existing – as he wills to be after that leap towards existence. Man is nothing else but that which he makes of himself. That is the first principle of existentialism.[3]

So we see here, in Sartre's definition, an anthropology that argues that 'Man is nothing else but that which he makes of himself.' Sartre's starting point is atheistic and so, once more, we have a reductionist, 'nothing but . . .', view of humankind. However, other existentialists, who are not necessarily atheists, stress, like Sartre, that you and I have lives to be lived and we are free to *choose* the way we will go. This openness to choice, it is said, means that life is unpredictable and that we are vulnerable to misfortune and suffering. To be human is to be individually unique and to experience both the pleasurable and the painful realities of existence. We exist, and by our decidingness we become essence.

We can see immediately that such an existential view of human nature has a certain amount in common with Rogers' anthropology, particularly with regard to its subjectivism and experience-centredness. However, although Sartre sought to show in his lecture that existentialism is a form of humanism in that it offers some hope for people by emphasising individual choice, on the whole existentialism is a more pessimistic, and at times more realistic, phenomenon than some of Rogers' more heady statements about humankind.

There are strong psychological components in the writings of Kierkegaard, Jaspers and other existentialists and so it is not surprising that many latter-day psychotherapists trace a measure of their thinking to existentialist authors.[4] Western existentialism has its origins in Europe and so I will concentrate mainly on the existential psychologies of Viktor Frankl, influenced by Kierkegaard, and R. D. Laing, who looks a great deal to Sartre.[5] Existential philosophy and psychology do not seem to have taken deep roots in the United States, where a pragmatic humanism, which perhaps has found a greater accord with American optimism, has been more pervasive from the 1950s onwards. Nonetheless, we have seen elements of existential thought in Rogers' insistence on living life fully in the 'here and now'. Furthermore, Rollo May (b 1909), another psychotherapist of Viennese extraction, has done a great deal to introduce an existential psychology to North America, although latterly he has moved towards a blend of existentialism, psychoanalysis and pragmatism.[6]

Viktor Frankl

Viktor Frankl (b 1905), of all the theorists we have so far considered, shares with Carl Jung views that are, in their different ways, perhaps most compatible with Judaism and Christianity. Frankl is said to have much in common with Kierkegaard's theistic views although he rejects the Danish philosopher's extreme subjectivity and argues a 'decisive commitment away from self to the objective world of meaning and values'.[7] Frankl's desire for objectivity also indicates his debt to Edmund Husserl (1859–1938) and other *phenomenologists*, who studied the phenomena of conscious experience as dispassionately as possible, respecting the validity of that experience to the subject.

Frankl was critical of both Freudian theory, with its tendency to devalue humanity, and Adlerian thinking, with its perpetuation of Freud's emphasis on instinct. Even so, he sought to establish a psychotherapy which was built on the foundations of Freud's psychoanalysis and Adler's individual psychology. This 'Third

Viennese School of Psychotherapy' offered the related therapies of *existential analysis* and *logotherapy*. Before examining Frankl's assumptions, aims and methods more fully it may be helpful to distinguish between these twin aspects of his therapeutic approach.

The term 'existential analysis' was first introduced by Frankl and others in 1938 and is used to interpret what it means for a patient to be human in terms of a sense of responsibility. The person being analysed is encouraged to make himself explicit with respect to 'spirituality, freedom, and responsibility'. Frankl regards existential analysis as a 'psychotherapeutic anthropology' which 'precedes all psychotherapy'.[8]

The concept of 'logotherapy' was first introduced in 1926 and is the clinical application of existential analysis, extending 'the scope of psychotherapy beyond the *psyche*, beyond the psychological dimension to include the noölogical dimension, or the *logos*'.[9]

What is meant by these latter, rather daunting terms? Noölogy refers to the study of the mind's understanding of life. Many of us will be much more familiar with the Greek word *logos*, particularly in its use in the New Testament where Jesus is referred to as the logos, the word. However, Frankl uses *logos* in its other main sense of 'meaning'. Logotherapy is a therapy which seeks to unearth 'meaningfulness' in the lives of men and women, carrying the quest for constructive change into the significance of human experience and its spiritual dimensions.

We can say that there is continuity between existential analysis and logotherapy in that the former helps to break the ground in the needy person's life so that the discussion acknowledges ultimate considerations, such as what it means to be human and the need to have a sense of responsibility; logotherapy then builds on that foundation of spiritual awareness to help the patient with his or her 'will to meaning'. To avoid unnecessary confusion I will mainly use the term 'logotherapy' to cover both aspects of Frankl's approach.

Assumptions

It has been said that logotherapy re-humanises psychotherapy and as we examine Frankl's view of humanity we detect a blend of realism and compassion which, so far in our exploration of mainstream psychology, has been rare. He seems to avoid the extremes of Freudian pessimism and Rogerian optimism when he writes:

> . . . in spite of our belief in the potential humanness of man we must not close our eyes to the fact that *humane* humans are, and probably will always remain, a minority. But it is precisely for this reason that each of us is challenged to *join* the minority. Things are bad. But unless we do our best to improve them, everything will become worse.[10]

Having experienced three years as a prisoner amidst the horrors of Auschwitz and Dachau in the Second World War, it is not surprising that Frankl freely acknowledges humankind's evil propensities. By the same token, this Viennese psychiatrist has emerged as a man who, through his own suffering and by observing the strength of the human spirit in the face of the Nazi holocaust, also has a message of hope for troubled men and women.

His diagnosis of the human condition comes through powerfully in the postscript to his book *The Unconscious God: psychotherapy and theology*, which was originally published in German in 1947 and not produced in English until 1975. He says that during the 1970s men and women were more and more experiencing an 'existential vacuum', in which the loss of a moral framework for life had led to a profound uncertainty as to what should be done and what must be done. Generally, he argues, people respond to this morass of indecisiveness by either being swamped by a grey conformity or by the machine of totalitarianism, or by floundering in the muddy waters of 'noögenic neurosis' – an anxiety with its roots in mental uncertainty. Frankl worked in both the United States and Austria and cites figures for his students in both countries. Amongst his European students, twenty-five percent had suffered this existential 'abyss experience' while as many as sixty percent of the Americans had been so afflicted. Frankl thinks that the high American figure relates to the subversive influence of reductionist anthropologies in the United States.[11] Once again, we see the way pervasive views of human nature filter through to the ways people think and act.

With his perspective on the cause and diagnosis of human plight, Frankl seeks to rescue us from despair by appealing to humankind's 'will to meaning'. He strongly criticises the deterministic theories of Freud's 'will to pleasure' and Adler's 'will to power' as implying a woefully inadequate view of human existence. He writes in a way that will warm the heart of the reader who believes more of human nature than that it is a bundle of instinctual drives:

> . . . human existence – at least as long as it has not been neurotically distorted – is always directed to something, or someone, other than itself – be it a meaning to fulfil or another human being to encounter lovingly.[12]

Countering the humanistic emphasis that the conscious goal of life is 'self-actualisation', Frankl argues that people are marked by 'self-transcendence'; and he declares that you and I find personal fulfilment, not by making a beeline for it, but as an 'unintentional by-product' of reaching out beyond ourselves. This encouraging view of the potential of human nature is well illustrated in Frankl's opinion that 'pleasure and happiness are by-products' and that 'the very pursuit of happiness . . . thwarts happiness'. With respect to contemporary ideas on sex, he rejects the hollow argument that 'the human potential of sex (is) actualized' by promiscuity; he sees such hedonism as the very obverse of loving another person:

> Grasping the uniqueness of a partner understandably results in a monogamous partnership. There are no longer interchangeable partners. Conversely, if one is not able to love he winds up with promiscuity.[13]

Frankl's concept of human 'self-transcendence' leads us to ask how he sees human nature with respect to its spiritual dimension. Based on a model by the phenomenologist Max Scheler, he regards a person as having a spiritual core surrounded by psychological and physical 'layers'. However, these layers are not discrete entities but are aspects of the individual. The dimensions of the mind and body are so clearly coordinated that we can talk of a 'psychophysicum'. Donald Tweedie, in his excellent critique of logotherapy, writes:

> Frankl likens the body to a piano, while the psyche is represented by the pianist, who can 'activate' the piano, and the spiritual dimension, in turn, is represented by the artistic 'necessity' of the pianist.[14]

However, the spiritual facet is primary to Frankl; he declares both the links between his three aspects of human nature and the priority of spirituality when he writes that 'The physical makes possible the psychological activation of a spiritual demand.'[15]

Frankl's view of human ontology is further expanded by his insistence on the importance of the unconscious. Unlike traditional Freudianism, he includes the spiritual as well as the instinctual within the concept of the unconscious. We can represent his ideas on the 'structure' of the person in an over-simplified way by the following diagram, in which individual being is shown as 'layered' in two dimensions, the spiritual core lying at the centre at the conscious, preconscious and unconscious levels:

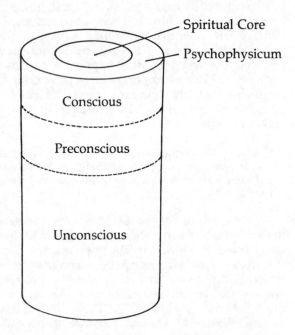

Figure 4   Representation of Frankl's view of personhood

Frankl's stress on the unconscious is seen when he writes that 'spiritual phenomena may be unconscious or conscious; the spiritual basis of human existence is ultimately unconscious'. Within the spiritual unconscious he postulates a transcendent perspective in which an individual may relate to God at an unconscious level. However, to avoid confusion, he adds: 'This . . . in no way implies that God is unconscious to himself, but rather that God may be unconscious to man and that man's relation to God may be unconscious.'[16]

Many of us will find some difficulty in Frankl's concept of the 'unconscious God' and may be reminded of Jungian supernaturalism. Here it is important to note that Frankl criticises Jung's way of allotting unconscious religiousness 'to the region of drives and instincts' where it 'no longer remained a matter of choice and decision'. Frankl sees Jung's perspective on the quest of humanity for God as instinctual, whereas his own view on the matter is that individuals are in a position of choice and responsibility. Frankl's anthropology is marked by 'deciding-ness', Jung's by 'driven-ness'.[17]

Less surprisingly, Frankl is also critical of Freud's belittling of religious belief. He cleverly reverses Freud's dictum: 'Religion is the universal compulsive neurosis of mankind' by declaring: 'Compulsive neurosis may well be diseased religiousness.' In this way he both argues the primary nature of human belief in God and yet acknowledges that 'repressed religion' can degenerate into superstition.[18]

In spite of his emphasis on human spirituality, Frankl seems to avoid the pietism of many supernaturalists. In his presuppositional basis he seems to earth his theism in a deep respect for humanity:

> Monotheism is not enough; it will not do. What we need is not only the belief in the one God but also the awareness of the one mankind, the awareness of the unity of humanity. I would call it mon-anthropism.[19]

Aims

The classical Freudian psychoanalyst has often been dismissed as a 'head shrinker' or 'shrink' and the traditional psychiatrist as a 'trick cyclist'. These and similar terms point to views that these professionals should be treated with caution and even suspicion. They are of course generalities which are grossly unfair on both individual psychotherapists and the psychological professions at large. However, behind these catch-phrases is a fear which can, on occasions, be well placed. In particular, the 'shrink' may well be an individual whose reductionist views actually threaten to diminish the personhood of the patient attending. Frankl contrasts Freudian 'depth-psychology' with his own 'height-psychology' in which the therapist is a 'stretch' rather than a 'shrink'. He seeks to 'stretch' people and make them 'shrink-resistant'![20]

In his attempts to 'humanise' psychiatry, Frankl, as has already been seen, tries to help the patient find meaning in his or her life. This aim of logotherapy includes three main focuses: the 'will to meaning'; meaning within suffering; and the freedom of the will.

Will to meaning.   We have already shown how Frankl argues that the human spirit has a thirst for significance that is achievable as it reaches out to ideas beyond itself, to other people and to God himself. This 'will to meaning' incorporates the determination to perceive facets of reality and to organise these aspects into 'meaningful wholes'. If in the course of logotherapy I am awakened to see the selfishness of my relationships with my friends, that I need to stir myself to be more reliable and considerate and that in so doing my friendships will be more harmonious and helpful to others, then I am beginning to realise my 'will to meaning'.

Meaning within suffering.   Frankl, with his profound experience of personal suffering, points out that logotherapy can help to combat that 'tragic triad' of human existence: 'pain, guilt and death'. As the person in need discovers new attitudes, these afflictions can be 'turned into something positive and creative'. The sufferer is changed for the better as he is awakened to new values by his suffering.[21]

Again, Frankl admits that there is nothing automatic in this constructive response to affliction. One person who suffers is refined thereby, another despairs. Frankl writes this of the person who gives up in the face of adversity: 'Anyone who is in despair, thereby betrays the fact that he had idolized something.'[22] If an individual is obsessed by self, another person, an idea, a hobby, a job, or whatever, then deprivation can lead to desperation. The idolator has so much to lose.

Freedom of the will.   The third focus of logotherapy is to help the patient exercise a freedom of the will. Unlike many modern existentialists who argue that men and women can be 'free from' all restraints, Frankl declares that true human freedom lies in being 'free for' responsible living. He departs from Sartre's view that 'man can choose and design himself by creating his own standards', likening this offer of autonomy to the spectacle of a fakir's trick in which a rope is thrown up into empty air. The idea of autonomous freedom is a delusion that leads nowhere.

Quoting Maria von Ebner-Eschenbach who said: 'Be the master of your will and the servant of your conscience!',[23] Frankl declares that responsible freedom entails a submission to conscience. Here he returns to the concept of the transcendent, seeing the conscience as an 'ethical instinct' that reaches down into the spiritual unconscious. He argues that this conscience is 'something individual, something concrete' for each person.[24]

Frankl brings the three strands of a 'will to meaning', a meaning in suffering and a freedom of will together when he writes: 'What can be changed should be changed.' Logotherapy seeks to be realistic in its aims; there are some things in our lives – certain inherited dispositions, a difficult job that we are committed to, a marriage that we have entered – that we cannot, or should not, expect to be removed. There are other perspectives – a tendency to be irritable with others, an attitude of jealousy towards a colleague, a self-centredness within a relationship – that we should seek to change. Frankl sums it all up by quoting a bill-board seen in the States:

> Calmly bear, without ado,
> That which fate imposed on you;
> But to bedbugs don't resign:
> Turn for help to Rosenstein.[25]

Methods

We have already indicated that existential analysis may be used to help the patient become aware of spiritual issues in his or her life, including a sense of responsibility. Here the technique embraces classical Freudian components such as free association and dream analysis. In this way, the patient is helped to discover and reveal his or her 'genuine religiousness'.

Unlike the more relentless of the exponents of psychoanalysis,

Frankl sees both the necessity for and the limitations of this process of unmasking. He readily identifies with the individual's anxiety that the therapist will not only expose his beliefs but will annihilate them too. Further, he is painfully aware of the propensity, that many of us have, to be too persistent in our attempt to uncover the tender plant of a client's value-system. He suggests at what point we should put the brake on:

> Unmasking is perfectly legitimate; but I would say that it must stop as soon as one confronts what is genuine, genuinely human, in man. If it does not stop there, the only thing that the 'unmasking psychologist' really unmasks is his own 'hidden motive' – namely, his unconscious need to debase and depreciate the humanness of man.[26]

In moving from this preliminary, but fundamental analysis, logotherapy proceeds in order to help the client towards a 'will to meaning'. Throughout therapy, Frankl stresses that the moment-by-moment, 'existential' relationship between the therapist and the person in need is primary. He argues that techniques are secondary and, as Tweedie writes, 'must not be allowed to obscure this relationship'.

Nonetheless, Frankl advocates certain techniques as well as a number of guidelines for effective logotherapy. You may have noticed the occasional use of the word 'patient' rather than 'client' in this section and it is important to note that Frankl's approach is essentially pursued within a medical framework. Even so, there is value for the non-medical reader in understanding some of the elements in the method of logotherapy as they include principles of more general application.

Over an average of eight sessions, the logotherapist seeks to help the patient to change his attitudes towards his difficulties. The relatively small number of contacts with the patient discourages dependence and encourages commitment to change. Within a relationship of trust, the therapist plays a more active role than in many of the personalistic psychologies. This more 'directive' approach does not actually give direction to the patient; rather, it appeals to the client's awakened insight and sense of responsibility.

Frankl uses two particular techniques in the treatment of the chronically anxious. The first of these, *paradoxical intention*, is potentially open to abuse and is therefore best used in a medical, or fully supportive context. In this method the patient is urged to meet head-on that which is feared. An integral part of this technique is in the use of humour; if a patient can laugh at himself and his illogical fears then there is progress. An example of this light touch is given by Tweedie where a stutterer can be encouraged to pass from saying, 'I'm afraid I'll stutter on "b"'s and "p"'s' to 'Today, I'll stutter my way through the whole alphabet!'[27]

The second method, *de-reflection*, is a form of the 'mind over matter' tack that is part and parcel of much home-spun advice. This technique is one which seeks to help shift the patient's attention from 'intensive, crippling self-consciousness' to 'self-transcending decisions in reference to the objective world'.[28] The student, whose preoccupation with inner conflicts can be turned towards attending the next lecture and offering coffee that evening to a group of friends, begins to feel more integrated into campus life and a little more the person he or she should be.

So we see that Frankl's logotherapy is a blended approach with both analytical and behavioural ingredients. The analytical element is wary of being too probing and too interpretative, while the behavioural component seeks to move the focus of the patient's conscious attention to less selfish patterns of behaviour. The dynamics of logotherapy tend to flow from the unconscious in the initial existential analysis into the conscious, as a new attitude of responsibility is awakened, and so to the unconscious once more as the person is liberated from 'stultifying "hyper-reflection"'. Frankl declares that the ultimate goal of logotherapy is 'to reinstate the spontaneity and naïveté of an unreflected existential act'.[29]

Critique

From a theistic, and even a Christian, point of view, Viktor Frankl's logotherapy is something of a high-point amongst the range of methodologies we have so far considered. His assumptions and aims seem to avoid both the biological determinism of Watson and Freud and the humanistic optimism of some of the neo-Freudians and personalistic psychologists like Rogers. Frankl's anthropology embraces, in some measure, both the glory and the ruin of Schaeffer's 'glorious ruin'.

Most Christians, on reflection, will feel at home with at least some aspects of the three focuses of logotherapy: a 'will to meaning', a meaning in suffering and a freedom of will. Frankl quotes research carried out in Czechoslovakia from which it has been declared that 'the will to meaning is really a specific need not reducible to other needs, and is in greater or smaller degree present in all human beings'.[30] In turn, Frankl has some criticism of Maslow, who we will meet again in the next chapter. Maslow has argued that an individual's lower needs, such as hunger and safety, must be met before higher needs, like a relationship of love, can be satisfied. However, Frankl points out that even amidst the horrors of a Nazi death camp, with its appalling deprivation of all the more basic personal needs, the human spirit could still soar to achieve a 'will to meaning'. He writes that people are more truly characterised by a 'search for meaning' than a 'search for self'.

The insights of logotherapy touch on the profound truth that Augustine declared so memorably in the opening of his prayer: 'Almighty God, in whom we live and move and have our being, who hast made us for thyself, so that our hearts are restless till they rest in thee . . .' Perhaps Frankl's psychological perception that human existence is more likely to find fulfilment when it is 'directed to something, or someone, other than itself'[31] catches a glimpse, in its generality, of the glorious and specific vision for humanity that Jesus gives when he said: 'He who finds his life will lose it, and he who loses his life for my sake will find it' (Matthew 10:39 RSV).

With respect to the reality and mystery of suffering, there is some accord between Frankl's views and the fuller, more explicit insights given through God's self-disclosure – in creation, the scriptures, history, human experience and, supremely, in and through Christ. Frankl puts his finger on the need for a theodicy (an understanding of God's justice in the face of evil) when he writes, 'The calculation of human suffering can be computed only in Transcendence; in immanence it remains an open question'.[32]

However, the Christian can be more definite. It is as we bring the pain and puzzle of our affliction to a God who suffers that we can begin to hold together both God's righteousness and the problem of evil. It was on the brow of the man of sorrows, God and perfect man, as he hung on the cross in the hours of darkness, that both the effective judgment of human rebellion by a holy God and the immeasurable weight of humankind's sin and suffering met. It is as we prayerfully 'consider him who endured from sinners such hostility against himself' (Hebrews 12:3) that we can be encouraged in our struggle against adversity.[33] As Christians we will want to modify Frankl's statement and say: 'The calculation of human suffering can be computed only in Transcendence, only in the mind and will of our omniscient God; however, in immanence, in Jesus Christ, the word made flesh, the open question of that suffering finds its ultimate answer.'

As with the 'will to meaning' and the 'meaning of suffering', we find in Frankl's understanding of a 'freedom of will' that his anthropology has some resonance with a biblical theology. Frankl eschews the hedonistic view of freedom, which tells us that we are free from all restraint, for a view that sees freedom as the state of being free to obey conscience and to be responsible. The scriptures move beyond this general statement to declare that true freedom is found in exchanging the old bondage of self-centred living for a new bondage of Christ-centredness, empowered by his Spirit. Here the individual is freed to obey a reawakened conscience and to live responsibly before God in his world.[34]

We can be grateful to Frankl for a methodology which, at a number of important levels, shares certain insights with a Christian perspective. However, as Tweedie points out, logotherapy is committed to the 'boundaries of transcendence', whereas Christianity, being revelational, is dedicated to the other side of those boundaries. He writes that '. . . whereas logotherapy in its philosophical observations only affirms the existence of transcendent reality, the Bible reveals it'.[35]

And yet, we are moving in the right direction. Here we have a theorist who, along with Jung, has lifted his eyes above and beyond the biological and person-centred frontiers of secular psychology towards the 'unknown God'. That God is thought to be not only unknown but unknowable is made explicit when Frankl declares that 'not only is man not able to comprehend the absolute meaning, but rather, he is also unable to know the Absolute in any other respect'.[36] Nevertheless, our gaze is lifted heavenwards. In the meantime, though, until we look more fully at a biblical anthropology and some of the methodologies used by certain Christians, we need to lower our sights once more – first to look at another existential psychotherapist and then to consider the obscurities of some of the transpersonal psychologies.

R. D. Laing

Viktor Frankl's relevance to Judaeo-Christian approaches in psychotherapy is self-evident; the methodology of R. D. Laing has been much more open to controversy amongst traditional psychiatrists, Marxist sociologists, mystic drop-outs and Christian thinkers alike.

Born in 1927 in Glasgow, training as a psychiatrist in the early 1950s, working subsequently at the Tavistock Clinic in London and carrying out research into schizophrenia and family dynamics during the late 1950s, and 1960s, Laing has become a widely known and unique influence in psychological, sociological and political circles. In recent years, the enigmas of the philosophical basis of Laing's thought have stimulated a fresh surge of interest and research, including books by the Marxist Andrew Collier and the sociologist Martin Howarth-Williams, both published in 1977, and, more recently, papers and aspects of a PhD thesis by J. N. Isbister, a Christian with a specialist interest in the history of psychology.[37]

Before looking more closely at the assumptions behind Laing's brand of existential psychology, it may be helpful to summarise some of the milestones that have been chronicled in the life of this individualistic Scottish psychiatrist.

J. N. Isbister, in his paper 'Anti-Psychiatry: Christian Roots in the Thought of R. D. Laing', cites some of Laing's declarations about his earlier years as recorded in Howarth-Williams' book. Laing describes how he 'grew up, theologically speaking, in the 19th century: lower middle-class Lowland Presbyterian, corroded by 19th century materialism, scientific rationalism and humanism . . .'[38] In *The Facts of Life*, Laing writes of 'when I was sixteen . . . among the Christian boys in my school, of whom I was counted as one'.[39] Subsequently, there was a loosening of his teenage commitment to conservative Christianity and he became increasingly influenced by the more liberal writings of Kierkegaard and Tillich (see below).[40]

Once medically qualified, Laing pursued his increasing interest in the causes and nature of schizophrenia.[41] His first book, *The Divided Self*, is a lucid account of his understanding of the deranged (psychotic) person. He writes that an 'absolute and obvious prerequisite in working with psychotics' is 'to be able to orientate oneself as a person in the other's scheme of things . . .'[42] His compassion for the schizophrenic is shown when he writes of such a person: 'We have to recognize all the time his distinctiveness, his separateness and loneliness and despair.'[43]

During the 1960s Laing, along with two other existential psychiatrists in particular (David Cooper, who had trained in Cape Town, and Aaron Esterson, a contemporary of Laing at the Glasgow Royal Infirmary), spearheaded a trend in Britain which attacked the *status quo* of traditional psychiatry. This movement of 'anti-psychiatry' was mirrored in the United States by Thomas Szasz, although Szasz has rejected any close identification with the anti-psychiatrists, accusing them of seeking 'to raise the "insane" above the "sane"'.[44]

In the early 1960s, Laing's psychoanalytic thinking came under the influence of Sartre's views on the nature of human groups and Gregory Bateson's concept of the *double-bind*. Bateson, who was director of research into schizophrenia at Palo Alto, California, pointed out the subversive and 'binding' effect that certain people have on others they relate to. In the 'double-bind', whatever the trapped party does he or she is wrong in the eyes of the one who spins the web. I remember a young student of English called Jim who was chronically anxious and described his mother as one who always tried to please others as long as, in doing so, she received pleasure herself. Jim's mother had told him that he could bring home 'any friend, any time' but when he attempted to do so his mother would disapprove and find some ruse to prevent opening her home to her son's guests. Jim was nearly driven to despair by this 'double-bind'.

In his books *The Self and Others, Sanity, Madness and the Family* (with Aaron Esterson) and *Interpersonal Perception* (with H. Phillipson and A. R. Lee), we see Laing widening his earlier concentration on the schizophrenic individual to include a study of relationships between two or more people and a survey of the whole family as contributing to the syndrome of schizophrenia respectively. From 1964 onwards, according to the Marxist psychologist Peter Sedgwick, Laing moved into the use of his 'psychedelic model' of schizophrenia. Sedgwick writes: 'schizophrenia was henceforth to be seen not as a psychiatric disability but as one stage in a natural psychic healing process . . .'[45]

In his *The Politics of Experience*, Laing bemoans the way our Western civilisation has caused a split between the 'inner' and 'outer' worlds of experience for all of us, therapists and patients included. He sees powerful pressures, working in society at large and in families in particular, which accentuate this splitting and its consequent feelings of alienation. For some individuals, ensnared by such psychological mantraps as the 'double-bind', there may be the development of what is described by the traditional psychiatrist as a schizophrenic breakdown, but by Laing as a 'journey'. He writes:

> This journey is experienced as going further 'in', as going back through one's personal life, in and back and through and beyond into the experience of all mankind, of the primal man, of Adam and perhaps even further into the being of animals, vegetables and minerals.[46]

In the same book, Laing compares the schizophrenic state and the 'transcendental experience', relating 'the transcendental experiences that *sometimes* break through in psychosis to those experiences of the divine that are the living fount of all religion'.[47] The influence of Eastern religion comes through strongly when Laing writes about the parallelism between the psychotic and mystical 'journeys'. He declares the magnetic pull of this philosophy in his aphorism: 'Orientation means to know where the orient is. For inner space, to know the east, the origin or source of our experience.'[48]

It was in the late 1960s and early 1970s that Laing became one of the prophets and gurus of the 'counter culture'. His charismatic and enigmatic figure seemed to stalk the corridors and campuses of the universities and colleges, while well-thumbed copies of *The Divided Self* and *The Politics of Experience* lay by the bed-sides of innumerable students. It appeared that many were disturbed by Laing's writings, many were enlightened and many bewitched. One formerly stable postgraduate student came to see me fearing her own incipient insanity after reading *Sanity, Madness and the Family*. A younger male student, whose range of personal difficulties I had been trying to help him with for some time, entered my consulting room one day with a beatific smile and declared, 'I've been reading Laing, and I *now* understand myself!' A French undergraduate we knew carried a photo of the beloved guru close to her heart.

In 1971, Laing left Britain for Ceylon where he committed

himself to Theravada Buddhist meditation. Subsequently he has made trips to India and Japan in order to continue his learning of meditative technique.

From the mid-1960s through the next two decades, Laing has been a key figure in the development of the Philadelphia Association, founded in 1964 and based in London. This charity has set up several communities, where people diagnosed as schizophrenic are allowed to experience the ramifications of their psychosis without let or hindrance. Within these caring settings no medical treatment is given without the individual's consent. Perhaps the best known of those who have profited from this still controversial approach is Mary Barnes, who tells her story, in collaboration with her psychiatrist, Dr Joseph Berke, in *Mary Barnes: Two Accounts of a Journey through Madness* (1971).

Mary Barnes, then in her forties, and a woman who had been labelled a chronic schizophrenic, was one of the first to enter the new 'anti-psychiatric' community of Kingsley Hall. She was allowed to go back to 'being a baby' again, to start her life all over again as it were. This 'journey' back in time to a point of 'rebirth' and gradual progress towards maturity has been described by her in these words:

> Flection: the act of bending or the state of being bent. That's how I was at Kingsley Hall, bent back into a womb of rebirth. From this cocoon I emerged, changed to the self I had almost lost. The buried me, entangled in guilt and choked with anger as a plant matted in weed, grew anew, freed from the knots of my past.[49]

She ascribes the success of this nightmarish journey to the patient help of her psychotherapist and the keeping of a faithful God: 'It's trusting God, through another person and no matter if so-called "mistakes" are made, God doesn't "drop us".'[50] In frightening contrast to this story is the tragedy of 'Anna', whose psychotic breakdown under the supervision of a Laingian psychotherapist was followed by her lingering death from severe self-burning.[51]

In trying to understand something of R. D. Laing's methodology, let us now examine more closely his assumptive world before briefly mentioning his aims and methods.

Laing, who puts himself in the company of those 'who follow Freud', is not only psychoanalytic in orientation but describes his approach variously as that of 'existential psychology', 'existential phenomenology' and 'social phenomenology'. In *The Divided Self*, he writes that 'Existential phenomenology attempts to characterize the nature of a person's experience of his world and himself.'[52] Throughout his writings, he has majored on the experiencing aspect of human existence and, in so doing, has sought to expose the reductionism of the more behaviouristic elements in the scientific method. In *The Voice of Experience* he attacks this scientism and its determination to brush aside the apparent vagaries of what you and I actually experience. For example, he exposes the limitations of 'total' objectivity in science when he writes:

> Total objectivity precludes itself from any possible explanation of experience. The most sophisticated neuroscientists are the most baffled at its very existence, and its inexplicable and capricious relation to the brain . . . The most sophisticated objective data on the correlation of reportable human psychic activity and objective physical events leaves us essentially as much in the dark or in the light as ever.[53]

In the same book Laing argues forcibly against the dehumanising and demoralising effects of scientific objectivity declaring: 'What is scientifically right may be morally wrong. An experiment may be scientifically impeccable and spiritually foul.' He carries his criticism of scientism into the controlling and over-interpretative aspects of traditional psychiatry, psychoanalysis and, even, existential analysis.[54] With respect to orthodox psychiatry, Laing questions strongly the 'medical model' of psychological disturbance (that is, that mental disorder is primarily *illness* which requires the careful diagnosis of signs and symptoms, the evaluation of prognosis and the administration of appropriate treatment). He seeks to show that this 'disease theory' is essentially *presupposition* in that the experiences it describes are assumed to be 'worthless, and destructive *per se*' so that 'the biological processes which accompany them *must* be pathological'.[55] Laing is exposing what seems to be a circular argument: a person has symptoms which are deemed 'sick' by the expert and so any bodily mechanisms behind these symptoms must be evidence of 'disease'. However, Laing does not, at least at this stage of the argument, give full weight to the fact that it is often the patient, rather than the psychiatrist, who sees his or her symptoms as a nuisance, as disruptive, as antisocial and, in a sense, as an indication of 'illness'. Laing is, of course, pointing out the danger of seeing most, if not all, psychological disturbances as primarily biological in their origin and therefore requiring purely physical treatment. Many psychiatrists would agree with the thrust of his argument while at the same time disputing its universal application. There *are* patients whose mental troubles seem to be rooted in their bodily functions and such are helped by chemical means. There are, of course, many others where medication is a useful adjunct that relieves unpleasant symptoms while emotional, psychological and spiritual causes of their malaise are explored and a measure of healing found.

Andrew Collier, in his *R. D. Laing: The Philosophy and Politics of Psychotherapy*, sees the atheistic existentialist, Sartre as the foremost influence on Laing's thought. Collier, himself a Marxist, argues that Laing's interest in the 'micro-politics' of such small groups as the family is apparently echoed in socialist and Marxist assumptions at the 'macro-political' level. Collier describes Laing's position in his early book *The Divided Self* as 'Left Personalist', in which an individual's ego is, although autonomous, a product of social constraints and only exists in relation to others; personal autonomy is lost due to the failure of society generally, and of the individual's parents more specifically, to recognise that autonomy.[56] In contrast to this earlier 'political' view held by Laing, Collier points out the development of 'Gnostic' leanings as expressed in *The Politics of Experience*. He notes that Laing has moved to the concept of the 'self' needing release from the ego ('an instrument of living in this world') and that this escape can be made through the use of drugs, religious experience or 'madness'.

Although acknowledging Collier's work as 'a fair attempt to chronicle and summarize the significance of Laing', J. N. Isbister has argued a very different case for Laing's assumptive world. As we have already noted, R. D. Laing grew up within a 'lower middle-class Lowland Presbyterian' environment and later turned his back on conservative Christianity. However, Isbister has shown that Laing continued with some level of Christian understanding before the increasing relativism and mysticism of his later thought took over. In 1957, a paper by Laing on Paul Tillich, the liberal theologian, was published in the *British Journal of Medical Psychology*. Isbister points out that the first draft of this paper was received in 1954 and concludes: 'The subject matter reveals Laing's continued interest in Christian concerns, and points to their primacy in undergirding his clinical studies.'[57]

What are Laing's aims in helping the person in need? The existential nature of his desire to aid the other towards a sense of individuality and inner harmony is seen when he writes: 'When the other is a patient, existential phenomenology becomes the attempt to reconstruct the patient's way of being himself in his world . . .'[58] Laing's aim is not only to foster this new feeling of integration but to do so through the medium of the 'therapeutic relationship'; this is the vehicle for recovering a person's humanness: 'Psychotherapy must remain an *obstinate attempt of two people to recover the wholeness of being human through the relationship between them.*'[59]

Within this humanising relationship, Laing emphasises the need for compassion, not least in the case of the schizophrenic, of whom he says: 'If we cannot understand him, one is hardly in a position to begin to "love" him in any effective way.'[60] For Laing, technique must be subservient to the caring relationship between the therapist and client:

> Any technique concerned with the other without the self, with behaviour to the exclusion of experience, with the relationship to the neglect of the persons in relation, with the individuals to the exclusion of their relationship, and most of all, with an object-to-be-changed rather than a person-to-be-accepted, simply perpetuates the disease it purports to cure.[61]

R. D. Laing's psychoanalytic thought, his existentialism and his mysticism, all springing from Christian roots and suffused, at times, with Christian imagery, are beyond easy categorisation. To take perhaps his best known stance, that of 'anti-psychiatry', we have seen, on the one hand, his discernment and compassion on behalf of the psychotic patient in particular and, on the other, an absolutising of his insights which has tended to antagonise the psychiatric profession. Although recognising the controversial nature of much Laingian thinking, I feel that we should take quite seriously both Frankl's and Laing's attempts to give psychiatry a 'human face'. Any opposition to biological determinism and scientific reductionism should be welcomed; any exposure of dehumanising elements in the diagnosis, treatment and prognosis of psychological disorder should be acclaimed.

Summary

As we have considered the personalistic psychologies we have observed an increasing concern with the numinous and otherworldly in the development of thought behind the methodologies. This same trend has been detectable in the work of some of the post-Freudians. And so, Erik Erikson's interest in Jesus and Gandhi, Rogers' acknowledgment in *A Way of Being* of a movement beyond the person, Frankl's firmly rooted theism and now R. D. Laing's own personal journey towards 'things Eastern' all point us, apparently, away from ourselves towards 'transcendence'. Sadly, we will find, as we look at transpersonal psychologies, that at least some of these outward routes seem to turn full circle back to the self and its bondage.

8

TRANSPERSONALISM: MAN BEYOND SELF

Orthodox, Western Christianity has dealt very poorly with the spiritual side of man's nature, choosing either to ignore its existence or to label it pathological.

Charles T. Tart

When the opposites are realized to be one, discord melts into concord, battles become dances, and old enemies become lovers. We are then in a position to make friends with all of our universe, and not just one half of it.

Ken Wilber

Men and women have always had longings that have led them to seek not only companionship in one another but also meaning and fulfilment beyond themselves. These age-old yearnings have been the mainspring of many forms of religion and magic and, although distracted for a season by the insights and blandishments of the Western secular psychologies, it is not surprising to see them re-emerging in the transpersonalism of the mid- and late twentieth century.

We have traced the growth, in our imaginary forest, of the somewhat stark tree of behaviourism, the contrastingly complex and shade-producing tree of psychoanalytic theory and the more self-evidently attractive tree of the personalistic psychologies. These three giants, springing from the soil of rationalism, materialism, humanism and existentialism, cluster around our ancient tree of Judaeo-Christianity and are now seen to be in the company of the tree of transpersonal psychology. On one side, the roots of this last tree commingle with those of the tree of pastoral care while, around the rest of its girth, it rises up from soil shared with a veritable thicket – the growth of the world's other religious systems. A substantial part of the canopies of the tree of psychoanalysis (in particular, its Jungian section) and the tree of personalism (through areas representing Rogers, Frankl and Laing) leans towards and mixes with the widespread branchings of the tree of transpersonal psychology. The linkage between these systems can be shown in the following way:

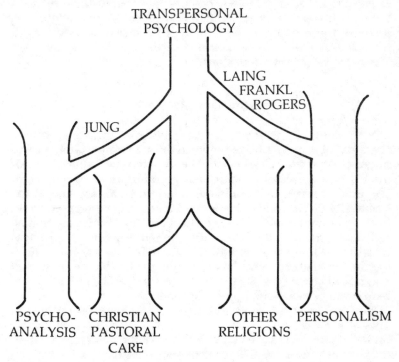

Figure 5 The rise of transpersonalism

In describing the transpersonal psychologies it is obvious that we are tackling a most complicated and motley assortment of influences and developments. This diversity is indicated by the subjects covered in *Transpersonal Psychologies*, edited by Charles T. Tart, which includes chapters on Zen Buddhism, Yoga psychology, contemporary Sufism, the Christian mystical tradition and patterns of Western magic. In his introduction, Tart acknowledges the omission of 'Taoism, Alchemy, the Cabalistic Tradition, Tibetan Buddhism, and so on'. In fact, it is impossible to do justice to even a sample of the psychological understandings of such a range of belief-systems and so I intend to examine, albeit briefly, some of the insights given by Maslow, from the humanistic stream, Assagioli, with his psychoanalytic and existential links, and Wilber, one of the leading protagonists of transpersonalism in the United States. Although mention is made of the importance of Christian mysticism in this area, a fuller assessment will be included in the later chapter entitled 'Reaching in' (chapter fourteen).

Abraham Maslow

The thinking of the American psychologist Abraham Maslow (1908–1970) forms a bridge between humanistic psychology and transpersonalism. Originally, like Rogers, he embraced humanistic views about human nature undergirded by a spirit of scientific enquiry – a spirit instilled in him by his teachers at the University of Wisconsin. He argued that men and women could find, through rational effort, a level of personal fulfilment that he called *self-actualisation*. In the 1950s he wrote against the human tendency to look for supernatural help in life's struggles, criticising the 'good many' who 'have thrown up their hands altogether and talked about original sin or intrinsic evil and concluded that man could be saved only by extrahuman forces'.[1]

However, a decade later, in the preface to the second edition of *Toward a Psychology of Being*, we find a shift towards an acknowledgment of the reality of evil and of the need for mankind to discover something 'bigger than we are'. Although he stopped short of supernaturalism, his desire to move beyond the limited horizons of behaviourism, Freudianism and humanism to a degree of transcendence in his 'Fourth Psychology' is clearly seen:

> I consider Humanistic, Third Force Psychology to be transitional, a preparation for a still 'higher' Fourth Psychology, transpersonal, transhuman, centred in the cosmos rather than in human needs and interest, going beyond humanness, identity, self-actualization, and

the like . . . Without the transcendent and the transpersonal, we get sick, violent, and nihilistic, or else hopeless and apathetic. We need something 'bigger that we are' to be awed by and to commit ourselves to in a new, naturalistic, empirical, non-churchly sense . . .[2]

Assumptions

Maslow's determination to stick to a ground-base that accords with his considerable experience, in comparative, developmental and social psychology, is seen in his reference to a commitment to 'something' beyond ourselves, 'in a new, naturalistic, empirical, non-churchly sense'. He seeks to advance into the realms of 'the problems of love, creativeness, value, beauty, imagination, ethics and joy' under the banner of science. In the area of inner conviction, 'only science can overcome characterological differences in seeing and believing. Only science can progress'.[3]

Here, it is important to see that Maslow is, on the one hand, acknowledging the primacy of science as *the* vehicle of investigation and, on the other hand, is extending its field of enquiry to include 'the problems and the data of personal and experiential psychology'. He readily declares the methodological difficulties in researching the aspirations, imaginations and beliefs of the human heart – and yet he insists in doing so from a naturalistic basis, that is from a viewpoint that the world is governed by purely natural (as distinct from supernatural) laws and forces.

Maslow's naturalism is less hidebound than the biological and instinctual determinisms of Skinner and Freud in that he sees human values as 'culturally developed' as well as 'biologically and genetically based'.[4] His humanistic and existential stance is shown in his grappling with an understanding of human nature. In his original 'Third Force Psychology', like Rogers, he espoused an optimistic view of humankind in which 'the basic needs . . . the basic human emotions and the basic human capacities are on their face either neutral, pre-moral or positively "good"'.[5] We see him moving towards 'the development of a humanistic and transpersonal psychology of evil' when he continues: 'destructiveness, sadism, cruelty, malice, etc. seem so far to be not intrinsic but rather they seem to be violent reactions against frustration of our intrinsic needs, emotions and capacities'. He concedes that anger, fear, laziness and ignorance 'can and do lead to evil behaviour, but they needn't. This result is not intrinsically necessary . . .' This sanguine view of the problem of evil is further expressed when he says that the 'literature of dynamic psychology and psychopathology' gives us the 'insight that human evil is largely (though not altogether) human weakness or ignorance, forgiveable, understandable and also curable'.[6] Maslow's perspective, that humanity is moving forwards to a bright future and yet is held back primarily by weakness and ignorance, is indicated by his whimsical quotation of a biologist who announced: 'I have discovered the missing link between the anthropoid apes and civilized men. It's us!'

Towards a transpersonal psychology

From his cautiously optimistic viewpoint on human nature, Maslow, in his *Toward a Psychology of Being*, seeks to integrate what he calls Being (or, B-) psychology, with its emphasis on mental health, and Deficiency (or, D-) psychology, which majors on mental illness. It may be helpful to consider these two psychologies under the headings of 'self-actualisation' and 'growth'. *Self-actualisation.* Maslow postulates that all human beings have a hierarchy of basic needs, beginning with the 'lower' needs of food, drink, sleep, shelter and clothing, and ascending through such requirements as a sense of belonging, friendship and self-esteem to the 'higher' needs of personal fulfilment, an integral system of values and an aesthetic dimension to life.[7] He argues that, broadly speaking, a gratification of the 'lower' physiological needs is required before a person is able to attend fully to questions of relating to others and developing his or her potential. Certainly, at the most fundamental level, someone dying of thirst is not going to be too concerned about the aesthetics of the surrounding desert landscape. In contrast, another individual, with terminal cancer, may well experience deep satisfaction of many of the basic needs within, say, the security of a hospice. Here, the caring and skilful attention of doctors and nurses, the love of visiting friends and relatives, the ability to reflect on God's grace and goodness as death approaches and the provision of a tasteful and reassuring environment all contribute to an example of Maslow's 'psychology of health'.

This B-psychology embraces the process of self-actualisation which Maslow has defined as:

... ongoing actualization of potentials, capacities and talents, as fulfilment of mission (or call, fate, destiny, or vocation), as a fuller knowledge of, and acceptance of, the person's own intrinsic nature, as an unceasing trend toward unity, integration or synergy within the person.[8]

He lists thirteen characteristics of the 'healthy' people who experience this 'unceasing trend' towards self-actualisation; these include: a superior perception of reality, an increased spontaneity, resistance to enculturation and a greatly increased creativeness.[9] Earlier, in 1954, he published a selection of well known personalities who were apparently free of neurotic and psychotic tendencies and displayed the full use of their talents; Lincoln, Einstein, William James and Spinoza were amongst the chosen few who showed the hallmarks of 'self-actualisation'.[10]

The general characteristics of the self-actualising person are summarised by Maslow under the terms 'B-love' and 'B-cognition'. He sees B-love as comprising an unselfish and generous concern which has the best interests of the other at heart. He contrasts this with the selfishness of 'D-love' in which a hunger for affection can be described as a 'deficiency disease'.[11]

Within B-love, Maslow continues, there is a B-cognition which is 'acutely and penetratingly perceptive'. This degree of awareness is, he argues, a distinguishing feature of moments of rapture like falling in love, experiencing some great or moving piece of music or poetry, and gaining inspirational or creative insight. He examined, through personal interviews with eighty individuals and written responses by 190 college students, a number of these *peak-experiences* in order to establish their characteristics. He summarises the effects of such experiences in somewhat fulsome, psychoanalytic terms; they are:

... a fusion of ego, id, super-ego and ego-ideal, of conscious, preconscious and unconscious ... a healthy regression without fear in the service of the greatest maturity, a true integration of the person at *all* levels.[12]

From these observations, Maslow concludes that peak-experiences both further the maturing process and also are experienced by self-actualising individuals 'more frequently, and intensely and perfectly than ... average people'.

Growth. As in Rogerian psychology, 'growth' is an important concept to Maslow because it indicates both the momentum and direction of the self-actualising process. He admits the difficulty of defining the term, declaring that 'its meaning can be *indicated* rather than defined' – for example, 'it is not the same as equilibrium, homeostasis, tension-reduction, etc.'. He prefers to see growth as synonymous with such ideas as 'individuation, autonomy, self-actualization, self-development, productiveness, self-realization'.[13] However we interpret these jargon words, we can see from statements like these that Maslow has a dynamic view of growth which includes the participation of the individual. Psychological growth is not inevitable; it requires effort.

He raises the question, 'Why do some grow and others not?' and concludes that every human being experiences two sets of forces: one that engenders fear, presses a person to cling to safety and may lead to regression; and one that urges the individual forwards to a 'full functioning of all his capacities'. This dialectic necessitates choice at every point throughout life 'between the delights of safety and growth, dependence and independence, regression and progression, immaturity and maturity'.[14] It is here that Maslow seeks to tread a middle way between pessimistic and optimistic views of human nature – between a Freudian attitude which sees everything through 'brown-coloured glasses', dwelling exclusively on 'evil and sin', and the more extreme positions of the 'growth school' that see through 'rose-coloured glasses' and declare that all is well with humanity.

However, Maslow does concede that the will to grow can be elusive and that the wise therapist will adopt a 'helpful let-be' approach towards the 'sick' person. Growth cannot be forced and the sensitive counsellor will recognise and respect 'the fear of growth, the slow pace of growth, the blocks, the pathology, the reasons for not growing'.[15] Maslow has also observed that growth could be most powerfully kindled through 'single life experiences such as tragedies, deaths, traumata, conversions, and sudden insights, which forced change on the life-outlook of the person and consequently in everything that he did'.[16]

The pathway of growth that leads towards the goal of self-actualisation is, then, a narrow route that few attain. Great strides may be made within life's peak-experiences, more modest steps forward may be taken through day-to-day decisions and choices, and the track may be unblocked with the help of a fellow-travelling friend or counsellor. This sometimes lonely route can, on the face of it, look like an elaborate ego-trip but, Maslow would assure us, 'the achievement of self-actualization . . . paradoxically makes more possible the transcendence of self, and of self-consciousness and of selfishness'.[17] Surely it is time to come back to the preface of the second edition of *Toward a Psychology of Being* and remind ourselves of Maslow's move towards transpersonalism – that 'we need something "bigger than we are"'.

Critique

In our exploration of the secular psychologies, we have seen an increasing humanisation of the therapist's views of men and women. In turn, Maslow seems, at first, to be pointing a way forward beyond humanistic and existential considerations to our need for something, or even someone, 'bigger than we are'. He writes, for example: 'The human being needs a framework of values, a philosophy of life, a religion or religion-surrogate to live by and understand by, in about the same sense that he needs sunlight, calcium or love.'[18] However, in spite of this concession to a religious need that exists at a similar level to our requirement for 'sunlight, calcium or love', Maslow persists with a naturalistic world view. We anticipate that he will lift his eyes towards the glory of the heavens and its creator, but his gaze is arrested by the sunset and its value as a self-actualising peak-experience. He sees something of the wonder of the 'significant moment' but seems not to admit the possibility of the greater Wonder beyond.

Nevertheless, Maslow does introduce us to some valuable observations in his hierarchy of needs and concept of growth. Firstly, the fact that we have a complex range of needs, from the more physiological to the more psychological, and that certain basic needs must be satisfied before our more sophisticated requirements can be entertained, is undeniable. As far as this hierarchy goes (and we will want to add spiritual perspectives to the list of needs), it has some degree of compatability with biblical views of human wholeness. Jesus came to save men and women and, in doing so, his concern was for the entire being of each individual. The Greek verb *sozo* (to save) and the noun *soteria* (salvation) are sometimes used in the synoptic gospels to indicate healing – and this healing is 'always of the whole man'.[19] Putting it differently, the Lord was committed to meet the needs of the hungry, thirsty, unclothed, imprisoned, oppressed and physically sick, as well as the 'higher' needs for love, respect, belongingness, forgiveness and a new life.[20]

Secondly, Maslow's concept of growth – in so far as it includes the necessity of choice – is worthy of consideration. The Christian, of course, will want to extend the need to choose to that most fundamental of decisions, voiced by Joshua to the people of Israel: 'choose this day whom you will serve' (Joshua 24:15 RSV). However, we can also readily agree with Maslow's conclusion that experiences such as 'tragedies, deaths, traumata, conversions, and sudden insights' can change a person's outlook and direction in life. Most of us can think of exceptions to the sweeping statement in Somerset Maugham's *The Moon and Sixpence*: 'It is not true that suffering ennobles the character; happiness does that sometimes, but suffering, for the most part, makes men petty and vindictive.'[21] A few years ago I heard of a young woman called Karrina who was blind in one eye from birth, partially deaf and who later became blind in both eyes. She also suffered from a bone deformity which gave her a height of only 4' 2". She had great problems with her earlier education because the various specialist establishments proved unsuitable. In spite of all her limitations, she eventually achieved a good upper second degree in philosophy – and then proceeded to train as a solicitor. She declared that it was her faith that saw her through.

It is perhaps with Maslow's notion of *self*-actualisation that the Christian has most difficulty. Even if we accept this 'ongoing actualization of potentials, capacities and talents' and this 'unceasing trend toward unity, integration or synergy' at face value, we may still have reservations about the self-directing nature of the process. Maslow points out that '*the* defining characteristics of full individuality, of true freedom, of the whole evolutionary process' are 'increasing autonomy and independence of environmental stimuli'.[22] Once again (see p. 121) we meet humankind's desire to 'go it alone' and to achieve an inner independence where both the journey and the destination are self-governed. This pursuit of self-actualisation, which, even on Maslow's reckoning, so few attain, is a far cry from another way – on whose royal road we have for company the King himself and his joy-filled people. Here the path and the prize is Christ; and along this route we experience an increasing measure of 'God-actualisation' – 'being transformed into his likeness with ever-increasing glory, which comes from the Lord, who is the Spirit' (2 Corinthians 3:18).

Roberto Assagioli

Whereas Abraham Maslow, reasoning from humanistic and existential presuppositions, has given form to a 'psychology of being' that acknowledges the need for something 'bigger than we are', Roberto Assagioli is an example of someone who has developed a highly systematic transpersonal *psychotherapy* – in his case, from existential and psychoanalytic roots. Assagioli (1888 –1974) wrote a doctoral thesis (1910) which included a critique of the limitations of Freud's views. His own approach to therapy, called *psychosynthesis*, led to the establishment of the *Istituto di Psicosintesi* in Rome in 1926 and, in 1957, the inception of the Psychosynthesis Research Foundation in Florence. A number of other centres of study and administration have grown up in London, Athens, Montreal and New York, while the work of Robert Gerard from Los Angeles is especially acknowledged by Assagioli.

Assumptions

Psychosynthesis shares a great deal of common ground with the assumptions, aims and techniques of a wide range of psychoanalytic and personalistic psychologies, including those of Erich Fromm, Erik Erikson, Abraham Maslow and Viktor Frankl. In his continental setting, Assagioli looks to the influences of Wilhelm Stern in Hamburg, A. Maeder in Zurich and C. Baudoin in Paris. Interestingly, from a Christian point of view, he rates Paul Tournier of Geneva, and his *Médecine de la Personne*, as a specially significant source (see chapter thirteen). In gathering interpretations from many schools of psychology, Assagioli writes, 'We arrive at a pluridimensional conception of the human personality which, though far from perfect or final, is . . . more inclusive and nearer to reality than previous foundations.'[23] In this view of the constitution of the human being we see important strands from the anthropologies of Freud, Jung and Frankl. Assagioli represents these insights in the following diagram, while admitting the difficulty of depicting the crucial dynamic aspect of our humanity.

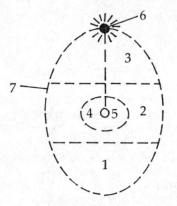

1 The lower unconscious
2 The middle unconscious
3 The higher unconscious
   (or superconscious)
4 The field of consciousness
5 The conscious self or 'I'
6 The higher Self
7 The collective unconscious

Figure 6   The human personality (after Assagioli)

It is worth clarifying these concepts a little in order to see something of the trends in transpersonalism from at least one individual's ideas about human personality. The *lower unconscious* (1), like Freud's unconscious, contains the 'elementary psychological activities which direct the life of the body' – including primitive urges and dreams, drives, phobias and certain complexes. The *middle unconscious* (2) is similar to the Freudian preconscious and includes those psychological elements that are readily available to consciousness. The *superconscious* (3) is the region in which 'are latent the higher psychic functions and spiritual energies' and from which 'we receive our higher intuitions and inspirations' (see also Frankl, pp. 129–130). The *field of consciousness* (4) is 'that part of our personality of which we are directly aware' and comprises 'the incessant flow of sensation, images, thoughts, feelings, desires, and impulses which we can observe, analyse, and judge'. The *conscious self* (5) is at the heart of this field of consciousness while the *higher Self* (6) is a permanent centre beyond or 'above' the conscious self. Finally, the *collective unconscious* (7), equivalent to the Jungian concept, is analogous 'to the membrane delimiting' a body cell, through which 'processes of "psychological osmosis" are going on all the time, both with other human beings and with the general psychic environment'.

Assagioli's ideas of 'the conscious self' and 'the higher Self' are part and parcel of many of the transpersonal psychologies. He insists that the higher Self (and, it seems, the concept of the superconscious) is not the same as Freud's superego. The higher Self is distinguished by a givenness and permanency, while the superego is that aspect of human personality that is acquired through inhibiting and judgmental 'parental' voices. Assagioli declares that the higher Self is not affected by 'the flow of the mind-stream or by bodily conditions' and the personal conscious self is 'merely its reflection'. He is keen to avoid a dualism of the higher Self and the conscious self, and argues that there is a 'real unity' between them. However, he admits that this unity is elusive, and touches on the human plight when he writes this of the individual:

> Feeling intuitively that he is 'one' and yet finding that he is 'divided unto himself', he is bewildered and fails to understand either himself or others. No wonder that he, not knowing or understanding himself, has no self-control and is continually involved in his own mistakes and weaknesses . . .[24]

As in Frankl's studies of the 'noölogical dimension' (pp. 127–128) and Maslow's examination of peak-experiences (p. 151), Assagioli seeks to assess the spiritual in men and women by the scientific method. He writes:

> Our position affirms that all the superior manifestations of the human psyche, such as creative imagination, intuition, aspiration, genius are facts which are as real and as important as are the conditioned reflexes, and therefore are susceptible to research and treatment just as scientifically as conditioned reflexes.[25]

He is careful to delineate his pragmatic attitude to 'spiritual experience and spiritual consciousness' when he declares that 'we will not attempt to define nor to discuss at the outset what "Spirit" in its essence may be'.[26] Citing Goethe's dictum that 'reality is that which is effective', he presupposes the existence of the superconscious, its value-systems and outworkings. Like Maslow, Assagioli looks to a 'study of genius' in his search for a scientific understanding of that superconscious. He contrasts the geniuses of people like Dante, Leonardo da Vinci and Einstein, who achieve 'a more or less permanent self-realization with many ways of expression', with those, like Mozart, who possess an extraordinary gift in one direction and in whom there may be little or no 'self-realization'.

Aims

As we have seen in Carl Rogers' later opinions, the aims and goals of transpersonalism are 'writ large'. Any psychological system which shifts its ground from Deficiency psychology to Being psychology is likely, if it is consistent, to move out eventually from a preoccupation with the individual through a focus on relationships and so to society itself – and thus become prescriptive in the areas of education, culture, religion, and civilisation generally. Assagioli is no exception to this trend:

> Let us feel and obey the urge aroused by the great need of humanity; let us realize the contribution we can make to the creation of a new civilization characterized by an harmonious integration and cooperation, pervaded by the spirit of synthesis.[27]

I propose to look mainly at this 'spirit of synthesis' as the aim of therapy for the individual, realising that the principles of psychosynthesis are seen to have universal application.

Assagioli writes that there are four stages on the path to psychosynthesis; the first three of these can be regarded as subsidiary objectives which should lead on to the primary aim of psychosynthesis itself:

(a) A thorough knowledge of one's personality;
(b) Control of the personality's various elements;
(c) A realisation of one's true Self – 'the discovery or creation of a unifying self';
(d) Psychosynthesis.[28]

Assagioli describes psychosynthesis as 'the formation or reconstruction of the personality around the new centre'. This freshly built personal core needs to be 'coherent, organized, and unified'. The 'ideal model' for this synthesis may be either a 'harmonious development, an all-round personal or spiritual perfection' or the full advancement of 'an ability or quality corresponding to the particular line of self-expression and the social role or roles which the individual has chosen'. The former, Assagioli argues, tends to be the aim of the introvert and can be endangered by passivity, and the latter is often the extravert's goal, which may be spoilt by rigidity. The inward-looking man or woman may well adopt a *laissez-faire* attitude to his or her 'harmonious development', reasoning, in effect, 'Circumstances *will* come together for me; decisions are difficult, choices impossible – I'll ride along on the crest of the wave and that wave will surely arrive.' The outgoing person, in the quest for synthesis, may become inflexible in daily living; he or she might say, 'I know where I'm going – nothing is going to stop me from getting to the top. *I'll* stick to the rules; others can go to the wall, for all I care.'

In spite of these polarised dangers, the unifying results of psychosynthesis, as we have already indicated, are said to be available to every aspect of human life. Their fruits can be sought for personal psychological development, in the treatment of those with 'complex conflicts between conscious and unconscious forces', within an education for integrated childhood and adolescence, in the ordering of relationships within groups and in the 'Supreme Synthesis'. It is in this last panoramic objective for 'all creation' that Assagioli is at his most all-embracing and optimistic:

> We seem to sense that – whether we conceive it as a divine Being or as cosmic energy – the Spirit working upon and within all creation is shaping it into order, harmony, and beauty, uniting all beings (some willing but the majority as yet blind and rebellious) with each other through links of love, achieving – slowly and silently, but powerfully and irresistibly – the Supreme Synthesis.[29]

Methods

In his planned 'reconstruction of the personality', Assagioli states three stages in the cooperation between the therapist and patient: initially, the therapist is at his or her most active; in the intermediate phase, the therapist is more catalytic, representing a 'model' for the patient; and, finally, the therapist becomes a more shadowy figure once more. In this third stage of withdrawal, the helper 'is replaced by the Self, with whom the patient establishes a growing relationship, a "dialogue", and an increasing (although never complete) identification'. Here the needy person is beginning to achieve psychosynthesis as the personal self and the higher Self move towards unity.

In order to reach this transformation of psychological forces and activation of 'superconscious energies', Assagioli declares the 'deliberate use of a large number of active techniques'.[30] Bearing in mind his three stages of active engagement, catalysis and withdrawal, we can examine something of this variety of method under the four headings (three subsidiary goals and one primary aim) given on page 158.

Knowledge of one's personality.   Assagioli argues that the path of psychosynthesis must begin with an 'extensive exploration of the vast regions of our unconscious'. This psychoanalytic venture *can* be embarked on by oneself but he acknowledges that the journey is easier with another's help. The search may be extended to the regions of the middle and higher unconscious (fig. 6 p. 156) to discover 'hitherto unknown abilities, our true vocations, our higher potentialities'; we thus tap our 'unlimited capacity to learn and to create'.

Control of the personality.   As with Frankl, the importance of the human will is integral to Assagioli's method. Having discovered the creative elements within, 'we have to take possession of them and acquire control over them'. The most effective technique for this end, Assagioli writes, is *disidentification*. Here, the client is urged to change attitudes towards negative emotions. Instead of declaring, 'I am discouraged' or 'I am irritated', he is to objectify the situation by stating, 'A wave of discouragement is *trying* to submerge me' or 'An impulse of anger is *attempting* to overpower me.' In this way, the 'vigilant self' is able to distance the wayward feeling, examining its origin and observing its deleterious potential. Where there are harmful images and complexes that lead to our ready anger or discouragement, these partially hidden elements need unmasking and understanding first. However, although some battles may be lost, Assagioli declares that, through disidentification, there will be victory in the end.

The discovery of the true self.   As greater objectivity is achieved, the discovery or creation of a 'unifying centre' becomes a possibility. Assagioli concedes that there is normally a 'natural inner growth' in this direction but the ascent is slow. 'Our deliberate conscious action' and 'the use of appropriate active techniques' can speed up the process. He argues that there can be 'intermediate stages' in which individuals identify strongly with an ideal. This ideal may be internalised as when a final-year medical student centres his life on becoming an alert and well-informed young doctor, or a newly qualified graduate from a college of art models her whole being on becoming a fashion designer; or there may, particularly in extraverted people, be projection, as when a newly-wed concentrates her love and ambition in her husband and so aspires to being the 'devoted wife', or a young soldier commits himself life and soul to his country as an 'ardent patriot'.

Psychosynthesis.   Once the 'unifying centre' is found, the client or patient needs to build around it his or her 'new personality'. This reconstruction requires both an *inner programme* and practical *techniques*. The 'inner programme' may be entirely at the level of developing and perfecting the personality (psychosynthesis) or it may embrace *spiritual psychosynthesis*, reaching into the super-conscious to seek an increasing unification between the personal self and the higher Self. A wide range of methods are used to help the individual realise these grand purposes – including dream analysis, disidentification, hypnosis, sublimation, meditation and contemplation. I propose to outline two techniques, put forward by Assagioli to aid people on the path to spiritual psychosynthesis: *inner dialogue* and *music therapy*.

In *inner dialogue*, Assagioli postulates that a person in difficulty can be helped by seeing his or her higher Self as 'personified'. This personification may be regarded as an 'Inner Teacher' with whom one needs to enter into dialogue following an imaginative 'Inner Journey'. The value of this quest does not lie in the experience itself but in its resulting creativity and self-abandonment.[31]

In order to effect this 'Inner Dialogue', Assagioli advocates a number of exercises based on certain myths and stories that are rich in symbolism. Amongst these, 'The Legend of the Grail', 'The Blossoming of the Rose' and Dante's *Divine Comedy* are seen as fertile resources for exploring the 'higher conscious'. In the third of these, the soul's descent and subsequent double ascent, of the mountain of purgatory and the heavens of paradise, are used as a basis for meditation. The patient is initially asked to visualise a journey downwards into the depths of the sea. As he descends in imagination, images may be evoked that relate to unacceptable material dredged up from the 'lower uncon-scious' – such as hitherto hidden resentments towards a mother or father. In turn, the patient is asked to begin his 'ascent' out of the deep waters and on to the slopes of a hill, in order to climb an imagined high mountain up to its very summit and so progress into the clouds above. This symbolic upward path, Assagioli asserts, may be accompanied by constructive feelings of 'love and wisdom', in which the person is in touch with his higher Self.

Music therapy also plays a part in therapy. Music has been regarded as potentially healing since ancient times. Pythagoras and Plato, amongst the Greeks, saw music as curative and the calming effect of David's lyre on the troubled Saul sets an oft-quoted precedent for 'music therapy'.[32] Music has been used for easing pain, as an adjunct to anaesthesia, for soothing the frayed nerves of psychiatric patients, and to aid rehabilitation in occupational therapy. Assagioli also recommends its use in spiritual psychosynthesis.[33]

In his technique, the patient or group is primed with information on the piece to be heard so that its possible effect can be anticipated. The participants are encouraged to sit in comfortable positions in a softly lit room, which is then filled with soothing introductory music played at a low volume. This relaxing atmosphere helps to 'open the doors of the unconscious'. In this way the listeners are prepared for the set-piece which, in turn, is relayed in stretches of short duration, so that fatigue and the arousal of defence reactions are avoided. The bombardment of the senses by, say, all the movements of a Mahler symphony could lead to an unproductive boredom, exhaustion or explosion of resentment. Relaxation, it is found, is engendered more readily by modest doses of the prescribed music.

Assagioli sees three stages to this psychosynthetic use of music therapy, each marked by the possible utilisation of a certain range of music:

1 *Spiritual psychosynthesis*, which 'recognizes the inclusion and integration into the conscious personality of higher psycho-spiritual elements of which it is not consciously aware'. Here, 'truly religious music', such as Gregorian chants and works by Palestrina, Bach, Handel and César Frank are recommended.

2 *Inter-individual psychosynthesis*, in which a level of cohesion is 'established between an individual and his fellow-men within a group of which he forms a part'. Assagioli says that this stage of psychosynthesis is fostered by music that expresses 'collective emotions and aspirations' and he thus includes national anthems, folk-songs, marches, some of the more rousing choruses in Verdi's operas and the stirring evocations of comradeship and brotherhood in Beethoven's ninth symphony in its repertoire.

3 *Cosmic psychosynthesis*, in which there is 'an ever increasing recognition and acceptance by the individual of the laws, the relationships and the rhythms governing life itself, in its widest

sense'. In considering these universal 'laws' and 'rhythms', Assagioli looks to Aleks Pontrik's *Fundamental Thoughts on the Psychic Healing Effect of Music*. Pontrik sees the healing process in people with neuroses as a 'progressive development which brings about, or restores, the fundamental harmonious chord'.[34] He cites Albert Schweitzer's view of a work by J. S. Bach as 'an expression of the Primal Power which manifests itself in the infinite rotating worlds'. Whether it is in the acceptance of the 'laws, the relationships and the rhythms' that govern life, in some deep harmony that is basic to existence, or in being in touch with the Primal Power 'which manifests itself' in the universe, Assagioli sees 'cosmic psychosynthesis' as the desired objective of his many techniques.

Critique

Assagioli's transpersonalism undergirds the assumptions, aims and methods of psychosynthesis. In his highly systematised methodology, we find everywhere the markers of a transcendentalism which somehow, as in many other purveyors of transpersonal psychology, seems to stop short of theism. Even so, in fairness, we have to see that Assagioli is quite open about the presuppositional limitations of his approach. He writes: 'Psychosynthesis does not aim nor attempt to give a metaphysical nor a theological explanation of the grand Mystery – it leads to the door, but stops there.'[35] On this side of the door to the 'grand Mystery', Assagioli postulates his 'pluridimensional' view of the human being, which includes the existence of a 'higher conscious' and its 'spiritual energies'. This acknowledgment of the reality of aspirational, intuitive and spiritual perspectives within the personhood of men and women is reassuring to the Christian. Furthermore, the observation that people are divided within and so experience their 'own mistakes and weaknesses', although falling short of the concept of human sinfulness, is at least a pointer towards our inherent fallibility.

However, for Assagioli, this disjunction is between 'the conscious self' and 'the higher Self', rather than between an individual's whole being and a separate and holy God who is both immanent and transcendent. He seems to move nearer to a theistic view when he writes of the 'Inner Christ' as experienced by certain Christians of a mystical persuasion. Nevertheless, he sees the Inner Christ 'as a personification of the Self' and quite distinct from 'the Biblical Christ as the world figure and Son of God' who speaks to the Christian's 'soul inwardly'.[36] He continues that it is 'not important' for the Christian mystic to distinguish between these two Christs.

Although Assagioli does not explicitly reject the notion of a trinitarian God, his emphasis on the Inner Teacher or Inner Christ seems to imply that fulfilment can be found purely through the Inner Journey. Once again we meet a view that men and women have all the needed resources for constructive change within. It is as if the humanistic brand of personalism has pushed out its boundary to include human superconsciousness. At first, it looks as if people are urged to look beyond themselves. However, this brand of transpersonalism appears, in its search for unity between the conscious self and the higher Self, to crowd God out of the picture by a sleight of hand. The idea of Self is so huge that all is encompassed – including God himself.

Nonetheless, psychosynthesis, apart from the obvious therapeutic value of many of its techniques, offers a great deal of challenge and stimulus to our thinking. It freely acknowledges the rich diversity of the human psyche and spirit, and urges us to a greater integration of our often fragmented lives. The Christian will want to reason that our need for a new 'unifying centre' can be supremely met in Christ, around whom and through whom we can experience the building of a 'new personality – coherent, organized, and unified'.

Ken Wilber

The American, Ken Wilber has been described as 'the foremost writer on consciousness and transpersonal psychology in the world today'.[37] We can see his thinking as a consistent and logical extension of the direction taken by Maslow's Fourth Psychology and Assagioli's psychosynthesis.

Assumptions

Wilber's basic thesis is that the range of alienations we experience – within ourselves, in relation to others and with the environment – is due to the 'boundaries' that we set. Our continual preoccupation with these boundaries and the opposites they engender – mind vs body, reason vs instinct, life vs death, and so on – is the source of our conflicts and unhappiness. He sees this obsession with divisions as a characteristic of human folly: 'nature, it seems, knows nothing of this world of opposites in which people live. Nature doesn't grow true frogs and false frogs, nor moral trees and immoral trees, nor right oceans and wrong oceans.'[38]

Wilber traces our perverse living in a 'world of opposites' to the wrong tack taken by the first man, who 'grew boundaries'. This tendency, at its most fateful, is seen here: 'And when Adam recognised the difference between the opposites of good and evil, that is, when he drew a fatal boundary, his world fell apart.'[39]

Since the world first 'fell apart', Wilber continues, humanity has perpetuated and elaborated the drawing of boundaries and the manufacture of opposites. Adam, the namer of creatures, drew dividing lines between one species of animal and another. Amongst the thinkers of ancient Greece, Pythagoras majored on the mathematical order of the universe, while Plato and Aristotle emphasised a dualism which has been a trendsetter for the last 2000 years. Wilber argues that the preoccupation with boundaries in humankind's history has included a progression from the particular to the general – from Adamic classifying, through Pythagorean counting (a 'meta-boundary') to Western scientific reckoning with variables (the 'meta-meta-boundary' of algebra).[40]

In spite of this human bias towards 'drawing boundaries', Wilber declares that parts of 'every major religion' have drawn our attention perennially to another perspective – the essential unity of all things. This cohesive awareness (the Supreme Identity, Unity Consciousness, or Cosmic Consciousness) is, in its various forms, 'the nature and condition of all sentient beings'. The tragedy for the descendents of Adam and Eve is that we have turned our backs, according to Wilber, on the world of 'no boundary'. In our restless need to qualify and quantify, we are in danger of muddling illusion with reality:

The ultimate metaphysical secret, if we dare state it so simply, is that there are no boundaries in the universe. Boundaries are illusions, products not of reality but of the way we map and edit reality. And while it is fine to map out the territory, it is fatal to confuse the two.[41]

Wilber backs his fundamental assumption that the cosmos is essentially a seamless garment by referring to both Buddhist mysticism and the theories of modern physics. He points out, for example, that the Buddhist doctrine of the Void 'maintains that reality is void of thoughts and void of things'. He adds to the Buddha's reflection: 'All in one and one in all' a quotation from the physicist, Fritjof Capra: 'Quantum theory . . . has come to see the universe as an interconnected web of relations whose parts are only defined through their connections to the whole.'[42]

Aims

Having established that our tensions and conflicts arise out of our obsession with setting boundaries, it comes as no surprise that the ultimate aim of Ken Wilber's philosophy is a restoration of 'unity consciousness' by the removal of those same boundaries. What does he mean by 'unity consciousness'? As we consider his definitions, undergirded as they are by quotations from the mystical writings of Hinduism, Buddhism and Christianity, we realise that, along with Assagioli's 'cosmic' or 'supreme synthesis', we have moved into something universal and all-pervasive. Wilber has left behind the tentative glimpses of the transcendent described in Maslow's 'peak-experiences' and the systematised quest of Assagioli's 'spiritual psychosynthesis'. We have moved beyond the realm of categorisation to a region where the very use of words creates boundaries that threaten to divide up the unified landscape.

Wilber declares that 'unity consciousness is the simple awareness of the real territory of no-boundary'. He emphasises the primarily experiential nature of this state by adding that 'no-boundary awareness is a direct, immediate, and non-verbal awareness, and not at all a mere philosophical theory'.[43] He concedes that on the path to unity consciousness, the last boundary to be erased is that between our sense of individual identity and the world around. He writes that 'in no-boundary awareness, the sense of self expands to totally include everything once thought to be not-self'. This expansion of consciousness is expressed by the Buddhist sage, Padma Sambhava: 'If the seeker himself, when sought, cannot be found, thereupon is attained the goal of seeking and also the end of the search itself.'

However, Wilber is realistic within his own frame of reference.

He knows that men and women, particularly in the West, are so riven by boundaries that their journey towards 'no-boundary awareness' is beset by obstacles. Here he is at his most helpful when he analyses (my desire for boundaries begins to show!) the various ways in which the many therapies try to 'dissolve a particular boundary or knot in consciousness'. He argues that therapeutic objectives can be seen in an ascending order: from the removal of divisions between one's 'narrowed self-image', or persona, and the shadow; through those between ego and body; between total organism and the environment; and so to 'unity consciousness'. With this schema in mind, Wilber asks, although the various therapies seem contradictory, 'could it be that these different approaches are *all* more or less correct when working with their own major level?'[44] Admitting, with Wilber, that the levels merge with one another, we can modify his spectrum of therapies as follows:

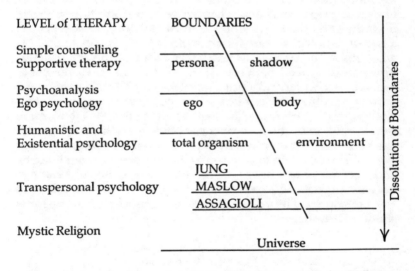

Figure 7   Levels of therapy and boundary dissolution (after Wilber)

With respect to the 'higher' aims within this framework, Wilber writes that in *transpersonal* experiences the person's identity expands beyond the 'skin-boundary' whereas in *unity consciousness*, 'the person's identity is with the All, with absolutely everything'.

Methods

Given the progressive nature of Wilber's goals on the road to the ultimate destination of 'no-boundary awareness', we find he includes a wide variety of techniques in his methodology.

Persona level. Wilber argues that most people in need are 'trapped in the persona', where inner boundaries are drawn to exclude the unwanted tendencies of the 'shadow'. We might give the example of a husband whose regular employment is very demanding and whose leisure hours are thus guarded jealously. His wife feels, not unreasonably, that at least some of his spare time should be spent cutting the lawn and weeding the borders. One particular Saturday afternoon, he leaves his wife washing up the lunch things while he vanishes into the garden 'to do one or two jobs'. Two hours later, when she returns from shopping, she finds the grass still uncut while her husband dozes in a deckchair, a favourite detective story open on his lap. He wakes to find his wife smiling accusingly as she gazes down at the sea of daisy flowers that spread between them. He throws down his book, kicks the deckchair and storms off to the garden shed to fetch the mower. His 'narrow self-image', or persona, is angry – ostensibly with the accusation he feels in his wife's look but, more profoundly, with the assertiveness of his own 'shadow', which has been nagging within him to prove himself a man by cutting the lawn in record time. In ignoring that subversive inner voice by choosing a lazy few hours, he has become doubly vulnerable to his wife's implied jibe. Wilber quotes a proverb that reminds us of the blindspots within, which are the product of a 'persona/shadow' boundary:

> I looked, and looked, and this I came to see:
> That what I thought was you and you,
> Was really me and me.[45]

It is said that the simpler styles of counselling operate at this first level where the client lives 'in the persona' and his or her defences are largely left undisturbed.

Ego level. However, at this second level, the therapist seeks to help the individual to see the link between the shadow and certain unacceptable symptoms – in the case of our reluctant gardener, the symptoms of sudden rushes of 'inexplicable' irritation. In therapy, such feelings are allowed to surface and display themselves. As part of this acknowledgment of the 'darker' areas of one's personality, Wilber also urges the need to see a unity between the apparent opposites of persona and shadow. The angry husband might need to become aware that his feelings towards his wife of 'I love you' and 'I couldn't care less about you and the lawn' are 'all of a piece'. Through such 'talking techniques' the client's split between persona and shadow can so be melted that the ego, or self-image, emerges with a new sense of integration. A wide range of approaches that explore the past are suitable, including classical psychoanalysis, the approaches of greater immediacy in neo-Freudianism and the concise methods of transactional analysis (see chapter nine).

The 'total organism' level.   Wilber sees the personality as occupying a 'cramped apartment' at the persona level, a 'comfortable home' at the ego level and a 'spacious mansion' at the level of the 'total organism'. This third level seeks the integration of body and ego, and is also called the 'Centaur Level' by Wilber because:

> A centaur is a legendary animal, half human and half horse, and so it well represents a perfect union and harmony of mental and physical. A centaur is not a horse rider in control of his horse, but a self-controlling, self-governing, psychosomatic unity.[46]

Wilber declares that, in the West, 'few of us have lost our minds, but most of us have long ago lost our bodies'.[47] In order to achieve an increasing sense of personal totality he urges the need for a greater awareness of the much neglected body. To effect this he advocates the development of a 'complete breathing cycle' in which the person, lying down with his arms at his side, imagines that the chest and abdomen are lined with a large balloon. He is encouraged to inhale gradually, drawing in a 'vital force from the throat to the abdomen, charging the body with energy and life'. Exhalation must be slow and smooth, while this 'vital force' is being released and radiated 'as subtle pleasure and joy throughout the bodymind itself'.[48] Once the breathing cycle is established, the client is asked to begin 'to allow all thinking to dissolve in the exhalation and pass to infinity'. Similarly, 'all distressful feelings . . . disease . . . suffering . . . pain' are to be breathed away.

Wilber, in his techniques at the Centaur level, looks a great deal to the *bioenergetic analysis* of Alexander Lowen (b 1910), an erstwhile pupil of Wilhelm Reich (see page 88) who works in the United States. Lowen is less intently preoccupied with the body than Reich and seeks to balance psychotherapeutic and biofunctional considerations.[49] Wilber, following Lowen, argues that we need to become aware of *blocks* – in this context, areas of tightness or numbness due to muscular overactivity which, in turn, point to the suppression of certain feelings. For example, tense muscles in the region of the neck, shoulders and arms may indicate the holding back of a desire to punch someone, and tension around the eyes may mean that tears are being held back.

These blocks can be released and dissolved, Wilber states, by simple technique. To start with, the muscles involved are tightened in order to make the matter conscious and so help the client realise that emotions are being held in check. Next, while relaxing the muscles, the person being helped is encouraged to surrender to 'whatever feeling would like to surface'. This release could lead to laughter, crying, screaming or even vomiting. Such a routine might need to be repeated for fifteen minutes or so each day for a month.

Wilber's aim at the Centaur level is that 'for the first time, you can embody your mind and mind your body'.

The self in transcendence. Having achieved a measure of integration between the body and the ego, the person is freed to move beyond his or her 'conscious self'. At this point, Wilber's thinking has parallels with Jung's exploration of the archetypes and Assagioli's search for the 'higher Self'. Wilber sees the 'transcendent self' as 'a centre and expansion of awareness which is creatively detached from one's personal mind, body, emotions, thoughts, and feelings'.[50]

As well as using, in common with Assagioli, the method of disidentification (page 160), Wilber also recommends a technique of reflection and affirmation in this pursuit of the transpersonal. Following the use of breathing exercises to help with 'Centaur' awareness, the client is advised to recite slowly such statements as 'I *have* a body, but I am *not* my body' and 'I *have* emotions, but I am *not* my emotions'. This disengagement from sensation is taken a step further by the affirmation: 'I am what remains, a pure centre of awareness, an unmoved witness of all these thoughts, emotions, feelings, and desires.'

Wilber argues that the cultivation of this 'deep inward sense of I-ness' can lead to a subjective experience of 'freedom, lightness, release, stability'. He likens this new sensibility to 'diving from the calamitous waves on the surface of a stormy ocean to the quiet and secure depths of the bottom'.[51]

Unity consciousness.   The quest for the 'transcendental self' can be seen as a 'jumping off point' for the realisation of unity consciousness – that 'simple awareness of the real territory of no-boundary'. In this mystical realm, questions of routine method and rigid technique stick out like sore thumbs. Wilber warns off our categorising Western minds when he writes: 'Since unity consciousness is of the timeless moment, it is entirely present now . . . Hence . . . there is no path to unity consciousness.'[52] The ultimate state of awareness is not so much a particular wave 'as it is the water itself'. In order to seek wetness there is no need to jump from one wave to another. In order to realise unity consciousness there is no need to move from one therapeutic level to another. Each level so far considered will help to break down the boundaries but the final loss of boundary is in the 'here and now'.

Wilber declares the value of *Gestalt therapy* in preparing the ground for unity consciousness. This approach, masterminded by Frederick (Fritz) Perls, seeks to 'suspend "mental chatter" and focus awareness on the immediate here and now'. Thinking is discouraged while present urges and sensations are concentrated on. This attempt to gain a sense of personal wholeness and oneness with the environment is supplemented by Wilber with a range of Eastern meditative techniques. Again, to Western thinking, the concepts are cryptic. Wilber states that the spiritual practice of, say, Zen Buddhism does not so much seek unity consciousness as express it. In fact, with this understanding, 'everything we do becomes our practice, our prayer . . .'[53]

In this pursuit of unity consciousness, Wilber acknowledges the inhibiting nature of the human desire to hold on to boundaries. There is a 'global unwillingness to look upon everything, as a whole, as it is, just as it is, now'.[54] Once this resistance is perceived and then relinquished, 'you no longer have a motive to separate yourself' from present experience. The final boundary between personhood and the environment dissolves and so 'the world and the self return as one single experience'. The individual is absorbed into a state of unity consciousness.

Critique

Because transpersonalism is, by definition and practice, so far-reaching and all-embracing, I propose a brief criticism of Wilber's concept of 'no boundary' as a fair representative of today's transcendent psychologies. I would like to follow this with a more general consideration of some of the dangers of this 'Fourth Force' in psychology.

First of all, Wilber provides us with a most valuable framework for assessing the bewildering range of psychotherapies (see fig. 7). This schema, based on the need to dissolve the various boundaries within our human existence, is also a helpful guide to the therapist as he or she seeks to encourage a client towards a greater sense of integration. Behind this useful model is the concept that our tensions and conflicts are the sad results of our boundary-filled lives. Up to a point, this view fits well with both biblical revelation and our day-to-day experience. Wilber's 'primary boundary' is original sin and this disruptive influence 'severs the unity of the organism-environment'.[55] The account of Adam and Eve's first disobedience in Genesis 3 vividly displays the resulting barriers between God and his children, between the man and the woman, and between each of them and the world around. This 'primary boundary' similarly leads to all manner of inner divisions, so that Paul, in Ephesians 4:18,19, can write of godless human life in these terms:

> They are darkened in their understanding and separated from the life of God because of the ignorance that is in them due to the hardening of their hearts. Having lost all sensitivity, they have given themselves over to sensuality so as to indulge in every kind of impurity, with a continual lust for more.

Wilber's thinking on the baleful influence of 'boundaries' also makes a lot of psychological sense when he writes: 'We dwell in yesterdays and dream forever of tomorrows, and thus bind ourselves with the tortuous chains of time and the ghosts of things not really present.'[56]

He argues that we are burdened by the 'boundary' of time,

within which we are heavy with guilt for the past and distracted by anxiety for the future. He urges us to live in the 'strict present'. At face value this advice accords well with our Lord's instruction in Matthew 6:34: '. . . do not worry about tomorrow, for tomorrow will worry about itself. Each day has enough trouble of its own.'

However, the linchpin of Wilber's hypothesis is that not only are boundaries, like time, the source of all our conflicts but these boundaries and conflicts *do not exist* as parts of reality. 'Boundaries are pure illusions in the sense that they create separations (and ultimately conflict) where there is none'.[57] This concept is all-pervasive and, in our example, excludes the true existence of time. It is with this perspective that the apparent similarity between Wilber's and Jesus's stress on living in the present breaks down. For the incarnate Lord the constraints of time were a daily reality; for Wilber, 'in the strict present there are no fundamental problems – for there is no time'.[58]

Moreover, Wilber's idea that 'boundaries are pure illusion' is in fact thoroughly monistic. His notion that there is only one, essentially impersonal element that makes up reality is truly Eastern in that it is also pantheistic. James Sire helpfully defines this Eastern pantheism in these terms: 'God *is* the cosmos. God is all that exists; nothing exists that is not God. If anything that is not God appears to exist, it is *maya*, illusion, and does not truly exist.'[59]

The discarding of temporal and spatial confines, and its consequent pantheism, is clearly seen when Wilber writes about the idea of a God who causes the beginning of all things:

> This first cause did not occur yesterday. Rather, it is a present occurrence, a present fact, a present activity. Furthermore, this first cause is not to be ascribed to a God apart from our being, for God is the real self of all that is. The primary boundary, this perpetually active first cause, is *our* doing in *this* moment.[60]

In this statement, we see the power of Wilber's monism. 'God is the real self of all that is'. You and I are the prime movers. This 'first cause is *our* doing'. We are God. God is us. All is God. God is all. We are all. Quoting Hindu, Buddhist and Christian mystical writing, as well as such apocryphal material as the Gospel of Thomas, Wilber pursues his argument that the boundary between self and not-self is illusion. When a person enters unity consciousness, he or she can say: '. . . a strange thing has now happened, for I realize that the real self within is actually the real world without, and vice versa . . . The world is my body, and what I am looking out of is what I am looking at.'[61]

As we consider Wilber's monism and pantheism, the Christian's theological hackles will rise. This is not simply because of differences between the East and the West for, after all, Judaeo-Christianity is rooted in the Near East and many Eastern philosophies are neither monistic nor pantheistic. The rising of saintly hackles relates more to the fundamental contrast between a belief in a personal God, who is creator and redeemer, and a system that, in rejecting all boundaries, robs both God and humanity of all distinctiveness and the possibility of 'I-Thou' relationships.

Wilber's dismissal of *all* boundaries as illusory removes the sort of God 'with whom we have to do' from the scene. By the same stroke, man's image-bearing, fallenness, guilt, salvation and hope of glory are all boldly swept away. Wilber's obliteration of distinctions promises us, it seems, anonymity and, at best, an amorphous destiny. These abstractions are a long way from our security in Christ, in which both the glorious certainty of a bodily resurrection and the present breaking down of divisive barriers are guaranteed. Although we know that racial, cultural and sexual characteristics are still part of everyday life, we are also aware that, for the Christian, the Lord's harmonising work is far-reaching. As Paul writes in Galatians 3:28, 'There is neither Jew nor Greek, slave nor free, male nor female, for you are all one in Christ Jesus.'

Wilber's methodology is one example amongst very many disparate approaches in transpersonalism. At first flush, the Christian will warm to the idea that men and women need perspectives in life that reach out beyond themselves. Supremely, the fact that 'God was reconciling the world to himself in Christ, not counting men's sins against them' (2 Corinthians 5:19) will be seen to offer the greatest hope to needy people. As we have seen, though, transcendent psychologies include many strange bed-fellows. Wilber himself, noting the widespread interest amongst our contemporaries in 'psychic phenomena, yoga, Oriental religions, altered states of consciousness, biofeedback, out-of-body experiences, near-death states', goes on to warn:

And because it has been generally repressed for so long, this urge to transcendence occasionally takes on bizarre or exaggerated forms, such as black magic, occultism, misuse of psychedelic drugs, and cultic guru worship.[62]

The point is well taken. The dangers of opening up ourselves to 'the powers of this dark world' and 'the spiritual forces of evil in the heavenly realms' (Ephesians 6:12) are well documented.[63] As well as the clear injunctions of scripture against the one who practises 'divination or sorcery, interprets omens, engages in witchcraft, or casts spells, or who is a medium or spiritist or who consults the dead' (Deuteronomy 18:10,11), we see many examples of trespassing into forbidden territory amongst the advocates of transpersonalism. Jung's unnerving experiences that arose out of his experiments with psychic material are well known. In his autobiographical *Memories, Dreams, Reflections*, he describes how in 1916, following several years' rumination and recording of his own fantasies and visions, this exploration of the supernatural came to a harrowing climax. On a bright Sunday afternoon that summer, the front door bell of his house began to ring frantically although no one stood at the door. He writes:

We all simply stared at one another. The atmosphere was thick, believe me! Then I knew that something had to happen. The whole house was filled as if there were a crowd present, crammed full of spirits. They were packed deep right up to the door, and the air was so thick it was scarcely possible to breathe. As for myself, I was all a-quiver with the question: 'For God's sake, what in the world is this?'[64]

Not only do we catch such grim glimpses of 'the powers of this dark world' in the pages of Jung's writings, but contemporary psychotherapeutic and counselling practice sometimes delves into esoteric areas that are, at the best, dubious and may, at the worst, be charged with malignity.

Generally, of course, the therapist is well intentioned in his or her use of psychic power. I know, for example, of an effective counsellor who uses certain forms of extra-sensory perception (ESP) in her work. Her methods include the use of a 'dowsing sense' – a mixture of reason, good sense and an extra-sensory power – to find the correct cause and treatment, and 'radionics' – in which a lock of hair or a blood sample is assessed for its 'electro-magnetic field' as indicative of actual or potential illness.[65]

Other transpersonalist therapists in the West look less overtly towards psychic power and more to the meditative traditions of the East. In an association of psychotherapists to which I belong, aids to personal development available include the possibility of attending a residential retreat to practise a form of Zen meditation, and a chance to learn relaxation and other techniques as put forward by Bhagwan Shree Rajneesh, a leading Indian therapist now working in England.[66] In the association's bulletin, a recent advert offered information on 'a wide variety of backgrounds, including transpersonal psychology, Zen, Marriage Guidance, Rajneesh, postural integration, and acupuncture'.

Other transpersonal methodologies

The influence of Eastern philosophical and religious thinking on the West has been seen clearly in Wilber's work and is hinted at in my brief mention of a British psychotherapy association's activities. Other key transpersonal movements have grown out of the teachings of the Caucasian, Gurdjieff (c.1875–1949), who in turn looked to Christian monasticism, Sufism and Tibetan Buddhism, and of the Bolivian, Oscar Ichazo (b 1931), who also travelled widely in the East, studying Yoga, Buddhism, Confucianism and the martial arts. Gurdjieff's influence, from the 1940s onwards, has spread out from centres in Paris and New York, while his former pupil, the Russian philosopher Peter Ouspensky (1878–1947), has left a group of students in London to continue his version of the work. Ichazo, following his initial lecturing and group-work in Africa, Chile, and subsequent travel, founded the Arica Institute in New York in 1971. His combining of Eastern mystical traditions of movement and meditation with Western psychology has spread to a number of centres in the United States and has had a more limited focus in England.[67]

In the West, *transcendental meditation* (TM), although regarded by many in India as an 'oversimplification' that is 'incapable of leading people beyond the spiritual kindergarten',[68] is probably the best known aspect of oriental psychology. Maharishi Mahesh Yogi, the founder of the TM movement, says that in this form of meditation he has rediscovered a 'technique as old as mankind'. He has defined that method as follows:

Transcendental Meditation is a natural technique which allows the conscious mind to experience increasingly more subtle states of thought until the source of thought, the unlimited reservoir of energy and creative intelligence, is reached. This simple practice expands the capacity of the conscious mind and a man is able to use his full potential in all fields of thought and action.[69]

By a 'natural technique', the Maharishi means that the mind is allowed to take 'whatever direction it may choose'.

The *assumptions* behind TM include the classical Eastern monism and pantheism we have seen in Wilber's thinking. The Maharishi declares that there is a boundless 'reservoir' or 'source of thought' that exists 'in all places at the same time'. This impersonal wellspring is called 'Creative Intelligence' or 'The Absolute' and it influences the human mind 'to grow, expand and develop'. The *aim* of TM is to help the individual experience directly 'the very source of thought' by moving beyond the everyday conditions of the normal waking state, dreaming and deep sleep to a series of expanding levels of awareness. These profounder states of consciousness are labelled by the Maharishi as 'Transcendental', 'Cosmic', 'God' and 'Unity' Consciousness. Of these progressive states, Cosmic Consciousness is hailed as the main goal for the 'average meditator'. Here the concept of the higher Self we have met in Assagioli and Wilber is paramount and Cosmic Consciousness is that state in which awareness of that Self is 'always present along with the waking, dreaming, and deep sleep states'. At this level of consciousness, it is claimed that a person is less tense and more resistant to life's stresses. Beyond TM's aims to help the individual to a more peaceful existence is the Maharishi's World Plan which has ambitious goals in the areas of politics, education, communal well-being, stewardship of the environment, and human spirituality.

The Maharishi has said that all that is required in TM's method 'is somewhere to sit and a pair of closed eyes'. As is implied, the initiate is instructed to approach meditation in a relaxed way and in a comfortable setting. Ideally, he is to sit upright, close his eyes and allow his thoughts to come and go. Early in the training the meditator is given a *mantra*, or 'instrument of thought', a word or phrase that is repeated as an aid to meditation. A great deal of mystique surrounds the choice of a person's mantra and the teachers of TM discourage the revealing of one's 'special word' to anyone else. After incanting the mantra for twenty minutes, the session of meditation is completed by sitting for a further two or three minutes with closed eyes.

Analysis of the writings and rituals of TM reveals that behind this apparently innocuous form of meditation lies a polytheistic religious system. Ronald L. Carlson has written a careful appraisal of this world view and points out that the Sanskrit hymn sung at the initiation ceremony is, in fact, a song of praise to Guru Dev, the departed master of Maharishi Mahesh Yogi. Further, the personal mantra that is received following this time of worship is shown to be a 'sound-symbol' which is connected in some way or other with the Hindu gods. Carlson warns would-be initiates with these words:

> The mantras meditated upon are not meaningless sounds but names or aspects of deities of nature, which are in reality demonic spirits. The mantra is part of classical Hinduism. To accept and recite it is to participate in an ancient religious practice with specific purposes. The result is an opening up to the occult world of demonic spirits and to the destruction of one's own soul and personality.[70]

This warning is timely in relation to the widespread interest in seeking relaxation amidst the hurly-burly of Western life. TM, correctly understood, *does* have strong religious components – its founder propounding a polytheistic and monistic system which incorporates the worship of Hindu deities, a cyclical understanding of history in which human 'souls' are reincarnated until personality is lost in 'cosmic existence' and a form of salvation that discounts Christ's sufferings and urges self effort on us all.[71] It is salutary for us to recall that the very afflictions which the Lord endured in the crucifixion are the source of victory over both the bonds of legalism and the powers of spiritual evil (see Colossians 2:13–15). Further, the passion we all have for inner peace is surely a challenge for a rediscovery of Christian forms of meditation;[72] we shall return to this theme in chapter fourteen.

Within the bewildering range of transpersonal methodologies – TM, Yoga psychology, the syncretism of Gurdjieff and the Arica Institute, the transcendentalism of Jung, Assagioli and Wilber, and the use of extra-sensory perception, including telepathy, divination, clairvoyance and the observation of auras – there are problems for both the Christian and the empirical scientist.[73] As we have tried to do, the believer needs to sift the assumptions, aims and methods of transpersonalism in the light of God's revelation. He or she will question monistic and pantheistic presuppositions, the goals of unity consciousness and 'enlightenment', and techniques which seem to open the personality to unknown spiritual and psychic forces.[74] Furthermore, the cautious observer will ask whether this or that transpersonal method actually works. Increasingly, the claims of such systems as TM have been rigorously assessed[75] and, for the first time in the United Kingdom, a chair of parapsychology (the Arthur Koestler chair in Edinburgh) has been set up to investigate paranormal activity. Although there is a fair amount of evidence to support at least some of the affirmations of transpersonalism, the Christian will not be lured by pragmatic considerations alone. He will be circumspect, remembering that the Adversary can appear 'as an angel of light', that there is a 'battle in the heavenlies' between the powers of good and evil, and, most of all, that Christ 'having disarmed the powers and authorities . . . made a public spectacle of them, triumphing over them by the cross' (Colossians 2:15).[76]

We have now completed our survey of the rise of the secular psychologies with a consideration of the fourth neighbour of our tree of pastoral care. Transpersonalism, sharing this tree's root system through its links with Christian mysticism, pushes its own growth heavenwards – but, in doing so, turns in upon itself. From the preoccupation with self within the humanistic psychologies, we have passed on to an absorption with the higher Self which, in the last analysis, is frequently a journey towards a Godless, formless terrain of 'no boundary'. However, before we consider the differing Christian reactions and responses to these psychologies we will look at the alluring progeny of the 'Human Potential Movement' – the schismatic 'New Therapies'.

9

THE NEW THERAPIES

*Existential humanism constitutes nothing less than a deter-
mined effort to salvage faith in a godless world. God has left
the world, the humanists claim, so that man can elevate
himself to the level of God.*

Joel Kovel

*Anything goes now in psychotherapy. The field is a
mess . . . Every few months we have a new technique or
approach . . .*

C. Patterson

During the 1950s and 1960s, the United States saw the emergence
of a whole array of new therapies, mostly spawned on the West
coast and strongly influenced by atheistic humanism and existentialism. Many of the founding fathers of this 'Human Potential
Movement' disowned their psychoanalytical training, with its
'excavation of the mind', and embraced both the 'here and now'
of everyday experience and the promise of a glorious future for
'self-regulating' men and women. Psychotherapy for the privileged few gave way to growth and fulfilment for the privileged
many. The utopic vision was exported to Western Europe during
the 1960s and 1970s and widely, and often uncritically, acclaimed
by both professionals and lay people. There is no doubt that
many of the insights and techniques introduced by these new
therapies have extended the range of ways of helping people
most usefully, although the world views that undergird the
approaches have been strangely neglected.

It is impossible, in the space of one chapter, to do justice to the
great range of methodologies that has been let loose on the
Western world during the last three decades,[1] including
bioenergetics, co-counselling, cognitive therapy, drama therapy,

encounter groups, *est*, family therapy,[2] the feminist psychotherapies,[3] Gestalt therapy, neurolinguistic programming, postural integration, psychodrama[4], primal therapy, rational-
emotive therapy, reality therapy, re-evaluation counselling,
Rolfing and transactional analysis. In this chapter I propose to
look at three important systems: rational-emotive therapy, one of
the primarily cognitive and behavioural therapies; transactional
analysis, a widely publicised approach that incorporates cognitive and analytic components; and Gestalt therapy, which is
strongly experiential. William Glasser's reality therapy and
Arthur Janov's primal therapy will be considered in Part II, in
their relevance to certain methodologies put forward by Christian
counsellors.

Rational-emotive therapy

Like so many of the charismatic figures who stepped on to the
American scene after the Second World War, *Albert Ellis* (b 1913),
although originally trained as a psychotherapist in marital, family
and sex counselling, was strongly influenced by psychoanalytic
thinking. Following his own experience of being analysed over
three years, he used the classical Freudian techniques of free
association, the interpretation of dreams and the resolution of the
transference neurosis. Averaging one hundred sessions with
each of his patients before finding 'distinct or considerable improvement', he became disillusioned with the longevity and
passivity of this piecemeal quarrying of the human mind.[5] He
found his results improved by shifting to the more active and
quickly interpretative approach of the neo-Freudians and was
able to reduce the number of sessions to an average of thirty-five
per person. During the early 1950s, he moved on to behaviouristic methods to force people to do things they were afraid of, like
riding on the Underground or sitting in the same room as a cat. In
this way, he became 'a much more eclectic, exhortative-
persuasive, activity-directive therapist'. However, Ellis still came
across patients who refused to do anything to help themselves
and so he had to face once more the inner complexity of the men
and women he was trying to counsel. Certain people just would
not respond to simple orders, unlike a Pavlovian dog. 'Why was
that?', Ellis asked. Quite simply, he concluded, because human

beings, being self-conscious, are powerfully influenced by what others tell them and by what they tell themselves. And so, by the beginning of 1955, 'the basic theory and practice of Rational (rational-emotive) therapy was fairly will formulated', by which approach Ellis sought to help people to 'un*say* and un*think*' in order to free themselves from neurosis. During his methodological pilgrimage Ellis claims that he progressed from an improvement rate of sixty percent over one hundred sessions, with his psychoanalytic techniques, to ninety percent in only ten or so encounters, with his new approach.[6]

Assumptions

In his *Reason and Emotion in Psychotherapy* Ellis describes himself as 'a clinician, a social psychologist, and a confirmed nonbeliever'.[7] His 'confirmed nonbelieving' is quite explicit when he writes: 'I do not, as a psychologist, believe that we can have any absolute, final, or God-given standards of morals or ethics.'[8] In rejecting absolutes, he declares that his thinking is essentially rationalistic in the modern, atheistic sense. More generally, he writes that, philosophically, his rational-emotive psychotherapy: 'takes some of the best elements of ancient and modern rationalism and tries to mate them with similarly workable elements of humanism, existentialism, and realism'.[9] The basic pragmatism and atheism of Ellis's stance surfaces when he reverses Voltaire's dictum by saying, from a mental health standpoint, 'If there were a God it would be necessary to uninvent Him.'[10]

As we have noted, Nikolai Berdyaev has said, 'Where there is no God, there is no man' and Ellis, inevitably, seems to move in this reductionist direction when he questions the idea of the 'intrinsic value' of human beings.[11] However, as we have already indicated, he does not fully embrace the behaviouristic views of Pavlov, Watson and Skinner and concedes that men and women are 'uniquely rational, as well as . . . uniquely irrational' animals[12]. Moreover, he argues that thinking and emotions are inextricably linked, writing that 'much of what we call emotion is nothing more nor less than a certain kind – a biased, prejudiced, or strongly evaluative kind – of thought'. Such 'illogical' thinking, Ellis notes, leads to our 'emotional or psychological disturbances'; in turn, we can rid ourselves of 'unhappiness, ineffectuality, and disturbance' if we learn 'to maximize (our) rational and minimize (our) irrational thinking'. Epictetus, the Stoic philosopher, had a similar perspective when he said, 'The chief concern of a wise and a good man is his own reason.'[13]

As well as human rationality, Ellis acknowledges human folly. He argues that people *can* control their self-defeating thoughts but, perversely, many do not do so; he suggests that they are too stupid, too ignorant, to neurotic or too psychotic.[14] He baulks at the possibility that they might be too sinful, seeing the concepts of sin and guilt as 'highly pernicious and antitherapeutic', adding that 'the rational therapist holds . . . that no human being should ever be blamed for anything he does . . .'[15] Ellis takes his conviction that a sense of blameworthiness is 'highly pernicious' to a crusading level when he says: 'The concept of sin is the direct and indirect cause of virtually all neurotic disturbance. The sooner psychotherapists forthrightly begin to attack it the better their patients will be.'[16]

Aims

The overall objective of rational-emotive therapy is to help the patient 'internalize a rational philosophy of life'.[17] Ellis seeks not so much to eradicate people's beliefs but to change them 'so that they become more closely rooted to information and to reason', developing 'a more consistent, fact-based, and workable set of constructs than they now may possess'.[18]

This achieving of an internalised rationality is worked towards through a set of subsidiary goals whereby the rational therapist 'shows his patients how to think straight and act effectively'.[19] Thinking and feeling are bound together and so there is a prime need to remove '*intense* and *sustained* negative emotions, such as enduring fear and strong hostility'. As the patient sees the illogical links in his 'internalized sentences', he learns to re-think these ways of talking to himself so that his thoughts become 'more logical and efficient'.

J. K. Galbraith wrote in *The Affluent Society* that 'in the world of minor lunacy the behaviour of both the utterly rational and the totally insane seems equally odd' and it is not surprising that Ellis, being a realist, avoids seeing people as just 'utterly rational'. He concedes that the rational therapist, as well as having a drive to help the patient 'internalize a rational philosophy of life', also needs to aid the needy towards the more Rogerian concepts of self-awareness and self-acceptance.[20] However, in this apparent loosening of the grip of rationality on a person's life, Ellis advocates a 'long-range or socialized hedonism' as the best way to achieve some sort of guidelines for living. In this circumspect pleasure-seeking 'one should primarily strive for one's own satisfactions', while at the same time trading, in most instances, 'immediate gratifications' for 'future gains' and being 'considerate of others'.[21]

Methods

Rational-emotive therapy, although discarding certain aspects of its Freudian and Pavlovian origins, is claimed to include strong elements of neo-Freudianism and neo-behaviourism. The ego-psychology of the former, which emphasises 'the cognitive processes and how they make and can unmake human emotional disturbance', and the 'liberalized view of perception', which characterises the latter in the writings of psychologists like Eysenck and Mowrer, are blended in Ellis's approach.[22] He owns a particularly close kinship with Adlerian therapy, where, for example, the therapist attacks beliefs of personal inferiority and encourages self-determination.[23]

In contrast to the interminable marathons of classical psychoanalysis, Ellis claims that almost all of his patients show 'distinct or considerable improvement' when seen once a week for only ten or so sessions. Concentrating on those emotions that are mediated through the thinking processes and the 'internalized sentences, or self-talk' that created these emotions in the first place, he seeks to re-educate the patient towards a deeper rationality. He shows the patient how both past and present illogical thinking are disrupting her life, before teaching her how to find her way to 'more logical and efficient' thoughts. The kind of unreasonable 'self-talk' that rational-emotive therapy will unearth and attack includes statements like: 'One should be thoroughly competent, adequate, and achieving in all possible respects if one is to consider oneself worthwhile'; and 'I can manage life only if I avoid, rather than face, difficulties and responsibilities.'[24]

The rational therapist seeks to change his or her patient's incorrect ways of thinking through a range of behavioural techniques such as deconditioning, desensitising and *homework assign-*

ments. In the last of these three, the client may be asked to look for his own particular 'self-defeating sentences' during the coming week and, on observing them, act deliberately and constructively in a way formerly avoided. For example, a young man may be hampered by 'self-talk' which says, 'It's no use, I can never stand up to anyone, even when I'm in the right.' During his week's homework, he may spot his usual inner response when he discovers that he has been sold, say, a dud battery at a local shop. In spite of his temptation to do nothing about it, his assignment will encourage him to return to the shop and deal with the situation straightforwardly.

Ellis argues that, although rational-emotive therapy has '*some* belief in the innate capacity of human beings to help themselves', the therapist needs to *teach* the patient new ways if success is to be experienced.[25] In marked contrast to Rogerian therapy, Ellis engages in a most vigorously didactic approach in moving his patients towards change. The therapist serves as a 'counter-propagandist' who attacks and dismisses the patient's illogicalities, prejudices and superstitions.[26] The flavour of Ellis's assertive style is seen when he writes:

> To the usual psychotherapeutic techniques of exploration, ventilation, excavation, and interpretation, the Rational therapist adds the more direct techniques of confrontation, confutation, deindoctrination, and reeducation. He thereby frankly faces and resolutely tackles the most deep-seated and recalcitrant patterns of emotional disturbance.[27]

Critique

Ellis writes that 'in accordance with their belief systems . . . therapists deliberately assume *some* kind of role with their patients . . .'; thus he acknowledges the link between the therapist's world view and his technique.[28] As we have seen, he also declares himself to be a 'confirmed nonbeliever' who leans heavily on the modern form of rationalism which sees reason alone as the guide to life, thereby disposing of the supernatural as a force to be reckoned with. In excluding God, Ellis draws a 'two-dimensional' man, a creature whose uniqueness is summed up in his rationality and for whom genuine spirituality is of no account. And yet, as G. K. Chesterton has pointed out: 'Reason is itself a matter of faith. It is an act of faith to assert that our thoughts have any relation to reality at all.' There is an arbitrariness (like Chesterton's 'act of faith'), born perhaps of human folly, ignorance or arrogance, about a view that exalts reason to the exclusion of even the possibility of divine revelation. Paradoxically, Psalm 14:1, repeated in Psalm 53:1, uses the Hebrew word *nabal* of the person who denies the existence of God, indicating someone whose mind is closed 'The fool (*nabal*) says in his heart, "There is no God."'[29]

However, in fairness to Ellis, his view of the personality is wider than that it comprises only rationality for he also acknowledges the reason's vital links with emotions. Further, his rationalism is tempered by a pinch or two of the more optimistic forms of humanism and existentialism, with their fuller perspective on personhood. Nonetheless, he argues that the concept of an individual's 'intrinsic worth' (so central to both humanistic and Christian thinking), is impossible to establish. He seems to be classically existentialist when he writes that, in discarding the idea of human value, it is better 'if men and women would spontaneously, unmoralistically, unself-consciously *be*'.[30]

In that Ellis rejects the existence of 'God-given standards of morals or ethics', he sees sin and guilt as 'highly pernicious' concepts. Like Freud, Ellis regards the blaming of self and others as 'the essence of virtually all emotional disturbances'.[31] He sees contrition as a travesty of human independence, in which bowing 'nauseatingly low' to 'some hypothetical deity' renders a patient 'proportionately less self-sufficient and self-confident'. Not for Ellis's patients the liberation that a realistic appraisal of wrongdoing, true repentance and the knowledge of forgiveness brings. The ruthless self-determination of rational-emotive therapy seems to bar the possibility of the life-changing experience of the Father's compassion in the client.[32]

Ellis's explanation of a person's 'irrationality' lies, again as with Freud, in the baleful influences of family, school, Church and government. Although he does not deny the effect of our 'biological inheritance' in producing 'illogical, neurotic views', it is 'powerful social propaganda' which is seen as the main culprit. We have, Ellis continues, a 'generally neuroticizing civilization'.[33] It is because such influences are primarily external that they are not 'fatal or irrevocable'. Ellis believes that men and women, untramelled by ideas of sin and guilt, and not too handicapped by what they inherit, can be changed radically by a re-education into right thinking.

There is no doubt, of course, that right thinking, right words and right action are intimately connected: wholesome thoughts can lead to wholesome activity, and loving behaviour can engender more caring attitudes. However, God's revelation clearly completes the chain of cause and effect in demonstrating the crucial influence of a 'right heart', a term used throughout the Bible for the centre of the personality.[34] The need for inner change is prophesied, for example, in Ezekiel 36:26, when the Lord promises, 'I will give you a new heart and put a new spirit in you'. We see the fulfilment of these words in the creative presence of the Spirit of Christ in his people, whereby we 'are controlled not by the sinful nature but by the Spirit' (Romans 8:9). It is in the context of Jesus's dying and rising again, opening the door to reconciliation with the Father and life in the Spirit, that Romans 12:1,2 can urge us to lives of sacrificial worship, within which we can 'be transformed by the renewing' of our mind, living out God's 'good, pleasing and perfect will'. Ellis, having disposed of human sinfulness, seeks change through right thinking alone. The Lord goes to the heart of men and women, seeing their waywardness and offering radical transformation in every part of life, including the areas of cognition and emotion.

As we have seen, the Christian will raise many questions over Ellis's presuppositions. Given his narrowed view of human nature, we can, nonetheless, appreciate the worthwhileness of his aim to change neurotic patterns of thinking in the lives of his patients. Within the sphere of God's common grace, it is surely better in terms of day-to-day human functioning for someone to change from saying to herself, 'I'm a born loser' to, 'I'm a human being and, like any other, I can influence life around me in positive and caring ways.'

What of Ellis's authoritative style of counselling? Is it right? Does it work? These are difficult questions because the evaluation of psychotherapeutic method bristles with problematic variables, such as the personality of both client and therapist, their expectations, and the parameters chosen to measure improvement. There is a great deal of truth in Ellis's opinion that *all* therapists, whatever their stance, exert powerful influences which can be seen as 'distinctly authoritative, technique-centred, controlling, and calculating'.[35] He continues that 'the real question is not *whether* the therapist is authoritative and controlling but *in what manner* he exerts his authority and his control'. Nevertheless, there is no doubt that Ellis takes this issue of control over the lives of others to an extreme. In the context of his 'questioning, challenging and reindoctrinating' approach, he writes: '. . . the more I persist, the more they usually come to admit that I am correct, and that they *can* help themselves much more than they first thought they could'.[36]

It is in the light of this cajoling method that one has to question Ellis's claim of a ninety percent success rate and his view that rational-emotive therapy is 'probably one of the *most effective* techniques that has yet been invented'.[37] Michael Balint, the psychoanalyst, has pointed out that in the healing art the doctor can be seen as the 'prescription'.[38] It may well be that rational-emotive therapy is exactly the approach that most suits Albert Ellis's personality; he is, perhaps, at his best as a specially effective 'prescription' while 'reindoctrinating' his wrong-thinking patients.

Transactional analysis

In all the wide variety of the 'new therapies', transactional analysis (TA) is the one that has most caught the public eye. Books like *Games People Play* by Eric Berne, *I'm OK – You're OK* by Thomas Harris and *Born to Win* by Muriel James and Dorothy Jongeward have become best-sellers, spreading at least the rudiments of TA into the vocabulary of hundreds of thousands of people on both sides of the Atlantic. Since the early 1960s the language of great numbers of men and women, both lay and professional, in the areas of psychology, psychiatry, sociology, education and the business world, has been coloured by talk of Parent, Adult, Child, positive and negative strokes, scripty behaviour, OK-ness and game-playing. Many Christians, both individually and in community, have taken on board the system of TA to stimulate personal growth and aid their care of others.[39] Let us then, according to our established pattern of 'assumptions, aims and methods' seek to evaluate this most popular of methodologies.

Assumptions

The psychiatrist *Eric Berne* (1910–1970), the founder of TA, graduated in medicine at McGill University in Canada and later moved to the United States where, like Albert Ellis, he received psychoanalytical training. However, in time, he parted company with Freudianism, looking more to the ego-psychology of Paul Federn, a patriarch of Viennese psychoanalysis, and his Italian pupil, Eduardo Weiss.[40] Berne has declared that TA makes only two assumptions: that 'human beings can change from one ego state to another'; and that transactions between people can be assessed and verified.[41] It may be most helpful to examine TA's basis by looking at these twin concepts of *ego states* and *transactions*.

Ego states

First, a *descriptive* analysis. Berne has defined an ego state as 'a system of feelings which motivates a related set of behaviour patterns'. As well as looking to Weiss's psychology, Berne also sees the research of Wilder Penfield, a neurosurgeon from McGill University, as crucial in confirming TA's understanding of ego states. In 1951 and the following years, Penfield found that, during brain surgery, a weak electrical stimulus applied to the temporal cortex of a conscious patient led to a 'reproduction of what the patient saw and heard and felt and understood' from a previous memory. It was as if the brain was acting as a 'high-fidelity tape recorder', playing back a 'tape' of the past, including both the meaning and emotions associated with the memory, *at the same time* as the patient's awareness of his or her present situation in the operating theatre. Such evidence seems to confirm that more than one 'ego state' can occupy consciousness synchronously.[42]

Through observation of his patients, Berne has identified three categories of ego state:

1 The *Parent* (or *exteropsyche*), 'a set of feelings, attitudes, and behaviour patterns which resemble those of a parental figure'.[43] This ego state is shown by either the *prejudiced Parent*, in which seemingly arbitrary values and prohibitive views reside, or the *nurturing Parent*, which has sympathy for others. The Parent says, in effect, either 'Do as I do' or 'Don't do as I do, do as I say.'

2 The *Adult* (or *neopsyche*), 'characterised by an autonomous set of feelings, attitudes, and behaviour patterns which are adapted to the current reality'. The Adult may say, 'Let us think carefully and act wisely.'

3 The *Child* (or *archaeopsyche*), 'a set of feelings, attitudes, and behaviour patterns which are relics of the individual's own childhood'. The two forms of Child are the *adapted Child*, which is dominated by parental influence and may either comply or withdraw, and the *natural Child*, which behaves independently either with rebellion or creativity. The Child says, 'Yes, I'll do whatever you ask', 'Nobody really cares for me', 'You just wait, I'll show you' or 'Life is wonderful and I'm going to really enjoy it.'

All of us, all of our lives, it is argued, have these three main aspects to our personality. Where these ego states are in harmony, 'each of them, Parent, Adult, and Child, is entitled to equal respect, and has its legitimate place in a full and productive life'.[44]

Ego states are also susceptible to an *historical* description. A key concept in TA's view of human development is that we each have a life-plan, or *script*, which is formed from parental directives and a childhood decision as to how one will live and die.[45] As with a theatrical script, Berne argues, there are important characters in the 'life-plan' who are obliged to play their roles as part of one another's destinies. Broadly, there are just two sorts of people, the 'winners' and the 'losers' which Berne, using a fairy-tale language, calls the 'princes and princesses', and 'frogs' respectively. A winner's script might say, 'There's always another chance in life'; a loser's might declare, 'Nothing ever goes right for me.'

It is here that we can suitably think about Thomas Harris's influential idea of the *life positions*. Harris, who particularly looks to the theories of Alfred Adler and Harry Stack Sullivan, was a co-founder of the Institute for Transactional Analysis in Sacramento, California and worked with Berne during the 1960s. Like Berne, Harris acknowledges the far-reaching 'decisions' of childhood and, further, he describes four 'life positions' which can result from these resolutions. The life positions, confirmed through dream material and by observing patients, are:

I'M NOT OK – YOU'RE OK. This first position, like the next two, is arrived at in the unconsciousness of the child usually during his or her third year.[46] Harris argues, with many others, that birth is invariably traumatic to the infant and so, initially, the experiences of external pressure, sudden release, a drop of temperature, the glare of light and the sound of voices lead the newborn to feel 'not OK'. In spite of the ensuing sensations from the mother's caressing and close proximity (*positive strokes*), the baby, according to Harris, is not fully reassured and continues to 'hold' an 'I'M NOT OK – YOU'RE OK' position. This stance can become more entrenched as the child becomes more mobile, provoking, at times, such *negative strokes* as nagging, scolding and smacking, which confirm the view of 'I'm not OK'.

I'M NOT OK – YOU'RE NOT OK. If a mother is cold and rejecting towards her child then, once baby days are over, he or she may conclude this second position. In this situation there are few, if any, positive strokes of cuddling, praise, encouragement and companionship, and the toddler may, unconsciously, decide there is no hope. Such a decision is 'deterministic' and so, subsequently, 'all experience is selectively interpreted to support it'. However lavishly attention is paid to the person who holds this doubly 'not OK' position, the level of positive stroking can never, in itself, undo this ingrained negative viewpoint.

I'M OK – YOU'RE NOT OK. Where a baby is battered or brutalised in other ways, this third position may be formulated. The child turns inwards 'to lick his wounds' and, perhaps, learns to cry himself to sleep. In effect, he says, 'Go away. Leave me alone. You're no good. I'll look after myself.' Harris points out that this position may lead to criminality later in life.

I'M OK – YOU'RE OK. This position is one of hope. The first three positions are arrived at early in life and are based on information from the Parent and the Child within the toddler's developing personality. The fourth position can only be achieved by the Adult and is a 'conscious and verbal decision'. 'The first three positions are based on feelings. The fourth is based on thought, faith, and the wager of action.' Sadly, Harris declares, most of us do not take this change of direction but persist with 'I'M NOT OK – YOU'RE OK.'

Transactions

Berne calls 'the unit of social intercourse . . . a transaction' and says that, in any encounter of two individuals, the transactions take place between their respective ego states. If someone's personality is represented by three distinct, yet touching, circles (each circle denoting an ego state – Parent, Adult or Child), then transactions between two people can be shown as follows:

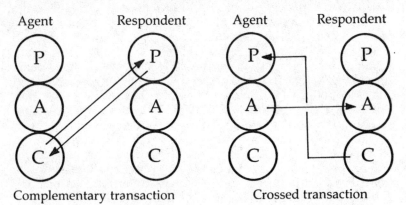

Figure 8   Transactions between ego states (after Berne).

In *complementary transactions* the response is 'appropriate and expected and follows the natural order of healthy human relationships'.[47] In our example depicted above, a young woman may say to her boyfriend, 'I'm cold! Please hold me' and he may respond with, 'Of course. You're always safe with me.' Here, her 'natural Child' has appealed to his 'nurturing Parent'.

In *crossed transactions* the communication is broken by an unexpected response. In the second diagram we can imagine a situation where a husband asks his wife, quite straightforwardly, 'What time will dinner be?' and is met by a tearful, 'Why do you always criticise me?' His Adult question has stimulated her 'adapted Child' which looks to his 'prejudiced Parent'.

Berne has classified transactions under a number of useful headings, including 'procedures', 'rituals', 'pastimes' and 'games'.[48] The first three of these are part and parcel of everyday social life but it is the fourth of these types of transaction that concerns us most in counselling. Berne has defined a *game* as 'an ongoing series of complementary ulterior transactions progressing to a well-defined, predictable outcome'. The basic dishonesty of a game is shown when, for example, an elderly man habitually feigns illness in order to gain the maximum attention from his wife and family.

Aims

As we have seen, TA presupposes not only the existence of scripts and life positions which result from the 'decisions' of childhood, but also the possibility of a further decision, made by the Adult, which leads to the 'fourth position of hope' – I'M OK – YOU'RE OK. Harris argues that 'the only way people get well or become OK is to expose the childhood predicament underlying the first three positions and prove how current behaviour perpetuates the positions'.[49] Berne makes a similar point when he presses the need for 'social control' in which the individual learns mastery over his or her tendency 'to manipulate or to be a prey to manipulation', over the propensity to listen to unhelpful Parent or Child voices. Put another way, we can say that the aim of TA is for the patient to achieve a 'script-free' life. Berne writes:

> While every human being faces the world initially as the captive of his script, the great hope and value of the human race is that the Adult can be dissatisfied with such strivings when they are unworthy.[50]

What are the marks of the person who is realising TA's social control and script-free living? Harris stresses the individual's emancipated ability to choose:

> The goal of TA is to enable a person to have freedom of choice, the freedom to change at will, to change the responses to recurring and new stimuli.[51]

Berne, writing in similar vein, declares that 'autonomy' is the 'ideal' of human behaviour and is known by its three capacities:

1 *Awareness*, in which a person 'knows how he feels, where he is and when it is', and lives with a full sense of appreciation of each immediate moment;[52]
2 *Spontaneity*, which means 'the freedom to choose' and 'liberation from the compulsion to play games';
3 *Intimacy*, which includes elements of candour and a childlike love towards another.

Berne answers his own question, 'After Games, What?' somewhat ruefully when he points out that it is only 'certain fortunate people' who achieve awareness, spontaneity and intimacy. The 'unprepared' may find these three capacities too daunting and may therefore clutch at 'togetherness' rather than 'autonomy'. He concludes his book *Games People Play* with something of an anticlimax: 'This may mean that there is no hope for the human race, but there is hope for individual members of it.'

Method

Berne argues that TA must be preceded by 'structural analysis', which seeks to clarify the varying roles of the patient's ego states and so help free the Adult from any unhealthy influences from the Parent and Child. For example, the recognition of a parental *prejudice*, 'You must avoid people from a different background', or an infantile *delusion*, 'Nobody can ever love me', may be an invaluable insight before moving on to the analysis of transactions.

Berne declares that the method of both structural and transactional analysis offers 'an actionistic, rational form of therapy which is suitable for, easily understood by, and naturally adapted to the great majority of psychiatric patients'.[53] He sees TA as having the best of both worlds, being 'actionistic', like the more 'parental' and directive forms of counselling, and 'rational', like the non-directive and psychoanalytic therapies. He seeks to hold these apparently contradictory elements of TA together by viewing its technique of analysing scripts as, initially, more like the activities of an engineer than a botanist.[54] If a hungry farmer is desperate to have a piece of land cleared to produce food, he will look to the engineer for help rather than the botanist: the former will take an 'actionist' line in removing undergrowth, improving drainage and levelling the ground, unlike the botanist who will ferret in the brushwood, examining each leaf and twig meticulously before allowing the bulldozers to move in. Berne says that once TA has helped the patient 'feel free as quickly as possible', then, if necessary, the 'rational' (more 'botanic') work of psychoanalysis can be turned to.

Structural and transactional analysis can be used to help people in a variety of ways, including individual counselling, marital therapy and group work. Generally speaking, TA is most effective in a group setting because it is in relation to others that transactions can be most faithfully observed and analysed.[55] Berne suggests that a maximum size for a worthwhile group is eight individuals; any larger gathering means a loss in the therapist's efficiency as observer and director. Let us look briefly at TA in action from both the patient's and the therapist's points of view.

The patient

As in all settings for counselling and psychotherapy, the motivation of the client or patient in seeking help will often be mixed. For most of us it is not easy to admit need and it can take a great deal of heart-searching, hesitancy and courage to make the first appointment with a therapist. There are, of course, others who become 'professional clients' and move eagerly from one counsellor to another. Within group therapy, such a person may be spotted by a fellow-client. Berne gives the example of a witty and perceptive patient who asked such a 'professional' in the group, 'Did you come for a treat or a treatment?'[56]

Whether it is primarily the Parent ('You really ought to get sorted out'), the Adult ('I need to think my situation through and make some important decisions') or the Child ('I'd be so much happier if I could get rid of some restrictions') that brings the client for counsel is an essential aspect of that person's life and forms a starting point for therapy. From then on, the patient needs to become increasingly willing to find insight into his or her 'games' and 'script'. Berne says that the success of this enterprise is not so much a matter of the patient's intelligence but rather his or her cultivation of an 'intuitive sensitivity' and the overall development of 'complete understanding between the patient and the therapist regarding the therapeutic situation'.[57] This obviously requires commitment from both parties.

The therapist

Within TA there is often a progressive element which carries the group from a type of transaction which is straightforward, and is a means of getting acquainted with the others (a *pastime*), through the exercise of ulterior transactions, known as games, to a consideration of scripts. The therapist throughout seeks to help the patients with an understanding of the games they play and of the scripts that bind their lives. Although TA may, for certain people, not need to enter the complex area of script analysis, it is, as we have seen, in becoming 'script-free' that the patient reaches the ultimate aim of therapy.

In the early sessions of a series of TA, the therapist will need to allow the games that the patient has brought to the group a certain range of freedom.[58] Initially, the mannerisms, gestures and postures adopted by the patient will be carefully observed because these can give valuable clues to the ways the patient is playing games and living in a script. Similarly, the therapist will listen most carefully (sometimes with closed eyes to exclude visual distraction and sometimes to a tape of a session) for tones of voice, details of vocabulary, and types of laughter, grunts, sighs and other non-verbal, vocal communication. From what he sees and hears, the experienced therapist will quickly discern the patient's script. To take a simple example, the husband, who is noticed to tighten his fist every time he mentions his wife and, at the same time, to speak in a harsh, vindictive 'parental' voice about her, is likely to be obeying some directive from his Parent, such as, 'Don't you stand any nonsense from others!' The scripted injunction needs to be uncovered. In this case, when the husband declares vehemently that of course he loves his wife, the therapist may ask, 'Then what is your clenched right fist saying about her?'

In ways like this the therapist aims to help patients recognise their Parent, Adult and Child 'voices'. Consequently, clients are given 'the option of choosing between' these 'voices', 'discarding the nonadaptive, useless, harmful, or misleading ones, and keeping the adaptive or useful ones'.[59] Berne argues that exposing the patients to such choices may include giving them *permission* 'to disobey the Parental directives, not in rebellion, but rather in autonomy'. In effect, the therapist sides with the patient's Adult to oppose the Parent, and so free the Child to do the forbidden thing. I well remember, in a TA group that I was part of, a young woman, whose Parent forbad her to trust herself physically to others, being encouraged by the therapist to permit her Child to 'take the prohibited risk'. A number of us joined hands to form a human stretcher upon which she allowed herself to collapse, thus overcoming – at least for a brief span – her innate resistance to close contact. Subsequent to such 'permission', Berne continues, the therapist needs to support the patient once more, this time to protect the Child against the Parent's 'retribution or jeers'. Through this therapy of the 'Three P's' – potency (the therapist's power to deal with the patient's Parent), permission and protection – the person in need is guided towards the objectives of 'social control', 'autonomy' and the 'script-free' life.

Critique

Harris has written that, in contrast to the complexity of psychoanalytic concepts, 'the vocabulary of Transactional Analysis is the precision tool of treatment because, in a language anyone can understand, it identifies things that really are, the reality of experiences that really happened in the lives of people who really existed'.[60] Although, as in any system, the vocabulary of TA sometimes degenerates into a mystifying jargonese, there is no doubt that its basic ideas of Parent, Adult, Child, transactions, games and scripts do offer a reasonably 'precise tool' in therapy. However, it is in its identifying of 'things that really are' that TA does, at times, seem to go overboard.

When Berne writes, 'It is incredible to think . . . that man's fate . . . is decided by a child not more than six years old, and usually three . . .', we have to agree. It *is* incredible! That is not to dispel the view that early childhood, in its adaptations, is powerfully relevant to the rest of one's life, but to question as to whether a child's 'decisions' cast the die of human destiny so irrevocably – unless, of course, a person is one of the few who can leave his or her script behind. This idea of a form of predestination that is instigated by a three-year-old seems highly presumptuous in the face of an all-knowing God who said, for instance, to Jeremiah, 'Before I formed you in the womb I knew you, before you were born I set you apart' (Jeremiah 1:5).

Moreover, even if we concede that the notion of a scripted life has a great deal of validity, TA makes some strong assumptions with regard to what we all need in life. This is perhaps most transparent in its idea of human OK-ness. Although we can reason that the life position of I'M OK – YOU'RE OK can be linked with the affirmation of self and others found in our Lord's command, 'Love your neighbour as yourself', TA, in its essential humanism, lacks the depth of understanding that the Bible has

on our basic 'not OK-ness'. Peter's insight into his own unworthiness before a holy and compassionate Lord is clear when he said
to Christ, 'Go away from me, Lord; I am a sinful man!' (Luke 5:8).
One's true 'OK-ness', we might say, is most deeply experienced
through the forgiving and transforming work of Jesus and his
Spirit. And yet, somehow the concept of 'OK-ness' can trivialise
the wonder of God's love in action. As Thomas Oden, the
American theologian, has written, 'OK-ness is hardly as profound as the holy self-giving love manifested in the cross.'[61]

Harris is more specific than Berne on the question of human
sinfulness. He writes, 'We simply cannot argue with the endemic
"cussedness" of man.'[62] However, quoting Paul Tillich's statement, 'Before sin is an act, it is a state', Harris concludes that
people should confess their 'state' rather than the actions that
flow from that condition. In TA terms, a person needs to
'"confess", or acknowledge, or comprehend' his or her 'not OK'
position rather than the 'sins' or games that express that position.
In contrast, the Bible does not seem to pit one aspect of sin against
the other but urges us to repent of both our fallen state and the
innumerable sinful acts that arise therefrom. The redemption
brought by Christ covers both our identification with Adam's
original sin (our 'state') and our personal sins (our 'acts').[63]

Oden also criticises TA's declaration that life is made up of
winners and losers because 'it imposes an ill-chosen image of
acquisitiveness upon the process of personal growth that it could
happily do without'.[64] Is it really better for us as people to be
always on the winning side? Are there not many 'losers' who
have a depth of character and measure of wholeness that eludes
the 'winners'? As Oden rightly points out, 'Jesus Christ may be
the prototypical loser . . . The resurrection is the final confound-
ing of the loser image.'

Finally, let us look at the objectives of TA. Although, as with
Ellis's rational-emotive therapy and Glasser's reality therapy,
(with its clearer perspective on issues of 'right and wrong' than
both TA and rational-emotive therapy), TA helpfully encourages
individual responsibility, it is in the humanistic concept of autonomy that we once more have difficulty (see pages 121–123). It is in
this state of liberation in which all classes of behaviour become,
for the patient, 'free choices subject only to his will' that TA offers
its greatest challenge to God's sovereignty and his call for our
subjection to *his* will. I was once part of a TA training weekend led

by an experienced therapist who, towards the end of our time with her, began to talk about her son and his potentials for the future. She was an excellent trainer and had helped to create a relaxed and caring atmosphere between the group members. Within the trust and openness of the group, I asked her how she would feel if, within his autonomy, her son one day freely chose to be a Christian. Her response was honest in that she declared that the question came as something of a shock to her, and the implication of the arising discussion seemed to be that humanistic autonomy and the decision to follow Christ were incompatible.

Gestalt therapy

Gestalt psychology has its origins in the thinking of continental phenomenologists like Heidegger and Husserl, who elaborated a 'science of experience'. The German word, *gestalt* was first used in a psychological context in 1890 by the Austrian psychologist and philosopher, Christian von Ehrenfels (1859–1932), who argued that there is a 'gestalt, or form' quality that is present in the *whole* of a structure and yet is absent in any of the parts which make up that whole. In 1912 three young German psychologists, who were particularly interested in human perception, joined forces to found the Berlin Gestalt school. These three friends – Max Wertheimer (1880–1943), Kurt Koffka (1886–1941) and Wolfgang Köhler (1887–1967) – reacted against the stark behaviourism of Watson and the narrow framework of Wundt's introspective analysis, reasoning that an individual should be understood as a 'meaningful whole'. Nonetheless, in due course many of the Gestalt psychologists left the University of Berlin for the United States where they capitulated to the extreme 'objectivism' of the Watsonian school and spent their time 'installing quantitative measures and excessive experimental restrictions'.[65]

Gestalt therapy, pioneered by *Frederick ('Fritz')* and *Laura Perls*, has sought to recover something of the original holism of the three Germans, as well as looking to psychoanalytic, humanistic, existential and transpersonal influences. Perls (1893–1970), whose 'flavour' has been described as 'lusty, energetic, colloquial, and charismatic',[66] was a key figure in the 'Human Potential Movement' based at Esalen in California in the 1960s.

In 1969, the year before his death, he founded a 'gestalt community' at Cowichan, Vancouver Island as a centre where therapists could stay and study for several months at a time.

Assumptions

Like Ellis and Berne, Perls both received training in psycho-analysis and later rejected some of the key tenets of classical Freudianism. In particular he argued that 'our blind spots and rigidities are in some aspect aware and not completely buried in an inaccessible "unconscious"'.[67] In tune with many other protagonists of the Human Potential Movement, his view of human nature is existential and humanistic; in his later years his thinking was further influenced by Eastern philosophy. We can see these ingredients, as well as Perls' acknowledgment of the promising origins of Gestalt psychology, as we consider his assumptions about our humanity.

Holism. Perls admits that there is no precise English word to translate the word *gestalt* but suggests that 'configuration, struc-ture, theme, structural relationship . . . or meaningful organized whole most closely approximate'.[68] The idea of the *figure* and the *ground*, first introduced by the Danish psychologist, Edgar Rubin in 1915, is an integral part of the gestalt. According to Perls, 'the context in which an element appears is called . . . the "ground" against which the "figure" stands out'.[69] When you next meet a close friend or a relative, allow yourself to notice the various features of your acquaintance's assumedly familiar face. When you concentrate on, for example, his or her nose (the 'figure') the rest of the face will briefly be the 'ground', or background. As your attention shifts to a new 'figure', say the left cheek, then the nose will become part of the new 'ground'. In fact, normally in conversation we are continually altering the exact contents of both figure and ground so that at any point we are perceiving a gestalt, or organisational whole. To see our friend's nose out of context, in, for example, the middle of a bowl of soup, would give a 'bad gestalt' (as well as a bout of nausea), a serious disruption of a sense of wholeness. This awareness of bizarre juxtaposition is one of the reasons that the art of a surrealist painter like Salvador Dali is so disturbing.

This argument about everyday observation is unnecessarily elaborate to most of us. However, the idea of the figure and the ground is the linchpin of Gestalt therapy. It is argued that 'each person is a complex arrangement of figure-ground relationships' and 'the healthy formation of gestalten is a continuous process of emerging figures and receding fields' in the life of the individual.[70] Gestalt therapists declare that this process is 'spontaneous' and is an existentialist response to the immediate situation. Two people might attend a flat-warming party. The one, because of a range of predispositions, might regard the company as genuine, well integrated, outgoing and caring; the other, holding different preconceptions, might see the party as made up of a bunch of showy, egocentric, untrustworthy and hypocritical people. The Gestaltist will point out that each has responded to his or her own set of 'figures' that stand out from the general 'ground' of the party, making up, for each, a satisfactory gestalt.

Gestalt therapy, then, seeks to hold a holistic approach to people which 'affirms the complexity of persons and of events' and includes 'all relevant dimensions'.[71] At the same time, this holism is said to be not only comprehensive but dynamic: 'the nature of reality – of life, humankind, and the world – can most profitably be regarded in terms of an ongoing constantly changing process'.[72]

Fragmentation.   Although Perls declares a belief that 'the Gestalt outlook is the original, undistorted, natural approach to life; that is, to man's thinking, acting, feeling', he also admits that the average person has 'lost his Wholeness, his Integrity'.[73] In Gestalt terms there is a loss of distinction between figure and ground in the person's experience. This condition of *confluence* may be the mark of certain marriages and long-term friendships, in which a healthy sense of individual distinctiveness is lost. Where two people have stagnated within a relationship of heavy routine and tedious predictability, then it is likely that there is a degree of 'confluence' between them. Here there is a loss of the 'excitement and growth' that feature a life of sharper identity – a life of a 'good gestalt', with figure and ground well defined and yet flexible.[74]

As well as causing loss between two people, or one person and the environment (as when someone is completely 'taken over' by a job or hobby), confluence also occurs within the individual. This may take the form of a diminished consciousness of physical function. Perls writes, 'almost all persons in our society have lost the proprioception of larges areas of their body', and this loss of awareness of the body's 'language' is a frequent accompaniment of neurotic illness.[75] In neurosis, the sufferer 'creates' symptoms by 'unaware manipulation of muscles' so that the tension headache or the difficulty in breathing, rather than the underlying need, becomes the focus of attention. In Gestalt language, for the anxious person the symptoms are the all-pervasive 'figure', while the 'ground' of the personality itself is ignored.

Perls is highly perceptive when he writes that 'in health and spontaneity . . . men appear most different, most unpredictable, most "eccentric"' whereas in neurosis 'men are more alike: this is the deadening effect of sickness'.[76] All of us will have had experience of contrasting the exuberant, well differentiated personality (with a 'good' gestalt) and the excessively anxious, and somewhat dull person caught in a confluent relationship (with a 'weak' gestalt).

Aims

Perls has written that the aim of Gestalt therapy is 'a unitary functioning of the whole man'.[77] As we have noted, many men and women are said to be in a state of fragmentation where they have lost their 'wholeness' and 'integrity'. And so, for the individual to 'come together' again 'he has to heal the dualism of his person, of his thinking, and of his language'.[78] In Gestalt language, it can be said that 'the achievement of a strong gestalt is itself the cure'.[79]

This healing of human disunity and experiencing of a sense of wholeness, or gestalt, is the outcome of 'creative adjustment', a process within which the individual wakes up to a fresh awareness of self and its potential. This road of self-discovery, the Gestaltists argue, can only be travelled by allowing inner, partially hidden conflicts to surface and to be faced. Progress is marked by what Köhler called the 'Aha!' experience in which the patient suddenly sees and understands what had long eluded him. Archimedes' 'Eureka!' ('I've got it!'), reputedly shouted out from his bath when he saw that the apparent loss of weight of an object in water equals the weight of water displaced, was an 'Aha!' experience. The 'figure' of insight stood out sharply from the 'ground' of his rumination and a 'good' gestalt was achieved.[80]

In his *The Gestalt Approach* Perls describes the intermediate objective of the 'fertile void', which is an 'awareness without speculation about the things of which one is aware'. In this trance-like state:

> Confusion is transformed into clarity, emergency into continuity, interpreting into experiencing. The fertile void increases self-support by making it apparent to the experimenter that he has much more available than he believed he had.[81]

Here we see, as part of the technique of Gestalt therapy, an aim for the individual which indicates Perls' links with Eastern trans-personalism. Nevertheless, such goals do not lead to a mystical isolationism for, it is argued, successful therapy opens the way to 'self-support' rather than 'self-sufficiency':

> When the patient is discharged from therapy he will not lose his need for other people. On the contrary, he will for the first time derive real satisfactions from his contact with them.[82]

Method

Gestalt therapy is essentially a 'here and now' approach – not 'an excavation of the past', as is psychoanalysis, but 'an experience in living in the present'.[83] As is suggested by this definition, this style of therapy is primarily experiential rather than verbal or interpretative, the past and future being continually brought into the present. Because of this 'here and now' emphasis, Gestalt therapy sees the need for 'creative experimentation' rather than 'set techniques'.[84]

In a one-to-one relationship or in a group setting, the therapist seeks to act as a *'catalyst* for change without taking all the responsibility for change within the client'. Although, ultimately, 'the therapist is only a resource for the client', there is no doubt that his or her role is an extremely active one. In group therapy, for example, the rest of the group acts as a 'Greek chorus' which may or may not be involved with the central 'drama' between the therapist and the patient: 'The therapist is a directive leader and orchestrates all aspects of the therapeutic interactions, with the advice and consent of the client who is working.'[85]

This 'stage management' stimulates other members of the group to work silently on their own conflicts or, in turn, to move to the centre of the therapeutic 'drama'.

The steps in the helping process are fourfold: expression, differentiation, affirmation, and choice and integration.

Expression.   The client is encouraged to express himself 'as fully as he can', becoming aware of 'his gestures, of his breathing, of his emotions, of his voice, and of his facial expressions as much as of his pressing thoughts'. He is urged to preface this expression with the key phrase, 'Now I am aware' – a reminder of immediacy ('Now'), responsibility ('I'), one's 'being' ('am') and a sense of personal ability ('aware').[86] The therapist may notice that every time a woman mentions her male friend she agitates her right foot. She, in turn, will be prompted to sense her mannerism and, when appropriate, declare, 'Now I am aware of moving my right foot.' This acknowledgment should lead to 'differentiation'.

Differentiation.   Once 'expression' has begun, the therapist starts to suggest certain experiments to help the client differentiate between the parts of his or her inner conflict. In our example, it might be proposed that the woman moves her foot even faster, exaggerating the movement as if the foot had a life and voice of its own. In so doing she may begin to realise that this particular mannerism points to her frustration with her friend's behaviour towards her. In effect, she may long to kick out at him!

Affirmation.   This is a crucial stage in therapy in which the client is urged to identify with 'all the parts' that are emerging into awareness. She may need to say, 'I am my foot – I'm frustrated!' It is here that the Gestalt therapist will allow the client a full expression of pent-up emotion. This release may be a powerful experience as is implied when Perls addresses the client in these words:

> you will permit yourself to express with full emotional force all the kicking, pounding and screaming of a child's tantrum. Despite conventional notions to the contrary, this is the healthy device by which the organism exteriorizes frustrated aggressions.[87]

This affirmation of recognised emotion may be aided by the 'empty chair' technique, in which the client, after giving vent to her feelings towards, in our example, her man friend, who is imagined to occupy an empty chair, in turn sits on that chair and so identifies with and voices his responses. In this way she may affirm her own frustration by saying, 'I feel so annoyed with you I could kick you' and she may then begin to gain insight and objectivity as she retorts on his behalf, 'I'm sick and tired of your over-sensitivity. Why can't you trust me?'

Choice and integration. Affirmation includes an awakening sense of responsibility for one's ways of feeling, so that, by this stage, our client can declare, 'I am responsible for my frustration and resentment.' However, as Perls put it, 'responsibility is really response-ability, the ability to choose one's reactions'[88] and so the client is encouraged to make choices appropriate to the insights gained. This need to deal with 'unfinished business' by decisive action may lead to an impasse and the client may then find it helpful to explore her fears and expectations by *rehearsal* within the group. This means testing out, or 'rehearsing', various sentences which attempt to express her feelings. She may, in our example, finally choose to confront her friend with the fact of her frustration. Often such decisiveness brings 'an internal integration . . . that releases tension and brings calmness'. This sense of peace may be a sign of 'a completed gestalt, the sense of satisfaction that comes when a situation is finished'.

Critique

The holistic nature of Gestalt therapy leads to some sweeping claims for its efficacy. Perls in the Introduction to his *Gestalt Therapy* declares his desire to lay the foundation for 'the full application of Gestaltism in psychotherapy as the only theory that adequately and consistently covers both normal and abnormal psychology'.[89] E. W. L. Smith writes in a similar vein:

> Perls' genius was demonstrated . . . in his creation of a new system which in its essence goes far beyond the constituent elements. Gestalt therapy is, in a very real sense, a Gestalt.[90]

In spite of these sweeping claims, Gestalt therapy, as with rational-emotive therapy and TA, points to some valuable insights about human nature and some most useful techniques for helping people with hidden conflicts. When Perls writes that 'the healthy person, with the present as reference-point, is free to look backwards or ahead as occasion warrants',[91] he is, however unwittingly, touching on the lasting truth that our Lord referred to when he urged his followers to avoid fruitless anxiety 'about

tomorrow; for tomorrow will worry about itself' (Matthew 6:34).
Further, we can see in the 'empty chair' method a far-sighted way
of helping an individual towards a 'sober judgment' of self and,
hopefully, a looking 'to the interests of others'.[92]

However, despite these helpful perspectives, the underlying
assumptions of Gestalt therapy about our humanity and the
nature of reality are greatly at variance with Christian theism.

Human nature.   Perls sees people in an essentially optimistic light
and as having the need to 'discover the potential of energy and
enthusiasm' that lies within.[93] He regards our nature as autonomous where 'the basic law of life is self-preservation and
growth'. He views the choices of 'self-regulation' as supreme,
overriding all ethical, medical and political considerations.[94]
Van De Riet *et al.* acclaim that the self is 'the arbiter of reality' and
the individual 'the creator of his or her own world view'.[95]

This arbitration about reality is entered upon, Gestalt therapy
declares, when emotion is seen as 'a guide which furnishes the
only basis on which human existence can be ordered rationally'.[96]
This exclusively existentialist view of daily life is coloured by a
'discovering-and-inventing as one goes along, engaged and
accepting' with 'no sense of oneself or of other things other than
one's experience of the situation'.[97]

The nature of reality.   The Gestaltist's view that human life only
makes sense when conducted on a foundation of extreme subjectivism is, inevitably, further based on a wholehearted rejection of
the existence of absolutes. Van De Riet *et al.* write:

> . . . the gestalt therapist believes that absolute and certain knowledge
> is a myth . . . Comparison does not exist outside the human
> framework, and without comparison certain knowledge is
> impossible.[98]

They add that the Gestalt therapist also denies that 'there is
a meaning in things, that a meaning exists'. Where there
are no absolutes and no meaning then ethics become entirely
'situational':

> In gestalt therapy there is no 'right' or 'wrong' built into any matter of
> question. There are rights and wrongs, but they are aspects of the
> stance and choices of an individual or of a society in particular
> situations . . .[99]

Once again, we see the sorry chain of interconnectedness where human experience is regarded as the yardstick that measures life, and human autonomy is viewed as the wherewithal to build something of substance. Anything 'out of sight' is not only out of mind but is ruled out of existence; therefore God, any moral order and ultimate meaning must go. Humanity is busy with its innumerable building projects, concentrating so very hard on the 'figures' of self-regulation but blind to the one whom Tillich called the 'Ground of our being.'

And so we have surveyed something of the essence of three of the numerous offshoots and hybridisations of our four main systems of psychology. As we have seen, the newer therapies have quite frequently grown from the stock of psychoanalysis. Sometimes, as in TA, some of the links with Freudianism are nurtured; sometimes, as with rational-emotive therapy and Gestalt therapy, those ties are severed. Generally, the strongest pairing is with the humanism and existentialism of the personalistic psychologies although, increasingly in many quarters, powerful elements of transpersonalism are introduced to lift the eyes of the needy and the questing beyond themselves.[100] As we consider Christian reactions and responses to the challenge of secular psychology in Part II we shall see both similarities and dissimilarities to the methodologies so far examined – similarities, because there must be a limited number of ways of viewing human nature, and dissimilarities, because God's self-revelation is both distinctive and corrective compared with 'man's study of man'.

PART II

CHRISTIAN REACTION AND RESPONSE

10

SINKERS, SWIMMERS AND STRUGGLERS

Believe in yourself! Have faith in your abilities! Without a humble but reasonable confidence in your own powers you cannot be successful or happy. But with sound self-confidence you can succeed.

Norman Vincent Peale

Psychotherapy is the counterfeit currency of the world and a substitute for the healing balm of Gilead. And Christian psychotherapy is a house divided against itself. How long shall we have one foot in the wilderness of the cure of minds and one in the promised land of the cure of souls?

Martin and Deirdre Bobgan

At the end of chapter one we saw how the Christian tradition of sustaining, guiding, healing and reconciling began to be exposed to the new science of psychology. Although pastoral care had been an important and intrinsic part in the life of God's people since the days of the Old Testament, it can be argued that the Church's caring has always been susceptible to the prevailing psychology of its environment. At times this influence has been imperceptible, at times blatant. When the wind of potential change has been detected the Church may have responded by resistance, acquiescence or compromise – with or without debate. With the rise of the secular psychologies from the Enlightenment onwards, Christianity in the West could not be oblivious to developments which threatened to rival its long established position as the prime source of solace and guidance. A response was demanded – sooner or later. Psychological science started to turn its gaze towards the Church and its claims and, for example, through the pragmatism of William James, a psychology of religion emerged as an academic discipline. God's people, as did Watson's rats and Skinner's pigeons, became the laboratory objects of empirical study. At the same time, atheistic and naturalistic views of human personality gained momentum and began to flood into the consciousness of countless thinking men and women. The Church had to sink or swim. If it swam, it had to choose between floating with the tide of secularism, striking out boldly against the flood and finding some sort of compromise route parallel to the shore of lost identity.

Inevitably, there has been a range of Christian response: sinking, floating, swimming and struggling. However, there are other people about in this sea of contrary views and so some Christians, mostly swimmers and strugglers, have proved fit enough to engage in dialogue. Such brave souls may thus find themselves swimming more confidently in the continuing stream of orthodox pastoral care, refreshed by insights shared with their new companions. It is likely that, sooner or later, those strugglers who shun prayer and honest discussion will become compromisers and, in time, find themselves either swelling the volume of flotsam or sinking without trace.

This analogy is, perhaps, over-defined, for the issues are complex. Nonetheless, we can trace these trends of running with the tide, of swimming vigorously (and sometimes unheedingly) away from trouble and, thirdly, of engaging in debate in order, hopefully, to swim with greater circumspection and confidence. We can see these responses to the powerful surge of the secular psychologies as those of *assimilation, reaction* and *dialogue*. Most of those who have moved into dialogue have been either assimilative or reactionary to start with. Their discussions may, of course, not change their direction but at least they are talking!

Assimilation

Towards the end of the nineteenth century in the United States the tradition of pastoral care began to look to scientific psychology in order to enhance its understanding of pastoral theology. Washington Gladden, a Congregationalist minister from Columbus, Ohio, for example, was amongst the first to urge cooperation between the clergy and the medical profession. In his book of 1891, *The Christian Pastor*, he showed considerable perception of the close ties between mental and physical health, arguing that the pastor is, above all, a 'friend' to the needy.[1]

As already indicated, the fraternisation between religious practice and psychological insight continued in both directions. Pastors, like Gladden, borrowed from the new perspectives to aid their caring for others; psychologists, like James, encouraged the close examination of religious experience. By the turn of the century both of these broad influences began to infiltrate the Church, through the teaching of the psychology of religion in theological seminaries and through an increasing openness amongst Christian leaders towards the messianic claims of Freud, Adler and Jung. Theologians and psychologists, clergy and doctors, pastors and psychotherapists entered into debate and partnership. Conferences were held, institutes were formed and training programmes launched – all under a common banner of 'healing for all'. Although, in terms of this book, our emphasis is on the mental aspects of this crusade, there has been, and still is, a more comprehensive desire to bring health to 'the whole man'.[2]

In spite of these complex trends developing on both sides of the Atlantic, it is in America that the overall movement to see pastoral counselling as a dominant facet of pastoral care has been most clearly systematised and documented. Many key figures have been involved, but I propose to concentrate primarily on just two of them: Boisen in the United States and Weatherhead in the United Kingdom.

Anton Boisen

Anton T. Boisen (1876–1966) is perhaps the best known of the founding fathers of a pastoral theology that has looked long and hard at theories of psychotherapy and counselling in order to sift and, where appropriate, assimilate insight. He is said to have been the 'first theologian to contribute to a number of American psychiatric, psychological and scientific journals'.

Boisen's father had left Germany in 1869 in order to complete his postgraduate studies.[3] In due course he was offered a chair in modern languages at Indiana University, where he met Boisen's mother, Louise Wylie. His parents were liberal Presbyterians and Anton's view of God was profoundly influenced by the aura of his dominant father as the 'great academic teacher'. Like his father, Anton Boisen graduated as a linguist, although his post-graduate studies on William James' *Principles of Psychology* were a forerunner of his lifelong interest in psychological matters.

Following some years of teaching French and German and a period working as a forester, Boisen responded to a call to the ministry in his late twenties. He spent three of his happiest years at the Union Theological Seminary, during the time of optimism when the American preacher, John R. Mott was calling for the world's evangelisation 'in this generation'. However, although this was Boisen's hey-day, he was disappointed at the dearth of psychological input on the seminary's curriculum.

In his delightfully frank autobiography *Out of the Depths* he traces the strands in his own emotional and psychological make-up which may have led to a shattering series of psychotic break-downs that began in 1920. In his earlier years he was haunted by the influence of his powerful father, who had died when Anton was seven and whose memory fuelled a loyalty that 'had become one with my religion'. Further, the young linguist was plagued by conflicting sexual desires which prompted the advice from an academic friend of his father that Boisen must 'look to Christ for help, and to some good woman'.[4] The 'good woman' he looked to was Alice Batchelder, a golden-haired girl from New Hampshire who swept him off his feet – although they were never to marry. There was very little reciprocation of affection for the love-lorn Anton and his inner turmoil and frustrations seemed to be strongly tied to his episodes of psychosis.

As with many before and since, Boisen's dark anguish para-doxically shed light, and he emerged 'out of the depths' with a fresh vision of the need to explore the links between mental disorder and religious experience. Following a further period of study, this time at Harvard, of the works of Freud, Jung and other psychoanalysts, Boisen, backed by Dr Richard C. Cabot, who lectured in social ethics at the university, took up a chaplaincy to the mentally ill at the Worcester State Hospital in 1924. A year later, still supported by Cabot, Boisen was the first to take theological students into a psychiatric hospital setting for further training. This innovative man, along with the chaplain, Russell L. Dicks, pioneered 'clinical pastoral training' in the world of the general hospital. Over the next decade Boisen and others estab-lished a range of centres at various mental hospitals in which ordinands were encouraged, under careful supervision, to have contact with patients and to take part in seminars and discussions on case histories along with the hospital staff.

Following the death of his beloved Alice, from cancer in 1935, Boisen moved into full-time writing and teaching at the Chicago Theological Seminary, maintaining a helpful link with the neo-Freudian, Harry Stack Sullivan throughout. During the late 1930s and early 1940s, Boisen made important studies on schizophrenia, conscientious objection and the rise of Pentecostalism in the United States.

Although Boisen has been rightly seen as the best known of the co-founders of clinical pastoral training, he was far from happy with the direction that this movement was taking. He had already castigated both liberal and 'fundamentalist' Christians for opting out of the full spectrum of people's needs – the former for denying their heritage and at the same time turning over the 'sick of soul' to the doctors, and the latter for concentrating only on 'saving souls'. He argued that 'fundamentalists' gave their limited 'treatment' without 'diagnosis', and the liberals offered neither 'treatment' nor 'diagnosis'.[5]

Having urged his fellow-Christians to pursue both 'diagnosis' and 'treatment', he was frustrated by the lack of theological and scientific acumen displayed by pastors and theologians alike. On the one hand, many accepted Freudian and post-Freudian thinking without theological reflection and, on the other hand, many eschewed the rigours of research in the pastoral fields they so blithely worked in. Furthermore, theological seminaries refused to alter the basic forms of their curricula, simply appending courses on 'person counselling' as a complete *non sequitur* to the more serious business of 'doing theology'. As a result, such profound issues as sin and salvation in the arena of pastoral care were soft-pedalled. Boisen writes of this Freud-inspired tendency to deal with people's feelings of guilt dismissively as follows:

> The solution offered by some of our chaplain-supervisors was that of getting rid of the conflict by lowering the conscience threshold. There were even those who accepted the later teachings of Wilhelm Reich, advocating a freedom quite at variance with the basic insights of the Hebrew-Christian religion.[6]

Leslie Weatherhead

Leslie Dixon Weatherhead (1893–1976) has been an important figure in the front line of the debate that took place in the United Kingdom between religion and psychology during the first half of this century. Like Boisen, Weatherhead was strongly influenced by a powerful parent – in his case by a dominating mother, whom he describes as a 'great forbidder' with respect to such optional activities as dancing, theatre-going, gambling, smoking and drinking. Weatherhead's father was a border Scot who had come south to London to work in a hosiery warehouse. The family were Methodists and Leslie grew up in Leicester amidst the strict 'methods' of Bible reading, prayers, chapel attendance and Sunday school, all presided over by his forbidding mother, characterised by a grandson as 'a Christian of terrible and serious aspect'.[7]

Perhaps not surprisingly, considering his upbringing, Leslie Weatherhead trained for the Methodist ministry and sailed for India in 1916 as a missionary. While working in Madras he applied for a commission in the Indian Army Reserve of Officers and, in due course, was sent to the deserts of Mesopotamia as part of an encampment guarding the port of Basra. During this term of service he was appointed as an army chaplain.

His year or so in the Middle East was important in that it gave him a great deal of time to mull over his faith, besides opening up his thinking to psychology. His reflections on Christianity tended towards liberalism – a reaction, perhaps, to his mother's systematised and disciplining beliefs. He wrote in his diary soon after: 'Let not the minister say, "This is wrong". It is a question of individual conscience . . . Right and wrong are matters of degree'.[8] Further, while in Mesopotamia, he became deeply impressed by a doctor who practised psychotherapy in a hospital setting and shared with Weatherhead his views on the psycho-somatic nature of much so-called physical illness. The medical man, who was killed in a riding accident shortly afterwards, insisted that it was the padres of the regiment who should be helping such people towards recovery.[9] During his remaining three years in India, Leslie Weatherhead turned to the writings of the psychoanalysts and psychological perspectives began to creep into his preaching. In 1920 he married Evelyn Triggs, an ex-missionary who was working as the vice-principal of a girls' boarding-school, and two years later the Weatherheads returned to England.

In 1925, the year that Anton Boisen begun his successful experiment of clinical pastoral training in the United States, Leslie Weatherhead started a decade of work as a Wesleyan minister in Leeds. Both there, and during a shorter period in Manchester previously, he put into practice his newly gained Freudian insights. Encouraged by his discussions with the army doctor in Mesopotamia, he interviewed patients who had been referred to him by the medical profession and adopted a number of psychoanalytic techniques, including the use of the couch, free association, the analysis of dreams and the occasional use of hypnotism. Weatherhead followed the Freudian tendency to see the repression and distortion of sexual desires as cardinal sources of anxiety. He declared that eighty percent of the people who came to him for help 'were in difficulties that derived originally from sex'.[10]

His most renowned work began in 1936 in London at the City Temple, a fine Congregationalist chapel built in 1640. It was here that he sought the help of those with 'a real Christian experience of their own, a psychological qualification and a medical degree'.[11] He soon enlisted the aid of five or six Christian doctors and psychotherapists for his 'psychological interviewing', besides starting intercessions for healing. Although the church was bombed in 1941, this caring ministry continued to prosper in various other centres in north and central London until the team and congregation were able to return to the rebuilt City Temple in Holborn Viaduct in 1958. During this time Leslie Weatherhead developed an international reputation. In addition to establishing his Psychological Clinic after the war, he was able to go on several lecturing tours in the United States, linking up with theologians and pastors whom he had admired for years, like the Niebuhrs, and Henry Emerson Fosdick at the Riverside Church, New York. In 1950 he gained a Ph D for a thesis which a year later appeared in his important book *Psychology, Religion and Healing*. It is here that we see his methodology spelt out.

Assumptions

Though clearly influenced by Freudian theory and practice, Weatherhead was not uncritical of psychoanalytic presuppositions. He questioned Freud's extreme emphases on the Oedipus complex and the place of sex, and argued that Adler, although showing his patients 'endless goodwill', exaggerated the importance of inferiority.[12] Weatherhead wrote of the founder of analysis:

> I feel that the fundamental weakness and condemnation of Freudian psycho-analysis is its entire lack of interest in a subsequent reorientation or synthesis. Christ's parable of the house swept and garnished and afterwards occupied by seven other devils is a most relevant comment here.[13]

Even though, like so many of his contemporaries in the 1930s and 1940s, Weatherhead used Freudian techniques, he reasoned powerfully for a Christian form of psychosynthesis, a building up through Christ's enabling after the dismantling process of analysis.

Furthermore, his view of human nature was more optimistic than Freud's, without falling into the Rogerian trap of elevating the ability of individuals to change themselves. Besides writing that 'it is the desire of most men and women, deep down, to be good', he also declared the need for people to find forgiveness and to surrender their jealousies and resentments.[14] However, as we noted in his desert musings, Leslie Weatherhead tended to play down the reality and gravity of human sinfulness, preferring, at times, to look at psychological explanations for human frailty. He was also uncomfortable with the orthodox Christian understanding of the atonement, particularly with its reference to the sacrificial aspect of Christ's death. One of his sons reports the storm of protests from believers when his father commented on the biblical statement, 'Without shedding of blood is no remission of sin' by saying, 'In our modern view this is simply not true'.[15]

Aims

Weatherhead sees the ultimate aim of his psychological interviewing as 'personal integration'. He equates this concept with Jung's objective of 'individuation', wherein there is 'the wise setting of the house of one's personality in order'.[16] This process of change is placed within the wider context of healing, of which Weatherhead writes:

> By healing . . . is meant the process of restoring the broken harmony which prevents personality, at any point of body, mind or spirit, from its perfect functioning in its relevant environment; the body in the material world; the mind in the realm of true ideas and the spirit in its relationship with God.[17]

Although this may suggest a tripartite view of human nature, he agrees with the Hebrew tradition when he declares that man must be seen as a 'unity of body-mind-spirit'.[18] The quest for health may emphasise this or that aspect of our being at any point of time, but in reality this overall unity is indivisible.

The road towards integration is marked, Weatherhead argues, by a 'religious interpretation of life on broad lines'.[19] More specifically he advocates that, if a man longs for health, '*first* he must desire to be right in his relationship with God, with man and with life'; health itself must be seen as a 'by-product' of this prior aim. He admits that, for those who have been deprived emotionally, the way forward will be aided by learning 'how to obtain love through the loving community, the Church, and how to find *through persons* the unfailing love of God'. Those of us who have counselled or befriended people who lack an experience of being loved will agree readily with Weatherhead that God's love can often only be made tangible through caring human contact.

Methods

Leslie Weatherhead's method of counselling was, as we have seen, strongly influenced by Freudianism and yet it was, in effect, a form of 'mini'-analysis, or 'brief' psychotherapy, avoiding the protracted commitment of classical psychoanalysis. He argued that the ideal setting for his approach is that of the local church and he urged that, in time, every Christian fellowship should have its 'psychological clinic where doctors and ministers can co-operate'. He envisaged that this aim could be modified initially by certain groups of churches, such as those of an Anglican diocese or a Methodist district, creating their own central clinic.[20]

At the City Temple, Weatherhead saw his 'patients' for six or seven sessions of one hour each, in which the whole problem was spread before the needy person so that he or she could understand what needed to be done and then, hopefully, do it. The first encounter or two sought to establish rapport and clarify the patient's family history and story. Subsequently, through the use of free association, emotionally charged areas were identified and catharsis encouraged through a re-living of difficult experiences. This process, where necessary, was further stimulated by dream analysis. Within this 'mini'-analysis, Weatherhead allowed the giving of 'simple explanations' and 'informal talks on psychological mechanisms, or even advice – not too dogmatically expressed – on ethical problems'.[21] He insists that he did not offer actual 'treatment' and, where a more thorough investigation was needed, Weatherhead referred the patient to one of his medical colleagues who would then, from time to time during therapy, report back briefly to the minister. Finally, Weatherhead would often see the patient once more in order to discuss how the needs of the 'integrated personality' might be met.

In this blend of 'directiveness' and 'non-directiveness', of analytic, cognitive and behavioural approaches, Weatherhead does not lose sight of spiritual aspects. He points to the value of confession – 'the pouring out from the soul of all its consciously repressed and hidden sins and poisons and burdens and griefs and sorrows'[22] – and sees the need for the praying, purified Church to rediscover its mission as 'an instrument which the Holy Spirit can use in the ministry of direct spiritual healing'.[23]

With his vision of the Church's healing ministry and his yearning to reach 'lovable pagans' for Christ we find Weatherhead at his most winsome. Nonetheless, his own theological thinking often seems to have been at odds with orthodox Christianity in spite of his Christ-centredness. Moreover, he had a lifelong interest in psychic phenomena, attended a number of séances and, during the 1950s, he received a series of messages, reputedly from dead persons, through the automatic writing of a Miss Geraldine Cummins.[24] His liberal view of biblical revelation, besides allowing such dabbling with sinister forces, led to a cavalier approach towards parts of the scriptures. In his last important book, *The Christian Agnostic* (1965), he proves, for example, 'to be annoyed at the upstaging in the church of the personality of Christ by that of the "neurotic" St Paul'.[25] William Temple was regarded as just as inspired as Paul and, on balance, the Romantic poets were seen as 'superior authorities' to the apostle to the Gentiles.

We have looked briefly at Boisen in the United States and Weatherhead in Britain as examples of Christian leaders in the first half of the century who assimilated a great deal of the psychological thinking of their contemporaries. Both were pastors, both were liberals and both sought to hold on to supernaturalism. Boisen seemed to maintain a more orthodox Christianity than Weatherhead and the American sounded louder warning bells about the pervasive influence of Freudianism than the Englishman. It is tempting to relate their different emphases to their relationships with their parents – Boisen's more cautious orthodoxy with his deep respect for his powerful and academic father, Weatherhead's often impish and iconoclastic heterodoxy with his early fear of his formidably methodical and disciplining mother. Be that as it may, both these men exerted important influences within the debate between psychology and theology – Boisen, as one of the founding fathers of clinical pastoral training, and Weatherhead, as a pioneer and populariser of cooperation between clergy and doctors in the area of mental health.

The rise of pastoral counselling

In the United States

Anton Boisen, in spite of his attempts to stem the tide of assimilation, was inspirational in the development of pastoral counselling in general and in the formation of Clinical Pastoral Education (CPE) in particular. Early definitions of the former quite simply emphasised that it is counselling which is carried out by the Christian minister. Seward Hiltner, of Princeton, wrote in the 1949 edition of his book *Pastoral Counseling* that pastoral counselling is 'the attempt by a pastor to help people help themselves through the process of gaining understanding of their inner conflicts'.[26] In the United States, the training of such a pastor 'to help people help themselves' has been carried, by and large, by the CPE movement. Mirroring Boisen's early work at the Worcester State Hospital, CPE encourages the relating of 'theological studies to interpersonal relationships through personal supervision' within 'a church, hospital, or other clinical facility for persons in church-related vocations'.[27] It has become a rigorous system of pastoral education with a stress on training, experience, supervision, accreditation and the support of Christian congregations.

In America in the 1930s, the literature on the psychology of

religion began to look towards the question of counselling. This
trend continued into the 1940s and 1950s with Rollo May's *The Art
of Counseling* (1939), Russell L. Dicks' *Pastoral Work and Counseling*
(1945), Seward Hiltner's *Pastoral Counseling* (1949), Carroll A.
Wise's *Pastoral Counseling: its theory and practice* (1951) and Wayne
E. Oates' (ed.) *An Introduction to Pastoral Counseling* (1959). It is
interesting to note that May, who looked primarily to
psychoanalysis and, later, existentialism, and Hiltner and Wise,
who are part of mainstream CPE, were all students under Anton
Boisen.

And so the prime tributaries of influence – the psychology of
religion; the chaplaincy and educational movement; and traditional pastoral care – flowed together to form the powerful river
of pastoral counselling. Seward Hiltner demonstrates that there
were two main outlooks on pastoral care – one seeing this function as simply 'everything the pastor does', the other regarding
this ministry as just *one* facet of the Church's work.[28] He sees
these perspectives as 'attitudinal' and 'structural' respectively
and needing to give way to a third view which is 'relational'. Thus
the pastor is recognised primarily as a 'shepherd' who, without
neglecting his more routine offices, relates caringly to the members of his 'flock'. Kenneth Leech views this move towards
Hiltner's 'shepherding perspective' as pivotal in the story of
pastoral theology, wherein the twin themes of the 'cure of souls'
and 'pastoral counselling' can now be discerned.[29] Leech, while
acknowledging overlap, distinguishes these two aspects of
pastoral care by markers which include:

1 The cure of souls, or *spiritual direction*, by a concern with
people's spiritual well being which is continuous and is based
within the life of the body of Christ;

2 *Pastoral counselling*, by an involvement with people, who are
under stress and sometimes in crises, which is thereby intermit-
tent and clinic- or office-based.[30]

Figure 9 may help to simplify this complexity of influences.

This range of trends, boosted by thinking assimilated from the
burgeoning secular psychologies – behaviouristic, analytic, personalistic and transpersonal – led to a prolific flowering of all
varieties of counselling, including pastoral, during the 1950s
and 1960s. This profusion is both anticipated and reflected in
the successful ministries of 'pastor-psychologists' like Harry
Emerson Fosdick and Norman Vincent Peale in New York. These

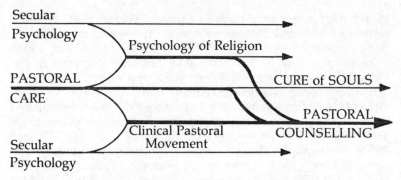

Figure 9   The rise of pastoral counselling.

liberal Protestants have seemingly assimilated a great deal of insight from Adlerian self-determinism and have disseminated their optimistic influence through such popular best-sellers as Fosdick's *On Being a Real Person* (1943) and Peale's *The Power of Positive Thinking* (1953).

Paul Halmos, writing in 1965, points out that, by 1960, there were 70,000 professional 'counsellors' in the United States, including psychiatrists, psychotherapists, psychologists, counsellors and social workers.[31] Although the legacy of pastoral counselling, as we have argued, has contributions from both secular psychology and the tradition of pastoral care, Halmos declares that counsellors, in general, 'act in lieu of the spiritual consultants and guides of former times'.[32] Whether we see pastoral counselling as an equal partner with 'spiritual direction' in the overall pastoral care of people or as a massive take-over bid for healing humanity's hurts, there is no doubt that the assimilation of secular psychologies is a dominant part of its history.

In the United Kingdom

There is some truth in the notion that the rise of Hitler led to the wholesale export of psychoanalytical talent to the United States where it cohabited with American humanism and pragmatism, producing a motley of energetic, and sometimes unruly, children. The most vociferous and venturesome of these, the so-called 'human potential' and 'counselling' movements, have found their eager way back to Europe. Within their assorted ranks can be heard the quieter speech of pastoral counselling – difficult to hear because of the babble of secular voices with which it keeps company. It has been said that what happens in the United States re-emerges in Western Europe ten years or so later. This trend is reflected in the dates of some of the key books on either side of the Atlantic. We have noted the predominance of seminal works on pastoral counselling in America in the 1940s and 1950s. In Europe we see a similar pattern in the 1950s and 1960s, for example: Harry Guntrip's *Psychology for Ministers and Social Workers* (1949), Leslie Weatherhead's *Psychology, Religion and Healing* (1951), Göte Bergsten's *Pastoral Psychology: a study in the care of souls* (1951), Eduard Thurneysen's *A Theology of Pastoral Care* (translated 1962) and Heije Faber and Ebel van der Schoots' *The Art of Pastoral Conversation* (1965).

However, it is easy to exaggerate this west-to-east transatlantic influence and ignore the fact that a great deal of thinking has been hammered out in European countries within their own national cultures. In Guntrip's book there is a lot of reference to Fairbairn and Klein, both working on British soil, and Bergsten alludes mainly to continental writers. It is fair, too, to say that the translation of European works, like Thurneysen's and Faber and van der Schoots', has done much to keep alive the debate on pastoral counselling in the United States.[33]

Just as Boisen was a pioneering figure in the clinical pastoral scene in America, so Weatherhead has been, in perhaps less direct ways, instrumental in the emergence of pastoral counselling in Britain. As we have seen, he looked to the influence of Harry Emerson Fosdick in New York, as well as to the rise of clinical training for ordinands in America. Weatherhead, in turn, was one of the leading encouragers behind the enterprising work of William H. Kyle in London in the 1960s.

Although born in Alabama, Bill Kyle grew up in the United Kingdom and identified primarily with the 'British scene'. He gained experience as a counsellor with the London Marriage Guidance Council and began to question why Christians could not offer counsel in and through the Church too.[34] Ordained into the Methodist ministry and backed by the friendship of Leslie Weatherhead, Kyle set up a Christian Counselling Centre in 1960 at Highgate Methodist Church in North London. With an advisory council of six drawn from 'professional or social work', an office staff, a team of four counsellors and a range of consultants from the medical, legal, educational and accounting professions, a training scheme was lined up and a counselling service launched.

At least initially, Bill Kyle seems to have insisted that Christians should counsel within a church-based framework. In response to the rise of secular counselling and 'the failure of the pastor or priest', he wrote, 'I feel strongly that this fact should drive the Church to repentance and renewal, and not to a ministry outside the Church.'[35] At the same time, he urged his fellow-pastors to see the value of training and learning from other disciplines: 'It is vital that our approach be acceptable to the medical profession and social workers, as without their help and approval our attempts in a healing ministry will be severely limited.'[36] And so, within the compass of a well informed and adequately trained team of Christian counsellors, Kyle stressed the mediation of Christ's concern for every aspect of a person's life. While acknowledging the value of a 'type of counselling work' which majors on the 'immediate power of God', as in a Billy Graham mission, Kyle argued that people's needs are often so deep-seated that improvement may have to be a more gradual affair.

Kyle's vision of a 'British expression of the best of pastoral psychology' led him to a period of preparatory work in the 1960s.[37] This included a training in Jungian analysis, a year or so at the American Foundation of Religion and Psychiatry in New York City and the gaining of a 'Doctor of Ministry' degree in Newton, Massachusetts. He returned to Britain in 1968 and founded the Westminster Pastoral Foundation (WPF) in 1970, initially based at the Central Hall, Westminster.

From the beginning the WPF looked to its American colleagues for inspiration. In the early days, John Maes, professor of pastoral counselling at Boston University, was invited over to guide in the establishing of training programmes and procedures for this important counselling centre. In 1978, Edward E. Thornton, professor of the psychology of religion at the Southern Baptist Theological Seminary, Louisville, came to Britain as consultant to Bill Kyle and the WPF. Although these American links have been formative, Thornton, in his address in 1980 following Kyle's death, criticised the British tendency to declare 'that in clinical pastoral counselling the power is in America and the innocence is in Britain and Europe'. He urged members of the WPF to be aware of 'the authentic power of positive self-esteem as the creators of a British institution responsive to the needs of the British people'.[38]

In time, WPF moved from Westminster to Kensington Square in West London and has, through the years, developed a highly reputable system of training in pastoral counselling – including a foundation course, which is usually full-time for one year, and a range of part-time courses that take two or three years and lead to varying degrees of accreditation under the Institute of Pastoral Education and Counselling. The courses offer personal therapy from an approved therapist, besides seminar workshops and the supervision of casework. Specialist training in group work, and family and marital therapy are also available. In recent years a number of other centres, affiliated to the WPF, have been established in the provinces, making training and counselling more widely accessible.

Even though the WPF continues to speak of 'pastoral' counselling, its roots in Bill Kyle's earlier vision seem to have loosened. The Rev David Porter, currently the Co-ordinator for Affiliated Centres, addresses himself to this issue.[39] He sees the adjective 'pastoral', in the context of counselling, as relating to 'the meaning given to life and to the values and attitudes which shape a person's destiny'. He insists that 'at no time is counselling an attempt to convert a client or to unduly influence a client to any particular creed or philosophy of life'. Nonetheless, Porter continues, 'pastoral counselling contains the possibility of the new life which is God's wish for his creatures whether or not this is recognised by those who are helped'.

Herein lies a dilemma which is perhaps at the heart of the fraternisation between liberal Christianity and the secular psychologies. While agreeing with Porter that God's grace and love can and do move in the lives of people who are oblivious of the source of their blessing, I wonder how far this thinking has shifted from the healing, sustaining, reconciling and guiding perspectives of traditional pastoral care. Although one cannot deny the excellence of WPF training in methods of counselling, the Christian origins of the movement seem to be largely bypassed in, for example, the Short Course Programme for 1982. This included seminars on our 'relationship to the Gods and Goddesses within', using the signs of the Zodiac and the Tarot as 'a map for the journey', and 'a weekend exploration of the inner world, brought to life through fairy tales'. The announcement of other courses, on such important subjects as communication, masculinity, mid-life crises, grief and self-awareness, gave no hint, at least in the official brochure, of the relevance of the Good Shepherd to people's needs.

Peter G. Liddell, director of pastoral counselling in the diocese of St Albans, writes that 'the whole exciting tradition' of psycho-analytic and humanistic thinking 'is available to the pastoral counsellor to accept, reject and refine'.[40] On the whole, from the 1920s through to the early 1970s there seems to have been more 'accepting' and 'rejecting' than 'refining' of secular insight by the Church. We have noted a strong tendency to 'accept' within the liberalism of many in the pastoral counselling movement. Let us now look at a Christian response which is primarily that of rejection, or reaction.

Reaction

Although many Christians seem to have hailed the secular psychologies with welcoming fervour as bringing in a new age of healing for humanity's ills, there were others in the Church who saw the dangers of a wholesale assimilation of this messianic dream. Anton Boisen's words of warning were largely unheeded by the rapidly flourishing CPE movement and well known pastors like Harry Emerson Fosdick in New York and Leslie Weatherhead in London seem to have absorbed all too readily the presuppositions of psychoanalysis. The trend was a Christian liberalism which drifted towards the shoals of seeing God as benignly permissive and regarding humankind as neurotic rather than sinful.

Hobart Mowrer

One of the most outspoken critics of this tide of opinion in the 1950s was the neo-behaviourist, O. Hobart Mowrer (1907–1982) of the University of Illinois. Describing himself as an 'active churchman', he inveighed against Freud, whom he regarded as 'the Pied Piper who beguiled us into serious misconceptions and practices'.[41] Changing the metaphor, Mowrer also referred to David Bakan's 1958 study *Freud and the Jewish Mystical Tradition* in which Freud is said to have seen himself as the new lawgiver destined to lead people 'out of slavery and oppression'.[42] Unlike Moses who, under God, sought the deliverance of the people from their sins, Freud seems to have sought humankind's release from the very idea of sin.

Mowrer, as early as 1947, attacked Freud's 'impulse theory' of anxiety in that it tends to explain away the notions of human sin, guilt and responsibility. The psychoanalyst's idea that we are neurotic rather than sinful, because there is a universal tendency to repress the things we want to do, is reversed by Mowrer's 'guilt theory' in which the blameworthy things we have actually done lead to our anxiety. Freud said we are unhappy because we give way neurotically to a harsh superego that stops us doing pleasurable things; Mowrer countered by saying that we are unhappy because we yield sinfully to our lower natures while ignoring the voice of conscience.[43]

Although orthodox belief will respond readily to Mowrer's diatribe against the sin of dismissing sin, closer scrutiny of his views reveals some important divergence from those of traditional Christianity. He helpfully points out, in fact, that guilty men and women not only need an opportunity to confess their failures but also an encouragement to make restitution where they have wronged others. Quoting Bonhoeffer, Mowrer rightly warns us against the danger of 'cheap grace':

> Cheap grace is the preaching of forgiveness without requiring repentance . . . Cheap grace is grace without discipleship, grace without the Cross, grace without Jesus Christ, living and incarnate . . .[44]

However, Mowrer comes across somewhat confusingly in the debate about the place of 'faith' and 'good works' in a person's salvation. For example, he advocates 'good works' to achieve 'atonement or restitution', presumably using the word 'atonement' to signify peace-making with other people rather than with God.[45] He criticises the doctrine of substitutionary atonement through Christ's sacrificial death as fostering a response of 'cheap grace' and attacks the concept of 'justification by faith' as causing demoralisation in people's lives by its apparent arbitrariness.[46] He writes, 'Salvation comes, if it comes at all, only by the grace and unpredictable favour of God'.[47] Mowrer carries his attack on divine bounty and apparent fickleness into a dismissal of the teaching in Ephesians 2:4–10, 14–16, in which Paul declares that the initiative for our salvation and reconciliation is entirely with a merciful God who 'made us alive with Christ even when we were dead in transgressions'. In reality, God's largesse need not lead to 'cheap grace'. Some awareness of the enormity of our sin and the boundlessness of God's grace can flow, rather, into the humbling realisation that 'we are God's workmanship, created in Christ Jesus to do good works, which God prepared in advance for us to do' (verse 10).

Mowrer shies away from Christian orthodoxy as the way forward. He feels that religion should stress 'principle' rather than 'God *as person*' and looks for a common ground between science and the world's faiths.[48] As a behaviourist he shows more than a streak of pragmatism when he advocates, with Richard Niebuhr, an 'empirical Christianity' which is validated by its 'accomplishments' instead of being reduced 'to a set of dogmatic asseverations which are to be taken purely on faith'.

Perhaps less controversially, Mowrer writes that pastoral counselling 'is surely a disguised return to the confessional'. Others have widened the point to include the whole of secular psychology, both in theory and practice, as having all the hall-marks of a new religion. Thomas Szasz, the 'anti-psychiatry' psychiatrist sees 'medical' psychiatry as a 'mutilation' of the 'religious and rhetorical nature of psychotherapy'.[49] Christian writers, including Jay Adams, Paul Vitz and William Kirk Kilpatrick, writing in the 1970s and early 1980s, have helped to form a strong critique of the messianic claims of the secular psychologies. Adams, influenced by Mowrer's anti-Freudianism and offering an important example of a Christian methodology of counselling, will be discussed more appropriately in chapter eleven.

Paul Vitz

Paul C. Vitz, writing as an associate professor of psychology at New York University, has made an outstanding contribution, to the view that psychology has overreached itself, in his book, *Psychology as Religion: the cult of self worship*. He describes how, during his work as an experimental psychologist in the mid 1960s, he began to see the fallacies of much of the humanistic thinking about personality. Becoming a Christian in the early

1970s, he began to disown the 'self-theories', seeing them as symptomatic of a 'form of secular humanism based on worship of the self'.[50]

Whereas Mowrer launches his main attack on Freud's dismissal of the importance of sin and guilt, Vitz tackles the 'selfism' of humanistic and existential viewpoints as represented in the works of Erich Fromm, Carl Rogers, Abraham Maslow and Rollo May. He traces the origins of their theories back to Ludwig Feuerbach (1804–1872), a theologian who studied philosophy in Berlin under Hegel. Feuerbach, in his *The Essence of Christianity* (1841), sums up his own essential atheism in the words: 'Theology is nothing else than anthropology – the knowledge of God nothing else than a knowledge of man.'[51] Although he does not clarify the historical links, Vitz shows how Feuerbach's God-denying man-centredness is mirrored in the selfism of latter day humanists.[52] The consequent shift from worshipping God to deifying the self received a powerful fillip, Vitz argues, in the writings and preaching of Harry Emerson Fosdick and Norman Vincent Peale, both nurtured within the liberal Protestantism of New York City in the 1930s and 1940s. Vitz describes this time of disillusionment in these words:

> The period of Fosdick and Peale was one of transition, in which a generation of faltering Christians, bored with and sceptical of basic Christian theology and ignorant of spiritual life, accepted an increasingly humanist notion of the self which had been dressed up with superficial Christian language and concepts.[53]

In his central critique of today's psychology, Vitz shows that humanistic selfism is, at heart, antithetical to Christianity at every point. Its 'idolatrous narcissism' leads to a love which leaves God out of the reckoning, to a creativity which is purely *self*-expressive and to a view that suffering always lacks meaning. In contrast, the Christian learns to love both God and others in response to the divine love, seeks to be creative as part of service and worship, and can, at times, see a redemptive purpose in affliction.[54]

In a fascinating chapter titled 'Beyond the secular self', Vitz demonstrates that 'the procedure of being objective is the fundamental psychological operation behind the growth of the self'.[55] It is humanistic psychology's craze of standing back in order to 'objectify' the self that, it is argued, leads to the grim results of a debased view of people and an emotional distancing from one another.[56] Not only does the observing subject begin to have power over the observed object, so that, for example, men and women become sex *objects*, but the subject, in time, is reduced to the level of the object. This power-conscious 'objectification' can lead to situations where 'the master becomes defined by his slaves, the subject by its objects, the psychologist by his rats or pigeons or cats'. This two-way dehumanising process inevitably yields estrangement and alienation, and is marked by an ugly self-centredness. To illustrate, Vitz cites a survey carried out on several hundred young people from Columbia and Barnard Colleges in the late 1960s and early 1970s and described in Herbert Hendin's *The Age of Sensation* (1975). Hendin writes of these students: 'This culture is marked by a self-interest and ego-centrism that increasingly reduces all relations to the question: What am I getting out of it?'[57]

And so, Vitz continues, persistent objectification leads to a 'painful double-bind', wherein individuals either exploit one another or withdraw from contact into a 'machine-like, emotion-free competence'. Either way, this 'existential narcissism' moves inexorably towards psychological death.

How can men and women escape the grim destiny that arises from determined selfism? Vitz answers:

> . . . the only way out is to lose the self, to let it go and once more willingly become an object again – not an object naively fused with the flow of life . . . nor an object to be controlled by other selves acting as subjects, but an object in the love and service of God.[58]

He admits that this 'letting-go' is 'no easy task' and that it is 'never perfect or complete'. It may begin through a sudden conversion or as a result of years of struggle. He argues that a major barrier to progress 'is not lack of knowledge but the presence of the selfist will to power'. It is this pride that must learn to give way to the humbling perspectives of God's revelation, wherein we are referred to as the Good Shepherd's sheep, called to be servants of all and urged to be childlike.[59] In this context, Vitz makes a moving personal plea for an 'updated orthodox theology' which will open up the paths of submission, humility, obedience and dependence on God more clearly – not least for proud and wilful academics and professionals.[60]

William Kilpatrick

William Kirk Kilpatrick, in his *Psychological Seduction: the failure of modern psychology* combines Mowrer's concern about the neglect of sin and Vitz's critique of selfism in an extended analysis of the rivalry between psychology and Christianity. An associate professor of educational psychology at Boston College, Kilpatrick, like Vitz, describes how he, once enamoured by humanistic psychology, slowly turned to 'real Christianity'.[61] In seeing psychology and Christianity as 'competing faiths' he shows how, at every turn, psychology has less to offer humanity than the Christian religion. He contrasts, for example, the arrogant assertiveness of self-love as advocated by humanistic psychology with the 'innocent' and valuable characteristics of a self-love that is compatible with Christian belief: a basis in our worth as God's handiwork; a simple wish for our own happiness; and a pleasure in serving a purpose in life.[62]

Further, Kilpatrick shows how secularism interferes with a sense of the sacred through three main habits of mind.[63] These are: *subjectivism*, wherein all ideas are given 'equal weight' and no area is permitted any intrinsic specialness; *reductionism*, in which everything is reduced to the lowest common factor; and psychological *naturalism*, by which Kilpatrick means an individualism that values spontaneity and treats social commitment as suspect. He feels that these subversive ways of handling life are given further impetus by the pervasive 'American Spirit' which is democratic, independent, optimistic, values 'positive' thinking and enterprise, and is impatient for results.[64] And so, Kilpatrick asserts, present-day psychology, imbued with American pragmatism, infiltrates the Church to produce: a *Christian subjectivism* which declares that nobody but the Holy Spirit can tell it what to believe; a *Christian reductionism* that tries to boil down the mystery of God into a few commonplaces; and a *Christian naturalism* that devalues social roles and is overfamiliar towards the sacred.

Kilpatrick, in common with Vitz but unlike Mowrer, declares a return to Christian orthodoxy in the face of the rival claims of secular psychology. Mowrer advises a form of universalism that plays down the idea of God as person, whereas both Vitz and Kilpatrick urge a bowing down before the Lord Jesus Christ. Kilpatrick completes his critique with a reminder of our glorious destiny in Christlikeness: 'We shall be most ourselves when we become the self God intends us to be. And that, truly, will be a self to marvel at.'[65]

Dialogue

Although Christian responses to the blandishments of secular psychology have tended to polarise into either an adoring fealty to the new 'messiah' or a staunch rejection of this latest 'tempter of the faithful', a number of psychologists and theologians have entered into a dialogue which seeks mutual understanding and respect. We have already noted a great deal of discussion and cooperation between the caring professions through the influences of people like Boisen, Weatherhead and Kyle, besides observing the carefully worded appraisals in the criticisms of modern psychology by such as Vitz and Kilpatrick. However, in recent years, the debate on the relation between psychological and theological ways of meeting humanity's needs has been sharpened. For instance, in spite of the strongly 'assimilative' element in the pastoral counselling movement, the European Conference on Pastoral Care and Counselling, meeting in Poland in 1981, considered 'Religious Values and Experience in Pastoral Care and Counselling', a theme which helped to correct the movement's 'neglect of theology and spirituality'.[66]

Let us consider, in outline, three of the recent contributors to this dialogue: the psychologists Malcolm Jeeves and Gary Collins; and the theologian Thomas Oden.

Malcolm Jeeves

Malcolm A. Jeeves, professor of psychology at St Andrews University, undertakes a clarifying exercise in his *Psychology and Christianity: the view both ways*. He aims to give guidelines for 'answering questions which arise as one seeks to relate what psychologists have discovered to what Christians believe and do'.[67] His approach is an open-minded one in which he points out that many 'pseudo-conflicts' between science and religion have arisen because neither side has made allowances for the concepts and language of the other.[68] He takes the example of 'guilt', where the psychologist and the Christian minister are likely to use the same word with quite different meanings. Jeeves urges a tolerance of each other's perceptions and writes, 'It would be a mistake to ask, is the patient a sinner or is he just neurotic? The point is that he is "both-and" simultaneously.'[69]

In an even-handed way Jeeves criticises psychology for its reductionism and Christianity for its paranoia. Along with Donald MacKay and others, Jeeves uses the term 'nothing-buttery' to indicate the regrettable trend in the behavioural sciences towards demeaning humanity by such formulae as 'man is "Nothing but" a complex animal, a complex machine, or the result of environmental forces'.[70] On the other hand, he advises the Christian to make the effort 'to assess the factual basis of any claims made in the name of psychology before rushing in to generate conflicts between such findings and Christian beliefs'.[71]

C. Stephen Evans sees Jeeves as a 'perspectivalist' with regard to the limitations of science.[72] In this view, Evans argues, there are dimensions to the reality which science explores that science cannot actually perceive. At the same time, both science and theology have their respective domains of inquiry and their own validity within those domains. Scientific and theological accounts of humanity are complementary and both are seen to be true. A clinical psychologist meeting the apostle Paul might note his prestigious background, singleness, intelligence, zeal over whatever cause he takes up, concern about his fellow-Christians and tendency to dominate. His 'scientific' appraisal might conclude that here is a gifted extravert of small stature who has become an over-compensated 'high achiever'. A theologian may or may not agree with the psychologist's conclusions but the fact that Paul can be viewed purely at sociological and psychological levels should not be disputed. These perspectives need not detract from the overarching claim that the pharisee Saul was challenged, called and turned around by the risen Lord on the Damascus road. His pedigree, personality and propensities were submitted to God for a life completely re-channelled as the 'apostle to the Gentiles'. As we consider this example, we can appreciate Evans' opinion that the 'perspectivalists', although holding a reasonable position, need to ask, 'concerning the various models in terms of which man can be viewed, "Which of these accounts is more ultimate?"[73]

Gary Collins

Although Malcolm Jeeves acknowledges the primacy of a biblical view of man, Gary R. Collins, in his *The Rebuilding of Psychology: an integration of psychology and Christianity*, does take the debate further by seeking to lay a 'new foundation' for psychology. Collins, professor of pastoral psychology at Trinity Evangelical Divinity School, Illinois, demonstrates the seriously faulted base of both experimental and clinical psychology by exposing the dehumanising trends in five of the main presuppositions: empiricism, determinism, relativism, reductionism and naturalism.[74] Having displayed the undermining features of each of these assumptions in their more extreme forms, he reasons that if we can improve on these fundamentals then 'we must be willing to replace some of our old foundations – even if that new core of psychology gets us into the area of religion'.[75]

In preparing the ground for his new basis for psychology, which does, believe it or not, 'get us into the area of religion', Collins looks at the framework set out in *Faith Seeks Understanding* (1971) by the philosopher, Arthur Holmes.[76] Holmes postulates that religion and science are related in three main ways:

1 *Both use 'models' in order to explain reality*, in which a model is a 'picture, analogy, or small copy of something that is too complicated to grasp directly'. Freud's use of a 'biological' model, wherein people are viewed primarily as complex animals, and the 'pastoral' model in the Bible, which uses the language of shepherd and sheep for the Lord and his followers, are examples of such analogies.

2 *Conflict between them is really over assumptions and interpretation.* Collins notes that the scientist 'seeks to give precise descriptions of a limited body of data' whereas the theologian, who also pursues accuracy, 'tends to use more picturesque and metaphysical terms to comprehend God and his creation'. This is the 'perspectivalist' view that Jeeves majors on.

3 *Science finds its 'ultimate meaning' in religion.* There are only two sources, Holmes argues, for scientific assumptions: theism, which is open to the 'vertical' dimension; and nontheistic naturalism, which can look solely to the 'horizontal'.

In his chapter 'Psychology in a Vertical Dimension', Collins acknowledges the difficulty of either proving God's existence or his 'nonexistence'. However, he continues, 'of the two alternatives . . . only the assumption that God exists gives a rationale for order in the universe and an explanation for the purpose, dignity, and destiny of man – who is, after all, the prime subject matter of psychology'.[77] In a carefully reasoned discussion, Collins seeks to establish a basic premise – *that God exists and is the source of all truth* – and a corollary – *that man who exists is able to know the truth*. He undergirds his argument by referring to both *general*, or *natural*, *revelation*, whereby God reveals truth through nature, history, science and human perception, and *special revelation*, in which God discloses himself through the biblical record. Although the 'biblical revelation has a higher priority' than natural revelation, Collins declares that, ultimately, truths from both these sources 'cannot contradict each other': 'God's Word and God's world are in perfect harmony.'

In building a 'new foundation' for psychology, Collins looks to both special and natural revelation to lay down six 'working assumptions' over the basic premise and corollary just mentioned.[78] The first five of these are revisions of secular psychology's 'raw material' of empiricism, determinism, relativism, reductionism and naturalism:

1 *Expanded empiricism*, in which empirical studies of people are still part of scientific investigation but where God's direct influence in the lives of men and women is also acknowledged.
2 *Determinism and free will*, whereby both perspectives are assented to and the place of the supernatural is included.
3 *Biblical absolutism*, wherein 'unlimited relativism' is rejected and God's unchanging ways and laws are submitted to.
4 *Modified reductionism*, in which the task of psychological research is not seen primarily as the fragmentation of human behaviour, but rather as the study of man in his wholeness and with as much precision as possible.
5 *Christian supernaturalism*, where nontheistic naturalism is discarded and all order is viewed as originating with 'a sovereign God who created the universe and holds it all together'.

The final 'working assumption' is:

6 *A biblical anthropology,* giving a 'model of man derived from the Bible' (see next chapter).

Finally, Collins gives some tentative conclusions in the complex field of the integration of psychology and theology. Looking to Richard Bube's *The Human Quest* (1971). Collins presents a 'levels of description' approach in which, as with Jeeves' 'perspectivalist' position, 'both theological and scientific explanations can be simultaneously valid and invalid'.[79] He is aware of the fear of obliteration in both disciplines but argues that, in building on his 'new foundation', 'each of the two fields stands to benefit from coming together' and 'there is enough uniqueness in each field to prevent the elimination of either'.

Thomas Oden

Thomas C. Oden, professor of theology and ethics at Drew University, New Jersey, is a key figure in the dialogue that has taken place between theology and psychology since the 1950s, partly because of his shrewd and vigorous theological thinking and partly because of his wide experience of the 'therapy explosion'. Throughout his academic career he has adventurously explored the interface between theology and psychology, revealing a refreshing courage and enthusiasm as each new pitch is tackled. Unfortunately, we can only allude to some of Oden's important insights in the space of this chapter and so I propose to concentrate mainly on two of his books, *Kerygma and Counseling* (1966) and *Agenda for Theology* (1979), which span his journey from a perceptive liberalism to what he calls 'postmodern Christian orthodoxy'.

In *Kerygma and Counseling,* Oden puts forward the central thesis that 'there is an implicit assumption hidden in all effective psychotherapy which is made explicit in the Christian proclamation'.[80] This 'implicit assumption', he claims, is that all men and women, whether they know it or not, are acceptable to God.

It is difficult to be sure what Oden, in line with many writers in the 1950s and 1960s, means by this 'acceptability' but he seems to argue that every individual is a recipient of the divine love, regardless of the counter-effects of sin and a lack of repentance. He writes:

> In our prodigality, alienation, estrangement, frustration, guilt, and hostility we find we are still loved by the Father and received into sonship. The divine love is not a reality we discover but a reality that discovers us. We do not win God, he wins us.[81]

Oden uses here the parable of the prodigal son but apparently soft-pedals the context of the 'rejoicing in the presence of the angels of God over one sinner who repents' (Luke 15:10). Nevertheless, Oden's implication that God's accepting love is always reaching out to needy people is surely a right one. Moreover, this 'implicit assumption' of man's acceptance is 'made explicit in the Christian proclamation' – the *kerygma*. This kerygma means the 'preaching or announcement of the good news that Jesus is the Christ', the 'expected deliverer'.[82] Although Oden is at this point muted on the question of human sinfulness, its reality is embedded in the 'making explicit' of this 'good news'.

A second mainstay of Oden's argument is the vital nature of 'self-disclosure' within the context of effective therapy. Looking to the psychologist, Sidney M. Jourard, in his *The Transparent Self: self disclosure as well-being* (1964), Oden points out that the psychotherapist needs to be open and honest if the client is to respond with 'self-disclosure'. This responsive sharing is therapeutic: Jourard writes, 'No man can come to know himself except as the outcome of disclosing himself to another person'.[83] As a result of Jourard's perception, Oden imaginatively extends the discussion by declaring the need to explore an 'analogy between the divine self-disclosure in the Christ event and human self-disclosure in effective counselling'. Daringly, he chooses the theology of Karl Barth and the client-centred therapy of Carl Rogers as the twin focus of his search.

Oden sees Barth's *analogia fidei*, analogy of faith, as giving a perspective that is refreshingly new in the debate between theology and psychology. The term 'analogy of faith' comes from Romans 12:6 where Paul encourages the use of God's gifts and urges that prophecy be used 'in proportion to our faith' (RSV). This indicates, for Barth, a relationship of analogy, proportion or correspondence 'in which human knowledge of God is converted into man's being known by God'.[84] As Oden writes: 'Faith then proceeds to use human language to reflect analogically upon itself as having been known and discovered by God. Hence, the analogy of faith.'[85]

The 'analogy of faith' is perhaps best understood by contrasting it with the *analogia entis*, the 'analogy of being'. Most of us, when searching for ways to show some sort of correlation between divine and human qualities or activities, argue from the human to the divine. We might say that being a human father can be compared with the fatherhood of God or that a psychotherapeutic interview corresponds to some extent to, say, God's healing activity. Here we are using the 'analogy of being', starting with a 'natural entity or relationship' and then searching for 'some attribute of God with which it corresponds'.[86] In the 'analogy of faith', advocated by both Barth and Oden, the direction of comparison is reversed. In this case the analogy 'begins with the divine word or activity as it is received and understood in faith and perceives the natural entity or relationship from the vantage point of the divine activity'. In this way of thinking, God's revelation about his fatherhood is studied and wondered at before seeing any correspondence in human fatherhood; similarly, we come to know of the Lord's healing action before turning to see the therapeutic situation as analogous.

Using Barth's 'analogy of faith', Oden turns his attention to Rogers' 'client-centredness' and postulates five main correlations between God's activity, the therapist's actions and the individual's response.[87] The 'most representative' of these analogies is that between the Lord's incarnation, a counsellor's empathy and a client's increase in self-understanding. In the incarnation 'God assumes our frame of reference, entering into our human situation of finitude and estrangement, sharing our human condition even unto death.' Oden sees a correlation with our Lord's 'self-emptying' (Philippians 2:5–7) in the therapeutic process of 'placing oneself in the frame of reference of another, perceiving the world as he perceives it, sharing his world with him', so that the client knows he is accepted and understood. Even though such analogous reasoning offers an enriched perspective on counselling, Oden admits that the 'analogy of faith' breaks down at certain crucial points – not least when we see that 'God takes our sin and estrangement upon himself', whereas the therapist can do no more than share imaginatively in the client's suffering.[88]

In the Preface to the 1978 edition of *Kerygma and Counseling*, Oden writes:

the promised theological revolutions of the messianic late 1960s and early 1970s have, by and large, misunderstood the perniciousness of sin, overestimated human potential, idealized autonomous individual freedom, and have in the meantime tended to become patricidal toward the Christian tradition.[89]

We see Oden's drive to reaffirm that 'Christian tradition' continuing through into the early 1980s. In his 1980 paper 'Recovering Lost Identity', he demonstrates how the 'classical pastoral tradition' of the Church has been grossly neglected in the twentieth century.[90] A survey of seven standard works on pastoral theology written at the turn of the century reveals a generous number of references to key historical figures in the realm of pastoral care, including Chrysostom, Augustine, Calvin, Luther and Baxter. A similar assessment of seven major contemporary writers on pastoral counselling – four Americans and three Europeans – shows a liberal sprinkling of the names of Freud, Jung, Rogers, Sullivan, Berne and Fromm – but not one reference to the luminaries of Christian pastoral history. In this paper, Oden urges an approach to Christian pastoral care which turns again to 'the classical tradition for its bearings, yet without disowning what it has learned from modern clinical experience'.[91] This rediscovery of our pastoral heritage is pursued further in his *Pastoral Theology: essentials of ministry* (Harper and Row 1983) and *Care of Souls in the Classic Tradition* (Philadelphia: Fortress 1984).

Oden's *Agenda for Theology* (1979) sets out both a critique of modernity and a basis for a reappraisal of traditional Christian care as a combined springboard for his later writings. Looking back at his personal history as a 'movement theologian' caught up in each new wave of secular therapy, Oden now sees the need for a stability of thinking which is 'better prepared to discern which movements are more or less an expression of Christ's ministry to the world'.[92] He attacks, in particular, modernity's tendency to declare of each innovation: 'New is good, newer is better, and newest is best', whereby an 'inner circle' of modernism has reached a 'dramatic movement of precipitous moral decline' following the hedonism of the 1960s and 1970s.[93] Although many modern minds seek to reassure us that we are on an upward path, 'the actual history of late modernity is increasingly brutal, barbarian, and malignant'. There is a desperate need to find our way back to the centre of gravity amidst the pendulum swings of societal trends – a centre 'which is the proclamation of God's steadfast love in Christ addressed to ever-changing human environments'.

Oden holds his theological position of 'postmodern Christian orthodoxy' as one who has 'been through the best and the worst that modernity has to offer' and declares that he is amongst those who 'have happened on classical Christianity'.[94] He compares this stance with that of the apostle Paul who had, prior to his conversion, experienced the 'full rigours of a hellenizing Judaism' and had 'opposed Christianity with all his might'. Consequently, Paul, the erstwhile persecutor, and today's 'postmodern' Christian are able to grasp the faith 'from the inside with a special intensity'.

Oden asks why 'neo-orthodoxy' failed and 'fundamentalism' did not stir in the face of modernity's challenge to classical Christianity.[95] He argues that the 'neo-orthodox' theologians, Paul Tillich, Karl Barth, Reinhold Niebuhr, Emil Brunner and Rudolf Bultmann, were 'reformist change agents rather than conservators of tradition'. In retrospect, Oden continues, we detect a 'slightly adolescent psychological tinge or quality to much of their writing' in their desire to break free from the restraints of both liberalism and orthodoxy. On the other hand, 'fundamentalists'[96] and 'charismatics' tend to have avoided even the risk of contamination by modernity and so, although usually orthodox in their beliefs, lack the biting edge for the 'postmodern' who has rediscovered the classical faith. In a sentence, post-modern orthodoxy 'seeks only to represent the *old* orthodoxy in a credible way amid the actual conditions of the modern world'.

The 'agenda' for this postmodern theology is to be Christ-centred. Oden castigates the liberalism of his own background by writing: 'In only one century of focussing on the ethical relevance of Jesus' teaching, we have almost forgotten how to speak of and pray to Jesus Christ, the Son of God and Saviour of the world.[97]

In the same vein, Oden sees the living Lord as the centre of the 'circle of Christian tradition', a circle with a wide circumference that embraces the rich diversity of orthodox belief and practice.[98] From this circle a truly christocentric theology needs to continue the dialogue with secular psychology. Oden, after two decades of personal 'bridge-building', feels that 'the traffic is moving on the bridge only one way: from psychological speculation to rapt religious attentiveness'. In this 'one-sided' conversation, theology has been the listener, drinking in the words of psychology. Oden hopes for a 'viable two-way dialogue' but fears that theology is less willing to speak out than psychology is to listen.[99]

And so we have traced a range of Christian responses to the rise of the secular psychologies. Many respondents have just run with the tide of modernity, others have struck out defiantly away from such muddied waters, while yet others have entered into dialogue with one another in order to clarify the best direction to swim in. Returning to our picture of the forest, we have observed, in effect, that the part of the tree of pastoral care which has grown during this century relates in three main ways with its surroundings. A large and important section has spread out its branches to interweave imperceptibly with the vigorous outgrowths of Freudianism, secular personalism and transpersonalism. This part of the forest presents an impenetrable wall of foliage where one tree cannot readily be distinguished from another. A further area of the tree of pastoral care has grown vigorously away from the other trees and sprouts distinctively, but in some isolation. The remaining part of the tree angles towards the trees of secular psychology and, although it will always risk hybridisation and assimilation, seems to be the section of the tree of pastoral care which is most commanding and available to the rest of the forest.

ROUTE-FINDING IN THE FOREST

The Western world begins by making splits, then drawing boundaries, then solidifying those boundaries.

Gregory Bateson

The map is not the territory.

Alfred Korzybski

. . . it is manifest that man will never obtain a perfect knowledge concerning himself, unless *he has first beheld God's countenance and then descends from his look to the contemplation of self.*

John Calvin

So far, in this book, we have tried to find our way through the forest of counselling methodologies. This woodland, although rooted deeply in the psychologies of early civilisation, has been the scene of a massive proliferation of growth during the last hundred years or so – a growth comprising the four main psychological systems of behaviourism, psychoanalysis, personalism and transpersonalism, which cluster around the ancient tree of pastoral care. As we have wandered to and fro in this forest of the 'helping methodologies' we have found our path dividing amongst the hybridisations and mergings of the five burgeoning systems. Furthermore, we have observed, in the last chapter, three primary Christian responses to the secular psychologies – assimilation, reaction and dialogue, each producing its own distinctive development within the complex of the tree of pastoral care. These responses each tend, as we shall see, to form their individual range of counselling methodologies.

Having explored and roughly mapped this complicated terrain, let us now attempt to devise some sort of compass so that, when we encounter this or that method of counselling or psychotherapy, we can have an idea of where we are on the map. As Korzybski has pointed out, 'The map is not the territory' and so we cannot expect to have guidelines that answer all our 'on the spot' questions. However, a compass that at least helps us to ask the *right* questions of our whereabouts will be useful. So equipped, we will be better able to evaluate both secular and Christian approaches to counselling and, at the same time, assess and, if necessary, correct our own particular bearings in helping others.

While surveying the various psychological systems, it is likely that we will have been most questioning with respect to the philosophical assumptions about human nature that each of them makes. What is believed about human behaviour, instinct, inclination, motivation, deciding, reflecting, feeling, memory, relatedness, mortality and spirituality is central to each method-ology's stance concerning people in need. Moreover, as Ellis has written, 'in accordance with their belief-systems . . . therapists deliberately assume *some* kind of role with their patients'.[1] In other words, the *aims* and *methods* of therapies grow out of the 'belief-systems' or *assumptions* of therapists. If a man or woman is simply regarded as a higher animal where patterns of behaviour are of greatest importance, then behaviour-modification by methods of desensitising and deconditioning become appropriate. When a person is viewed primarily in terms of a 'will to meaning' then some form of existential analysis is likely to be applied. And so, I suggest, in our assessment of the many approaches in counselling, whether secular or religious, Christian or otherwise, we need to evaluate them from the vantage-point of a theology which includes a God-given understanding of human existence, i.e. a well reasoned *biblical anthropology*.

A biblical anthropology for evaluating methodologies

I realise that, in declaring the need for a 'well reasoned biblical anthropology', I am presupposing some resolution of two crucial questions: 'Why a *biblical* anthropology?' and, if the requirement of a scriptural perspective is granted, '*Which* biblical anthropology?' With respect to the first query, it must be evident from this book that I hold a 'high view' of the inspiration of the scriptures, seeing them as the trustworthy vehicle of God's explicit self-declaration. With regard to the second, I am aware of some aspects of the great debate that has taken place throughout Church history on the nature of man, including the divergence of views between Eastern and Western Christendom, Pelagius and Augustine, Arminius and Calvin, and, in this century, between Karl Barth and Emil Brunner. However, along with recent writers like H. D. McDonald and David Clines, I would like to argue that the following dimensions should be included in building up a biblical perspective on our humanity: we have *supreme value*; we are *living unities*; we have *broken relationships*; we are *restorable*.

Supreme value

Special creation

There is a conversation described in P. G. Wodehouse's *The Code of the Woosters* which goes:

> 'Have you ever seen Spode eat asparagus?'
> 'No.'
> 'Revolting. It alters one's whole conception of Man as Nature's last word.'[2]

In spite of our frailty and ineptness, including the way certain of us might eat asparagus, we human beings *are* 'Nature's last word' – or, better still, God's 'last word', the very peak of creation.

As McDonald points out, the specialness of the creation of humankind is underlined by the use of the adverb 'then' in Genesis 1 and 2.[3] In Genesis 1:26, God having completed his making of the vast and wonderful material universe, we read: '*Then* God said, "Let us make man . . ."' (RSV). Further, in Genesis 2:7, following the Lord's provision of a mist to relieve the earth's barrenness, we meet the same climactic word: '*then* the Lord God formed man of dust from the ground, and breathed into his nostrils the breath of life; and man became a living being' (RSV). The scene was set, the once arid ground was now watered, and some special being was needed to till the verdant land.

The uniqueness of man's creation is further suggested by the assumedly trinitarian and personal nature of the phrase, 'Let *us* make man . . .' (1:26), in contrast to the more general introductions, 'Let there be . . .' and 'Let the earth bring forth', which precede the earlier stages of the creation.

Thirdly, as has often been noted, the refrain, 'and God saw that it was good', which rounds off each creational phase, is superseded, following the advent of humanity, by the concluding, 'And God saw everything that he had made, and behold, it was *very* good' (1:31 RSV).

Special relation

Francis of Assisi once said, 'What a man is in the sight of God, so much he is and no more', and it is in their special relation to God that men and women are seen to have supreme value. This specialness is indicated in the evocative and mysterious statement that 'man' is created in the 'image of God'. We read in Genesis 1: 'Let us make man in our image, after our likeness' (verse 26, RSV) and 'So God created man in his own image, in the image of God he created him; male and female he created them' (verse 27).

From the earliest days of the Church, theologians have striven to find the precise meaning of the idea of man being made in God's image (*tselem*) and after his likeness (*demuth*). Although in the past a great deal has been made of distinguishing these two terms, scholarship today generally argues that the Hebrew words *tselem* and *demuth* are synonymous.[4] Further, many have concluded that the Bible 'never gives us any kind of systematic theory about man as the image of God'.[5]

Nevertheless, there have been innumerable attempts to nail the concept of humanity as image-bearer. Some, such as the sixteenth-century theologian Socinius, have emphasised that human *dominion* over the created order is implied; others have urged a view that people reflect God in their so-called '*higher*', or more *spiritual*, *qualities* only; others again, including G. von Rad writing in the 1950s, have declared a more holistic perspective urging that the human body must be included in the 'image'; and yet others have taken one particular aspect of our humanity as the main focus of being made after God's likeness, including *rationality*, *morality* and *personality*.[6]

Perhaps the most all-embracing views are those which emphasise *relationship* together with a *christological* dimension. Karl

Barth argues from Genesis 1:26 that the phrase, 'Let us make man in *our* image' gives a priority to relatedness within the Godhead – and that therefore the 'image' is most clearly seen in *partnership* between men and women, and in *community* between fellow human beings.[7] Paul K. Jewett in his *Man as Male and Female*, following this Barthian line, majors powerfully on the theme that the declaration 'male and female he created them' in Genesis 1:27b is an 'exposition' of 1:27a, 'So God created man in his own image'. Jewett affirms that 'Man, as created in the divine image, is Man-in-fellowship' and that 'the primary form of this fellowship is that of male and female'. From this understanding he points out the obligation to preserve 'one's own sexual integrity' and accept 'sexual partnership' as an integral part of human life. This 'sexual partnership' is a wider concept than marriage and includes the many aspects of a 'complex, creative, dynamic, all-pervasive human fellowship' between men and women.[8]

Calvin sought to plumb the depths of the mystery of *imago Dei* by exploring the restoring of that image in Christ and declaring that the 'likeness' contains the hallmarks of righteousness and holiness (Ephesians 4:24) and knowledge (Colossians 3:10). The Dutch theologian, G. C. Berkouwer has pursued this Christ-centred understanding of our humanity 'as the image of God' and writes that in the new life in Christ, 'which can be described in very different ways – newness, community, peace, joy – man is re-created in the image of God'.[9]

These important themes of 'Man-in-fellowship' and restoration in Christ are helpfully brought together by contemporary writers like David Clines, Derek Kidner and H. D. McDonald. Clines has noted, like others, that men and women are not only God's 'representatives' on earth but also his 'representations'. He writes, 'A representative may have little or nothing in common with the one he represents, but a representation resembles the original, and re-presents its original.'[10] Derek Kidner indicates this representational element when he declares that 'man . . . is an expression or transcription' of the creator – 'as one might attempt a transcription of, say, an epic into a sculpture, or a symphony into a sonnet'.[11]

H. D. McDonald brings all these threads of interpretation together and argues that they can be subsumed 'under the concept of sonship'.[12] Like Calvin and Berkouwer, McDonald looks to the New Testament to validate his view. He points out that Adam is called 'son of God' as the first of all forbears in the genealogical list at the end of Luke 3, and backs up his argument by a consideration of Christ as the true Son of the Father. McDonald suggests that the 'relationship of the Second Person of the Trinity to the Father in terms of sonship provides the pattern – the original image – in which man was created'. Other aspects of man's image-bearing, such as 'dominion over the world order', are included within the original unbroken filial relationship of Adam and Eve with their God.

Firstly, then, in assessing methodologies of counselling we need to ask whether the assumptions behind their theory and practice fit with the biblical view that people have supreme value – in that they are a special creation by God, made for a special relation with their creator, from which they are called into relationship with others as they exercise a responsible stewardship over God's world. Immediately, we can see that many approaches to therapy which imply purely biological or mechanistic ways of seeing people, or emphasise autonomy and individualism overmuch, are deficient in their basic anthropology.

Living unities

In everyday language we often show a view of human nature that seems to split the individual into different parts. It was once fashionable in evangelistic circles to talk of saving someone's 'soul' and it is not unusual to hear such comments as 'My "body" needs at least eight hours' sleep a night' and 'Sorry I can't make it – but I'll be there in "spirit"!' A further symptom of compartmentalised attitudes is shown in the contemporary tendency to speak of one's 'social life' and 'sex life' as if these aspects of living were dismembered from the mainstream of existence – rather like a hobby that is picked up and given up at will.

Such partitioning ways of thinking about our humanity are more Greek than Hebrew, more pagan than Christian. Plato held that the person is made up of three parts – body, soul and spirit – and this tripartite view has permeated the theology of Eastern Orthodox Christianity. Similarly, Stoicism, with its dichotomous thinking, influenced the Western Church primarily so that, for example, Tertullian, at the turn of the second century, could write, 'the entire man consists of two substances', referring to 'soul' and 'body'.[13]

However, many biblical scholars today argue that the scriptures point away from a stark trichotomy or dichotomy and towards a unitary view of the person. Stacey writes: 'The Hebrew did not see man as a combination of contrasted elements, but as a unity that might be seen under a number of different aspects. Behind each aspect was the whole personality.'[14] At a quick read, the Bible seems to regard human nature as divided up into a host of 'different aspects' and, in fact, something like eighty distinct parts of the body are mentioned in the Old Testament when human existence and activity are being described. And yet, as Stacey observes, 'behind each aspect was the whole personality'. These figure amongst the more frequently used terms: *soul*, often seen in the context of personal stress or deep desire; *spirit*, commonly found denoting supernatural influence; *flesh*, generally indicating that aspect of human life that is earth-bound; and *heart*, occurring both where thinking, intention or resolve are alluded to and where the individual's totality is stressed.[15] Similarly, in the New Testament, the Greek words *psyche, pneuma, sarx, soma*, etc. are used in ways that usually refer to certain aspects in the life of the whole person. Further, the promise of the bodily resurrection guarantees, for the Christian, continuity of life for one's entire being and complete transformation into Christ's likeness.[16] We might sum up this multi-dimensional view of human nature in the phrase 'plurality-in-unity': you and I are creatures of both great complexity and deep indissolubility. As McDonald says, man is a 'unity of dust and deity'.[17] Karl Barth makes the same attempt to capture the essence of our humanity when he writes that 'man is completely soul and completely body through the action of the living Creator'.[18]

And so, *secondly*, in our evaluation of approaches to counselling and therapy it is worth asking how adequately men and women are viewed in terms of their essential 'plurality-in-unity'. How much importance is given to all aspects of human life, and how readily are clients seen and treated as whole people? It is worth noting that many secular psychologies are reductionist in one way or another, in effect majoring on either the 'outer' aspect of a person, as in behaviourism and the so-called 'body' therapies, or on the 'inner' dimension, as with a number of analytical and transpersonal therapies. This is not to deny that many methodologies within these traditions seek a more holistic view, although they may, for practical reasons, emphasise a particular facet of personhood during therapy. In spite of biblical teaching on the unity of personality, there are a number of Christian approaches to counselling which seem to ignore whole areas of human existence. We see this trend, for instance, in styles of therapy which stress the cognitive and volitional to the neglect of the more feeling and creative aspects of the people they seek to help.

Broken relationships

Sadly, we cannot conclude the discussion at this stage by simply declaring that we are of 'supreme value' and that we are 'living unities'. The 'sonship' with which we were endowed at the creation has been abused and forfeited, and our sense of 'plurality-in-unity' has been severely fragmented. Although Mark Twain has, somewhat wistfully, said that 'Man is the creature made at the end of a week's work when God was tired', we cannot, although our rebellious nature would have it otherwise, blame any other being for our 'fall from grace'. We see, in the pages of scripture and of history, and in our everyday lives, that the seeds of disharmony have spread to all our relationships: with our creator God, with one another, with the created order, and within ourselves.

With God

The account in Genesis 3 of the initial, profoundly far-reaching break between the Lord God and his 'special creation' is a graphic one. We witness the shattering of man's filial fellowship with God and see the forging of the first links in a chain of grim consequences for humanity: a guilty fear ('they hid from the Lord God'); acute self-consciousness ('I was afraid because I was naked'); blaming others ('she gave me some fruit from the tree, and I ate it' and 'The serpent deceived me, and I ate'); a continuing bias towards wrongdoing and arrogant independence ('The man has now become like one of us, knowing good and evil. He must not be allowed to reach out his hand and take also from the tree of life and eat, and live for ever') and removal from the Lord's presence ('So the Lord God banished him from the Garden of Eden').

The effect of this rebellion permeates every aspect of human existence. This doctrine of 'total corruption' is derived from such statements as 'All have turned aside, they have together become corrupt; there is no-one who does good, not even one' (Psalm 14:3); 'The heart is deceitful above all things and beyond cure. Who can understand it?' (Jeremiah 17:9); and 'They are darkened in their understanding and separated from the life of God because of the ignorance that is in them due to the hardening of their hearts' (Ephesians 4:18). Berkouwer writes of the pervasiveness of sin: 'Scripture constantly makes it clear that sin is not something which corrupts relatively and partially, but a corruption which fully affects the radix, the root, of man's existence, and therefore man himself.'[19]

However, if sin is so corrupting, how is it that we see honour, altruism, beauty, loyalty and caring in the lives of those around us as well as lying, backbiting, pride, betrayal and selfishness? Here it is vital that we take note that the scriptures refer to men and women as divine image-bearers even *after* the fall. For example, in the covenant with Noah the Lord declares: 'Whoever sheds the blood of man, by man shall his blood be shed; for in the image of God has God made man' (Genesis 9:6) and James, writing of the dangers of an idle tongue, says: 'With it we bless the Lord and Father, and with it we curse men, who are made in the likeness of God' (James 3:9 RSV). Moreover, there are abundant references in the Bible which demonstrate that even sinful humankind is the object of the Lord God's love and workmanship.[20] It is here that we can speak of God's 'common grace' (also called 'general', 'preserving' and 'conserving' grace) wherein he endows us with a variety of 'natural' gifts, holds in check the ravages of evil within our humanity and enables many to achieve what is worthwhile in any and every walk of life. It is the apparent contradiction between human corruption and giftedness that has led Calvin to point out that 'in man's perverted and degenerate nature some sparks still gleam', Pascal to write that 'Man is only a reed, the weakest thing in nature; but he is a thinking reed' and Francis Schaeffer to refer to man as a 'glorious ruin'.[21]

With others

Although we have looked at Genesis 3 to demonstrate the rift between God and his 'special creation', it is in the same chapter that we also see the immediate and the predicted outcomes of disharmony between one person and another. In verse 16 the tragic distortion of the God-given equality and mutuality between men and women is forecast when the Lord says to the woman, 'Your desire will be for your husband, and he will rule over you'; as Kidner has said 'to love and to cherish' becomes 'to desire and to dominate'.[22] In Genesis 4 sin's productivity continues within the next generation as Cain's attitudes and actions towards his brother Abel bear the ugly fruit of envy, selfish anger, hatred and murder. The rest of the biblical record, history and human experience unfold the sorry tale of poisoned relationships: parent and child; husband and wife; brother and sister; friend and friend; neighbour and neighbour; ruler and subject; employer and employee; colleague and colleague; one race or nation and another. As we know, such discord can be expressed in the trivial and mundane as well as in the horror of murder, rape and torture. John V. Taylor refers to the banality of our alienation when he writes that God 'has made us little lower than gods, while our highest ambition is to be a little above the Joneses'.[23]

There is no doubt that our sin drives us towards isolation and yet, once more, our God is graciously at work limiting the degree of lostness and loneliness between one person and another. He has created us for relatedness and for community, and, in spite of our fallenness, we can still find a great deal of consolation and hope in our common humanity. Family life, friendships, camaraderie, the joining of clubs and societies, the playing of team games, working or sharing in groups, and even being driven together against a common enemy or because of a common need, are still part of our overall human experience. 'Sin indeed disturbs the whole of man's life, but in the midst of corruption sinful man again and again escapes the isolation which threatens him and again lives in the richness of his common humanity, divinely preserved'.[24]

With the created order

Mark Twain once said: 'Man is the only animal that blushes. Or needs to!' It is a hallmark of our forfeited 'sonship' that, in our moments of greatest sensitivity, we stand ashamed within the created order. Called to have dominion 'over all the earth' (Genesis 1:26, Psalm 8:5–8) and yet, through disobedience, committed to wearying toil (Genesis 3:17–19), men and women live their lives both in and out of harmony with 'Nature'. Once more we see two 'principles' at work: the leaven of human corruption – squandering, exploiting, poisoning and destroying the environment; and God's 'preserving grace' – checking the evil and endowing people with the abilities and the will to investigate, develop, husband, share and conserve natural resources with sensitivity and wisdom.

Within ourselves

Inevitably, because our sense of completeness is linked with our unbroken state of 'sonship', we lose our inner peace in losing our fellowship with the creator. We see, for example, this state of turmoil in Job when he cries in the midst of his afflictions: 'Why did I not die at birth?' (Job 3:11 RSV) and in Jeremiah's anguished statement: 'my soul is bereft of peace, I have forgotten what happiness is' (Lamentations 3:17 RSV). This sense of inner disintegration, although largely held back by God's 'common grace', is well portrayed by George Herbert, the seventeenth-century poet:

> Oh, what a thing is man! how far from power,
> From set'led peace and rest!
> He is some twenty sev'ral men at least
> Each sev'ral hour.[25]

And so, *thirdly*, in looking at any system of counselling, it is worth asking how its methodology views the seamier side of human nature. Do questions of personal sin, true guilt and individual responsibility give way, for instance, to a deterministic emphasis on the power of the instincts and the neurotic nature of all guilt? Or, within a more humanistic framework, are human beings seen as essentially good and well motivated for constructive change, or is their propensity for self-centredness acknowledged? Further, what does the approach considered say, not only about inner conflicts, but about disharmony between one person and another, about irresponsible attitudes to the community, and about misuse of the wider environment?

It is in this area of human fallenness that there is considerable difference of opinion between Christian styles of counselling and many of the secular therapies – particularly because the latter so often play down or deny the relevance of personal culpability. At the other extreme, there are certain schools of thought amongst Christian counsellors which seem to so stress man's 'total corruption' that divine 'common grace' is neglected, ignored or even rejected. Here there is a tendency to link every human problem to the individual's sin and to frown on any suggestion that the sovereign Lord might work in and through the 'unredeemed'.

Restorable

Just as a valuable old painting, begrimed through years of neglect and misuse in a dusty attic, can be restored to its former glory once it is found and rescued, so men and women, although sullied in every aspect of their being by sin, can find restoration in Christ to a 'former glory' that brings honour to the Father. Both David Cairns and H. D. McDonald refer back to this restorable 'former glory' when they present a close link between the ideas of the 'glory of God', the 'image of God' and the 'sonship' of God's 'special creation'. McDonald writes:

> Man's chief end is to glorify God. Such was God's intention for the man he made. But man could only respond to the divine desire in so far as he reflected God's glory. And it was in him so to do because he was created in the image of God with the gift of sonship.[26]

Through humankind's rebellion, all 'fall short of the glory of God', the image of God is obscured, although not lost, and the gift of sonship is spurned. It is through people becoming 'new creations' in Christ that God can be glorified once more, his image restored and adoption into the Father's new family effected.[27] Our resources and inspiration, mediated by the Spirit, are in the Lord Jesus Christ who is the perfect image of God, the unique Son and the one who supremely glorifies the Father.[28] Some of these strands are gathered together in 2 Corinthians 3:18: 'And we, who with unveiled faces all reflect the Lord's glory, are being transformed into his likeness with ever-increasing glory, which comes from the Lord, who is the Spirit.' It is the Christian's destiny 'to be conformed to the likeness of (God's) Son' (Romans 8:29) and it is the Father's good pleasure to bring 'many sons (and daughters!) to glory' (Hebrews 2:10). Herein is something so wonderful that it is almost incomprehensible. We sense some-thing of the believer's hesitancy before these mysteries in what has been called the 'Johannine stammering' of 1 John 3:2,3. Here the apostle declares both uncertainty: 'what we will be has not yet been made known' and certainty: 'we know that when (God) appears, we shall be like him'.

In the meantime, Christ's reconciling work in our lives restores not only our fellowship with the Father but our relationships with one another as we are adopted into a new community. This reconciliation is a deep work and makes possible the breaking down of every barrier of sin and misunderstanding.[29] The per-spective is cosmic, for we read that 'the creation itself will be set free from its bondage to decay and obtain the glorious liberty of the children of God' (Romans 8:21).

Fourthly, then, in our appraisal of both secular and Christian methodologies, we should query what hope is given for needy men and women within the assumptions held, and the aims and techniques used. We have already conceded that there is a great deal of everyday encouragement available to people as they respond to God's 'preserving grace'. However, it is in the almighty's 'special grace', reaching to us through his Son, that the only hope lies for radical and lasting change in human lives. It is in the consideration of such revolutionary new beginnings that most of the secular psychologies are woefully inadequate. Christ-ian approaches in counselling may also founder where either the expectation of possible change is pitifully low, thus belittling the Spirit's redeeming and sanctifying work, or where the anticipa-tion of healing presses for immediate results, thus demanding of God that he complete *now* what he has promised as our destiny in Christ.

Evaluating the methodologies

We have taken some time to establish the need for a valid biblical anthropology as a major part of an orthodox Christian approach to the vast array of counselling and psychotherapeutic methods. We can sum up our reasoning by posing this question of any methodology we seek to evaluate:

Do the assumptions, aims and methods of this particular methodology accord with divine revelation about human nature?

In other words, we should ask how the theory and practice of this or that approach squares up against the plumbline of God's self-disclosure about humankind – its *raison d'être*, 'plurality-in-unity', fallenness, giftedness, aspirations, redeemability and future.

Further, and we shall argue the point more fully in the coming pages, we need to raise a secondary question:

Do the assumptions, aims and methods of this particular methodology accord with scientific investigation where practicable?

Behind this query lies the presupposition that this is God's world and that scientific enterprise is a right use of human talent to explore and understand that world. In this respect, the oft-repeated phrase, 'all truth is God's truth' is in danger of becoming a cliché, not least because the concept of 'truth' is open to so many interpretations. Such statements as 'I love my wife', 'That is a beautiful sunset', 'The gravitational pull of the Earth is roughly six times that of the Moon' and 'Christopher Columbus sailed to America in 1492' are all valid, although their truth may be discussed on quite different grounds – experiential, aesthetic, scientific and historical. Without entering a philosophical debate, we can, nonetheless, maintain that scientific truth is one important aspect of the whole.[30] Further, where a certain methodology of therapy can be examined scientifically with regard to its concepts and effectiveness, then the thinking Christian will take note.

Christian responses to the methodologies

Although we have offered two questions to guide us in the assessment of the methodologies, we have to admit that we are rarely that tidy-minded in our appraisals. Christian responses to the secular psychologies and the counselling ways of fellow-believers spring from a variety of reason and unreason. Both the 'assimilation' and 'reaction' we explored in the last chapter can arise from clear or muddled thinking, perceptive or misguided intuition, identifying or rejecting emotions, firm or weak convictions. Furthermore, the 'dialogue' of the more open-minded may be carried out from fiercely contended positions or from readily relinquished viewpoints.

Behind the variety of more respectable reasons we might give for our own responses, and our own personal approaches to counselling and pastoral care, we need to see that we are all creatures of past and present experiences, as well as individual make-up. It is realistic to acknowledge that a Christian may choose a style of counselling which is, for example, directive and authoritarian for a variety of reasons. Ostensibly, the choice may be made because it is believed to be a thoroughly biblical one, while other people may quietly observe that here is a form of therapy that suits the counsellor's robust personality and fits well with upbringing, background and experience of life. Similarly, another may counsel in a less confrontational and more reflective way, arguing that this is surely a more Christian tack, while friends may notice the link between the style of counselling and a type of person who is fearful of authority and disagreement.

Nevertheless, whatever the range of reasons for our choices in counselling theory and practice, I would like to put forward a conceptual framework for analysing Christian responses to the methodologies. This seems to me to be a useful exercise on several grounds. Hopefully, it will help us evaluate our own reactions to other methods and understand why we follow our particular brand of counselling. Secondly, it should aid our assessment of the bewildering array of approaches adopted by other Christian counsellors and therapists. Thirdly, it will help us re-evaluate and, if necessary, change our assumptions, aims and techniques as we seek to help the needy.

Bases for response

As we survey the contemporary scene of counselling methods used by Christians, we are struck most of all by its diversity, ranging from a number of positions held by evangelicals – each purporting to hold a truly biblical view – through a variety of mystical and sacramental emphases, to opinions which embrace more liberal and open-minded understandings. I would like to suggest that there are three cardinal parameters which may help us differentiate one stance from another. Each guideline is closely allied to the other two. All three, in turn, are an extension of the two questions we posited on pages 255–256.

The emphasis given to general and special revelation

We have already proposed the need to ask of a methodology whether its assumptions, aims and methods 'accord with divine revelation about human nature'. Having postulated some of the main ingredients of a biblical anthropology, let us now turn our attention to the phrase 'divine revelation' for it is on this concept that so much of the debate between Christian counsellors hinges.

It is because this book is looking primarily at *psychology* that we have concentrated on the 'divine revelation about *human nature*'; and yet, of course, directly we mention God's self-disclosure we move into the realm of *theology*. We cannot in fact divorce the true knowledge of our humanity from the knowledge of God, and the theologian, in studying the knowledge of God, looks to divine revelation. As Bernard Ramm puts it: *'Revelation is the auto-biography of God*, i.e. it is the story which God narrates about himself. It is that knowledge *about* God which is *from* God'.[31] This 'autobiography of God' has been traditionally subdivided into general and special revelation.

General revelation has been variously defined but is basically God's 'general' revelation for all people. Calvin regarded the 'skilful ordering of the universe' as a 'sort of mirror in which we can contemplate God, who is otherwise invisible'.[32] Berkouwer, writing in a Calvinist tradition, shows how 'man is . . . confronted with the reality of God's revelation . . . with the sovereign working of God in nature, in history, and in human existence'.[33] Ramm declares that 'general revelation . . . is both the fundamental witness of the Creator *to* the creature and the primal witness of the Creator *in* the creature'.[34]

It is as we study the scriptures that we discover the origins of this theology of general revelation. In the so-called 'nature psalms' we find a paean of praise towards the God who reveals himself in and through his creation: in Psalm 19:1-6 we read how 'The heavens declare the glory of God; the skies proclaim the work of his hands'; Psalm 29 tells of the Lord who 'thunders over the mighty waters' and whose voice 'strikes with flashes of lightning'; Psalm 93 rejoices in the God whose 'world is firmly established'; and Psalm 104 concludes its doxology of the creator-Lord with the response: 'I will sing praise to my God as long as I live'. The books of Job and Isaiah strike similar notes of wonder at the Lord of the universe and all his works.

In the New Testament, John 1:9 speaks of 'The true light that gives light to every man'; Acts 14:17 comments that God 'has not left himself without testimony' in his provision for humankind; Romans 1:20 declares that 'men are without any excuse' in the face of God's self-revelation in the created order; Romans 2:15 points to the presence of God's law 'written on' the 'hearts' of unbelieving Gentiles; and Revelation 4:11 resounds with praise to the one whose worth is shown in his creation of 'all things'.

Special revelation is special in the sense that it is 'historical, concrete, and personal'.[35] Whereas general revelation is God disclosing himself generally to all mankind through the wonder of the created order, special revelation is concerned with specific times, places and people. Further, 'special revelation is remedial because it is God's means of reaching the *sinner* with saving, restorative truth'.[36] This gracious disclosure of the Father's redemptive love is mediated through visions, dreams, angels, the prophets, through the words and grammar of human languages, and, supremely, through the coming of Jesus Christ, the Son of God, the 'Word made flesh'. Hebrews 1:1,2 give a panoramic view of this special revelation: 'In the past God spoke to our forefathers through the prophets at many times and in various ways, but in these last days he has spoken to us by his Son, whom he appointed heir of all things, and through whom he made the universe.'

Special revelation is trinitarian. The Spirit makes known what belongs to the Son, and whoever has seen the Son has seen the Father.[37] Moreover, the divine self-disclosure is effected by the Spirit who illuminates the scriptures which, in turn, speak of God.[38]

General and special revelation. Church history has been bedevilled by polarisation between these two aspects of divine self-disclosure. In *natural theology*, given intellectual respectability amongst Christians by Thomas Aquinas in the thirteenth century, it is argued that God can be known by a 'rational reflection on the nature of things' and, therefore, special revelation tends to be seen as secondary.[39] Although Reformed religion eschewed Aquinas's views, natural theology resurfaced during the Enlightenment of the seventeenth and eighteenth centuries and has also persisted as an integral part of much Roman Catholic thinking. In contrast, there has been an unfortunate tendency to see natural theology and general revelation hand-in-glove and, conse-quently, Reformed Christianity's desire to reject the former has led at times, as in the case of Karl Barth, to a reaction against the latter.[40] Both natural theology and Barthianism are in danger of narrowing the full breadth of God's self-disclosure.

However, as we have seen, the scriptures endorse *both* general and special revelation; they are 'all of a piece' and the Bible displays no embarrassment at their juxtaposition. Nevertheless, it is clear that, as far as unregenerate men and women are concerned, general revelation and God's common grace speak in muffled tones. They point to the creator's 'eternal power and divine nature', as Romans 1 demonstrates, but cannot break through humanity's fallen understanding and so, ultimately, leave humankind 'without any excuse' before a holy God. It is here that special revelation in Christ makes a true knowledge of God possible. The Spirit illuminates the scriptures and in turn, as Calvin argues, the Bible aids our shortsightedness like an effec-tive pair of 'spectacles': 'So Scripture, gathering up the otherwise confused knowledge of God in our minds, having dispersed our dullness, clearly shows us the true God'.[41]

And so we can say that general and special revelation are not in competition. As Berkouwer puts it: 'No one comes to the Father but by *Christ*, but neither to the understanding of the works of his hands. But in his *light* we see the light of creation . . .'[42] The work of God and the word of God are interwoven.[43] The psalmists can proclaim a Lord who is both creator and redeemer, who speaks through both his works and his special words of salvation offered. And it is in Christ himself that we see the integration point of both general and special revelation:

> He is the image of the invisible God, the firstborn over all creation . . .
> all things were created by him and for him. He is before all things, and
> in him all things hold together . . . For God was pleased to have all his
> fulness dwell in him, and through him to reconcile to himself all
> things, whether things on earth or things in heaven, by making peace
> through his blood, shed on the cross.
>
> (Colossians 1:15–20)

If, as we have argued, the scriptures declare that the Lord God reveals himself through and exercises his gracious bounty within his created order, then the way is open to humankind for the legitimate exploration of all that the creator has made. Thomas Torrance, formerly professor of Christian dogmatics at Edinburgh, rightly indicates that this path of inquiry is accessible to both science and theology: 'The natural scientist inquires into the processes and patterns of nature, and man himself is a part of nature; and the theologian inquires of God the Creator of nature and the source of its created rationalities, to which man also belongs'.[44]

Such considerations show us that humanity itself is an appropriate focus for study – not only by the biologists and theologians, but by the anthropologists, sociologists and psychologists too. Men and women, made in the image of God, fallen and yet glorious, are open to investigation and understanding *by* men and women, made in the image of God, fallen and yet glorious. None of this is to deny that we all (psychologists included!) desperately need redemption in Christ. It is simply to argue that God is a God of general as well as special revelation, of common as well as special grace. Consequently, we can say that the Christian psychologist, psychotherapist or counsellor does not hold the sole rights to insight into the human *psyche*. His or her non-Christian colleague is also made in God's image, is similarly the recipient of God's common grace and may well discern and share valuable perceptions about human nature.

The emphasis given to deductive and inductive argument

In any *reasoned* argument we say both what we think and why we think it. A statement like 'I believe abortion is wrong because it outrages the sanctity of life' is much more likely to lead to rational discussion than a wilfully unsupported declaration such as 'I believe abortion is wrong. So there!' In other words, 'every argument must contain both a conclusion and at least one premise'.[45]

Philosophers tell us that statements can be divided into *deductive* and *inductive* types, depending on how the argument is carried from the premise to the conclusion.

Deductive reasoning. A number of definitions of deductive thinking have been given but it is perhaps simplest to view it as an argument which is carried *from the general to the particular*. The 'general' may include, for example, a clear perspective gained from studying the Bible, a conclusion drawn from examining history, or a principle of wide application that has been established within a science. In counselling, if you or I reason as follows we are drawing 'deductive inferences': 'Because the Scriptures declare that all are sinners, then this particular client I am trying to help must be a sinner'; 'Because it is understood generally that babies need love, warmth and food, then this particular infant, who is rejected, left exposed and starved, will not thrive'.

Bell and Staines point out that a deductive argument is one 'in which the premises purport to *guarantee the truth of the conclusion*'.[46] If the biblical affirmation that all men and women are sinners is true, then *necessarily* this client is also a sinner.

Inductive reasoning.   In this type of argument, the reasoning runs *from the particular to the general*. Inductive inferences are being drawn when you or I make statements like these: 'Because I have observed, in a number of instances, that people following a personal tragedy, are more prone to illness, then I conclude that, generally, those who experience adverse crises are more likely to become unwell afterwards'; 'Because I have found that certain people who suffer are particularly open to the significance of Christ's experiences in Gethsemane and at Calvary, then I conclude that the Son of God's suffering can be recalled helpfully by those in affliction'.

In inductive reasoning, the argument is one in which the 'premises purport to *support*' the conclusion and not, as in deductive reasoning, to guarantee its truth. An inductive inference is often marked by such phrases as 'it is likely that' or 'it seems that'.[47]

Although Christian counsellors and psychotherapists tend to value deductive statements more highly ('The scriptures say . . .', 'The Church declares . . .', 'Theology argues . . .' or 'Christian experience shows . . .'), we can maintain, from biblical premises concerning general revelation and common grace, that inductive argument has a valid, although more tentative, basis.

The credence given to the secular systems

In our consideration of Christian thinking on the methodologies, this third parameter is a necessary rider to our points about God's self-disclosure and the categories of argument used. Where a

Christian counsellor insists that special revelation alone holds the stage and that any vestige of general revelation and common grace smacks of a natural theology, then there is a tendency to exalt a narrowly 'biblical' deductive reasoning and dismiss inductive thought. This 'biblical' thinking is narrow in the sense that it seems to ignore the scriptural perspective of a God who speaks through his works as well as by his word. Consequently, this position tends to reject all secular insight as, at best, suspect or, at worst, evil. (In chapter twelve we will see something of these views mirrored in Jay Adams' approach to counselling.)

At the other extreme, when a Christian psychotherapist regards God's special revelation in Christ as barely relevant to psychological matters, then there is a danger of embracing inductive thinking exclusively and of seeing the secular therapies from purely scientific and pragmatic viewpoints. (We have commented on similar elements within the Clinical Pastoral Education movement in the United States and the Westminster Pastoral Foundation in Britain in chapter ten.)

A fully scriptural understanding of both general and special revelation will enable the Christian counsellor to give due weight to both deductive and inductive reasoning and help in the careful evaluation of the methodologies.

A framework of responses

Having outlined three important aspects of the basis from which many Christians in the world of counselling and psychotherapy seem to argue – sometimes knowingly, sometimes unwittingly – I would like to suggest a framework of Christian responses to the secular methodologies.

In recent years there have been a number of attempts to describe the range of possible positions which can be adopted in a theological consideration of the place of psychology in the understanding and healing of humankind. Some, if not most, of these derive from the seminal work *Christ and Culture* (1951), written by Richard Niebuhr and based on a series of lectures given in the United States in 1949. Here, Niebuhr gives three broad categories of Christian thinking on the relationship between Christ and human cultural activity; the third of which is further subdivided:

1 Christ *against* culture
2 Christ *of* culture
3 Christ *above* culture
   a. *Synthesis*, in which *both* Christ *and* culture are affirmed;
   b. *Dualism*, in which Christ and culture are in tension and each of us is seen as a 'citizen of two conflicting worlds';
   c. *Conversionism*, in which Christ is the *transformer* of culture.

There is not the space here to develop more fully Niebuhr's formative analysis although we will refer back to his categories as we clarify our own framework.

Amongst subsequent writers there have been both expansions and contractions of Niebuhr's categorisation. Charles Kraft in his *Christianity in Culture* (1979) presents two further positions under the heading of 'God *above* culture'; adding these to Niebuhr's list, we have:

   d. *Deism*, in which God is unconcerned with human beings in culture;
   e. *Kraft's own position*, in which God uses culture 'as the vehicle for interaction' with people. Unlike 'conversionism', which sees culture as 'corrupted but convertible', Kraft's view regards culture as *neutral* in its forms and functions (although the *use* of forms and, in time, the actual structures of culture may be changed through human redemption).[48] We might use the term *instrumentalism* of this position, in the sense that God uses culture as a 'means' or 'instrument' for his work.

As we turn our attention from these foundational views on the relation between God and human culture to the question of the links between theology and psychology, we need to exercise due care – because these two disciplines are themselves part of culture. However, *revealed* theology is, by definition, open to God's self-disclosure and is therefore in a position to evaluate psychology from theological premises. Further, as we have already argued, general revelation and God's common grace justify our careful exploration of his world and, by inference, psychology is as entitled to look at and respond to theology as *vice versa*.

John Carter and Bruce Narramore of the Rosemead Graduate

School of Professional Psychology, in the United States, have usefully probed the range of relationships between theology and psychology in *The Integration of Psychology and Theology*. Acknowledging Niebuhr, they offer four 'models' which summarise the variety of stances from both psychological and theological vantage points:

1 The *against* model
2 The *of* model
3 The *parallels* model
   a. *Isolation*, wherein there is little or no overlap between theology and psychology;
   b. *Correlation*, in which parallels are drawn between concepts in each of the disciplines;
4 The *integrates* model.

While agreeing with the basis of Carter and Narramore's classification, I would like to suggest the following outline, with its inclusion of 'eclecticism', as a useful alternative. Categorisations tend to be either so complex, by trying to delineate every exception and variation, that they are useless, or so simple that they can be accused of ignoring diversity. In presenting this analysis, I realise that many Christian counsellors and psychotherapists either fit into more than one category or, as their ideas alter, move from one position to another.

Excluding

Niebuhr declares that the 'Christ *against* culture position' was held with particular conviction by Tertullian, who once wrote in relation to Greek philosophies: 'We want no curious disputation after possessing Jesus Christ . . . With our faith we desire no further belief'.[49] This *excluding* view was integral to the mainstream of the monastic movement and, both Niebuhr and Kraft suggest, can be traced to a misreading of such passages as 1 John 2:15–17, which begins: 'Do not love the world or anything in the world. If anyone loves the world, the love of the Father is not in him'.[50] This position tends to see the Greek word *kosmos* in only negative terms, so that the Johannine prohibition is related to the whole of human culture rather than to the 'allegiance to the Satanic use of that same culture'.[51]

We can also argue that an 'excluding' stance is encouraged by an inadequate view of general revelation and God's common grace. There is a tendency to believe that divine self-disclosure is purely through special revelation and it is therefore only the Lord's people who hold valid insights into the deeper things of life. As in certain aspects of monasticism, a beleaguered mentality can arise wherein the unredeemed are seen as beyond shouting distance from the walls of the embattled Church, and therefore outside the realm of daily discourse and dialogue. This drift towards polarisation can lead to anti-intellectualism, a limited view of the deep-rooted nature of sin in the believer's life, and legalism.[52] Nonetheless, certain Christians have always been drawn to this fiercely entrenched position, from which the saints behold the surrounding culture with undivided suspicion. Their separateness can be magnetic. As Niebuhr writes, 'the single-heartedness and sincerity of the great representatives of this type are among their most attractive qualities'.

In the last chapter, we indicated the existence of this position in the sometimes vehement rejection of the secular psychologies by certain theistic writers. On analysis, though, we often find a *partially* excluding view, in which a system or an aspect of psychology is evaluated and dismissed. Examples of these discriminating exclusions include Mowrer's repudiation of Freudianism and Vitz's critique of humanistic 'selfism'. Kilpatrick's reaction to psychology as a 'social force' that 'competes' with Christianity is more sweeping; however, his main contention seems to be with a psychology which over-reaches itself.[53] Christians who adopt more fully excluding opinions include Jay Adams, and Martin and Deirdre Bobgan (see next chapter).

Assimilative

Niebuhr traces the rise of the 'Christ *of* culture' position to the influence of such theological and philosophical 'heavyweights' as Kant, Schleiermacher, Hegel and Ritschl. Their attempts to harmonise Christ and culture merges, Niebuhr says, with the 'social gospel' of the first half of the twentieth century – a 'popular theology' which 'condenses the whole of Christian thought into the formula: The Fatherhood of God and the Brotherhood of Man'.[54] In the previous chapter, we noted these liberal trends in the *assimilative* views espoused by the Clinical Pastoral Education movement in the United States and, in Britain, within a line of influence running through Leslie Weatherhead, William Kyle and the Westminster Pastoral Foundation.

As we examine the tendency for certain Christian therapists to assimilate the thinking of the secular psychologies, we can differentiate three main levels of appropriation:

1 *Where a whole methodology is taken on board.* Here *presuppositions* seem to be accepted (if only as 'working hypotheses'), as well as *objectives* and *techniques.* Inevitably, the assimilation of heavily deterministic, mechanistic, humanistic or existential assumptions is problematic for the Christian. Something has to give – and this means either the underlying psychology or the believer's theology. As Carter and Narramore have written: 'Proponents of this view selectively translate or interpret various passages or concepts from the Bible for use in their particular psychology.'[55] Amongst 'assimilators' we may find tendencies to reject the supernatural, the reality of sin and hope for humankind in Christ, as well as trends towards elevating environmental and instinctual factors, and the power of humanity to change itself.[56]

It is, of course, where a methodology argues or permits a theistic basis that the Christian counsellor is more likely to be drawn to it. Thus the presuppositions of Jungianism, Frankl's logotherapy and a number of the transpersonal therapies seem to leave an open door to many Christian thinkers. Quite a few, in particular, have been taken up by Jung's supernaturalism and views on the 'shadow', including Morton Kelsey in the United States and Christopher Bryant in Britain (see chapter fourteen).

2 *Where assumptions are discarded, but aims and methods are retained.* Here there may still be conflict between psychological and theological understanding with respect to the *objectives* of therapy. This predicament may again be resolved by a more liberal theology, or by an unthinking acceptance of such goals as self-actualisation, autonomy or cosmic consciousness. Others may regard certain aims, such as Jung's individuation, Frankl's discovery of meaning or Assagioli's psychosynthesis, as compatible with Christian insight.

3 *Where assumptions and objectives are rejected or modified* and the basic *techniques* are appropriated. This is probably the commonest position adopted by 'assimilating' Christian therapists. Where a

method offers a coherent and accurate tool for helping others, then its techniques may be pursued even though its premises may be strongly questioned. Both TA and Gestalt therapy, for example, present routines that are used by many Christian counsellors and psychotherapists, although the humanistic assumptions and quest for autonomy within their methodologies may be seen as suspect. H. Newton Mahony of Fuller Theological Seminary is one of a number of Christians who look to TA; he has written: 'Christian counsellors can appropriate TA technique without hesitation so long as they can find ways to incorporate into their basic assumptions the elements of Christian faith.'[57]

However, jut as theological perception is needed in evaluating the assumptions and aims of the secular psychologies, so too therapeutic techniques require scrutiny. There are times when technique is not neutral and questions should be asked. As we have already suggested, the fundamental query lies in asking how the method being assessed measures up against a biblical anthropology. Are the specialness, 'plurality-in-unity', fallenness and redeemability of men and women acknowledged in this or that psychological technique? The Christian, surely, will be uneasy where a method threatens human integrity. This consideration makes suspect the more reductionist and manipulative techniques – as in some forms of Reichian therapy, which regard the sexual orgasm as *the* key to health, and in Erhard Seminars Training (*est*). *Est* was founded by a former sales executive, Werner Erhard and its 'training' sessions usually involve a couple of hundred people based in a hotel for two consecutive weekends. Centred in a large room for up to sixteen hours at a stretch, sitting on hard, wooden seats and deprived of food and toilet facilities, the participants are browbeaten corporately and, from time to time, confronted individually. People's defences are broken down while they are being urged to see life in terms of personal choice. In this exposed and vulnerable state of mind, the trainees feel at one with the overall group and are susceptible to every suggestion.[58]

Eclectic

Many Christians in the psychological and sociological professions, when asked about their personal approach to their work, describe themselves as 'eclectic'. The word comes from the

Greek *eklektikos* and was used in the ancient world to distinguish
a group of philosophers who 'selected such doctrines as pleased
them in every school'.[59] Eclecticism is essentially a borrowing of
ideas and approaches from a variety of sources. In terms of our
categorisation, we can see eclecticism as the 'partial assimilation'
of a range of methodologies.

Many of us adopt an eclectic stance in our counselling. Mostly,
it is because we pick and choose what seems to work best – not
only to suit our personal style but in order to find the most
appropriate way of helping a particular client. In my counselling
work I have employed a range of techniques within a 'brief
psychotherapy' framework, including delving into the past and
the use of transference, more 'here-and-now' forms of therapy,
TA and certain ideas from Gestalt therapy. A great deal of
research, in fact, supports eclecticism in counselling. Frederick C.
Thorne, for example, writing in 1969 as editor of the *Journal of
Clinical Psychology*, summarises earlier work which shows that
adherence to a particular methodology is less important in helping needy people than the therapist's experience. Thorne concludes that commitment to a specific system disadvantages the
client or patient, and he urges a greater flexibility in both training
and practice.[60] Amongst Christian therapists, the methodologies
of Paul Tournier, Frank Lake and Howard Clinebell show
elements of eclecticism.

Following our guidelines for evaluating the secular psychologies, we can argue the need for a 'circumspect eclecticism' which
pursues its approaches with theological and psychological discernment and discards pure pragmatism. Generally, for reasons
already explained, a Christian counsellor who is eclectic will
eschew secular presuppositions but will be more open to a
methodology's objectives and techniques. In assessing systems
of counselling, therefore, I suggest that we can add the following
to the two questions we considered earlier (pages 255–256):

*Which particular aims and methods are most appropriate for this client or
patient?*

Compartmentalised

This heading covers a range of attitudes towards theology and
psychology which are classified by Niebuhr and Kraft under
'synthesis' and 'dualism', and by Carter and Narramore under

their two forms of the 'parallels' model – 'isolation' and 'correlation'. With respect to Christ and culture, Niebuhr sees the
synthetic position as one in which *both* the divine *and* the human
are valued. He cites Matthew 22:21, 'Then (Jesus) said to them,
"Give to Caesar what is Caesar's, and to God what is God's."',
and the philosophy of Thomas Aquinas, who saw the Church as
the 'guardian of culture', as representative of this view.[61] However, as we shall see, there is also a strong 'integrational' element
in Niebuhr's 'synthesism'.

In the dualistic stance, Niebuhr postulates the idea of tension
between Christ and culture where culture is seen as thoroughly
evil. Kraft highlights the believer's dilemma, within the conflict
between God and his creation, when he writes that 'the Christian
is like an amphibian living in two realms'.[62] This amphibian may
be happy in both elements (synthesism) or only content in the
one (dualism). In either case, 'compartmentalisation' may arise
where interpenetration between the two realms is rigidly
avoided.

In the context of our main discussion, by 'compartmentalisation' I mean a view of theology and psychology which sees both
disciplines as valid and valuable within their own frames of
reference – and yet having little or no conceptual and practical
common ground. As Carter and Narramore rightly argue, such
thinking may lead towards a position of 'isolation', in which
'psychology and theology are independent and uncorrelated', or
to a stance of 'correlation', wherein there is an attempt to draw
parallels between the two perspectives.[63] Paul Meehl and others,
in *What, Then, is Man?*, seem to be forced towards a 'compartmentalised' view; they wrestle with the confusion of concepts and
language between theology and psychology, and are obliged to
ask whether *'any* valid equations can be written between
theological and psychological categories'.[64]

Many Christians in the caring professions have a 'compartmentalised' perspective. Sometimes this is a well thought out position
in which theology and psychology are seen as disparate, each
having its own assumptions and vocabulary. Perhaps more commonly, others are trapped into viewing their Christian understanding and their day-to-day work as separate functions with
little or no overlap: life divides the world of Sunday worship and
mid-week fellowship from the world of out-patient clinics and
counselling sessions, and so thinking is kept watertight too.

Within this framework there is a tendency for a rigid differentiation, wherein spiritual and pastoral problems are exclusively the province of the Christian minister, and psychological and emotional difficulties are strictly under the aegis of general practitioner, psychiatrist, psychotherapist, clinical psychologist, social worker and trained counsellor.

While acknowledging that everyday professionalism often demands a 'tidy-minded' channelling of people towards this or that 'expert', I would question whether our reasoning needs to be as compartmentalised as our social institutions. Given that we do have to fathom the meaning in our workaday lives of our Lord's injunction to give to Caesar *and* to God, we can jeopardise people's well-being by applying this command inappropriately. It is unlikely that Jesus's words were a call to splitting the secular from the sacred; rather, they are to be seen as an invitation to distinguish our various duties and loyalties within life's complexities.[65] The Lord's mandate does not exclude God from his dominion over human government. Likewise, we should seek that his lordship and influence be known in the realm of psychology as well as theology. Thus, affirming that our sovereign God is at work through his common grace in hospital ward, consulting room and counselling clinic, our unduly compartmentalised views can be opened up.

Integrational

Writing in 1951, Niebuhr observes 'many yearnings' amongst believers for a synthesis between 'Christ and culture'.[66] He writes: 'Man's search for unity is unconquerable, and the Christian has a special reason for seeking integrity because of his fundamental faith in the God who is One.'[67] Further, Niebuhr, in his 'conversionist' position, raises hope for culture when, although under divine judgment, it is also seen as 'under God's sovereign rule' and, therefore, open to a 'transformed life in and to the glory of God'.[68] Kraft, even though he postulates its neutral nature, likewise views culture as redeemable and accessible to divine influence.

Carter and Narramore, with regard to theology and psychology, push beyond Niebuhr's tentative words about synthesis and Kraft's exploratory thoughts on a 'God-above-but-through-Culture' position, to argue for integration. They write:

When God created humanity, He created the possibility for psychology. The integrated approach emphasizes both psychology and the Scriptures because they are allies. Psychology here is the psychology that existed before the word was coined . . .[69]

Herein they seek to demonstrate a unity (which, in essence, already exists) between theology and a God-given psychology, stripped of its atheistic and humanistic accretions. In this quest for integration, they want to avoid 'violating the methodology or level of analysis of either' discipline.[70]

Apart from themselves, Carter and Narramore also refer to William Hulme, Maurice Wagner and A. van Kamm as writers with integrational approaches.[71] In the previous chapter, we noted similar unifying trends in the thinking of Gary Collins and Thomas Oden. Other counsellors, whom we shall consider in the following pages and who have also contributed to the search for unity, include Lawrence Crabb, Paul Tournier and Frank Lake.

Niebuhr, while appreciating the Christian's quest for synthesis, urges us to be wary of idealism. He warns against the 'Absolutizing of what is relative, the reduction of the infinite to a finite form, and the materialization of the dynamic'.[72] Although Niebuhr refers to the broader canvas of 'Christ and culture', we need a similar caution in pursuing the integration of theology and psychology. Here we are often dealing with imponderables. How *do* we assess psychological theory and practice in the light of God's self-disclosure? In what ways is a theological understanding of sin and guilt compatible with psychopathology? Is there any identification between spiritual and psychological growth? What light, if any, do God's covenants with his people throw on the counselling relationship? How do the psychological processes of group therapy link with Christian fellowship?

All in all, we can argue for the reasonableness of seeking a degree of integration between theology and psychology from the vantage point of the essential unity of general and special revelation. We have a God who speaks through both his works and word, inviting men and women to explore and appreciate the created order through the 'spectacles' of his self-disclosure in Christ. However, we must never see this search for a unified view as an easy matter. God reveals himself, but his thoughts are still far above ours; we have guidelines for comprehending human nature, but we are still faced with mystery and complexity. Many of us, while we look for integration, do so from assimilative or eclectic positions. We perceive a great deal that is of value in this or that aspect of the methodologies and seek to hold assumptions, aims and methods up before the lamp of God's word. In the meantime we may be cautiously assimilative, embracing the system that seems most compatible with our beliefs, or circumspectly eclectic, continually refining and adapting objectives and techniques. This search calls for humility amidst the uncertainties. As Carter and Narramore put it:

> Closely related to humility is the ability to tolerate ambiguity. In a new and essentially pioneering venture it is essential to keep an open mind. We must be able to see alternative perspectives, look for new relationships, and, above all, not be too quick to throw aside apparently conflicting information. It is out of seeming contradictions and unresolvable dilemmas that new insights frequently emerge. If we attempt to close the book on integration, we shut off this process of personal creativity.[73]

Conclusion

We have drawn our map of the forest of the secular psychologies and made our compass of Christian response. Before we look at a sample of important Christian practitioners in the remaining chapters, I would like to suggest three points by way of a summary to help us evaluate both our own theory and practice of counselling, and that of others. In doing so let us recall once more that many of us straddle two or more positions. We may, for instance, be eclectic in our choice of techniques and compartmentalised in our attitude to theology and psychology. Or again, we may be assimilating towards a particular method and yet also look for a measure of integration between that system and our Christian understanding. Others of us may hold excluding or compartmentalised stances and, at the same time, feel uneasy about our isolated viewpoints. The three points are these:

1 The need to question strongly excluding and fully compartmentalised positions as possibly deficient in a 'common grace' theology;

2 A constant sifting of the methodologies so that assimilative and eclectic views have their theological and psychological rationale;

3 A diligent search for an integration between theology and psychology which is comprehensive enough to avoid a partisan approach and humble enough to be open to fresh insight.[74]

REACHING TO THE WORD: BIBLICAL COUNSELLING

> *Biblicism may fail to see the literary character of Scripture and treat Scripture like a code book of theological ordinances. Criticism may be so preoccupied with the literary aspects of Scripture that it fails to see the substance of which literature happens to be the vehicle.*
>
> Bernard Ramm

> *The Bible is alive, it speaks to me; it has feet, it runs after me; it has hands, it lays hold on me.*
>
> Martin Luther

> *For the word of God is living and active, sharper than any two-edged sword, piercing to the division of soul and spirit, of joints and marrow, and discerning the thoughts and intentions of the heart.*
>
> Hebrews 4:12 (RSV)

Having established five main categories of Christian response to the secular psychologies and their associated therapies, let us, in the next four chapters, look at some of the methodologies held by Christians and do so from the point of view of the main *focus* of counselling: the Bible; the relationship between the counsellor and client; inner exploration; and primal experience. These sub-divisions are, of course, over-simplified in that any truly Christian approach to therapy will look to one or more of a whole array of resources – the Holy Spirit and his gifts, the scriptures, the sacraments, the fellowship of the Lord's people, spiritual direction, discipling, and personal experience. However, although there is a rich variety of 'aids' to caring, we can discern at least four streams of counselling amongst Christians on the rather broad bases of reaching to the word, the relationship, the inner life, and the past. Each of these *directions* of attention will, if they are truly Christian, be Christ-centred, Spirit-filled and Bible-based. Within these groupings, following our argument of the last chapter, we will expect to meet a range of views that contain excluding, assimilative, eclectic, compartmentalised and integrational positions.

Under our first heading of 'biblical counselling', I want to include those methodologies which lay a great and well publicised emphasis on their scriptural basis. Counsellors holding such 'high views' of the Bible tend, by definition, to come from Reformed and evangelical stock. The main systematisation of these 'biblical' approaches has grown up in the United States, particularly from the late 1960s onwards, partly as reaction to the secularising influence of the psychotherapies and partly as an attempt to find a degree of integration between psychology and a conservative theology. Evangelicalism in Britain has been slow to respond to American brands of 'biblical' counselling, although the impact of their evangelistic equivalents in the Billy Graham Evangelistic Association, Campus Crusade for Christ and the Navigators has been considerable.

As we examine 'biblical' counselling, we find a spectrum of characteristics depending on, amongst other things, the stresses given to general and special revelation, ranging from Jay Adams' *nouthetic counselling* and the Bobgans' *spiritual counselling*, through the variant brands of *biblical counselling* of Jim Craddock and Lawrence Crabb, and the *Christian counselling* of Selwyn Hughes, to the *discipleship counselling* of both Gary Collins and Gary Sweeten. These American figures, together with Selwyn Hughes in the United Kingdom, are important representatives of a much greater army of counsellors who quite openly claim a scriptural basis to their work.

Not surprisingly, 'biblical' counsellors tend to hold either an 'excluding' or an 'integrational' stance. This is because their doctrinal position is often sharply conceived and so secular psychology is either roundly condemned (from an exclusively 'special revelational' perspective) or cautiously evaluated (where God's revelation is seen to be through his word and works). However, in passing, there are other Christians who are more 'assimilative' or 'eclectic' in their desire to be biblical. Such have often turned to secular theorists who present methodologies which seem to resonate with scriptural perspectives. Amongst these, there has been quite a vogue in looking to William Glasser's reality therapy with its triple emphasis on 'reality', 'responsibility' and 'right and wrong'.[1] Although Glasser's themes are, on the surface, compatible with biblical concepts of objective truth, personal accountability and moral absolutes, the assumptive basis is highly subjective. He writes:

> We believe that almost all behaviour which leads to fulfilling our needs within the bounds of reality is right, or good, or moral behaviour, according to the following definition: When a man acts in such a way that he gives and receives love, and feels worthwhile to himself and others, his behaviour is right or wrong.[2]

A number admit the importance of O. Hobart Mowrer and Thomas Szasz in shaping their early disillusionment with psychiatry and psychotherapy, some look to Albert Ellis and his stress on the way our thinking affects our feeling, while other biblical counsellors, such as James Dobson, acknowledge the influence of behaviourists like Thorndike and Skinner on their handling of needy people.[3]

Let us now examine a selection of the methodologies of some of the leading biblical counsellors.

Nouthetic counselling

Jay E. Adams, dean of the Institute of Pastoral Studies and visiting professor of practical theology at Westminster Theological Seminary in Philadelphia, is an influential figure amongst evangelical counsellors on both sides of the Atlantic. Since the introduction of his distinctive *nouthetic counselling* in 1969, training has become available at a number of centres – including the Christian Counselling and Educational Centre at Laverock in Pennsylvania, under the directorship of Adams' colleague, John Bettler. In 1977, the National Association of Nouthetic Counsellors was founded to 'promote and upgrade biblical counselling by certifying counsellors, counselling centres, and training centres'.[4] In the early 1980s Jay Adams began a series of summer schools on nouthetic counselling at Hildenborough Hall in Kent, at the invitation of its new general director, Peter Letchford, who had worked with Adams in the United States. Of

Adams' internationally known writings, his *Competent to Counsel* (1970) has been especially formative in this country.

Jay Adams, with degrees in homiletics and speech, and as a pastor in various branches of the Presbyterian Church in Pennsylvania and New Jersey, experienced a great deal of frustration as he sought to counsel needy Christians by Freudian and Rogerian methods. A turning point came in his pastoral understanding in the summer of 1965, as a result of taking up an Eli Lilly Fellowship in psychology at the University of Illinois under the supervision of O. Hobart Mowrer. Reading Mowrer's *The Crisis in Psychiatry and Religion* proved to be an 'earth-shaking experience' for Adams as he eagerly responded to Mowrer's dismissal of the 'medical model' of 'mental illness' and his proclamation of a 'moral model', in which real guilt and personal responsibility are acknowledged. Adams' work with Mowrer at two mental institutions confirmed this 'discovery' so that he, like his mentor, repudiated the validity of such terms as 'neurosis' and 'psychosis' and, further, concluded that people were inmates there 'because of their unforgiven and unaltered sinful behaviour'. Although rejecting Mowrer's man-centred stance, Adams returned from his summer in Illinois resolved to bring 'the ministry of God's Word' to the so-called 'mentally ill'.[5]

Assumptions

Adams declares that 'counselling methodology must grow out of and always be appropriate to the biblical view of God, man, and the creation'. From this vantage-point, he argues that, in the area of counselling, 'at bottom, the Christian believes that there are only *two* approaches: the Christian; the non-Christian'.[6] He presents this polarisation more fully when he writes:

> It is clear . . . that from Adam's time on there have been two counsels in this world: divine counsel and devilish counsel; the two are in competition. The Bible's position is that all counsel that is not revelational (biblical), or based upon God's revelation, is Satanic.[7]

Here there is no middle-ground. 'Divine' and 'devilish' counsel are pitted against each other, the former being 'revelational' and the latter somehow outside 'God's revelation'. In his *Competent to Counsel*, as well as in private discussion, Jay Adams acknowledges the importance of Van Til to his theological re-flection.[8] Cornelius Van Til, formerly professor of apologetics at Westminster Theological Seminary, has argued a similar view to Adams' on the clear-cut dichotomy between the bases for living of the believer, who is part of 'a world run by the counsel of God' and the unbeliever, who presupposes 'a world of Chance'.[9] Van Til reasons that scientific methodologies (and here we can include psychological systems) are never neutral; they grow out of 'conceptions of reality' – either Christian or non-Christian.[10] He summarises uncompromisingly: 'All men are either in covenant with Satan or in covenant with God.'[11]

We will come back to these far-reaching presuppositions when we attempt a critique of Adams' approach.

Adams' view of two polarised kingdoms is accompanied by another 'either-or' perspective – in which human malaise is seen to be due to either personal sin or bodily malfunction. There is no intermediate territory of 'mental illness' or psychological disturbance that is not sin-induced. He writes: 'All nonorganically caused problems are considered to be hamartigenic (sin-caused). Sinful living is at the heart of the counselling focus.'[12] Adams is consistent: if a psychological perspective to people's difficulties is irrelevant, then so are those professionals who seek to help others on that very basis. He declares:

> Biblically, there is no warrant for acknowledging the existence of a separate and distinct discipline called psychiatry. There are, in the Scriptures, only three specified sources of personal problems in living; demonic activity (principally possession), personal sin, and organic illness. These three are interrelated. All options are covered under these heads, leaving no room for a fourth: non-organic mental illness.[13]

I agree with Van Til and Adams that our conceptions of reality have a direct affect on our methodologies. This linkage is as clear with Adams as anybody in that he seeks to argue his case with precision and circumspection from his understanding of the scriptures. His declarations that the Bible is unequivocal in emphasising two opposing counsels, 'divine' and 'devilish', and in underlining that human affliction is either physical or sinful (and sometimes *both*), the demonic excepted, permeate the aims and techniques of his nouthetic counselling.

Aims

Adams frequently refers to the overall objective of helping others as 'biblical change'. Given that every man, woman and child who seeks advice belongs either to the kingdom of light or the kingdom of darkness, then 'biblical change' means the process of sanctification for the former and the reality of conversion for the latter. Adams writes of 'precounselling' for the non-Christian in which the counsellor's work is 'to confront unsaved men with the universal offer of the gospel'.[14] If successfully evangelised, then the regenerate client can be counselled. This point is strongly made: '. . . you can't *counsel* unbelievers in the biblical sense of the word (changing them, sanctifying them through the work of the Holy Spirit, as His Word is ministered to their hearts) so long as they remain unbelievers.'[15] 'Biblical change' for the Christian is described variously as sanctification, being made more like Christ, bearing the fruit of the Spirit, experiencing the restoring of God's image and becoming 'more normal'.[16] The overarching aim of counselling is 'love to the glory of God', in which love is seen as a 'relationship conditioned upon . . . responsible observance of the commandments of God'.[17]

This goal of discovering a 'loving conformity to the law of God' is expressed in very practical terms, wherein wrong patterns of living are rejected, and replaced by 'biblical' ways of thinking and behaving.[18] The objective of 'biblical change' is anticipated with confidence in an all-powerful God: the Christian counsellor '*knows* that God is in the business of changing lives. Every change that God promises is possible. Every quality that God requires in His redeemed children can be attained. Every resource that is needed God has supplied.'[19] And, for the nouthetic counsellor, the reality of individual transformation has an immediacy about it: '. . . the Christian cheerfully asserts the possibility of thorough, rapid change . . . He believes in conversion and in the sanctifying power of the Spirit.'[20]

Method

Adams seeks to base his style of counselling on the Spirit's activity and on biblical understanding. He sees these two foundations as inextricably linked: '. . . since the Holy Spirit employs his Word as the principal means by which Christians may grow in sanctification, counselling cannot be effective (in any biblical sense of that term) apart from the use of the Scriptures'.[21] This 'use of the Scriptures' is obligatory for the Christian who counsels because, Adams argues, the Bible is *the* text book for counselling. He writes: 'All that is needed to form values, beliefs, attitudes, and behavioural styles is in the Scriptures. Indeed, no other book can do so, and all other books that attempt to do so thereby become competitive.'[22] And so Adams' method claims the stamp of Holy Writ in the sense that: 'A biblical technique is one that is commanded in the Scriptures . . . commended in the Scriptures . . . or grows out of a Scriptural principle.'[23]

For Adams, *the* 'biblical technique' is, undoubtedly, what he calls *nouthetic counselling*. This term derives from the Greek verb *noutheteo* and the noun *nouthesia*, words that occur primarily in the writings of Paul. Adams describes *nouthesia* as a 'rich term with no exact English equivalent' but, nonetheless, declares three 'basic elements' within the practice of nouthetic counselling:

1 The effecting of personality and behavioural change;
2 Person-to-person verbal confrontation;
3 Motivation by love – for the client's good, and to God's glory.[24]

Paul's inclusive statement in 2 Timothy 3:15–17 is seen by Adams as the touchstone for biblical counselling. He says, 'The whole process of counselling, plus the resources and methodology to be used, is either stated or implied in this passage.'[25] He sees the declaration that 'All scripture is inspired by God and profitable for teaching, for reproof, for correction, and for training in righteousness' (verse 16 RSV) as indicative that 'the Scriptures themselves are nouthetically oriented'.[26]

What qualifications are needed by the nouthetic counsellor? Adams argues that the triple requirements of *change, confrontation* and *care* within the counselling process are best met by the possession of 'extensive knowledge of the Scriptures, divine wisdom, and good will toward others'.[27] Quoting Romans 15:14 (NASB), in which Paul declares that his readers are 'able . . . to admonish (nouthetically confront) one another', Adams says that all Christians should be 'competent to counsel'.[28] However, he also declares that, as a 'life calling', counselling should be the prerogative of the 'ordained minister'. He sees the proclamation of the apostle Paul in Colossians 1:28 as confirming this view:

'Him we proclaim, warning (*noutheteo*) every man and teaching every man in all wisdom, that we may present every man mature in Christ' (RSV). By implication the full-time nouthetic counsellor will be, like Paul, set apart for his ministry. Adams concludes that this work is best carried out by an associate pastor within a congregation or by pastors who assist several churches.[29]

Because nouthetic counselling is biblical, Adams reasons, it is also *authoritative* in that it mediates 'the authority of God'. Further, 'because it is authoritative, biblical counselling is *directive*' (my italics). Adams completes the circle of his argument by writing: 'The New Testament word for counselling (*nouthesia*) implies scriptural direction. Counselling *as* directing was universal in biblical times.'[30] By the same token we can see that nouthetic counselling is also *disciplining*. To expose the client to God's authoritative word in a directive way is a challenge to personal discipleship and, by implication, to the possibility of church discipline. Adams makes this point clearly when he writes: 'If a counselee refuses to do God's will, the best that the centre counsellor can do is to dismiss him or, in necessary situations, inform his pastor.'[31] However, aware of the dangers of dependency, the nouthetic counsellor seeks throughout to lead the client towards *self*-discipline.[32]

How, then, is this authoritative, directive and disciplining form of counselling to be carried out? At the first session a 'Personal Data Inventory' is completed by the client to give the counsellor a factual baseline on the client's health, religious background, type of personality, marital status, family history and perception of 'the main problem'. Before this 'main problem' is tackled, be it marital breakdown, feelings of inferiority or homosexual leanings, the client's standing before God is ascertained. If he or she is a believer then counselling can proceed; if not, the gospel is first offered, because, with respect to the unbeliever:

1 'God has not authorized us to reform people outwardly';
2 'To do so would misrepresent the true nature of His magnificent redemption in Christ';
3 Clients may rely on any outward change 'with false assurance that problems have been solved'.[33]

This 'precounselling' is a 'problem-oriented evangelism' in which in any immediate crisis initial advice may be given in order to present the good news in Christ. If an unbelieving husband is threatening to leave a Christian wife that very day, then a nouthetic counsellor may urge both parties to at least agree to attend the counselling centre on the morrow. Such minimal intervention prepares the way for evangelism. If, after faithful presentation of the gospel, response to the Lord is refused, then the nouthetic counsellor declines to proceed with counselling. He may need to say, 'We're up against a brick wall . . . There is only one way to get through it – through the Door, through the One Who said, "I am the Door" . . . I can do no more for you until you go through that Door.'[34]

The method used in nouthetic counselling is both cognitive and behavioural, seeking changes in ways of thinking and patterns of behaviour. The main thrust is to tackle wrong habits of thought and action by the 'two-factored process' of *dehabituation* and *rehabituation*. Adams points out the frequency of the biblical imagery of 'putting off' and 'putting on' with respect to Christian living. Ephesians 4:22–32, for example, demonstrates the need to 'put off' our 'old self' with its 'deceitful desires', 'falsehood', unrighteous anger and 'unwholesome talk', and to 'put on the new self, created to be like God in true righteousness and holiness'. With this two-fold principle in mind, counsellors must help their clients so that 'the old sinful ways, as they are discovered' can be 'replaced by new patterns from God's Word'.[35]

The techniques employed to achieve dehabituation and rehabituation include a wide range of behavioural approaches to spur motivation and galvanise action: *rewards* and *punishments*, encouraging 'good' responses and discouraging 'bad' ones; *modelling*, in which the counsellor might share something of his own story in seeking to live a 'godly, disciplined life'; and the use of *assignments*.[36]

The assigning of 'homework' is a crucial aspect of nouthetic counselling and is started from the first session. Throughout counselling there is an attempt to move the focus from problems of *presentation* ('I feel down') and *performance* ('I'm not coping with my work') to those of *preconditioning* ('I always find it difficult to handle responsibility').[37] The initial assignment might seek to relieve the presenting complaint by tackling 'performance' at a simple level: 'Be punctual at the office every morning during the coming week' or 'Make sure you dust the living room before you see me next.' To aid the monitoring of patterns of behaviour a

'Problem-Solving Sheet' may be given, on which the client records relevant incidents, how they were handled, what should have been done, and what ought to have been done next. By confronting the 'smaller' self-evident problems first, it is argued that the 'larger' preconditioning difficulties will surface as homework is completed and discussed with the counsellor. In this 'iceberg' method of giving priority to the visible, the client is encouraged 'to focus not on feelings (symptoms) but on behaviour'.[38]

After about six weeks, it is expected that the client will be entering the 'more positive work of establishing biblical patterns' of living. By the end of another two to four weeks the 'counselling ought to be well on its way toward reaching solutions to specific problems'.[39] Clients are offered hope and encouragement throughout, are urged to find and use their spiritual gifts, and are helped to move from their problems to 'God's solutions'. Within this process, every effort is made to see both parties, where appropriate, and to challenge them with the needs of reconciliation and restitution.

Discussion

Adams' views on counselling are controversial and a considerable body of literature has grown up during the last decade to chart the course of analysis and response.[40] Although a number of opinions have been expressed adversarially, behind the polemics there are some extremely important points of issue. Adams has a great influence amongst many Christians who counsel and so we should give at least some of his perspectives an airing.

There is no doubt that Adams' bold insistence on the primacy of the scriptures has been of great value in encouraging the re-evaluation of counselling methodologies in the light of the Bible. Further, his emphasis on right thinking and action, stimulated by behavioural techniques, has done much to help needy Christians break with sinful habits and move forward into more obedient patterns of living. However, it is in Adams' way of handling the scriptures with respect to God's influence in the created order that there is room for discussion. I realise that the whole question of *how* to interpret the Bible for use in the world today is a hotbed of theological debate, but we cannot give up on the hermeneutical task – not least in our understandings of human nature and how God speaks to us, both of which are highly relevant to a biblical perspective on counselling. In following Van Til, Adams seems to enter a controversy over 'common grace' and general revelation. Both men, in emphasising, quite reasonably, the two counsels – 'divine' and 'devilish', seem in danger of neglecting the biblical dimension that proclaims a God who speaks through both word *and* works (see our discussion on general revelation on pages 258–261).

In his writings, as well as in personal conversation, Jay Adams acknowledges the existence of divine common grace as contributory to, for example: 'an element of truth reflected by every false position'; the unearthing of certain 'nuggets' of insight by an unbeliever; and, with the Westminster Confession, the worth-whileness of doing 'that which is of good use, both to the unbeliever and to others'.[41] At the same time, however, a number of his other statements appear to demonstrate a much more restricted view of God's dealings in and through our common humanity. Adams' understanding of 'man as the image of God' seems to major on the 'fallenness' at the expense of any residual 'glory'. He writes: 'The image of God in man was distorted by the fall. Man as a communicating, holy, knowledgeable, righteous being, reflecting God, his creator, became rather a reflection of the Father of lies' and, elsewhere: 'The image of God was ruined by the fall . . .'[42] It may be argued that such comments are simply a matter of emphasis within particular contexts but, on the other hand, Adams' seeming neglect of the biblical dimensions of general revelation and common grace *as a developed argument* is, I believe, the main root of at least some of his more disputed opinions. I would like to explore this influence in three cardinal areas of Adams' thinking: the place of *psychology, evangelism* and his particular brand of *counselling*.

Psychology

Adams' position is essentially 'excluding' with regard to the concepts and practice of psychology and the allied disciplines. Arguing that the Bible only considers *two* aspects of our humanity, the 'inner life' and the physical, he dismisses 'the so-called psychological' by writing:

> Nor is there the slightest *hint* in the Bible that there is *another* inorganic, amoral aspect of man in addition to the heart (the so-called psycho-

logical) which (according to the advocates of the view) is so important
for living . . . Biblically, the emphasis is the *Bible* for living.[43]

Adams is very aware of the blanket criticism that 'nouthetic
counselling considers all human problems the direct result of
actual sins of particular counselees' and he calls this view a 'gross
misrepresentation of the facts'.[44] It is essential, therefore, that we
try to understand with care Adams' thoughts on the linkage
between sin and human nature.

As far as I can discern, he holds to the following propositions:

1 Human nature is 'duplex' – a 'twofold' unity which comprises
   an outer (visible) and an inner (called the 'heart' in the Bible)
   aspect;[45]
2 All parts of human life are blighted by sin;[46]
3 Physical sickness is, originally, a consequence of the fall but, in
   specific cases, may or may not be due to personal sin;[47]
4 The 'heart' or *whole* inner life' is evil, wicked and 'totally
   corrupt' without Christ;[48]
5 There is no 'non-bodily psychological area' which is either
   unaffected by sin or is not a source of further sin.[49]

From these premises Adams reasons that there is no such thing
as mental *illness*. We are not allowed to draw a parallel with
physical disease, in which the cause is not necessarily due to
personal sin, because, according to Adams, *there is no comparable
psychological area to consider*. The analogy, he would insist, can
only be made between the body and our 'inner nature', and the
latter is so corrupt that we can only talk of its sinfulness, and not
of its sickness. It seems to me that it is here that Adams oversim-
plifies the biblical witness in a way that forces him towards some
inconsistency in dealing with our inner and outer natures. We
can, in agreement with Adams, declare that we have an intrinsic
unity but further, at seeming variance with Adams, own that we
are also multi-faceted and that the Bible uses a wide and rich
range of words and imagery to describe us. Moreover, as we have
also seen, we can affirm, with Adams, humankind's 'total corruption' – its fallenness in every aspect of being – but we need to
announce too that we are still referred to as 'in the image of God'
within that corruption and that glimmers of glory still break
through. God is a God who gives gifts to humanity, speaks within

and through his creation and is concerned about justice and mercy in the lives of *all* people.

It is, I suggest, Adams' somewhat limited view of human nature that leads to his rejection of the validity of psychiatrists, clinical psychologists and others working in the realm of psychological and emotional problems. Experimental psychologists and physicians are seen to have their place in the scheme of things in that they deal with the more acceptable domains of behaviour and the organic. It is apparent that this 'excluding' position cannot countenance the viability of what I have called 'circumspect eclecticism' and of working towards an integration of psychology and theology.[50] Such ventures, by implication, are seen as parleying with the devil in that they are regarded as excursions into rival enemy territory. A fuller acknowledgment of general revelation, along with special revelation, invites, I believe, such pioneer work as we seek to claim *every* aspect of our humanity for Christ. We labour in *God's* world where we strive to bring his kingdom into regions sabotaged, but not possessed, by the Adversary.[51]

Evangelism

Adams' powerfully expressed view that evangelism must precede counselling accords with his perspectives on both the inaccessibility of the unredeemed to 'godly counsel' and the equation that 'biblical counselling' concerns sanctification – in the sense of replacing wrong patterns of living with right ones. While agreeing that the men and women we aim to help in our Lord's name desperately need regeneration and growth towards Christlikeness, I am not convinced, from biblical perspectives, that we can *only* see clients in such specific terms. With respect to limiting counselling to the Christian, Adams writes:

> (God) is not in the business of *reforming* lives, but in the business of *renewing* His image in them. God does not want His counsellors to aid and abet non-Christians in exchanging one sinful pattern for another (that is reformation); He has called us, rather, to a ministry of reconciliation and renewal.[52]

It seems to me that the scriptures demonstrate that God is concerned with reconciliation, renewal *and* reformation. To take but one example, God's wrath, expressed through the prophet Amos, thundered against oppression and injustice in the lives of both his people and of other nations. To Israel, awaiting the possibility of full reconciliation and renewal with the coming of the Messiah, God still says: '. . . let justice roll on like a river, righteousness like a never-failing stream!' (Amos 5:24). And so, in our counselling, where a husband remains faithful to his wife, a mother shows less favouritism towards one of her children, one friend learns to be more forgiving towards another, a man wrongly dismissed from his job is reinstated, and a woman becomes a more just employer, then we should rejoice, acknowledging that God's restraining hand is at work.

Counselling

Adams' use of the Greek words *noutheteo* and *nouthesia* to advance an approach to counselling is a reasonable one. It is in his tendency to present his confrontative style of counselling as *the* biblical method that difficulties arise. He writes, for instance, of Paul's instructions to Timothy 'to use the Scriptures concretely in accordance with their nouthetic purposes'; he continues by quoting 2 Timothy 4:2 (NASB): 'preach the word; be ready in season and out of season; reprove, rebuke, exhort, with great patience and instruction'; and concludes: 'Timothy could fulfil that mandate only by using the Scriptures nouthetically. So nouthetic confrontation must be scriptural confrontation.'[53] At times Adams agrees that there are other Greek words in the New Testament than *nouthesia* that can also be used for the idea of counselling. In one such instance, he nevertheless concludes that 'nouthetic counselling . . . is simply another designation for biblical counselling'.[54] In choosing the 'nouthetic' words (*noutheteo* occurring eight times and *nouthesia* three times in the New Testament) and neglecting a range of alternatives, including *parakaleo* (109 occurrences) and *paraklesis* (twenty-nine times), Adams seems to favour the more directive and admonishing stance of the former to the more encouraging and consoling style of the latter (see chapter sixteen for a fuller treatment of these words).

Interestingly, Donald Capps, professor of pastoral theology at Princeton, notes a similar selectivity in Adams' handling of the book of Proverbs: '. . . Proverbs is paradigmatic for Adams because it provides a basic model for pastoral counselling. This model is based, in part, on Proverbs' use of the phrase "my son", which Adams takes to mean approval of a paternal approach to the counsellee.'[55] Although Capps agrees with Adams that Proverbs is a book of instruction, especially for the young, and that it says more about behaviour than feelings and is positive about discipline and reproof, he feels that Adams has misconstrued 'its *instructional*, *behavioural*, and *disciplinary* emphasis'.[56] In contrast to Adams' view that the book presents discrete 'segments of life', Capps argues that Proverbs stresses the 'interconnections of all aspects of life (social, psychological, natural)' and 'resistance to viewing life in terms of "segments"'. Capps concludes that 'these proverbs do not provide the clearest support for directive counselling that Adams thinks they do'.

Let us finally examine one area of human experience that Adams seems dismissive towards in his nouthetic approach to counselling – that of 'feelings and emotions'. He does not deny the existence of feelings but appears to regard them as entirely the servant of behaviour. He declares that 'nobody has *emotional* problems; there is no such thing as an emotional problem . . . The problem is a behavioural problem . . .'[57] He seeks to translate such declarations as 'I *feel* inferior' to 'I *am* inferior.'[58] Adams, of course, has a point here. It is easy for us, in labelling our dilemmas as 'emotional' to sidestep our irresponsible behaviour. But do we need to adopt such 'either-or' statements about human personality? Again, Adams' thinking here appears to arise from his exclusion of psychological and emotional factors as being rather untidy in his scheme of things. Such inconvenient perspectives must somehow be tied into the realms of the physical or the behavioural – if problematic, they must be swiftly related to organic illness or sin. This straightjacketing seems a far cry from the complex interweaving of feelings, experiences, thinking and action found in such Proverbs as 'An anxious heart weighs a man down, but a kind word cheers him up' (12:25), 'Hope deferred makes the heart sick, but a longing fulfilled is a tree of life' (13:12) and 'A happy heart makes the face cheerful, but heartache crushes the spirit' (15:13).

Adams' contribution to counselling is immensely important in its urgent quest to be biblical, in its challenging of the secularisation of psychology, in its confrontation of sin and in its practical help in forming new patterns of living in the power of the Spirit and to the glory of God. Many of us would be so much happier if nouthetic counselling could be seen for what it is: one attempt, amongst others, to put forward a particular style of counselling that has its roots in biblical understanding. God's revelation, in both word and created order, with respect to caring for one another is somehow wider than the constraints of one particular methodology of counselling.

I hope I have not been unfair on Adams' opinions as expressed in his writing; I have said all in brotherly love and with respect for his singlemindedness in serving the Lord in and through nouthetic counselling. We have spent some time looking at Jay Adams' approach to counselling because his methodology presents an influential and distinctive contribution to the range of various forms of 'biblical' counselling. Other examples include the 'spiritual' counselling of Martin and Deirdre Bobgan, the 'biblical' counselling of Jim Craddock and Larry Crabb, and the 'discipleship' counselling of Gary Collins and Gary Sweeten. All these – and they are simply instances of a widespread movement emanating from the United States and achieving international status – seek to base their methodology fairly and squarely on biblical revelation. Crabb's statement is typical of the ground rules of this grouping:

> Every concept of biblical counselling must build upon the fundamental premise that there really is an infinite and personal God who has revealed Himself propositionally in the written word, the Bible, and personally in the living word, Jesus Christ'.[59]

I propose to write a brief summary of the approaches of these particular counsellors to give the 'flavour' of American brands of biblical counselling. Apart from Jay Adams and Gary Collins, Larry Crabb is probably the best known to evangelical Christians in Britain, I will add an outline of the work of Selwyn Hughes, an important contributor to the British counselling scene and someone who acknowledges his links with Crabb and other Christian counsellors in the United States. In considering the protagonists of biblical counselling it will become evident that some, like Jay Adams, adopt a more 'excluding' position towards the world of psychology, whereas others seek a measure of integration between a biblical theology and psychology.

'Spiritual' counselling

Martin Bobgan, who is an educational psychologist, and his wife Deirdre Bobgan are the co-directors of 'Counseling Ministry', based at Santa Barbara in California. Their book *The Psychological Way/The Spiritual Way* puts forward a telling case that 'there is a psychological way and a spiritual way to mental-emotional health' and that the former's basis and effectiveness are found wanting compared with the solid premises and transforming power of the latter. The Bobgans declare that they are not opposing, or criticising, the whole area of psychology, 'but rather the practice of psychotherapy based on ideologies which contradict Scripture'. With this proviso understood, they argue that 'all nonorganically related mental-emotional disorders have a spiritual, Christ-centred solution rather than a psychological, self-centred solution'.[60]

Analysing the four 'polluted streams' of psychoanalysis, behaviourism, humanism and transpersonalism, the Bobgans warn the Christian counsellor against the ensnaring characteristics of Rogers, Glasser and Harris in particular. They write that psychotherapy 'is a field that is filled with speculative and spurious thought, which sometimes ends up killing one's confidence, confession, and convictions in Christianity'. They criticise the Christian psychotherapist, in effect, for 'believing in combining both the spiritual way and the psychological way'. Here they seem to be attacking an unthinking 'assimilation' and 'eclecticism' rather than an 'integration' that seeks to evaluate psychological insight in the light of the scriptures.[61]

Quoting Galatians 6:1–2, the Bobgans point out that it is those who are 'spiritual' who are called to be 'burden bearers with the ministry of restoration and sanctification or spiritual growth'. In other words, such 'spiritual' counsellors need, besides being able to 'bring nonbelievers into (the) new life of relationship with God', to be adept at ministering to 'the spiritual nature of Christians'. Overall, the aim of 'spiritual' counselling is to lead the needy 'from self-centredness (which is a major cause of mental-emotional suffering) to God-centredness'.[62]

Who are the 'spiritual' counsellors? The Bobgans declare that they are ministers or lay people who centre their counselling in Jesus and whose 'main reference book is the Bible'. Although observations made by others about our humanity may be used, they are to be tested 'with Scripture', since the Bible is seen to be 'the most accurate treatise on the human condition'.[63] Spiritual counsellors are regarded as better off without the potential contamination of 'exposure to psychotherapeutic theories and techniques', because these facilities can condition the counsellor-counsellee relationship unhelpfully, by creating unbiblical expectations. Rather, the prerequisites for effective Christian counselling are: the Lord's training in 'the Christian walk'; 'ministering to one another'; a 'knowledge of the Word with an emphasis on Scriptures which relate to the mental-emotional-behavioural realm'; and sharing from one's own 'experience and knowledge'.[64]

This ministry is carried out in the atmosphere of 'faith, hope, and love', with dependence 'upon the Word of God' and in accordance with three principles:

1 *Listening/talking*, where listening is seen as a 'response of the entire person' and where both dimensions are seen to include the Lord's listening and speaking;
2 *Confessing/accepting*, in which Christ's acceptance of the client, without condoning his or her sin, paves the way for confession, forgiveness and cleansing;
3 *Thinking/understanding*, where godly wisdom and a spirit of discernment are exercised.[65]

The assumptions, aims and method of spiritual counselling are expressed when the Bobgans conclude: 'The perfect value system lies within the Word of God. And along with His value system, God has supplied the Holy Spirit to enable the Christian to live by biblical standards and the blood of Jesus to take away sin and guilt.'[66]

'Biblical' counselling

Scope Ministries

Jim and Doris Craddock established Scope Ministries in the early 1970s as an enterprise 'committed to the development of Biblical Counselling'. Jim became a Christian in Okinawa in 1954 through the work of the Navigators. He returned to Colorado to complete his studies in political science and, subsequently, he joined Campus Crusade for Christ, with which he worked for the next fifteen years. During the early years of his ministry on American college campuses he was challenged to consider meeting people's 'spiritual and emotional needs . . . through the Bible alone' and, in due course, Scope Ministries was founded.[67]

This body, which seeks to 'minister to the emotional, spiritual, and physical needs of the Church through the strategic, yet practical use of the Word of God alone', has grown from just one counsellor in 1973 to a staff of fifty or so twelve years later. Scope Ministries is an interdenominational 'para-church' organisation which, besides vital counselling work, also offers one and a half years of training for its staff. From its base in Oklahoma City, in 'the buckle of the Bible Belt', this counselling service has developed centres in Tulsa (Oklahoma), Alabama, Louisiana and Washington DC. Its expectation 'to make a significant contribution to the needs of the Body of Christ worldwide' has been partly met in Scope's participation in the training provided for the Billy Graham missions in Amsterdam in 1983 and England in 1984.

Craddock defines biblical counselling as 'an approach to counselling based upon the inspired, inerrant Word of God (literally and in principle), which utilizes the Bible as its foundation in the development of its theology, its philosophy, its therapies, its techniques, its tools and its materials'. Although he distances himself from an 'integrational' position, he feels that his brand of biblical counselling is closely allied to that of Larry Crabb. Like Adams and the Bobgans, Craddock is wary of so-called 'psychological truth', arguing that it must be 'viewed through the grid of Scripture as the absolute standard of truth'.

As with all the forms of biblical counselling considered in this chapter, the thrust of Scope Ministries is both evangelistic and a call to godliness. In accordance with the seminal influence of Campus Crusade on Jim Craddock and other members of the team, there is a strong emphasis on the 'Spirit-filled life' and the 'Lordship of Christ' for both the counsellor and the counsellee. Within these far-reaching objectives, the biblical counsellor seeks to encourage 'life-changing habits' in both thinking and behaviour, according to biblical principles. Craddock sees Paul's injunctions in Philippians 4:9 as an important guide for the counselling process: 'Whatever you have learned or received or heard from me, or seen in me – put it into practice. And the God of peace will be with you.'

In order to establish such new patterns of living, Scope Ministries uses a range of cognitive and behavioural 'tools' and techniques. The counsellor is provided with an instructive desk manual which gives guidance on a wide spectrum of subjects, including alcoholism, anxiety, depression, fear, grief, guilt and suffering. This reference book is comprehensive and aims to help the counsellor in both the recognition of symptoms and in biblical understanding of both problems and solutions. The client is seen for fifty minutes a session over six to eight weeks before reassessment. Within the context of a caring relationship, full use is made of an initial 'In-Take' information form filled in by the client, general reading material, cassettes and achievable assignments, which include the memorising, studying and writing out of scriptures.

Lawrence Crabb

Lawrence Crabb, like Jim Craddock, pioneered his approach to biblical counselling in the early 1970s. Trained as a clinical psychologist, he had worked as a professional counsellor in both a university setting and in private practice. However, 'aware of a deep sense of uneasiness', he came to admit that, 'as a Christian committed to a biblical view of man', he could not make his 'psychological thinking . . . dovetail with basic biblical beliefs'.[68] Encouraged by the wise counsel of a friend who was pastor at a nearby church in Boca Raton, Florida, Crabb left his secular employment to spend a year collecting his ideas 'on what the Bible says about counselling'. Following further years in Florida in private practice and as the director of the Institute of Biblical Counselling, he is now assistant professor in and chairman of the Department of Counselling, Grace Theological Seminary at Winona Lake in Indiana. His earlier books, *Basic Principles of Biblical Counseling* (1975) and *Effective Biblical Counseling* (1977) have been influential on both sides of the Atlantic.

Assumptions

Larry Crabb's methodology 'asserts the authority of Scripture and the necessity and adequacy of Christ'. We may describe his position as cautiously 'integrational' in that he seeks to develop 'a solidly biblical approach to counselling' which 'draws from secular psychology without betraying its Scriptural premise' – a premise that stimulates belief in 'an inerrant Bible and an all-sufficient Christ'.[69] In analysing the attempts of evangelical Christians to relate to both Christianity and psychology, he aligns his own thinking with a 'spoiling the Egyptians' stance. Crabb cites the incident mentioned in Exodus 12 in which the Israelites, sanctioned by the Lord, plundered the Egyptians of clothing and articles of silver and gold for their journey towards the Red Sea. However, the people of God also took some apparently doubtful company in the 'mixed multitude'. It is these people who appear to have been the main rabble-rousers amidst the disaffected Israelites in the wilderness. Consequently, of all God's people who had left Egypt, it was only Joshua and Caleb who survived the journeyings to reach the promised land. Crabb uses this involved story to emphasise the dangers of taking from secular psychology (spoiling the Egyptians) in that unsavoury elements may by assimilated (the mixed multitude) and, worst of all, Christian perspectives on psychology (the bulk of the Israelites) may perish. He therefore urges on integrationists a circumspection in the 'delicate and risky task' of screening the insights of secular psychology.[70]

As part of his watchful integration of psychological perspectives and biblical truth, Crabb declares two further premises:

1 People desperately need both meaning and love (*significance* and *security*);
2 Both these needs can be fully met by the all-sufficient Lord Jesus Christ.[71]

Before we consider the second of these statements as we look at the goals of Crabb's methodology, let us examine his view on people's basic needs. He argues that, before the fall, Adam and Eve knew significance and security. In other words, they experienced 'purpose, importance, adequacy . . . meaningfulness, impact' and 'love – unconditional and consistently expressed; permanent acceptance'.[72] Mankind's rebellion against God has led people to explore 'alternative strategies' for finding significance and security. Behind this sometimes feverish search for meaning, Crabb observes faulty thinking. He writes, 'Personal problems begin with a wrong belief which leads to behaviours and feelings which deny us the satisfaction of our deep personal needs.'[73] Furthermore, these inappropriate 'behaviours and feelings' are readily translated into symptoms when the individual meets 'obstacles' to his or her 'chosen goal'. Crabb declares that there are three main hurdles which may thwart a person in the particular race he or she has entered on; each of these tends to lead to a particular form of frustration:

1 *Unreached goals*, where the impossibility of the ambition gives way to feelings of *guilt*. Here we might postulate someone who wants to be acceptable to everyone around him. He cannot, of course, achieve perfection and his obsessive apologies, explanations and 'niceness' lose him friends. This failure, in turn, leads to self-recrimination.

2 *External circumstances*, where the goal seems attainable but people, things and incidents block the path; *resentment* is the result. For example, a rather average teacher sees her own training, experience and ability as more than a cut above anyone else's. She feels she is the obvious choice for a forthcoming post as head of the department and her deep irritation knows no bounds when an outsider is appointed.

3 *Fear of failure*, where the goal is a reasonable one but crippling fear generates *anxiety*. In this instance we could envisage a young man who has profound doubts about his virility. His aim is to find a girl whose company he can enjoy and whom he might eventually marry. His concern that he might be rejected is such that he never quite makes an initial phone-call. The more he prevaricates, the more anxious he becomes.

Crabb makes the point that many of us live in these 'pre-neurotic' states, where efforts are being made to overcome life's frustrations. Neurosis arises, he argues, when the individual gives up the unequal struggle and withdraws into the 'safety' of symptoms.[74] In the above examples this might mean: (i) compulsive acts such as excessive hand-washing or the development of nervous ticks that begin to lead to avoiding others; (ii) feelings of depression due to unresolved resentment; and (iii) excessive palpitations and feelings that he will faint, which 'enable' him to avoid social gatherings where he would meet female company.

Aims

In the face of the tragic loss of a sense of significance and security in the lives of many who seek help, Crabb declares the objectives of biblical counselling at a number of levels. Ultimately, its aim is Christlikeness: he writes that the 'goal of all true counselling' is 'to free people to better worship and serve God by helping them become more like the Lord'.[75] This maturing process, based as it is on 'our acceptance' through the 'atoning work of Christ', entails, in Crabb's language, moving both 'over' and 'up'. The client needs help both to move 'over' on to the path of obedience and to journey 'up' towards 'inward newness, a renewed way of thinking and perceiving, a changed set of goals, a transformed personality'. Crabb contrasts the radical nature of God's life-changing work with the goals of other therapists: 'Rogers renews feelings. Glasser renews behaviour. Skinner renews circumstances. Christ renews minds.'[76]

Method

Larry Crabb sees the local church as 'the primary instrument to tend to our personal aches and pains' and, therefore, the main context for biblical counselling. Within this setting he describes three levels of counselling:[77]

1 *Encouragement*, which deals primarily with 'problem feelings' and endeavours to replace these with 'biblical feelings'. He sees this level of caring as a calling for every member within the church family, to be exercised in an 'attitude of compassion and concern for the person who hurts'. This entails a sensitivity to 'those valid (opportunities) which cross our paths'.

2 *Exhortation*, wherein 'problem behaviour' becomes 'biblical behaviour'. Within the local church, a number of 'spiritually mature and responsible people' need to be trained in 'basic principles of Christian living', an ability to 'think biblically' and in 'general interviewing skills'. Pastors, elders and church leaders, who might thus be trained, need to be 'facile in thinking through complex situations and discussing the approach which would be the most consistent and biblical teaching'.

3 *Enlightenment*, in which 'problem thinking' gives way to 'biblical thinking'. Here there is a need for a thorough training for a 'few selected individuals who could be equipped to handle the

deeper, more stubborn, complicated problems'. It is this level of counselling that Crabb's *Effective Biblical Counselling* addresses and that we are considering primarily in this chapter.

Larry Crabb follows John Carter's suggestion that *parakaleo* and its cognates supply a 'much more adequate model of counselling (than *noutheteo*) from a biblical perspective'.[78] Crabb sees the concept within *parakaleo* of 'coming to one's aid in a variety of different ways depending on the problems' as providing a 'broad and accurate model for counselling'. His approach emphasises the relationship between the counsellor and the client wherein 'interactions vary depending on the temperaments, problems, personalities of the people involved'. 'Confrontation' will thus be one of a number of counselling styles that will need to operate from time to time.

Crabb delineates seven stages in his model for 'enlightenment' counselling:[79]

1 *Identify problem feelings.* Initially, such negative emotions as 'anxiety, resentment, guilt, despair, or a vague sense of emptiness' are identified.

2 *Identify problem behaviour.* Next, the counsellor seeks to clarify what the client was doing when he or she became frustrated at meeting an obstacle in the chosen path.

3 *Identify problem thinking.* This may involve Adler's 'Early Recollection Technique' in which the client is asked to recall his or her earliest memory, completing the sentence, 'One day I . . .' It is argued that people tend to remember most readily those incidents that specially shaped their psychological development.

4 *Change the assumptions.* At this stage the 'hard work begins' because firmly held beliefs are often overlaid with powerful emotions that resist probing. Here the client needs to be taken forward gently as these guardian feelings are expressed and as the possibility of changing wrong assumptions is considered. This process may be helped by the 'Tape Recorder' technique in which two cards are carried by the client – one declaring the faulty presupposition, the other the contrasting biblical perspective. When emotional upset arises the client is encouraged to read both cards, choosing to 'replay at top volume the biblical sentence'.

5 *Secure commitment.* The client is urged towards a commitment to right action however he or she may feel at the time of temptation. It is at this stage in counselling that an awareness of wrong

thinking, emotions and behaviour can be turned into confession and assurance of forgiveness.

6 *Plan and carry out biblical behaviour.* Here the counsellor and client agree specifically on new patterns of behaviour which need to be lived out.

7 *Identify Spirit-controlled feelings.* The client is encouraged to look for and rejoice in 'evidence of the Spirit's work' in his or her life. As thinking is renewed, a commitment to change followed and obedience practised, then, in time, a 'wonderful sense of improved adjustment' should be realised. This new peacefulness will not exclude such 'godly' emotions as anguish, constructive sorrow, concern and righteous anger.[80]

Such a system of counselling hopes to help the client join Larry Crabb in saying: 'God loves me enough to straighten me out, to smooth off the rough edges, to chip away until the brilliance of His Son shines through my life.'[81]

Selwyn Hughes

Selwyn Hughes is probably the best known British proponent of biblical counselling. His father having been converted in the Welsh Revival, Hughes became a pastor in the branch of Pentecostalism known as the Assemblies of God. Through the early 1950s he served the Lord in churches in Cornwall, Wales and Yorkshire. In 1958, while carrying out evangelistic work in Sheffield, he experienced what he has described as a 'breakdown'. This 'breakdown' became a 'breakthrough' for it seemed that Christ intervened miraculously, speaking powerfully through the words of John 10:10: 'I have come that they may have life, and have it to the full'. Hughes tells how he began to appreciate for the first time the 'strange world of damaged emotions'. Formerly he had seen human need purely in terms of 'sin' or 'sickness'; now he started to understand that the Greek biblical word *astheneia* may indicate weakness or infirmity as a third area of human susceptibility – an area that may engender sin but does not necessarily do so.[82]

With his interest in emotional and psychological matters awakened, Selwyn Hughes attended appropriate courses at Sheffield University and at the Rosemead Graduate School in the United States. Through the years his links with Clyde and Bruce Narramore, and with Lawrence Crabb have been formative in his thinking. In 1965, Hughes, deeply concerned for a revival of God's work, founded the Crusade for World Revival (CWR). By the early 1970s this organisation was expanding rapidly through Hughes' widely read *Every Day With Jesus* Bible notes, a prayer chain and the sales of *Revival* magazine. In 1975, Selwyn Hughes and his colleague, Trevor Partridge initiated a 'teaching and training ministry' which has become incorporated into the Institute of Christian Counselling – based, along with CWR, in Walton on Thames, Surrey. This body offers training at Larry Crabb's three levels of counselling:

1 An introductory day course entitled 'How to Help a Friend' for the work of *encouragement*;
2 A day course called 'Dynamic Christian Living' to help with the level of *exhortation*;
3 Residential courses on 'Christian Counselling' to train for the deeper ministry of *enlightenment*.

At the end of 1983, CWR bought Waverley Abbey House at Farnham, Surrey, as a centre for administration, the building up of resource material and for more comprehensive training in counselling.

Broadly speaking, Hughes' methodology has many parallels in the range of approaches to biblical counselling we have so far considered. In his *A Friend in Need* (1981), written to help Christians with the 'encouragement' and 'exhortation' levels of care, he declares that he believes 'the Bible, in its original form, to be divinely inspired and without error in all its parts'.[83] However, not least because of his own personal pilgrimage, he is not 'excluding' in his attitude to secular psychology; like Crabb, he seeks to evaluate other therapies from a 'spoiling the Egyptians' stance. He regards the deepest needs of people as security, self-worth and significance, and aims to see these deficits fulfilled in Christ. The goal of counselling is to help the client move 'from self-centredness to Christ-centredness'.[84]

As part of his strategy for helping someone, Hughes postulates a 'layer' theory of human function in which personality can be depicted as a series of concentric spheres – the outer coat comprising the physical and then each successive layer made up of the emotional, volitional, and rational, surrounding a spiritual core. During counselling, the counsellor evaluates each 'layer' diagnostically: medical check-ups are advised where necessary; negative feelings are identified; goals and choices explored; patterns of thinking assessed; and spiritual certainty checked. The quest for solutions is pursued by working back out through the 'layers', seeking to establish right ways of thinking, convictions, decisions, and the recognition and harnessing of the emotions. Like Ellis, he gives an emphasis on the importance of the right 'tapes' in the thought processes; unlike Ellis, Hughes stresses the vital use of the scriptures in creating those 'tapes'. Within the counselling relationship, he advocates the sharing of 'carefully selected Scripture passages' and has produced *The Christian Counsellor's Pocket Guide* (1977) as a ready reference to matching certain problems with appropriate texts.

Hughes' style of helping tends to shift from the identifying and encouraging elements of *parakaleo* towards the more confrontative nature of *noutheteo* as counselling proceeds. He says that Christian counselling is 'largely *directive*' in that, using the Bible readily, it is essentially 'telling people, with deep compassion and genuine love, what God requires of them'.[85]

'Discipleship' counselling

A final broad grouping within biblical counselling is the 'discipleship' counselling of such practitioners as Gary R. Collins and Gary R. Sweeten. We have already noticed the importance of 'making disciples' in other methodologies, particularly in those of Adams, the Bobgans and Craddock, and so the assessment of a separate category called 'discipleship' counselling may seem superfluous. However, in contrast to these other methods, but in line with Crabb and Hughes, both Collins and Sweeten argue for an 'integrational' approach to theology and psychology. As we gave space to Gary Collins' valuable work on integration in chapter ten, I would like to concentrate on Gary Sweeten's form of discipleship counselling at this stage.

Sweeten, who has an academic background in adult education, declares his Christian roots to be 'fighting Fundamentalist', origins which hold an attitude, to quote him, that 'loves Jesus and can't stand anyone else'![86] At a seminar in 1969, four years after Adams' formative summer with O. Hobart Mowrer, Gary Sweeten was challenged on hearing Mowrer say that 'the early

Christian church was the most powerful therapeutic community that ever existed'. Sweeten, in time, took on board Mowrer's thesis and concludes:

> Rather than reject Biblical Christianity as a counselling tool, we need to better learn our traditions and translate them into appropriate pastoral care . . . and pastoral counselling. This rediscovery I call 'Discipleship Counselling'.

In 1975 he began a 'Skills Training Programme' at College Hill Presbyterian Church in Cincinnati, Ohio in order to help people with interpersonal skills so that a 'total community of love, nurture, health, and life' might be built up. As this venture has prospered, Gary Sweeten and his colleague, Rev Alice Petersen now conduct workshops on the 'Integration of Psychology, Theology, and the Power of the Holy Spirit' besides offering practical advice on lay counselling. There has been a worldwide development of ministries based on a 'Teleios Model' (teleios, complete or mature) similar to that exercised at College Hill, in which small or large churches can learn to pastor their people more effectively.

Sweeten's assumptive basis holds the validity of both special and general revelation. His view of the Bible is expressed with unifying wisdom:

> We get into no debate or arguments with anyone over terms such as 'inerrancy' or 'infallibility' because they so often lead to dividing the Body of Christ. We simply believe that the Scripture is a true, reliable, trustworthy, and accurate guide to moral, spiritual and community life.

He follows the Reformers in seeing science as 'the handmaiden of the Lord for it teaches us to systematically examine nature to discover her organization and laws'. He reasons from an integrational position when he declares that the 'discipleship counselling' model is not only 'firmly grounded in Biblical and practical theology' but is also 'congruent with the most recent studies in counselling, counsellor education, pastoral psychology, and community psychology'.

The objectives within Sweeten's methodology are for both personal and communal change, achieved by training and mobilising the people of God. He writes:

Discipleship counselling is aimed at training people to be *effective* agents in the growth of believers toward wholeness in Christ. It is learning to work cooperatively with the Holy Spirit in the sanctification process. For that reason, we must learn to combine Discipleship and Counselling.

Discipleship, for both Sweeten and Collins, is the response to the great commission in which our Lord commanded his followers to 'go and make disciples of all nations' (see Matthew 28:18–20). Sweeten sees this edict as incorporating: growth in numbers through evangelism; growth in Christian maturity of individual church members; growth in the efficiency and effectiveness of the body of Christ; and growth in impact on the community and its range of needs. Within this high calling, the 'disciples' are allowing the Lord to rule over the whole of life. This yielding includes 'learning to be submissive to those in authority' and the releasing of 'the gifts of the Holy Spirit in their lives and ministries'.

In 'discipleship' counselling, the first goal is to train the pastors and other leaders to be able to disciple and counsel their flock. Both initial and subsequent training programmes are based on a theoretical foundation which looks to 'the truth of God in special and natural revelation'. In turn, the participants are encouraged to grow in 'personal awareness' as they discover their 'strengths, weaknesses, gifts, talents, and abilities'. The next layer of training is in the development of 'interpersonal skills', including such 'core conditions' as empathy, respect, non-possessive warmth, the ability to share one's own experience, genuineness, the skill of confrontation, the art of being specific (concreteness) and honesty about the counselling relationship (immediacy). The final level of training concerns the 'power to change' and seeks to aid the church members in the continuing 'development of the fruit of the Spirit' and in the identification and the use of the Spirit's gifts. This schedule is enhanced by the 'Apples of Gold', 'Rational Christian Thinking' and 'Breaking Free from the Past' courses, which, respectively, foster the assimilation of the 'core conditions', the overcoming of negative emotions, and the learning 'to release God's love and power' to set people free of inner bondage.

Discussion

We have considered a range of approaches to counselling which, in one way or another, claim to be thoroughly biblical. Sometimes, as with nouthetic counselling, the remit seems to be too narrow but, nonetheless, attempts to bring all aspects of caring to the touchstone of scripture are wholly commendable. At other times, the tendency to restrict the vista to one aspect of revelation can lead to an adversarial stance. Yet 'excluding' views have a resoluteness which can be a great challenge and stimulus to those of us who fish in the muddier waters of 'assimilation' and 'eclecticism' or, to change the metaphor, are busy spoiling too many Egyptians for safety's sake.

All of these styles of biblical counselling lend themselves to systematisation in a way that is alien to many British sensibilities. This is not to deny that, in a do-it-yourself world, most of us have recourse to handbooks at some stage or other, whether it is in servicing a car, trying out a new recipe, decorating a complicated room or learning to spin. Some of us, though, hesitate to apply a similar 'how to do it' approach to activities which largely concern 'relationships'. Sexual intercourse may no doubt be enhanced, where difficulties are primarily technical, with the help of the appropriate manual, but try developing a friendship by numbers or relating to a workmate according to a checklist! Similarly, in counselling, the dynamics of a growing relationship are not always best served by the sort of precise mental inventory that categorisation can produce. It is interesting to note that the more directive a counselling method is, the more directions are offered to the trainee. Conversely, those varieties of biblical counselling that stress more the counsellor-counsellee relationship seem to be less dependent on workbooks. Nevertheless, many of us do need guidelines, particularly if we are new to counselling, and are grateful for the analyses, schedules and manuals of people like Adams, Craddock, Hughes and Sweeten.

The trend for biblical counselling generally to centre its activity in the local church, and in the concept of discipleship, surely has strong precedents in scriptural teaching on the people of God. Amongst the handful of models we have briefly surveyed, I warm especially to Gary Sweeten's stress on the threefold aspects of a powerful and effective church life: '. . . the necessity of the truth of God; the fruit of the Spirit as validation of those who know the truth; and the essential nature of the power of God in the release of His charisma to combat sickness, sin and other forms of evil'. His comment that it is rare for 'a person, church, or congregation' to be 'mature and whole enough to give all three themes equal importance' is salutary. I suspect that where biblical counselling is open to this triple perspective it is most likely to communicate the wonder and power of our triune God.

It is probable that all of the schemes we have thought about in this chapter (most using adjectives which seem to claim much for their brand of counselling – 'biblical', 'spiritual', 'discipleship' and 'Christian') leave an impressive trail of lives challenged, restored and renewed in Christ. As with all methodologies, it is very difficult to know about those who cease attending, who dissemble a measure of improvement or who keep well clear of all advertised 'biblical counsellors'. If there are casualties, then it strikes me that these will at least include those who find certain of the approaches too insensitive, too controlling or too simplistic. Such criticisms may at times be justified. We can shrug them off by declaring that some clients are clearly resisting discipleship, trying to hide their sins from scrutiny or seeking to evade a straightforward word from the Lord. Reactions like these may, at times, be the case. It is also possible that the counsellor or the method is at fault: neither may be as Spirit-inspired, Christ-centred or biblically-oriented as we would wish.

There are many aspects to the dilemma. One of these is our great need for what has been grandly termed 'hermeneutical sagacity'. We should be obliged to listen more carefully to those theologians and Bible scholars who wrestle with interpreting the scriptures and we should study the Bible more comprehensively ourselves, continually checking our assumptions and prejudices with what the text *really* says, all the while seeking to glorify the Father, as we obey the Lord in the power of the Spirit. In this way of wisdom our understanding and use of the scriptures as counsellors will be a humble and sensitive enterprise. At times, we will need to draw our client's attention to specific biblical passages, but we should avoid a 'push-button' mentality where particular texts are *automatically* displayed as certain problems crop up. We are not dealing in computation – or in magic. Rather, we should listen to the living word as we counsel so that he may guide us in the use of the written word. The Bible may be the 'sword of the Spirit' but we are not, as Gary Sweeten puts it, to wield it to 'perform open heart surgery at every turn' – a heavy-handed approach to people in need that 'exudes death'. Behind our sharing of this or that portion of scripture with the person we try to help lies the more fundamental task of learning to 'think biblically' amidst the convoluted problems and searing anguish of the fallen lives we try to minister to. We need to move away from the dangerous shoals of bibliolatry (elevating the scriptures to the station of their author) and biblicism (tying thinking to the literal text regardless of any consideration of literary form, geographical setting and historical context) without denying that the words of the Bible, as originally given, are God-breathed and therefore trustworthy. Richard Lovelace sounds the right note of caution, I believe, for our handling of scripture as we seek to counsel according to biblical principles:

> We must guard against the assumption that all the truth that is needed for the most effective counselling is contained in Scripture. Biblical truth is not a compendium of all necessary knowledge, but a touchstone for testing and verifying other kinds of truth and a structure for integrating them. It is not an encyclopedia, but a tool for making encyclopedias.[87]

13

REACHING OUT: RELATIONSHIP COUNSELLING

Man seeks man and flees from him.
Jean de Rougement

Listening is an art that must be developed, not a technique that can be applied as a monkey-wrench to nuts and bolts. It needs the full and real presence of people to each other.
Henri Nouwen

Bear one another's burdens, and so fulfil the law of Christ.
Galatians 6:2 (RSV)

From the beginning, there has been a certain two-way bridge of communication between the healer and the healed, the spiritual guide and the disciple, the one who mediates forgiveness and the forgiven, the pastor and the sustained. These four-fold aspects of pastoral care – healing, guidance, reconciling and sustaining – have, as we have seen, been enhanced by, and in some cases supplanted by, the twentieth-century preoccupation with counselling and psychotherapy. As we noted in chapter two, the *relationship* between the counsellor and client, the therapist and the patient, is at the heart of the effectiveness of the helping therapies. Fiedler (1950), Rogers (1957), Truax and Carkhuff (1967) and others have researched and elaborated the prime importance of the qualities that both parties bring to that relationship. Nelson-Jones, summarising this theme, describes 'basic empathy' (made up of Rogers' triad – genuineness, non-possessive warmth and empathic understanding) as a 'necessary ingredient of virtually all successful counselling relationships' – not only in personalistic approaches but also in psychoanalysis,

Adlerian therapy and, to a lesser extent, rational-emotive and behavioural therapies.[1]

Christians who counsel do so not only in harmony with modern research but also in a time-honoured tradition when they emphasise that a caring relationship is integral to the help they offer. (The example given by Jesus as he related to the needy is something we shall look at more fully in chapter sixteen). This is not to deny the importance of relationship in the types of 'biblical counselling' we considered in the last chapter, although the more confrontational forms of these approaches major on God's propositional word rather than on the dynamics of personal interaction. Other Christian therapists have given a fuller focus on the face-to-face encounter in their methods of counselling. Such include a wide range of professional helpers from evangelical, liberal and Catholic backgrounds. Some are integrationist, seeking to blend a biblical theology with psychological understanding, some seem to be 'compartmentalised', separating their writings on therapy from overt Christian considerations, and others are eclectic, looking particularly to the personalism of Rogers and the existentialists. This broad grouping includes people as diverse as Gary Collins (also a 'biblical counsellor'), Paul Tournier, Seward Hiltner, Wayne Oates, Howard Clinebell, Tom Oden and, on the Catholic wing, Jack Dominian, Gerard Egan, Eugene Kennedy, Henri Nouwen and John Powell.[2] I propose to concentrate on Howard Clinebell and Paul Tournier as important representatives of this wide-ranging section.

Howard Clinebell

Howard Clinebell, following studies at Columbia University and Union Theological Seminary, has worked as a parish pastor in Indiana and New York, as a minister of counselling in a downtown church in Southern California and, latterly, as professor of pastoral counselling at the School of Theology at Claremont, California. His influence on the training of seminary students in the United States is considerable and he has become internationally known through conducting workshops on counselling and through his writing. His books include *The Intimate Marriage* (1970), co-authored with his wife, Charlotte H. Clinebell, and the widely read *Basic Types of Pastoral Counseling* (1966), now revised and reissued as *Basic Types of Pastoral Care and Counseling* (1984).

Along with David and Vera Mace, the Clinebells have been key contributors to the rise and spread of the Marriage Enrichment movement, designed to help 'good marriages become better' by encouraging a greater openness and mutuality of sharing within marriage. Working in small groups, each couple explores ways of communicating, the handling of anger and resentment, and the setting of realistic goals for the coming months. The idea of 'growth', both individually and as a 'partnership', is emphasised. In Britain, this movement is linked with the Westminster Pastoral Foundation and through residential weekends led by Hugh and Rachel Fielder, and others, many couples have been enabled to discover a new vitality to enrich their marriages. My wife, Joy and I have taken part in the Fielders' courses a couple of times and been greatly helped in our understanding of each other; in turn we, amongst others, have taken similar weekends under the auspices of Care and Counsel, a Christian counselling service based in London.

Assumptions

Clinebell is an integrationist, seeking to bring together resources from 'the psycho-social sciences and psychotherapy' and from 'our theological heritage'.[3] He is also widely eclectic, looking to the personalistic and transcendental views of, for example, Rogers, Maslow, May, Frankl and Assagioli, and the more confrontational approaches of Ellis and Glasser. Clinebell's commitment to the idea of psychological growth means that he is open to learn from the whole panoply of the humanistic growth movement, as well as from the various 'radical' therapies, which aim to bridge personal maturing and social change.[4]

Theologically, Clinebell seems to have been influenced to some extent by his teacher, Paul Tillich, the German existentialist theologian who taught in New York, Chicago and at Harvard from the late 1930s through to his death in 1965. Although Clinebell quotes Tillich quite freely in *Basic Types*, it is not clear how profoundly he follows the more liberal aspects of the German's thinking. It appears, rather, that Clinebell sees Tillichian concepts – God as the 'ground of being', people as estranged from that being, and humanity as needing 'new being' – as confirming more traditionally expressed beliefs. More fundamentally, Clinebell esteems the Bible highly without, as far as I am aware, deeming it necessary to present a detailed view of its inspiration and reliability. The scriptures are regarded as giving a unique and comprehensive insight into human nature. They are also viewed as a cardinal source of healing, teaching and comfort in the process of counselling.

Clinebell sees the dimension of *growth* as written deeply into the biblical record. He cites, for example, the beautiful imagery of the righteous person being like 'a tree planted by streams of water' (Psalm 1), our Lord's injunction to become 'like a little child' in order to enter the kingdom of God (Luke 18:17) and Paul's picture of growth towards Christlikeness (Ephesians 4:11–16).[5] The momentum of growth is regarded as a 'gift from God' and integral to our created nature. Clinebell views this 'potentializing' in somewhat Rogerian terms when he writes 'that persons have tremendous untapped creativity, intelligence, and capacity for socially useful and personally fulfilling lives . . .' However, he is aware of the 'superficial optimism' of some aspects of the 'human potential movement' and argues that 'biblical insights about the nature of being human and of growing' can enrich, inform and correct these misapprehensions.[6]

Nonetheless, Clinebell does at times seem overly optimistic about human nature, seeing both individual and collective sin as simply 'blocked potentializing' and 'resistance' to growth. He questions 'classical theology's interpretation of the "fall" as describing some deep irreparable flaw in our humanity' and dismisses a view that human evil is 'inherent and inevitable'. However, Clinebell's understanding of our fallenness does not deny the prevalence and destructiveness of our wicked ways; it affirms, rather, the need to be active and responsive to God in the face of our sinfulness.[7]

Aims

The objectives of Clinebell's *growth counselling* are depicted in terms of *growth*, *liberation* and *wholeness*. These overlapping goals are pursued at personal, relational and institutional levels.

Growth

The 'integrating core' of all personal development is, according to Clinebell, an individual's 'spiritual growth' – a growth which includes 'awareness, decision, freedom, meaning, commitment, and the quality of one's spiritual life and relation to God'. This 'lifelong process' of growth is to be encouraged within churches, schools and counselling agencies as people are helped to realise their own potentials and so become 'change agents' to enable others to mature.[8]

Liberation

Personal and societal liberation are important themes to Clinebell who (rightly, I believe) argues that a crucial feature of biblical revelation is to show humanity's need for relief from all manner of oppressions. At the individual level, a new freedom should be sought in what Clinebell describes as 'androgynous wholeness'. He points out that Jesus both showed characteristics that we tend to identify more with men – 'courage, strength, leadership, and concern for justice' – and those we see as womanly – 'caring, compassion, tenderness, and responsiveness to the needs of others'. Clinebell declares that the Lord 'demonstrated that both sets of qualities are neither masculine nor feminine but *human* capacities'. Growth counselling seeks to help the client feel free to develop the neglected aspects of the personality, moving towards 'androgynous wholeness'.[9] Certainly, the feminist movement has allowed many women to discover the more analytical and assertive sides to their nature. And yet, I have often found a deep resistance amongst male clients to acknowledge and express the more tender, nurturing, vulnerable and intuitive facets of their personalities. Such would benefit greatly, both within themselves and in their friendships, if they could let the guard slip and live out the richness of their inner selves more fully.

By extension, growth counselling is also strongly concerned about release within society from all racist, sexist and economically unjust trends. Clinebell is disarming when he urges us to 'transcend the Anglo-European, middle-class, white male orientation' of our pastoral care. He rightly argues that our traditional methods of 'introspection' and 'insight' are often useless amongst those who are 'economically disadvantaged' or from 'authority-centred ethnic and cultural groups'. Here the primary goal of counselling must be to help people discover 'practical ways of resolving their economic, employment, or health crises' and to make such discoveries 'fairly soon'.[10]

Wholeness

In growth counselling, the processes of 'growth' and 'liberation' help the client advance towards the 'unifying goal' of 'wholeness'.[11] Clinebell sees this objective as a 'growth journey' rather than a 'fixed goal'. He equates this 'wholeness' with partaking in the 'life . . . in all its fullness' which Jesus offered (John 10:10 NEB). Clinebell further links this quality of living with the Hebrew concept of *shalom*, meaning 'whole, sound, or healthy (as well as peace)' and correctly regards the context of such wholeness as both personal and communal.[12]

In counselling, 'growth toward wholeness' is sought in six 'interdependent aspects': the enlivening of the *mind*, aiming for increased awareness, perception and creativity; the refreshment of the *body*, including 'learning to experience and enjoy one's body more fully'; the 'renewing and enriching' of *intimate relationships*; a 'deepening' rapport with and caring for the *environment*; progress in relation to *institutions* and improvement in working with others; and, as a unifying factor in all areas, an enhancement of a *personal relationship with God*.[13]

Method

Clinebell's growth counselling is nothing if not comprehensive and it is therefore difficult to summarise its methods succinctly. Nevertheless, there are three notable dimensions to this system that we should consider: it is *pastoral*; it is based on *relationship*; and it is *holistic*.

Pastoral

Clinebell sets his growth counselling firmly in the context of pastoral care as the 'utilization of a variety of healing (therapeutic) methods to help people handle their problems and crises more growthfully and thus experience healing of their brokenness'.[14] This pastoral counselling includes the healing, sustaining, guiding and reconciling roles outlined by Clebsch and Jaekle (see chapter one), as well as Clinebell's additional 'nurturing', or 'sanctifying', function.[15] Such caring is carried out both by individuals, and in groups within the congregation, including 'marriage-and-family-enrichment groups, grief-growth groups, creative-singlehood groups, spiritual-discovery groups, and growth-action groups'.[16] Here the emphasis is on 'people helping people' within the fabric of everyday life.

The *pastoral* counsellor is someone who can often dispense with the formality of the 'office' setting, reaching out to others on the street, in their homes or at work. The pastoral calling means that initiatives can be taken in ways quite inappropriate to 'secular' counselling. A minister, for instance, is entitled to call in to enquire of a parishioner's well-being in an unsolicited way that would be greatly threatening to both parties in traditional counselling, where fears of dependency and the compromising situation may be real.[17]

Based on relationship

Clinebell regards the importance of the relationship between therapist and patient, and counsellor and client as paramount; he writes:

> Pastoral psychotherapy uses the relationship as the *foundation* on which uncovering methods are based . . . In supportive care and counselling the relationship *per se* is the primary instrument of change. Maintaining a dependable, nurturing relationship is the heart of the process.[18]

He sees this instrumental relationship as a vehicle for 'the grace of God'. In a moving passage, Clinebell paints a picture of himself as having an 'inner irrigation channel' which carries refreshing water to the parched areas in the lives he seeks to help. He views the 'Source of the flow' as residing far beyond himself and prays for 'openness to the presence of the Holy Spirit' – the one who works 'in and through our relationships'.[19]

Even so, Clinebell does not regard the therapeutic encounter as a passive affair in which the counsellor simply sits back and watches the contact between God and the client take place. The 'relationship *per se* is the primary instrument of change' and the delicate network of relating requires building up, maintaining and repairing.

Clinebell is particularly helpful here with respect to the sex and background of both client and counsellor.[20] Pastoral counsellors within a church setting are frequently male and, as such, Clinebell argues, are disadvantaged on two accounts when dealing with women clients. However liberated his thinking, a man is unable to know the experience of a woman in a sexist society 'from the inside' and, further, he cannot function as a 'role model' of a 'strong, competent, caring woman'. Clinebell is thus declaring that the male counsellor is not able to enter fully into the dilemma of many women in the West today, who feel victimised, misunderstood and demeaned, and who need the inspiration of other women who are confident and achieving. Nonetheless, men who counsel and who are 'warm, open, vulnerable, and growing (as well as competent)', besides being aware of sexist issues, can be effective in helping both male and female clients. By implication, as 'androgynous wholeness' is sought, then counsellors of either sex will be better fitted to counsel both women and men. In the meantime, Clinebell lays bare the need for more female pastoral counsellors.

He also points out that there should be more counsellors from ethnic minorities if the therapeutic relationship is to be truly effective in all circumstances. How readily, for example, can a clergyman from London's 'stockbroker' belt or a pastor from America's 'Bible' belt identify with and respond to a Sikh from the Punjab or a poor immigrant from Mexico or Puerto Rico? Clearly those who have lived with and made close friends of people from different ethnic origins will be better able to relate, but such counsellors seem to be few and far between. For most of us, it is easy to be blind to 'subtle but significant differences in the ways counsellees from other backgrounds perceive, conceptualize, feel, solve problems, and create their worldview'. Clinebell adds that, in our counselling, it is good for us to declare that we are aware of differences in background and to ask for help from our clients when there is misunderstanding.

Holistic

Clinebell portrays his approach as a 'new holistic growth and liberation centred paradigm for pastoral care and liberation counselling with spiritual and ethical wholeness at its centre'.[21] Holism, from the Greek *holos* and a word coined by Field Marshal Smuts in the 1920s, is defined as 'the tendency in nature to produce wholes from the ordered grouping of units'.[22] We have already seen how Clinebell refers to biblical concepts of wholeness as he tries to help people towards well-being in every part of life. This comprehensiveness is apparent not only in the objectives of growth counselling but in Clinebell's openness to a wide range of methodological insight. We shall look briefly at this inclusiveness with regard to the counsellor's *attitudes, resources* and *focus of attention.*

Attitudes. Clinebell follows the psychologist, Elias H. Porter in describing a spectrum of attitudes found amongst counsellors in their response to their clients.[23] Porter outlines five main categories:

1 *Evaluative,* involving both judgment and the implication of what the client '*might* or *ought* to do'; here, a counsellor might say, 'It seems to me that you are to blame in this situation';

2 *Interpretive,* in which there is an explaining and teaching component, which might lead to a statement like, 'What you have just said relates to your distrust of your father';

3 *Supportive,* wherein the counsellor seeks to reassure and undergird the client, saying, for example, 'I shall be able to see you regularly, so that if difficulties arise we will be able to discuss them promptly';

4 *Probing,* where there is an investigative and exploring spirit, raising such questions as 'You seem to be flustered whenever I mention your boss; can you tell me just how you feel about the way he treats you?';

5 *Understanding,* in which the counsellor shows his or her comprehension of the client's situation, indicated by such words as, 'Yes, thank you for explaining what happened last night. As I see it, you felt that you were being deceived. Have I got that right?'

Clinebell adds a sixth attitude:

6 *Advising,* where constructive suggestions are made, as in, 'I propose that you and your wife spend half-an-hour together each evening – really listening to each other.'

Taking the first letters of these six attitudes, Clinebell talks of the EISPUA categories and argues that the pastoral counsellor should be able to use any or all of these responses in the course of counselling. He sums up the diversity of these approaches in his 'growth formula', in which there is a balance of both caring and challenging. In harmony with the Pauline phrase 'speaking the truth in love' (Ephesians 4:15), Clinebell asserts that 'growth occurs in any relationship when one experiences both accepting love and honest confrontation'.[24]

Resources.   Growth counselling seeks to mobilise a wide range of resources within congregation and community to enhance the 'primary instrument of change' in the therapeutic relationship. Clinebell views the enabling of 'spiritual healing and growth' as the 'core task of all pastoral care and counselling', and so he sets a great deal of store in the use of 'religious resources' to achieve this end.[25]

However, prayer, the scriptures, sacraments, theological concepts and Bible stories are all to be handled 'with precision and care'.[26] There is no place for unthinking, insensitive or heavy-handed usage of these precious aids to spiritual health. They are only to be used when an understanding of the client's background has been attained, because 'religious' resources mean different things to different people. Further, caution is essential to prevent an unhealthy dependency in those who are looking for 'magic cures' and the avoidance of personal responsibility. In this context, I have found, at times, that it is best *not* to pray aloud with a client when to do so would somehow sidestep the challenge that he or she needs to go away with. I agree with Clinebell too when he says that these spiritual 'helps' should not be resorted to in a way that makes them a substitute for the counselling relationship. It seems to me that, within therapy, to deal with the Bible or prayer in a manner which deliberately distances another is basically wrong.

It is in his handling of the Bible with regard to counselling that we see once more Clinebell's all-inclusive approach. He appears to avoid the more 'prescriptive' style of using scriptural texts that we have noted amongst 'biblical' counsellors and, instead, outlines some more general ways of applying the Bible. These comprise: allowing 'biblical wisdom to inform the process, spirit, and goals' of counselling; comforting and strengthening people in crises with, for example, the perspectives of Psalm 23; as a means of diagnosis; as a corrective to wrong beliefs and attitudes; and as instruction. Clinebell has found a valuable diagnostic technique in inviting clients to share with him the Bible story they most like and the one they most dislike. By this method inner conflicts within Christian people may be exposed as they identify with or reject certain biblical characters. Someone who admires Jacob's scheming or Ruth's compliance may be telling us a great deal about themselves!

Focus of Attention.   Clinebell's comprehensiveness is found not only in the holism of his aims and therapeutic styles but in the varying foci of attention he offers. Broadly, his system includes a wide range of forms of therapy, embracing supportive, crisis, referral, educative and group counselling. Within these main groupings, the major focus may be, for instance, on bereavement, problem-solving, guilt feelings, spiritual understanding or ethical issues.

As the client is helped towards growth and wholeness, the counsellor keeps the emphasis on the present and the future. Elaborate probing into the past is not part of the remit and those earlier decisions, events and encounters that are still relevant are dealt with in the present. The future is viewed as exerting a strong pulling power on the client's will to change and make responsible choices.[27] The immediacy of Clinebell's approach is shown in his handling of a client who has 'intentionally violated the values' that his or her maturer side holds dear.[28] The 'growth formula' of love and *confrontation* is applied to encourage self-confrontation in this area of 'appropriate' guilt. As the expression of present emotions takes place *confession* will become a crucial part of the 'cleansing, healing process'. The pastoral counsellor may then have the privilege of being instrumental in the declaring of God's *forgiveness*. The client, in facing the 'living past' in present reality, is now supported while he or she plans to do all that can be done to make amends with those harmed. As human friendships are repaired, this *restitution* gives way to the reality of *reconciliation* – with God, others and oneself. Growth counselling, by this systematic concentration on the present opens up genuine hope for the future.

Paul Tournier

The gentle wisdom and therapeutic skill of Paul Tournier, the retired Swiss doctor, is known worldwide – largely through his twenty or so books, written from 1940 onwards and translated into eleven languages.[29] Born in Geneva in 1898, he was the son of Louis, an elderly pastor, and his second wife, Elizabeth, then in her late twenties. The death of his father, when Paul was only a few months old, and of his much-loved mother, when he was six, left a deeply imprinted 'orphan complex' in Tournier's life. When in his eighties, he wrote that it is possible to describe the whole of his writings as 'a long search for maternal tenderness'.[30]

Paul and his older sister were thus torn from 'the loving, intellectual and religious influence' of their home-life and brought up by an aunt and uncle. At the age of eleven or twelve, the young Tournier made two far-reaching decisions: to commit his life to the Lord; and, in due course, to become a doctor. In later years, he reflected that his purposing to read medicine was 'to avenge the death of my parents, especially that of my mother'.[31] He was a shy and lonely child who found solace in the companionship of his uncle's hunting dogs and in his own private retreat in a tree-house.

In *The Gift of Feeling* (1979), Tournier tells how his mediocrity at school was radically changed by his 'first psychotherapist', a classics master who befriended the sixteen-year-old by inviting him home.[32] Weekly visits to the teacher's house built up a valuable relationship of which Tournier writes, 'someone was listening to me . . . as a human being, a person'. Stimulated by a new sense of worth, Paul entered into a whirlwind of activity for the rest of his school years and while at medical school. He founded the students' union at the University of Geneva, worked in Vienna for the repatriation of Russian, Austrian and German prisoners-of-war, organised international aid for destitute children, and became an enthusiastic church member, speaking out for orthodox Calvinism and against modernism. In 1923 he graduated as a doctor and married Nelly Bouvier, the wife who was to become his close and loving companion until her death in the 1970s – a bereavement in which Tournier felt 'orphaned for the third time'.[33]

When Tournier was thirty-four he met his 'second psychotherapist', a Dutch financial expert who held a high office in the League of Nations and was a member of the Oxford Group. This movement had been started by Frank Buchman, an American pastor, at Oxford University in 1921 and taught a 'concrete obedience to God's inspiration in daily life, both private and public' and complete openness between one Christian and another. At the home of his new Dutch friend, Tournier was able to share his suffering as an orphan for the first time, experiencing the novelty of a 'truly personal, emotional dialogue'. His wife, Nelly soon became his 'third psychotherapist' for she encouraged him to move from his tendency 'to instruct her and explain everything to her intellectually' to a 'real personal relationship'. Tournier sought to make amends with those on the church governing body whom he had resisted and, in time, found that his relationships with family, friends, colleagues and patients became richer and warmer. He and Nelly became very active in the Oxford Group, travelling throughout Europe during the 1930s to help others to declare hidden emotions and commit their lives to God and his daily guidance. At the end of the Second World War, the Tourniers severed their links with the movement as they disagreed with the political emphasis of the newly formed Moral Rearmament, which grew out of the group.

In the summer of 1935, Paul Tournier was driving the family car when the vehicle skidded on a wet road and crashed, killing his uncle and badly injuring Nelly. Tournier was shattered by the accident, searching his conscience through the night as to whether he was guilty or not. He concluded that he was both culpable and, at the same time, a 'victim', discovering forgiveness and a new peace 'at the foot of the Cross'.[34] This was a 'watershed' experience, coinciding with a new emphasis in his work as a general practitioner in which he would invite patients into his home to chat by the fireside. Two years later, as a result of a 'divine call', he decided to devote himself to 'a Christian view of medicine', seeking to open 'the door to the grace of God' in the lives of those he tried to help.[35]

In 1947, Paul Tournier, along with the psychoanalyst, Dr Alphonse Maeder of Zurich, and Dr Jean de Rougement of Lyons, organised the first of the International Conferences on the Medicine of the Person. Meeting in the old castle at Bossey, near Geneva, doctors from a broad range of medical and denominational backgrounds shared their concern for their profession's 'excessive specialization' and the premium it placed on technique at the expense of humanity. Tournier's contribution to the annual meetings of the 'Bossey Group' has included regular lectures on medical and psychological understanding in the light of the Bible – series which have provided material for his books. Other important pioneers in this 'medicine of the person' were Théo Bovet of Zurich, Aloys von Orelli in Basle, Roberto Assagioli of Florence, the founder of psychosynthesis, and Assagioli's collaborator in Los Angeles, Robert Gerard.[36]

Paul Tournier has always been at great pains to point out his lack of specialist training. His own distinctive perception of people's psychological needs has come about through his willingness to learn in his encounters with patients, and in his wide reading. Persuaded against becoming a psychoanalyst by his friends, Tournier, the general practitioner, has revelled in his freedom to cultivate 'an interest in the whole of medicine and not in psychiatry alone'. His numerous writings reflect a prime concern for the rich field of his relationships with his patients. Although many of his earlier books have an anecdotal and discursive style which I, for one, have sometimes found difficult to persist with, his later works reveal thorough scholarship and an orderly presentation, shot through with his characteristic warmth and disarming honesty.

In *Creative Suffering* he refers to his generalism with waggish humour:

> So, for forty years now, in all my books, I have been trampling regardless over all the barriers which the analytical spirit of our civilization has carefully been erecting between the various disciplines; not only the medicine of the body, genetics, and psychology, but also sociology, education, economics, history, literature, theology, and philosophy. Of course I lack competence in each of these individual disciplines, and the experts find it easy to denounce my mistakes and see me as a perpetual heretic.[37]

In spite of being dubbed a 'heretic' by the experts, Tournier's insatiable curiosity and creative mind have kept him 'trampling regardless over all the barriers' from his teen years right through to old age. Re-reading Sophocles and Plato in his seventies and excited by 'data processing, cybernetics, and electronics' in his eighties, Tournier is the quintessential amateur – that is, 'someone who thoroughly enjoys what he is doing and takes his work seriously'.[38]

Assumptions

Psychological

Like Howard Clinebell, Paul Tournier is both eclectic in his sources and integrational in the direction he takes. In contrast to

Clinebell, who is influenced by the American pragmatism of the neo-behaviourists and cognitive therapists, Tournier, not surprisingly, has been more open to European systems of thought. Although both men look to the existentialists and psychosynthesists, the analytical theories of Freud, Jung and Adler play a distinctive part in Tournier's thinking. Whereas Clinebell focuses on the present and the future in therapy, Tournier gives a great deal of attention to the past and the realm of the unconscious.

However, the Swiss doctor is not uncritical of the views of the pioneers of psychoanalysis. He points out, for example, Freud's tendency to reduce human diversity 'to a standardized schema' and the way Freudians have 'formulated a doctrine of aggressiveness and set it up in opposition to Christianity'.[39] Further, Tournier expresses his concern that 'scientific psychological methods', such as those of Freud, Jung and Adler, can be 'elevated into systems', in which problems are seen to be about 'mechanisms' and not 'values', and about 'functions' rather than 'the person'.[40] He manages to avoid such systematisation in his own methodology, declaring that he belongs 'to no particular school of thought'.[41] At the same time, as Collins has noted, Tournier 'believes that every method can help, so long as the therapist has a positive attitude toward his patient'.[42]

Since his earliest writings Paul Tournier has been a protagonist for integration between science and the Bible, between psychology and theology. Writing in his eighties, he looks back on his 'personal vocation' of attempting 'a synthesis between psychology and classical medicine – and even religious belief'.[43] This quest has been undergirded by Tournier's conviction that God speaks through both general and special revelation, although the latter has the primacy. He writes: 'Nature has a meaning. It speaks to us of God; not only of His greatness or His wisdom, but also of His love'[44] and, in another place: 'But it is above all through the Bible, the book of the Word revealed and incarnate, that God speaks, and personal contact with him is established.'[45]

Even so, Tournier does not see this call to integration as a simple affair. He acknowledges that the public often senses a deep contradiction between matters psychological and spiritual so that there appear to be 'two gospels' – 'a gospel of psychology, and a biblical gospel; a gospel of self-fulfilment, and a gospel of

self-denial; a gospel of self-assertion, and a gospel of renunciation; a gospel of sincerity, and a gospel of charity'. This apparent
division is further deepened by the fear and criticism which can
exist between doctors and theologians. Tournier urges the professionals to enter into a 'true dialogue' where not only ideas are
exchanged but 'personal problems' and 'intimate difficulties'
are aired.[46]

Theological

Just as the psychological roots of Tournier's thinking are diverse
and even fragmentary so we do not find a clearly defined theological position in his books. Collins puts it that Tournier holds a
'loosely organized collection of religious beliefs, many but not all
of which are similar to the beliefs of Calvin'.[47] His Calvinist
upbringing, his close study of the Bible, his friendship with Emil
Brunner, his personal contacts with Karl Barth, and his admira-
tion for the Jewish theologian, Martin Buber have all contributed
to Tournier's 'collection of religious beliefs'. Gary Collins quotes
The Person Reborn (1946) in which Paul Tournier indicates an inner
call to link 'orthodoxy', which he sees as 'a personal evangelistic
faith completely subject to the authority of the Bible', and 'tolerance', viewed as the 'definitive renunciation of any attempt to
propagate that faith by doctrinal argument or controversy'.[48]

How does Tournier view the scriptures? From his writings we
are shown a man who has a deep love for the practical wisdom of
the Bible. He regards the biblical record as giving answers for our
daily concerns, 'more poetic, more intuitive, and above all more
dynamic, than we are', full of psychological insight and 'burn-
ingly up-to-date' in condemning modern society.[49] Collins notes
that Tournier is not explicit about biblical inspiration and says of
him that 'he is more interested in determining how the Bible can
give a practical answer to the questions that are raised in his own
life and work'.[50]

Even the most cursory reading of Tournier's works reveals that
he believes in a trinitarian God, to whom he is irrevocably
committed. Following his exposure to the Oxford Group in 1932,
he realised that his faith had been 'too intellectual and theological, and very poor in personal experiences'; he saw that he 'had
been preoccupied with the need to have the right ideas about
God, and very little with the ideas that God might have about

(him)'.[51] He has spent the rest of his days listening to those divine 'ideas', in close companionship with Jesus Christ and open to the Spirit's leading.

Human nature

Tournier sees humankind as created in God's image and yet prone to destructiveness: men and women, although made for fellowship with the Father, rebel wilfully and experience lostness. He likens humanity's general state to the perversity of the prodigal son. He writes: 'All men are exiled, impoverished and all feel guilty; all yearn for the wealth of the home they have abandoned, and for forgiveness.'[52]

This longed-for return to the Father's home is effected through a personal relationship with the Lord made possible by his death on the cross: 'Salvation is no longer some remote ideal of perfection, for ever inaccessible, it is a person, Jesus Christ, who comes to us, comes to be with us, in our homes and in our hearts. Remorse is silenced by His absolution.'[53]

For Tournier, however, the Bible 'announces the collective salvation of the whole human race, and not only that of Christian believers'; he declares that it is 'rather uncharitable' to think otherwise. He argues a universalism that regards Christians as simply the ones who *know* the liberator of all mankind.[54]

Within his copious writings, Paul Tournier displays a vast repository of wisdom about the human condition. Our humanity is often viewed as having two contrasting elements which need to be brought under the lordship of Christ. The themes are many, and include: the 'two gospels' of psychology and biblical theology; the 'two movements' of self-assertion and self-denial; the 'strong' and the 'weak'; 'true' and 'false' guilt; 'benign' and 'improper' violence; intellect and feeling; privilege and deprivation. I propose to look briefly at just two of his twinned concepts: *person* and *personage*, foundational to many of the other ideas; and *masculinity* and *femininity*, a perspective that emerges most strongly in Tournier's later books.

Person and personage. Tournier's notion of the person is so deeply rooted that his whole approach to people as a doctor is widely known as 'the medicine of the person'. As well as the stimulus from the thinking of such contemporaries as Maeder, Bovet and de Rougement, Tournier acknowledges his indebtedness to the personalistic philosophy of Emmanuel Mounier – a Christian who challenged both bourgeois society and communism during the first half of the century.[55]

Tournier says that each of us has both a personage and a person.[56] He equates the personage with Jung's *persona*, as that part of us which is seen most readily by others. This personage – the external appearance made up from the clothes we wear, the way we wear them, our bearing, behaviour, mannerisms, occupation, leisure pursuits and lifestyle – is the expression of our person, or inner self. Conversely, 'our personage moulds our person' or, as Tournier quotes Napoleon as saying: 'One becomes the man of one's uniform'. What you and I say, the gestures we use, the impressions we give can mould and modify the persons we are.

Consequently, Tournier urges us to bring the personage 'into harmony with the person', not by turning inwards, 'where the true nature of the person always eludes us', but by looking outwards, 'towards the world, towards our neighbour, towards God'. Indeed it is only in relationship with God that you or I can be made a person, 'a free and responsible being' – and that dialogue can only be re-established through Jesus Christ who 'alone is a person without a personage'. This seems to mean that there is no 'front' with Jesus; he alone is fully a person through and through, consistent, integrated, a man without a mask. And this Christ is 'God coming to us because we cannot go to him'.[57]

Male and female.   Like Clinebell, Tournier addresses himself to the crucial debate about human nature raised by the issues of sexism and feminism – issues that are important for every member of society, and therefore for both counsellor and client. In *The Gift of Feeling*, he explores the 'complementary poles' of 'the taste for things' and 'the sense of the person', which, respectively, 'more or less correspond to the complementarity between man and woman'. Tournier writes, 'more or less' because he appreciates that there are men with a great capacity for personal relationships and women who have well developed technological skills and a primary interest in things. Further, he acknowledges that there are 'masculine' and 'feminine' tendencies within each of us.[58]

In seeking to trace the roots of nineteenth- and twentieth-century sexism, Tournier looks to the writing of Régine Pernoud, a woman historian who specialises in the Middle Ages.[59] She argues that, before the Renaissance, women in Western civilisation enjoyed a measure of political, economic and occupational equality. This is not to say that women in the medieval period experienced full freedom but their liberation was 'more advanced than it had been throughout antiquity'. However, the Renaissance saw the re-establishment of Roman law, with its view that women are of a lower status than men, and the emergence of a male-dominated, power-hungry society. The prevalence of intellect over body, and of things over the person, has been carried into our modern era. Tournier concludes that 'a kind of repression took place': '. . . the repression of affectivity, of sensitivity, of the emotions, of tenderness, of kindness, of respect for others, of personal relationship, of mystical communion – and of woman, with whom all the terms in this list are linked by spontaneous association of ideas'.[60]

Tournier feels that the first stage of the feminist movement in this century has been to establish 'the similarity of men and women'. He now declares that the time is ripe for moving into a second phase, within which we ask 'if there is something that we can expect of women which men are less capable of providing'. This 'something', he suggests, is to be found in woman's greater endowment 'for personal contact, for the emotional life, for concrete attention to the personal needs of each individual'.[61]

Here Tournier strikes a most serious note. He believes that the power-crazy strategy of the Renaissance is 'unstable in the long run' and that we are now in the grip of 'the fear of a civilization devoid of all humanity, in which the person is stifled by things'. Our chauvinism has thrust aside 'one half of the human race' and, in doing so, is in danger of losing the more important half of life, 'since, as psychology has taught us, man is not guided by reason but by his emotions'.[62]

Tournier concludes his moving and prophetic book, *The Gift of Feeling* by urging women to recognise their mission 'to bring warmth back into our frozen world of objectivity, to give our mechanized society a soul', and by calling both men and women 'to build the world together'.[63]

Aims

Gary Collins has shown that Tournier is often imprecise and diffident on the question of objectives in counselling.[64] For example, in *A Place for You* Tournier writes with disarming frankness: 'I do not know what to say to all the people who bring me their dilemmas, for they seem to me generally to be insoluble.'[65] Nevertheless, his hesitancy becomes resolve when he believes he 'can see what God's will is' for the patient. Herein, perhaps, lies the key to Tournier's aims for those in need, for he seems to be open to the Spirit's guidance in a fresh way for each new individual who comes to see him. Even so, we can discern at least four objectives in his methodology. These are, broadly following Collins: *insight; liberation; acceptance;* and *'soul-healing'*.

Insight

Unless the patient can be helped to sense something of the reality of hidden anger, the yearning for recognition, the presence of true guilt or the suppression of tenderness, there is not much hope for radical change. Where 'unconscious impulses' are unmasked, then there is the possibility of learning to master them.

Liberation

When a measure of new self-understanding is achieved, the way is open for liberation from those things that drag us down. The range of possible release is wide:

> (liberation) means freeing men, as far as in us lies, from suffering; but it also means freeing them from their loneliness, from their anxieties, their remorse, from their rebelliousness, and from all the enslavements that compromise their physical, psychological, and spiritual health.[66]

'To live is to choose' is an aphorism that Tournier uses frequently, and he prevails upon those who seek freedom to make their own choices. And such choosing 'also means renouncing', a 'letting go' of those attitudes, conditions, things or people that would hold us back. He likens this need to relinquish certain elements in life to the trapeze artiste, who must have the confidence to let go of one support before he can swing through the air to catch hold of another. Therein lies a dilemma for those who seek help. Liberation involves letting go. To refuse to budge is 'to die a little. It is to remain attached to one's trapeze instead of jumping as life calls us to do.'[67]

Acceptance

However, Tournier is realistic. Many of us find, even in 'letting go', that there are certain given aspects of life which stay with us as we leap towards our next 'support'. We do not necessarily find dramatic psychological or circumstantial liberation in our bid for freedom; the challenge for us may be one of acceptance – 'of one's age, one's sex, a spouse, or a parent, an affliction, a failure, a mistake'. And yet, as we well know, such acceptance of one's lot is much more difficult for some than others. Many find a chronic illness, a difficult relative, a prolonged state of unemployment, or an unjust situation quite intolerable, and such cannot helpfully be told, particularly by a well attuned and well-heeled therapist, that they *must* accept their circumstances. Tournier adds that adjustment can only come 'from a slow inner evolution'.[68]

More radically, Christian faith can be the key to acceptance where, for instance, 'there are physical and psychic infirmities from which no medical or psychological treatment can free us'. Tournier gives the example of a colleague who suffered from a sexual abnormality which precluded marriage. This man had discovered that 'the goal of life is not health, but to bring forth fruit' and he had been enabled through faith to see that celibacy and a life devoted to scientific research was God's way forward.[69]

Soul-healing

Most fundamentally, Tournier's objective in counselling is to bring 'soul-healing' to the men and women who come to him for help. And yet this desire to bring others into lifelong fellowship with a loving God is never lightly pursued. Tournier is very wary of an approach to the needy which tends to 'brush aside even the gravest problems by resorting to religious exhortation'. However, he realises that so often an individual is helped with profound psychological difficulties solely to be brought face to face with issues 'which can be solved only through true forgiveness and true renunciation'.[70] Where the conscience is awakened, the only valid solution is 'the acceptance of our responsibilities, genuine recognition of our guilt, and repentance and the receiving of God's forgiveness in response to this repentance'.[71] This 'soul-healing' is part and parcel of the encounter with the living Lord in which people in need bind themselves 'ever more closely to Him through faith'.[72]

Method

Dialogue counselling

Tournier's 'medicine of the person' is characterised by the Socratic method of *dialogue*, in which there is a frank interchange that seeks to enable others to view themselves clearly and acquire personal convictions.[73] This interchange is truly reciprocal. As Tournier puts it: 'I think what distinguishes me most clearly from the specialists in psychotherapy of all the varying schools is this commitment of my person in the dialogue with the patient, my readiness to talk to him about my own problems.'[74]

Here there is communication between two persons, rather than simply an association of two personages. This 'true personal relationship . . . involves both choice and risk; it lays open to a reply, and to the necessity of replying in turn: it is a dialogue'. Choosing to expose one's inner self *is* risky, for the grim possibilities of a rejecting judgment and the betrayal of confidence lurk behind every frank encounter.

In addition to this 'true personal relationship' between counsellor and client is the equally important 'inner dialogue' between each of them and God. In the discussion, in the silences, in the reading of the Bible, in prayer and in moments of decision, God is speaking. Moreover, Tournier believes that this inner dialogue can take place 'even if the man concerned is not a believer and thinks he is wrestling only with himself'.[75]

The route to the establishing of dialogue within the counselling relationship is, at least initially, through the objectivity of psychotherapeutic technique. As we have seen, Tournier is truly eclectic in that technique, looking to the analytical methods of Freud, Jung and Adler, as well as the personalistic insights of humanist and existential therapies. Dream analysis, for instance, is an integral part of Tournier's methodology and yet his 'circumspect eclecticism' permits him to use both Freudian and Jungian perceptions. He often uses interpretations from each of these schools to shed light on the dreams of one particular patient. He likens Freud's instinctual understanding and Jung's purposive view of the dream-world to back-wheel and front-wheel drive respectively. However, these perspectives are partial. It is the Bible which reveals that human nature is 'a four-wheel-drive vehicle', in which both instincts, 'thrusting from behind', and aspirations, 'pulling from in front', are God-given.[76]

Even though Tournier uses analytical approaches, his technique is always subject to relationship. In analysing dreams, rather than seeking a 'scientific interpretation', he is 'much more concerned to get inside the dream . . . to feel it, to appropriate it to (himself)' so that 'real fellowship' is created between him and the patient.[77]

From what we have said so far, it is clear that 'dialogue counselling' is centred upon a relationship between just two people. Unlike Clinebell's 'growth counselling', there is no place for group therapy in Tournier's method: the scale is too intimate and the level of personal investment too deep for the interplay of a network of relationships. Further, as with Rogerian therapy, dialogue is non-judgmental and, by and large, non-directive. Tournier argues that 'God knows so much better' than he does with respect to the patient's situation. Moreover, giving advice is eschewed in that, if it is followed, the recipients 'remain children' and, if it is not followed, they are 'isolated'. Nevertheless, although Tournier's intention is to be non-directive, he is level-headed enough to acknowledge that the therapist's 'implicit beliefs' are bound to be influential.[78]

Let us look now at two other distinctive features of Tournier's 'dialogue counselling': *confession* and *meditation*.

Confession. Within his medical practice, Tournier has noticed time and time again that the patient's need for confession is basic to a change in direction. He has observed that 'many functional disturbances, and, in the long run, many organic lesions as well, are the direct consequence of unresolved remorse'. The admission of a lie or an illicit love-affair can bring the relief of headaches, insomnia or palpitations – as well as the joy of forgiveness. Tournier is aware that numerous people are searching for a confessor and, where he or she is 'willingly trusted', the doctor may be called to be that person. In the case of Roman Catholic patients, Tournier is at pains to encourage them to seek priestly absolution under the ruling of their faith.[79]

However, the picture of a doctor or counsellor who sits back somewhat smugly and exacts painful confessions from patients or clients is far from Tournier's mind. The one who offers help is also a sinner and needs confession too. Tournier writes of himself and the patient: 'I am as guilty, as powerless, as inferior and as desperate as he is . . . I am his companion in repentance and in waiting for grace.'[80] And this is not just a token admission of guilt, for the dialogue counsellor should be open to confessing his or her shortcomings to the client.

Tournier knows that 'we all feel a formidable inner resistance to entering . . . into true confession, the sort which really humbles'. He had himself been protected by the defences of an arid and intellectualising Christianity until he was disarmed by the genuine admissions of fallibility amongst his new friends in the Oxford Group. As he sustained 'the regular practice of confession', he found a 'spiritual ministry opened' before him.[81]

Amongst the examples Tournier gives of the way confession to the patient can facilitate counselling is the occasion of a referral from a 'highly regarded' colleague. Tournier found that weeks passed without progress in the attempted dialogue with the woman patient. A time of prayer revealed that he was personally at fault in that he was concerning himself 'too much with being successful' in the eyes of his colleague. He realised that his fear of failure had made him less relaxed, which in turn had produced an unnaturalness that made success even less likely. He shared his thoughts with his patient and discovered that the atmosphere between them improved considerably.[82]

Meditation.   A second legacy which Tournier inherited from the Oxford Group is that of meditation, in which the individual keeps silence before God in 'adoration and spiritual communion'. It has been Tournier's habit to spend an hour or so every day, usually alone but sometimes with his wife Nelly or a close friend, in silent fellowship with the Lord. Having placed himself firmly in God's hands, he reflects on whatever comes to mind – something he has said or done, a snatch of conversation, a piece that he has read, someone he has met, yesterday's disappointments, today's plans and tomorrow's hopes. He consciously thinks about these things in God's presence, seeking his guidance as he meditates and moves towards practical decisions and new resolutions. Tournier finds that writing down his thoughts helps him to be more precise and committed to action. He discovers too that God often reminds him of people during meditation so that his reflections are 'a sort of school for fidelity in intercession'.[83]

Just as both counsellor and client need confession, so meditation is regarded as of value to both parties. During therapy, Tournier is sensitive to the inner dialogue that is taking place within himself and in his patient. At times there may be a spontaneous silence when God is clearly speaking to the patient. These moments of 'silentiotherapy' are sacred and are enhanced by Tournier's own quiet meditation. He observes that a 'prolonged silence can become the highest form of personal communication, real communion, especially if we both feel we are in God's presence'. This responsiveness is practical. Patients may be helped by writing down fresh insights or lines of action. Moreover, they may be advised to meditate before seeing the therapist and so be enabled 'to come at once to the things that really matter'.[84]

As well as meditation, Tournier also emphasises the importance of prayer and Bible study in both everyday life and within the counselling process. He is quite open to a 'straightforward declaration of his faith' to the patient and admits that, at times, a verse from the Bible may afford 'the only true relief'. On the other hand, Tournier does not feel obliged to talk to every patient about Christ, aiming to adapt his approach to the nature and needs of each person he helps.[85]

Discussion

In this chapter we have considered the methodologies of two Christian counsellors for whom the therapeutic relationship is the prime focus of the counselling process. They come to this crucial encounter from different backgrounds and with different styles of therapy. Clinebell stands within an American pastoral tradition which looks a great deal to the 'human potential movement' and its quest for personal and communal growth, where attention is given primarily to the present and the future, and where the units for counselling and nurture are diverse in size and content. In contrast, Tournier has trained as a doctor within the psychoanalytical climate of Central Europe. He and others have pioneered a distinctive 'medicine of the person', where the past and the unconscious are recognised as powerful forces in the patient's condition, and where the intimate and confessional nature of dialogue requires a counselling unit of no more than two.

Both therapists are eclectic in their methods and both seek an integration of psychology and theology. Clinebell presents a greater systematisation of his comprehensive range of approaches, perhaps not least because of his considerable involvement in training and education. Tournier is aware that his emphasis on the nuances of dialogue is 'impossible to teach' and, as a result, admits a certain embarrassment, 'more especially in America, for Americans like a clearly formulated doctrine and a technique that can be taught'.[86]

It is probably fair to say that neither Clinebell nor Tournier offer a fully developed theology in their major writings.[87] Although both lay claim to the cardinal tenets of orthodox Christianity, there is a tendency in Clinebell to play down the pervasiveness of sin and, in Tournier, to dismiss the reality of hell and proclaim a universalistic gospel.[88] The apparent reasons for these beliefs include, for Clinebell, his desire that people should not be hampered by morbidity and defeatism, and, for Tournier, his deep compassion for all men and women, coupled with his concern about an unwanted exclusivism amongst certain strands of Christianity.

Both 'growth' and 'dialogue' counselling value biblical insight about the nature of God and our humanity, besides viewing it as a tool in therapy. Unlike 'biblical' counsellors, Clinebell and Tournier appear not to spell out their understanding of the inspiration of the Bible and, generally, they decline to use scriptural texts in a prescriptive way. During counselling, they seek to impart biblical wisdom in a manner that does not threaten the encounter. Bible, prayer, meditation and sacraments may mediate God's blessing, but it is the *relationship* between counsellor and client that is the context of that blessing.

My own view is that Clinebell and Tournier, as representatives of 'relationship' counselling, make a most valuable contribution to the ways of caring for people in need. I believe their stress on the encounter between counsellor and client, and between each of these and God, is thoroughly scriptural in that our God is a God who makes covenants with his people and is one who calls us into fellowship with him and one another. Clinebell (like Crabb, Collins and Sweeten, amongst other 'biblical' counsellors) emphasises biblical concepts of community most helpfully, while Tournier's focus on personhood highlights God's care for the individual. Their insights into sexist and feminist issues are most perceptive and their call for an integration of feminine and masculine qualities is salutary.

Although some 'biblical' counsellors may run the risk of biblicism, or even bibliolatry, the 'relationship' counsellors we have considered may be in danger of expecting too little from God's word. Nevertheless, Clinebell's and Tournier's attempts to allow scriptural concepts to permeate every aspect of their method are commendable. Moreover, I share their caution about the too-ready prescriptive use of the Bible with its dangers of seeing texts as 'magic' formulae and of distancing the client from the counsellor. Their limited views on the far-reaching effects of human sin seem to undermine the Christian authenticity of their approaches but, in fact, Clinebell's optimism and Tournier's large-heartedness may offset this deficiency as they encourage their clients to listen to God's voice.

We shall pick up the central theme of 'relationship' in our last chapter as we study some of the ways that Jesus helped others. In the meantime we shall examine Christian approaches to counselling which delve into the interior life and deeply into the hidden past.

14

REACHING IN: THE INNER JOURNEY

The contemplative is not needy or greedy for human contacts,
but is guided by a vision of what he has seen beyond the trivial
concerns of a possessive world.

Henri J. M. Nouwen

Most modern life is a studied attempt to avoid ever being
alone, faced with the reality of the inner world.

Morton Kelsey

(Jesus) did not need man's testimony about man, for he knew
what was in a man.

John 2:25

Although there is much overlap between 'biblical' and 'relationship' counselling, there are also clear differences of emphasis. Amongst these, we have noted the more cognitive and behavioural approaches of the former and the strong personalism of the latter. We now shift our focus from the written word and the counselling relationship to consider the 'inner journey', or 'mystic way'. All Christian styles of therapy have, by definition, important supernatural dimensions but it is in the 'pilgrimage inward' that we find the greatest resonance with the transpersonalism of Assagioli, Wilber and, most of all, Carl Jung.

Just as the Bible-centred and 'dialogue' forms of counselling have their roots in God's earlier dealings with his covenant people, so the Christian transpersonalism of the 'inward path' has a long and hallowed tradition with an important part of its origins, so it is argued, in the incarnation of the Lord Jesus Christ.[1] In recent decades there have been a number of key people in Western Christianity, mostly Roman Catholics, Anglo-Catholics and Episcopalians, who have exercised a prophetic role in bringing a more mystical spirituality to the attention of many people. These visionaries include Victor White, Harry Williams, Christopher Bryant, Martin Israel and Kenneth Leech in the United Kingdom, William Johnston working in Japan, Catherine de Hueck Doherty in Canada, and Thomas Merton, Henri Nouwen and Morton Kelsey in the United States.[2] In our chapter on transpersonalism we noticed that today's counselling tends to merge with concepts of a way of life, and the same applies as we consider Catholic pastoral care. Kenneth Leech points out that, although there are distinctive features, pastoral counselling and spiritual direction have considerable common ground in their commitment to change in people's lives.[3] As we examine some of the cardinal features of 'meditative' forms of counselling, much of our discussion will range over issues relevant to therapist, counsellor and spiritual director alike.

In studying Christian understanding of the 'inner journey' we find thematic material that is shared by the methodologies of a number of different proponents. Many of the approaches, for example, look both to the mystical tradition within Christianity and to Jungian psychology. I propose, therefore, to abandon our normal pattern of focusing primarily on individual theoreticians and to look instead at some of the *themes* of Christian trans-personalism under our familiar headings of assumptions, aims and method. In doing so, I will look mainly at the work of Christopher Bryant, William Johnston and Morton Kelsey, as representatives of these important perspectives.

Christopher Bryant, a member of the Society of St John the Evangelist, the Anglican religious community known as the Cowley Fathers, has written a number of books combining spiritual insight and psychological understanding. At the age of seventeen, his teenage agnosticism began to dissipate on reading William James' *Varieties of Religious Experience*, although it was not until Bryant was in his early thirties that he started to 'realize the meaning and relevance of Christian doctrine', to which he had previously given only 'intellectual assent'. This awakening came primarily not through the Bible or the sacraments but through reading Carl Jung. As a theological student, Bryant had a passing acquaintance with the thinking of the founders of analytical theory but it was Jung's *Modern Man in Search of a Soul* that gave the breakthrough. Other important influences on Bryant's thought are the theologians Austin Farrer, former warden of Keble College, Oxford, Victor White, a Dominican who wrote *God and the Unconscious* (1952), and Harry Williams, a member of the Community of the Resurrection, Mirfield in Yorkshire. It was White who helped to allay Bryant's anxieties about the compatibility of Jung and Christianity, and Williams' book *The True Wilderness*, with its clear Jungianism, that prompted Bryant further in his commitment to the Swiss analyst. Although not under analysis himself, Bryant readily acknowledges the value of his membership of a small group of clergy and Jungian psychoanalysts who met four or five times a year over a period of six years or so.[4]

Where Bryant seeks an integration between Christian belief and Jung's psychology, *William Johnston*, although admitting Jung's importance, has pioneered a dialogue between Christianity and Zen Buddhism. Born in Belfast, Northern Ireland, he has lived in Japan since 1951, holding the professorship in religious studies at Sophia University, Tokyo, and lecturing widely on East-West mysticism throughout the world. Johnston, a member of the Jesuit Order, repudiates the rigid scholasticism of medieval Catholicism and hails the greater freedom for dialogue with other faiths that was given birth to by the Second Vatican Council in the early 1960s.[5]

Morton Kelsey, an Episcopalian priest and counsellor now based in California, is well known through his thoroughly researched books on healing, speaking in tongues, dreams, Christian meditation, the afterlife and psychology. Growing up with his father's view that we exist in a purely physical universe, Kelsey's agnosticism as a young man was reinforced by his study of Immanuel Kant's rationalistic philosophy. Seeking some sort of answer in life, he proceeded to train at one of the more liberal Episcopalian seminaries during the early 1940s, graduating with the conviction that 'there were equally good reasons for not believing in a meaning to the universe as for believing'.

It was some years later that, as a parish priest, Kelsey was overcome by depression and anxiety. He could no longer live a lie, proclaiming a Good News that he did not believe in, and so he began to search for help. Ironically, he could find no suitable confidant amongst his Christian contacts although, eventually, a parishioner encouraged him to see Max Zeller, a Jewish Jungian analyst. This remarkable man, who ascribed his release from a Nazi concentration camp to God's providence, taught Kelsey 'that God was real' and 'how to pray'. Continuing in analysis,

Morton Kelsey reckons that it was ten years after his ordination before he discovered 'the real significance of the Christian faith'.

It is not surprising that Kelsey, like Bryant and other Christian transpersonalists, regards Jung very highly. Rescued from a liberal and arid Christianity and from a psychological breakdown through the caring ministrations of a Jungian, Kelsey writes: 'In some respects, I see Jung and his followers as having been raised up out of stones when the church failed to do its job.' When asked whether he is a Jungian, he replies, 'No, I am a Christian who has found the thinking of Jung helpful in communicating the world view and message of Jesus to seeking, educated, modern men and women.' Morton Kelsey and his wife, Barbara, between them working for twenty-five years in analysis, are committed to 'both the saving power of the Christian God of love and the insights of depth psychology' as they seek to proclaim Christ's transforming message.[6]

Assumptions

We can consider the theological and psychological assumptions behind the methodologies of our three representatives under the headings: *Christian tradition*; *Jungian influence*; and *Openness to the East*. As we examine these presuppositions, we will find that the theology tends to be 'natural' rather than 'revealed' (although at times it seems to be both), and the reasoning 'inductive' rather than 'deductive' (see pages 261–262). Even though the psychological methods are inclined to be 'assimilative', there are also degrees of integration achieved between Jungianism and Christian belief, and a modest eclecticism towards transpersonalists like Assagioli.

Christian tradition

Mysticism

Before we outline a brief history of some of the strands that make up Christian transpersonalism today, we need to clarify one or two terms. This is easier said than done since human words are notoriously inadequate for describing the blissful transportations of the mystical tradition: prosaic definitions are 'all thumbs' as they try to handle the ineffable. However, Evelyn Underhill in her classic book *Mysticism* points out that 'all mystics . . . speak the same language and come from the same country'. There is a common denominator in mysticism which leads her to write: 'Broadly speaking, I understand it to be the expression of the innate tendency of the human spirit towards complete harmony with the transcendental order; whatever be the theological formula under which that order is understood . . .'[7]

The attainment of this 'complete harmony' may be in the 'God of Christianity', the 'World-soul of Pantheism' or in the 'Absolute of Philosophy'. She comments further that such 'mystic union' is not a matter for discussion, but for experience. 'Not to *know about*, but to *Be*, is the mark of the real practitioner.'[8]

Morton Kelsey helpfully picks up this crucial ingredient of subjectivism when he suggests the value of the wider term 'religious experience'. He cites the purveyor of situation ethics, Joseph Fletcher, as saying that 'mysticism is something that begins in mist and ends in schism'; the word is too vague and ill-understood to be useful. Kelsey, writing in a Christian context, shows further that 'religious experience' has three primary aspects – *sacramental, contemplative* and *meditative*.[9]

Sacramental. Here there is experience 'in which the divine comes into focus directly through some element of the outer, physical world'. The use of sacraments is rooted in the biblical record and includes, for instance, circumcision under the old covenant and the Lord's supper as a mark of the new. Sacramental experience gives continuity and stability to the spiritual life, although familiarity with the form may lead to a loss of the meaning, resulting in inflexibility and stagnation.

Contemplative. The contemplative experience is one of 'union with the divine in which no outside elements are involved' and, to many minds, is mysticism *par excellence*. This form of encounter with God is distinguished by 'passivity, openness and waiting'. It is 'an experience of losing one's ego, of dissolving into the very marrow of the universe. It gives a sense of identity, oneness, ecstasy and bliss.' We have seen a similar quest in the desire for 'unity-consciousness' described by Ken Wilber (see pp. 171–172).

Kelsey indicates that the origins of this 'imageless' form of mysticism are not found within the pages of scripture but, rather, are to be sought in the teachings of the third-century, neo-Platonist philosopher, Plotinus, who, based in Alexandria, promulgated a 'way of negation', a merging with the One that is defined by what it is *not* like. This *apophatic*, or 'negative' theology, in which God is deemed to be unknowable, was taken up by a more orthodox Christianity and became the mainspring in the lives of ascetics like Anthony and Evagrius in the deserts of Egypt. This mystical stream flowed on through the writings of 'Dionysius the Areopagite', early in the sixth century, and so, eventually, into the medieval Church and on to the great Spanish mystics of the Counter-Reformation, St Teresa of Avila and St John of the Cross.

Meditative. In the meditative tradition, Kelsey points to a 'turning inward and using one's imagination as a tool with which to contact the reality of the spiritual world'. Within this experience images from both the personal psyche and beyond are faced and, in time, at least partially understood. This form of 'mysticism' is part of Morton Kelsey's overall approach and we shall return to it when we consider the methods of Christian transpersonalism. Unlike contemplative experience, the meditative way is seen as rooted in the incarnation of Jesus, so that 'access to the Risen Christ' can be known through 'inner images'. God is not remote and purely transcendent, as he appears to be in apophatic theology; he is immanent too – and can be known in Christ. Kelsey traces this emphasis in the devotional works of Origen, Gregory of Nyssa and Augustine, observes its continuation later in *The Spiritual Exercises* of Ignatius of Loyola and notices its embodiment in the practice of a listening silence in the Society of Friends, or Quakers.

World view

There is an understandable tendency amongst Christians, with a more mystical understanding of spiritual direction and pastoral counselling, to look back wistfully to elements in Plato's philosophy and, at the same time, to regret much of Aristotle's influence within the Church.

Morton Kelsey, in particular, argues such a position in his *Encounter with God*. He shows how Plato's view of the existence of two realms of reality was very influential in early Christianity: a physical reality which was known through the five senses and reason; and a spiritual reality which was 'reached through a direct contact and participation in the realm of the eternal'. The latter could be discovered through 'prophecy', 'healing', 'artistic inspiration' and 'love' – experiences which, Kelsey argues, accord with the Holy Spirit's work as shown in the New Testament.[10] This Platonic supernaturalism has been carried by the Eastern Church to this very day, while in the West, although Augustine developed the implications of man as both spirit and body, medieval Christianity turned its gaze to a revival of Aristotelian thinking.

Aristotle, in contrast to Plato, had held that 'man receives direct knowledge only through sense experience and reason' and this rationalist philosophy began its powerful hold on the Western Church in the thirteenth century through the teaching of Thomas Aquinas.[11] Kelsey regards this Thomist scholasticism as highly influential amongst Protestants as well as Catholics, and sees the modernism of scientific naturalism and liberal Christianity as by-products of Aristotle's premises.

And so, Kelsey, in the face of hard-headed and sceptical Aristotelian views, seeks to recover something of Plato's twin perspective of a physical and a spiritual world, the latter breaking through to the former through dreams, visions and 'coincidences'.[12] However, Kelsey avoids any Platonic notion that matter is inferior to spirit, declaring that the incarnation of Christ shows that there is 'no opposition between the divine and the physical, between the spiritual and the secular, the human'.[13]

The nature of God

Christian mysticism of the variety we have been considering lays stress on certain distinctive attributes of God. Of particular importance to the idea of the 'inner journey' are his *providence* and *immanence*. Christopher Bryant emphasises that God's hand is upon everything that happens to us – in the people we meet, the events that come our way, the moods that overtake us, the dreams we dream, and the hopes and fears of our daily lives. Bryant sees this providential action 'as a kind of invisible pressure setting a bias towards the choices and decisions which will lead a person to greater freedom and fulfilment'.[14]

This divine influence that orders our ways is both transcendent, beyond us in its autonomy, and immanent. It is the neglect of the latter – God's closeness and 'ever-present quality' – that Kelsey feels is the hallmark of 'many of the classical Western

writers'.[15] The meditative life that he portrays seeks to correct the
imbalance. Kelsey says that Christian meditation is 'something
we undertake in order to bring the totality of our being into
relationship with a person, an Other to whom we can relate'. This
immanent God can be described as 'a prodigal, spendthrift love'.
Like the bereft father in the parable he receives us back without
chiding as we 'turn to Him for relationship'.[16]

By the same token, Jesus Christ is seen as both within and
beyond the Christian. Bryant argues that the Christ who is 'the
divine Word through whom the universe came into being' is
indeed the 'same Jesus who walked and taught in Palestine . . .
transformed by his dying and rising again . . .'[17] The Christian is
called to identify with this crucified and risen Lord, a Lord who,
Kelsey says, brings victory in 'the battle against evil and
danger'.[18] On this 'battlefield of opposing cosmic forces', the
Holy Spirit wants to draw us 'into the orbit of love and transformation', to bring us 'to unity and wholeness', and to enable us
to attain our 'eternal destiny'.[19]

Human nature

Christopher Bryant believes that God 'is present within all men
without exception' and has given 'to all men in germ the capacity
to respond to him'. For the Christian, the responsive attitudes
inherent in all humankind can be developed and integrated
through 'what God has said and is saying through Jesus Christ'.[20]
Coupled with this view of God's omnipresence and accessibility,
Bryant has an optimistic understanding of human destiny. In the
light of his evolutionary beliefs, he strongly questions the significance of the story of the Garden of Eden and mankind's fall
from an unsullied fellowship with the creator. He writes that,
'instead of having been created perfect, man is in the making'.
Moreover, he feels that the teaching of Jesus gives an emphasis
on 'man's weakness and need, his inability to help himself, rather
than on his wickedness' and suggests that the traditional doctrine
of hell is suspect in that it signifies 'the weakness of omnipotent
love'.[21]

In spite of this playing down of orthodox Christian teaching on
human sinfulness, Bryant admits that there is 'something wrong
with man as he is'. Kelsey takes up similar themes of human
potential and human estrangement. He declares that, as we turn

inward, ninety percent of the opposing forces we encounter are 'the pure gold of our naturalness waiting to be redeemed'; it is only the remaining ten percent that is 'radical and unredeemable evil'.[22] Kelsey is candid about an Enemy power that is able to monopolise these 'redeemable' and 'unredeemable' elements within the human psyche. He reminds us of Paul's words in Ephesians 6:11–12 that we fight 'against cosmic powers, against the authorities and potentates of this dark world, against the superhuman forces of evil in the heavens' (NEB). Even so, the armour of God is at hand for the Christian. In the face of this provision for a most daunting battle, Kelsey writes:

> But the message of Christianity is that if we will first try the inner way – dangerous as it is – and seek the kingdom of God, we will find help on the road ahead. The way of Christianity . . . provides solution, hopes, and victory, and the Good News is for both the outer world and the one we can find within.[23]

Jungian influence

We have already seen the enormous importance of Jungian thinking in the spiritual pilgrimages of both Christopher Bryant and Morton Kelsey. Bryant declares an indebtedness to Jung 'for the light he has shed for (him) on the Christian faith and way of life' and Kelsey, who spent three months in Zurich in order to meet the Swiss doctor, expresses gratitude to him for opening his eyes 'to the power, the liberty, and the value of real religion and of the Christian faith in particular'.[24]

Why is Carl Jung so crucial to these two men? Is it that *something* needed to break through their agnosticism and spiritual dryness, and that something happened to be an analyst from Zurich with views on the supernatural? Have they been taken over by 'another' religion – a religion that has Christian overtones but is at heart a compulsive adventure into forbidden territory? Or is it, rather, that Bryant, Kelsey, and many other deeply committed Christians of a Catholic and mystical persuasion, have stumbled across a psychological insight that is profoundly compatible with Christianity? It is the latter case that they make, and we need to see that their argument, within the theological framework we have briefly examined, is perceptive and discriminating.

World view

We noted in our short account of Jungian thinking in chapter five that Jung, perhaps reacting to the sterility of his clergyman father's faith, largely dismisses the propositional aspects of Christian belief. Bryant points out that Jung, leaving behind an early agnostic phase by the 1930s, accepted the existence of God and, at the same time, acknowledged the impossibility of confirming this conviction by scientific proof. Jung's famous reply 'I do not believe; I know' to the BBC interviewer's question about belief in God indicates the Swiss analyst's extreme emphasis on an inner assurance. Bryant criticises Jung for the 'one-sidedness' of his disregard for 'intellectual beliefs' and his espousal of the 'importance of religious experience'.[25]

It is this same stress on experiencing the spiritual domain that seems to be one of the major reasons for Kelsey's appreciation of Jung. He declares that Jung's world-view is 'fundamentally the same as that of Jesus and the early church fathers'. The context of this sweeping claim is Kelsey's discovery that both the scriptures and early Church history show that God speaks to us in dreams, thus confirming Jung's view that some 'deep inner reality' is seeking to help us towards our 'destiny'.[26]

Divine and human nature

It is in the area of Jung's opinions on the relationship between God and our humanity that the greatest confusion comes for many of us. Bryant grasps this nettle when he tries to explain Jung's understanding of the *Self*. He points out that Jung uses this term in two senses: to denote the *total personality*, conscious and unconscious; and to indicate the *centre* of the personality (a concept similar to Assagioli's 'higher self'). Bryant admits that, on occasions, Jung 'with characteristic verbal imprecision is led to speak of the Self as God'. This seems to be taking the idea of God's immanence too far! However, Bryant points out that it is more consistent with Jung's 'usual language' to see the Self, the total personality or its centre, as 'that through which God makes his presence known to the conscious personality'.[27]

Another fundamental concept in Jung's thinking that we need to understand is that of the *symbol*, which Bryant describes as 'the best available statement of an unknown reality'. More pertinently, a *living symbol* can be explained as 'a powerful image, focussing the imagination, releasing the emotions, moving to action'. Jung regards the living symbol as a 'psychological machine' which releases energy from the unconscious, transforming it into action – like the great turbines which change the power of the Niagara Falls into light and heat for millions of people. Bryant, altering the simile, adds that an effective symbol is comparable to a bridge in that it is able to link the 'two worlds' of everyday life and 'the mysterious depths'. Jesus, although 'more than just a symbol', is *the* 'living symbol' of the Christian faith, transforming our dull existence by his mighty power and bridging the apparent gulf between our daily lives and the 'being of God'.[28]

It is in mentioning the 'mysterious depths', which Jesus is seen to make accessible, that we need to look once more at Jung's distinctive notion of the *archetypes*. These can be defined as those innate ideas in the unconscious which 'organize experience in . . . predetermined patterns'.[29] These 'innate ideas' are formless in themselves but they are able to be represented by the images and figures of fairy tales, myths and dreams. As Bryant writes: 'The archetype is asleep until the appropriate image awakens it.' Kelsey lists the archetypes that emerge most pressingly from his own unconscious as he pursues the 'inner way'. These include the 'inner mother', the 'divine youth', the 'professor' and the 'priest-shaman', or mediator. He views these archetypes as both personal and transpersonal, as open to both good and evil forces, and is aware that there is 'a principle of darkness that seeks to undermine (his) soul by tempting (him) to identify with one of the archetypes'. Jung regarded Hitler, for example, as a 'shaman' who worshipped the pagan god, Wotan rather than Christ; the analyst saw this archetypal possession as 'the basic problem of Nazi Germany'. Kelsey gladly proclaims that it is only and through Jesus Christ that he can find an inner harmony.[30]

Stepping out of these dangerous waters, let us look in outline at Jung's less controversial theory of *personality types*. Morton and Barbara Kelsey, in particular, argue that an understanding of this range of groupings can sometimes, for instance, explain divisions in the Church as well as give valuable clues in guiding others on their 'inner journey'. Although sixteen psychological categories can be described, it is appreciated that we each show a wide range of functioning from time to time, while tending to develop some functions more than others.[31] Jung's types come under three headings: *attitudes*; *perceiving*; and *assessing*, or judging.

Attitudes.   Jung's division of humankind into *introverts* and *extraverts* is his most generally known contribution to popular psychology. Barbara Kelsey says that an introvert 'prefers to deal with the inner world of ideas and concepts and finds his or her renewal of energy coming during a period of inward turning and aloneness'. In contrast, the extravert's interest is centred in 'the outer world of actions, objects, and persons' and he or she tends to be revitalised by others. An introvert may enjoy a party to a certain extent, is inclined to concentrate on one or two people, who are known to share some appreciation of subjective things, but may well slip away early, feeling quite exhausted and longing for some solitude. An extravert at the same party will arrive early and leave late, entering wholeheartedly into every aspect of the evening, relating readily to anyone and everyone, and increasing in vitality into the small hours. Extraverts assume that their first, rather negative impressions of introverts are correct and will find it difficult to revise their views on closer acquaintance. Introverts can respond very enthusiastically on first meeting extraverts, since the latter's outgoing nature is so winsome, but may be disappointed in time by a lack of depth. It is important that the counsellor evaluates both his own and the client's basic personality type 'in order to avoid imposing standards that do not fit'.

Perceiving.   Another parameter within each personality is that of perceptive function whereby we 'take in information about the world'. It is said that each of us perceives life's issues primarily as either a 'sensation' or 'intuitive' type. The *sensation*-type lives busily in the present, developing a skill and handling it well, using the five senses readily and disliking change. Such a person can have a clear awareness of God's immediate nearness and responds straightforwardly to the sacraments. Those repressed parts of the psyche, the *shadow*, tend to give the sensation-type some misgivings about negative possibilities in the world around; these apprehensions come from the neglected 'intuitive' aspects of the personality.

The *intuitive*-type takes in information through the unconscious, works with bursts of enthusiasm interspersed with slack periods, enjoys developing new skills but does not persist with their use, and likes to keep options open in any discussion. In contrast to the sensation-type, the intuitive is not good at remembering faces, names and the details of what people wear; however, although facts may be elusive, the person with intuition is able to make many suggestions with half-forgotten material. The shadow may lead to a crude hedonism which rises up from suppressed 'sensation' characteristics.

Assessing.   Jung argues that we assess, judge and organise what we perceive in two main ways: 'feeling' and 'thinking'. Here he uses the word 'feeling' to denote a type of reasoning rather than to refer to the emotions. The *feeling*-type uses value systems in order to come to conclusions, taking both the self and others into consideration, whereas the *thinking*-type utilises a 'cause-and-effect logic to reach decisions'. In working situations both these types are needed: the feeling-type is good with people, able to spur others into action and adept at bringing reconciliation to warring parties; the thinking-type is efficient and highly organisational, well able to continue working in bad atmospheres, does not like too much talking, needs his or her ideas to be accepted and tends to inflexibility. The feeling-type's shadow may emerge with an overpowering system of thought which insists on acknowledgment, while the thinking-type may erupt with a show of unruly feelings.

Barbara Kelsey argues that the balanced personality needs to specialise in one of these four functions, cultivating a second, or 'auxiliary function', to support the first. She mentions that John Sanford, in his book *The Kingdom Within*, writes that Jesus Christ is the only one who held the four functions of sensation, intuition, feeling and thinking in perfect harmony.

Openness to the East

Jung urged that Western civilisation should learn to listen to the voices of Eastern religion without disowning its own roots.[32] We have already noted a tendency for many Western psychologists amongst post-Freudian analysts, personalists and transpersonalists to bend an ear eastwards as their careers develop, and at times we have suspected that their origins in a Judaeo-Christian tradition are either neglected or spurned. William Johnston, amongst our trio of Christian transpersonalists, is the one who has followed Jung's advice most fully, establishing a dialogue with Eastern mysticism while maintaining his Christian standpoint.

Johnston is glad to leave behind the rigid objectivity of the traditional Aristotelian scholasticism which pre-dates the Second Vatican Council. Instead, he likens theology to a flowing river that is 'open-ended, progressing, ongoing and dynamic'. He sees the way clear for dialogue with other faiths, given that 'our knowledge of God is always open to development'. He writes:

> For if our grasp of truth is partial, can we not envisage the possibility that there is partial truth in non-Christian religions also? May they not possess aspects of the truth that we have not seen? Is it not possible that they will even cast light on the mystery of God and Christ?[33]

However, in his quest for truth, Johnston admits that the only real hope for dialogue between Christianity and, in this case, Zen Buddhism is to base the discussion 'above all on religious experience and, ideally speaking, upon mysticism'. Nonetheless, in doing this, words have to be used at some stage in order to find common ground. Johnston speaks tentatively of five 'transcendental precepts' which need to be kept, he suggests, by the Christian who approaches Buddhism 'sympathetically': *be attentive*, to both the Buddhist viewpoint and the Holy Spirit; *be intelligent* in gaining insight; *be reasonable*, as an attempt is made to assimilate 'new elements of truth'; *be responsible*, recognising the good in the other religion; and *be committed*, to the integration of newly perceived truth.

It is in 'being reasonable' that the greatest difficulty is anticipated because a Zen Buddhist world view 'inveighs against the discriminating intellect, against words and letters, against any kind of theory, against statements either of affirmation or denial'. Johnston challenges this anti-intellectualism by asserting that 'the formation of judgments is quite compatible' with the Eastern experience of 'enlightenment'.[34]

How does Johnston handle the deity and uniqueness of Christ in the face of Eastern mysticism? Without denying who Jesus is, he distinguishes between 'Jesus Christ as the *mediator of grace* and Jesus Christ as the *mediator of meaning*.' He reasons that the Lord brings grace to 'the whole human race' but that same Lord does not carry meaning to Buddhists and others who do not believe in him. 'In short', he writes 'we can say that Christ mediates *meaning* to the Christian and Buddha mediates *meaning* to the Buddhist'. Johnston is aware of inconsistencies in Christian approaches to the East but seems prepared to 'refrain from pushing logic to its ultimate point' out of sensitivity towards those with whom he debates.[35]

Aims

The objectives of the 'mystic way' or 'inner journey' are variously expressed by our three authors and can be considered under the three main groupings of *wholeness*, *individuation* and *self-realisation*. These Christian, Jungian and Eastern ways, respectively, have their own distinctive language although dialogue attempts to find concepts in common.

Wholeness

The ultimate goal of the Christian path is described by Bryant as 'personal salvation or wholeness',[36]. This road to glorious completeness is marked by progress in relation to God, others and the Self. As we have previously argued, it is an openness to God in the 'total personality', or the 'centre' of that personality, that leads to the transformation of that Self. Bryant declares that 'to be one with Christ means to be at one with one's own centre' or, to use Pauline language, 'I live, yet not I but Christ lives in me'.[37]

Bryant is thoroughly scriptural when he sees an integral link between union with Christ and a responsiveness to others. He says that there are 'two kinds of growth' nurtured by the Spirit as we take the 'spiritual journey': 'growth in the awareness of God, which is in part psychological'; and the much more important 'growth in a loving committedness to God in heart and will and action'. It is the latter which 'overflows in the love of other people'.[38] Many similar statements are made by the apostle John, including: 'Everyone who loves has been born of God and knows God' (1 John 4:7b).

Morton Kelsey shows that *freedom* and *inner-directedness* are key 'intermediary' goals on the journey towards wholeness. These marks of psychological maturity display a release 'from relationships of actual dependency' and an 'ability to give love without expecting anything in return'; the individual is thus allowed 'to find new and richer attachments to God and to other human beings'.[39]

Such a process of transformation can never be automatic; it requires choice, commitment and the exposure of wrong ways. Bryant, seeking to avoid the connotation of 'sin' in the word 'repentance', prefers to use *metanoia*, the Greek term which means 'change of mind or change of attitude'. He argues that this understanding of *metanoia* brings hope on life's journey – a hope for personal growth and for peaceful co-existence. Within the individual there may be the need to face 'one by one the unfinished tasks of earlier life' and those inner elements which have been repressed. Thus there can be a move away from childish selfishness and pettiness to the childlike qualities of trust, spontaneity and straightforwardness.[40]

Kelsey gives some concrete suggestions for discerning the outcomes of the 'inner way', for clarifying whether the prime influence in the journey's battles is divine or demonic. God's work is shown by love and harmony rather than hate and schism, by the authority of Jesus rather than a brainwashed inflexibility, by humility rather than pride, by peace rather than a destructive depression and, most generally, by the Spirit's fruit rather than personal disintegration and human bondage.[41]

Individuation

Bryant defines Jung's maturing process of individuation as 'the acceptance and living out by the individual of his own specific nature, the becoming more and more what he truly is, the living out of his own truth'.[42] He regards an appreciation of Jungian thinking here as 'powerful and liberating' in that God is seen to guide us from the very centre of our being. Bryant writes: 'If the authority to which I have to submit is within me, then the more I conform myself to its directions the more at one I shall be in myself and the more inner-directed.'[43]

Within the conscious part of Jung's concept of the Self is the *ego*, which has an 'executive' function for the whole personality. In the first half of life 'ego-consciousness' is built up as this controlling and deciding agent gains in strength and self-awareness. In one's middle and later years this ego 'should learn to discover and submit to the deep centre' of the Self as part of the process of integration and individuation.[44]

One important aspect of psychological maturing that we have seen spelt out by Clinebell and Tournier is the coming to terms with the 'contra-sexual elements' in the psyche. As we saw in chapter five, each man carries an *anima* within his unconscious which is the 'eternal image of woman', and, similarly, every woman possesses an archetypal *animus*, the image of maleness. The first part of life is taken up with identifying with an ideal appropriate to one's own sex. Falling in love can be seen as a deep responding to one's hidden contrasexual side; this movement towards the 'ideal woman' or 'ideal man' hopefully gives way in time to a caring for the real person.[45] For example, a young man who, as an only son, was mollycoddled by his mother may have repressed a formidable archetypal 'mother figure' into his unconscious. Without awareness of its significance he falls in love with a series of young women who delight to mother and smother him. Fortunately, through a psychological crisis and some perceptive therapy, he begins to face and accept his powerful anima, eventually becoming emotionally free enough to marry someone (not too like his mother!) whom he relates to in a mature and caring way.

Self-realisation

William Johnston states that 'self-realization is found in self-transcendence', that the way to 'finding ourselves' is in 'losing ourselves' – in venturing beyond self. He acknowledges that this ultimate goal, rightly understood, can be seen as an objective of Christian commitment, of Jungian individuation and of Buddhism.[46]

Johnston points out that 'the Buddha' actually means 'the true self' and the self-realisation, or enlightenment, is at the heart of the Buddhist religion. Within Zen Buddhism the possession of 'the mirror mind' is an objective. Here the enlightened mind is likened to an unblemished and polished mirror which receives 'everything into itself without distortion' and reflects 'all objects as if they were appearing in it for the first time'. This 'mirror mind' can be compared to the mind of a child in its receptiveness and sense of wonder in seeing everything anew. Johnston lines up this imagery with that of our Lord's call for us to 'become like little children'. He writes:

> When I become the child I realize existentially in the depths of my being that God my Father is love and that we did not first love him but that he first loved us. And having realized this I cry out: 'Abba, Father!'[47]

Method

As we have already noted, the 'inward journey' is one that can be made in both the contexts of counselling and spiritual direction. Morton Kelsey offers each of these ministries, giving therapy for those in 'pain' and spiritual direction for those who primarily seek to bring the whole of life 'into congruence with God'. Kelsey and his colleague, John Sanford see their main interest as 'walking with people on the inner journey'. Even though this book's theme is the methodologies of counselling and psychotherapy, it is important here for us to examine some of the techniques of helping others on the 'inner way' since, in practice, a counselling situation may merge into one of spiritual direction. However, Kelsey is very cautious about taking people along the path towards 'inner wholeness' and feels that he cannot accompany others in that direction further than he has travelled himself. Because of the demands and dangers of the 'mystic way' he aims to direct only those who have a 'strong, well-disciplined ego', are well motivated for the inward journey and are prepared to persist with practicalities. An initial counselling session of not more than one hour is used so that the possibility of spiritual direction can be assessed. [48]

It is the intuitive-types who profit most from guidance on the inner path. (Both Carl Jung and Morton Kelsey are 'intuitives'). For those who are more 'sensate' in the way they view life, Kelsey points to the equally valid route of sacramentalism. In their greater need for 'images, symbols, and rituals of the church', sensation-types can learn to submit their lives to God in the context of, for example, a daily Eucharist, 'frequent and searching confessions', Bible study and Christian fellowship. Kelsey alludes to Jung's affirmation of the Catholic 'sacramental way' and urges his Protestant brethren to 'reconsider the place of the sacraments in their life and fellowship'. [49]

Although, as we have seen, there is a great deal of confusion in the language of mysticism, we can distil the various approaches to realising God's presence into those of *contemplation* and *meditation*.

Contemplation

Traditionally, contemplation can be divided into its 'passive' and 'active' forms but, to the purist, it is the former that is meant by the general term. William H. Shannon summarises the explanation of passive contemplation given by the Cistercian contemplative, Thomas Merton in these words:

> This is a gift of God that we simply cannot achieve by our own efforts; it is a pure gift of God that involves a direct and experimental contact with God as He is in himself. It means emptying oneself of every created love to be filled with the love of God. It means going beyond all created images to receive the simple light of God's substantial presence.[50]

This is the path of 'contemplative experience' we have already picked up in Kelsey's analysis of mysticism, where he traces its origins to Plotinus and the Desert Fathers. This apophatic path, 'way of negation' or 'way of unknowing' is marked by its 'imagelessness'. Christopher Bryant helpfully simplifies the discussion when he tells the story of an old peasant, a parishioner of the curé d'Ars. He was observed by the curé to kneel nightly for one hour, gazing at the altar with wrapt attention. When asked what he said in his vigil, the old man replied, 'I don't say anything. I look at him and he looks at me.' Bryant sums up this essentially 'imageless' contemplation as 'looking and loving'.[51]

It should not surprise us that this abstract form of devotion has a greater appeal to Jung's 'intuitive' and 'feeling' types. Bryant shows how access to this 'intuitive' contemplation may, initially, be through using images in a distinctive way. Attention is focused on a picture, crucifix, lighted candle, word, phrase or idea, while the contemplative 'looks through the image towards the Unknown'. This contemplation may become more intuitive by using words 'as a windscreen to protect the flame of prayer within . . . from being blown out by distractions'. Many Christians use the 'Jesus Prayer' of the Eastern Orthodox Church in this way. The words 'Lord Jesus Christ, son of God, have mercy upon me' are slowly repeated so that its truths gradually 'penetrate from the head to the heart'. In time, conscious thinking is suspended so that Bryant can write of the words: 'I know what they mean but I don't think what they mean'. Instead, he continues, 'I attend to a presence in my heart', knowing 'a yearning towards an indwelling companion whom I trust and love.'[52]

We saw in chapter eight how, since the mid-1960s, many in the

West have turned for peace of mind towards Eastern mysticism. In doing so, many other 'mental devices' for reducing 'active, controlled thinking' have been disseminated widely. The reiterative use of the Jesus Prayer we have just considered is remarkably similar to the repetition of the *mantra* in Transcendental Meditation (see pp. 176–179). Zen Buddhism silences conscious thought by repeating a *koan*, 'an insoluble riddle that defeats reason' – such as the famous question 'What is the sound of one hand clapping?'[53] Johnston elaborates the importance in the East of a slow, rhythmical form of breathing which utilises the abdominal muscles primarily. 'The way of the breath' can become a way of life as the novitiate seeks enlightenment. An oriental master is reputed to say to his disciples: 'Your breathing is your greatest friend. Return to it in all your troubles and you will find comfort and guidance.'[54]

Meditation

'Active' contemplation, or 'imaginative' meditation, Kelsey argues, also needs to be a 'way of life'. He writes:

> The inner meditative journey is not a weekend excursion to a land of sun and happiness. It is a way of life for people who actually feel a need for it and who become conscious of their need. In the final analysis this is a way for people who have been unable to find meaning by other methods.[55]

As well as the prerequisite of a deep sense of need, those who venture on the 'inner way' must be safeguarded by a belief in 'a higher, loving will that has already conquered evil' and a determination to work at forming 'real human relationships'. Kelsey is in no doubt that hope to win through is supremely given by the victory bought by Christ in his death and rising again, and support for the journey is best found through a spiritual director or a caring group of praying friends.[56]

Morton Kelsey draws a number of parallels between Jung's process of psychological individuation and the Christian's path towards spiritual maturity. These analogies are fourfold: abreaction and *confession*; transference and *love*; psychological and spiritual *integration*; and resolution and *wholeness*.[57] We will look at the first three in their movement towards the ultimate goal of the fourth (already considered on pp. 348–349).

Confession

Like Tournier, Kelsey recognises the fundamental importance of 'knowing one's faults and owning them, usually in the presence of another person'. This confession, or abreaction, can only take place where the counsellor is seen to be a good and trustworthy listener who will not 'pass moral judgment'. Although the counsellor may need to point out certain possible consequences of the client's attitudes or actions, Kelsey agrees with Jung that 'condemnation does not liberate, it oppresses'. The climate for confession can only be created where the counsellor knows and faces his or her own failures and negative ways.

The process of abreaction can be furthered by *keeping a journal*. During regular times of quiet reflection, a record is kept of all that preoccupies consciousness, making a note of interrupting thoughts and ideas without trying to find a logical sequence. Emotional reactions, lapses and mistakes can all be recorded and subsequently shared with the counsellor or spiritual director. I found within a period of thinking over resolutions for a new year that the writing down of some complicated feelings about a friend led to a modest letter of confession and reconciliation.

Love

Self-giving love is, of course, a prerequisite for all relating under God's hand. However, we need to recognise our own limitations and the particular difficulty a counsellor who is, say, an 'introverted intuitive-feeling' type might have in identifying with a client of an 'extraverted sensory-thinking' disposition. Kelsey writes that one of the tasks of spiritual direction 'is to make the unlovable person lovable through loving them'; to this end, he needs to pray: 'Lord, I cannot love them, but maybe you can love them through me.'

One of the most crucial psychological aspects of caring for our clients is that of transference and counter-transference (see pages 24, 81). Once more, Kelsey is cautious. He does not believe that transference is an essential part of therapy and limits the number of counselling sessions initially in order to evaluate whether a potential transference will be constructive or destructive. He realises that clergy, doctors and therapists are sitting targets for psychological projection where, for instance, a woman parishioner or patient may invest such 'authority' figures with all the strong feelings that are displaced from the repressed animus. The counsellor must tread warily, avoiding deceit or sarcasm towards the enamoured client. Even so, rightly managed, Kelsey regards transference as 'one of the most creative forces in the world' – a force which, 'like dynamite . . . needs to be handled with care'.[58]

Integration

Progress along the road to an increasing integration of the inner depths and the outer world can be aided by attention to some important ways and means. Kelsey rightly stresses the indispensable nature of adequate *time* for reflection and listening. He admits that many of us who fill our days with a ceaseless activity are afraid of being alone: the clamouring voices within have too much to say for us to stop and listen. Kelsey repeats a favourite story of Jung's in which an excessively busy pastor, facing a nervous breakdown, sought the Swiss doctor's help. Jung offered the simple remedy of a daily routine of eight hours work, eight hours sleep and eight hours in the quiet of his study. The clergyman spent the next two days following Jung's suggestion carefully. He used his time well in his study, playing some relaxing music and reading parts of some weighty novels. He returned to see his analyst on the third day feeling disgruntled with his lack of progress. He explained what he had done but received the rebuke that he had not been asked to spend his time with Herman Hesse, Thomas Mann, Chopin and Mozart. He had been asked to be alone with himself. At this the pastor, with fear in his voice, exclaimed, 'Oh, but I can't think of any worse company!' Jung's reply was devastating: 'And yet this is the self you inflict on other people fourteen hours a day'. It is surely better for us all to make time to be alone and to look within 'before life catches up with us'.[59]

Having established a regular stretch of uninterrupted time, preferably when we are at our most alert, we need to learn to come to terms with *silence* – in order to listen to 'the deepest needs' of our inner selves and 'the prompting of the creative Spirit', whichever way he may lead. This is ideally a period of *detachment*, in which 'action, planning, desiring are all suspended, entrusted to the One in silence, while the thoughts and emotions and realities that surround them are given a chance to regroup'. Each part of the body is gently told to relax in turn, while the meditator waits in the quietness. Focusing the eyes on a single object or repeating the Jesus Prayer are said to help initially in establishing an inner stillness.

At this point, there may be 'contact with a flow of images' that well up from the unconscious – images 'charged with emotion', having 'a life and power of their own'. However painful the experience, Kelsey argues, we are to avoid repressing these emotions yet again. They are a part of our total being and need to be brought into the open and exposed to God's transforming love. Kelsey suggests that we should resist attaching our anger, fear, and anxiety to other people and situations, realising that these negative emotions are intrinsic within our own hidden make-up. A renewing experience of God's love for us – 'warts and all' – can 'begin to change our old feelings into new strengths'. An inflexible control over our children may become a more compassionate 'letting go', a deep hostility to an employer may give way to an understanding of his troubled domestic life, and an envy of a successful workmate may be replaced by an attitude of generosity.[60]

It is as we begin to consider the *archetypal images* which, along with powerful emotions, may emerge in the meditative silence, that we enter once more into a mysterious and controversial area. Kelsey, like Jung, regards *dreams* as extremely important signposts on the road to integration. Kelsey, as a result of his studies and personal experiences, believes that all dreams, although varying greatly in significance, are from God.[61] Less explicitly, he writes: 'Through dreams, some deep inner reality that is greater than my psyche is trying to help me toward my destiny.'

In counselling or spiritual direction, he encourages the person he seeks to help to keep a detailed record of his or her dreams, learning to reflect on them and attempt tentative interpretations. As a client recounts a dream, Kelsey tries to listen to both the narrator and the narrative as if listening to God. An awareness of the immediate circumstances of the client's life may, of course, be invaluable in understanding the dream. He is circumspect in his approach, asking for the client's view of its meaning; suggestions are made by the counsellor but Kelsey reckons that an interpretation is only correct if it makes sense to the dreamer. As archetypes begin to be recognised and understood, Kelsey stresses again the profound need that both counsellor and client have for divine aid.[62]

The last method of coming to terms with these unconscious forces which I want to consider is that of Jung's *active imagination*. His is a technique in which 'the mental image of some impressive figure', perhaps from a dream, a fantasy or in everyday life, is questioned in the imagination and then allowed to give some 'answer' to the listener. Kelsey and Bryant propose that the Christian might like to use a similarly imaginative approach in reflecting on, say, a Bible story. You might, I suggest, imagine being a close companion of Jacob as he settles down for the night at a lonely spot on his way from Beersheba to Haran, where he hopes to find a wife from his uncle's family. You can sense the sharp drop in temperature as you curl up in a robe on the stony ground. In the middle of the night Jacob's restlessness is noticed and you suddenly see that he is sitting up, wide-eyed and terror-struck. You then begin to ask the imaginary figure, 'What's the matter, Jacob? What have you seen?' and, as he begins to explain his overpowering dream, you ask, 'How do you understand this dream, Jacob? What does it tell you about the God of Abraham and of Isaac?' (see Genesis 28:10–22). Bryant makes the suggestion that such an exercise 'may speak with power to your depths and enable you to realize at a deeper level both your own profound need and the healing power of Christ'.[63]

Perhaps the most transforming of all images that we can meditate upon, as we try to come to terms with our inner turmoil, is that of the crucified Messiah. Kelsey concludes:

> If we will once live through the betrayal and crucifixion of Christ in our imaginations, we will realize that there is no reason to fear showing the worst of our images of violence and defeat and pain to Him.[64]

Discussion

There is no doubt in my mind that many of us have a great deal to learn from the Christian mystical tradition in terms of devotional practice and godliness of life. The sense of God's loving presence and his concern for every department of both everyday living and the depths of one's personality is exemplary. The blend of adoration towards our creator-redeemer and a preparedness for his searching glance, even amongst the muddiest waters of the unconscious, displays a singleminded commitment to go God's way in life that few of us can match. Contemplative and meditative prayer, and the use of images to aid attention to the Lord, may be means of grace to which non-Catholic Christians should be more open. Certainly the practice of meditation has become more widely used by Protestants in recent years. However, at these practical levels there do seem to be real dangers in the 'inner way' for those who are unstable, those who are tempted to withdraw from others, those who are readily self-absorbed and those who are drawn easily by various techniques into a spurious spirituality. Bryant, Johnston and Kelsey seem well aware of these potential follies and are at pains to prevent them.

Those of us who look primarily to the authority of the scriptures may be nonplussed by the power of apophatic, Jungian and Eastern mystical influences on the amalgam of Christian transpersonalism. Although Bryant and Johnston allude frequently to biblical passages and Kelsey has made some very thorough studies of scriptural insight, it seems inevitable that Plotinus, Jung and the Buddha will give some variant readings! The 'way of negation', for example, so stresses God's transcendence that he can be seen as unknowable, whereas Jungian psychology is in danger of so emphasising divine immanence that God can become equated with the Self. Although the full divinity of Christ is given assent to, there appears to be a tendency to see the Spirit as an impersonal, yet all-pervasive, influence.

We have commented on the optimistic views concerning human nature amongst our three writers and noted an inclination to stress a person's essential integrity and to play down the deep-rootedness of individual and corporate sin. Personal evil is sometimes identified with the 'shadow', those rejected elements of the personality, although, at the same time, the redeemable aspects of that shadow are given the preeminence. I am not sure that the gravity of such biblical statements as Paul's 'everything that does not come from faith is sin' and John's 'If we claim we have not sinned, we make him out to be a liar' is always acknowledged by Kelsey, Bryant and Johnston (see Romans 14:23 and 1 John 1:10).

It is perhaps in the cautious but determined exploration of the unconscious that the 'inward passage' is most open to debate. All three of our authors rightly warn us of the dangers of this pursuit and of our profound need of the crucified and risen Christ in overcoming the dark forces. But we have to ask who exactly are these dark forces and does God really call those 'intuitives' amongst us to engage in such skirmishes, whether through the interpretation of our dreams or in an 'active imagination' which engages unknown figures dredged up from the depths? We have already seen something of Jung's unnerving experience at the family house in Küsnacht in the summer of 1916 (see page 175) and there is no doubt that the Swiss analyst's encounters with the numinous through apocalyptic visions and deeply disturbing dreams and fantasies can serve as a warning to us. He writes this of his confrontation with the unconscious:

> An incessant stream of fantasies had been released, and I did my best not to lose my head but to find some way to understand these strange things. I stood helpless before an alien world; everything in it seemed difficult and incomprehensible. I was living in a constant state of tension; often I felt as if gigantic blocks of stone were tumbling down upon me.[65]

Morton Kelsey is fully aware of the opposing spiritual powers that can do battle in the hidden region of the psyche. He urges on us discernment 'in the realm of archetypes'. He declares further that the New Testament 'speaks of angels and demons', which are 'powers and messengers of creation and destruction', and adds that 'archetypes are angels in the hands of Christ and devils in the hands of the Evil One'. Reassuringly, he reminds us that the demonic has 'no ultimate power over us when we are in Christ's presence'.[66] I am not sure of Kelsey's demonology here but his point is well taken. We do indeed struggle against 'the powers of this dark world' and are called to 'stand against the devil's schemes', clad in 'the full armour of God' (see Ephesians 6:10–18). I can see that waiting on God in the silence, allowing him to deal with those negative emotions that surface and being open to his voice speaking to us in our dreams and prayerful imaginings are some of the many valuable ways that we can commune with our Lord. I am less than sure about the archetypes! I appreciate something of the mystery of the unconscious and believe that the hidden depths of the Christian are as accessible to the Holy Spirit as any other aspect of the psyche. I can accept, to some extent, the idea of a collective unconscious as a vast repository of myth, fantasy and submerged memory which is part of our common humanity, and is therefore, in some sense or other, both fallen and redeemable. Like Kelsey, I believe that these cryptic areas must be accessible to both the Lord God's rule and to Enemy subversion. In allowing the Spirit's revealing and transforming activity in the deep places we should, I suggest, seek his protection of our imagination and be wary of all techniques which encourage an openness to images of unknown origin and intention.

In the dialogue between Christianity and the East, many of us will have similarly strong reservations. We have raised some of these at the end of chapter eight. There is the same objection in the rhythmic chanting of a *mantra* or *koan* (or, for that matter, the Jesus Prayer) that we have met in considering the archetypes: the danger of opening ourselves to Enemy influence, partly through the suspension of conscious appraisal and partly through a temptation to resort to a form of magic. This is, for many of us, an obscure and puzzling area but Evelyn Underhill's distinction between 'magic' and 'mysticism' may be helpful. She classifies broadly as magical 'all forms of self-seeking transcendentalism', declaring that, fundamentally, 'magic wants to get, mysticism wants to give'.[67] Furthermore, Johnston's argument in *The Mirror Mind* poses well the dilemma present in dialogue between the revealed theology of Christianity and the philosophy of Zen Buddhism, described by Christmas Humphreys, the well known English Buddhist, as 'the religion of "self-effort"'.[68] Johnston's solution of proclaiming a Jesus who 'mediates meaning' to Christians and 'mediates grace' to all others, although it has some accord with a biblical doctrine of common grace, seems in danger of watering down our Lord's uncompromising statement: 'I am the way and the truth and the life' (John 14:6). Kelsey perhaps strikes at the heart of the distinction between Christian belief and Eastern mysticism when he writes that the former sees ultimate reality as 'a Lover to whom one responds' and the latter as 'a pool of consciousness in which one seeks to lose identity'.[69] It is here, once more, that we return to the uniqueness of God's call to us – a call into fellowship with our loving Lord and his people, and to an increasing individual and corporate Christlikeness, in contrast to the amorphous destiny of cosmic-consciousness that draws many who listen to the voices of Eastern mysticism.

In our penultimate chapter, if you feel game for one more expedition, we shall take a journey both inwards and backwards in time.

REACHING BACK: HEALING THE PAST

*For you created my inmost being; you knit me together in my
mother's womb.*

Psalm 139:13

*I've been born, and once is enough. You don't remember, but
I remember. Once is enough.*

T. S. Eliot

*For by the vehemence of His cry in the darkness on Golgotha,
He affirms for ever the divinity of all the pain and all the cries
of protest at the absence of love.*

John Fletcher

One of the cardinal discoveries in the field of counselling made by
the charismatic and renewal movements from the 1960s onwards
is the need that many have for a journey backwards in time – a
journey which seeks to expose to the restorative power of Christ
what is hidden. The methodology of this reaching back comes in
many guises, including 'inner healing', the 'healing of the
memories', 'primal integration' and the 'healing of the family
tree'. Before examining some aspects of this important range of
Christian approaches, I would like to look briefly at two secular
theorists whose work has some relevance to this therapeutic
unearthing of the past: Otto Rank and Arthur Janov.

Otto Rank, the Austrian psychoanalyst, was a personal
favourite of Freud in the 1920s. Rank, whose father had a drink
problem and whose parents split up when he was in his teens,
looked to Freud as something of a 'father-substitute'. In return,
Rank was treated like an adopted son and was generally believed
to be the heir apparent of Freudian analytical society. Although
Freud already saw 'the act of birth as a source of anxiety' and, at

one point, judged Rank's views as 'the most important progress since the discovery of psychoanalysis', it was Rank's resolute belief that *all* anxiety has its source in the trauma of birth which eventually led to the parting of 'father' and 'son'. Rank's thinking excluded the role of the Oedipus complex in creating conflict and paved the way for a prime emphasis on the nurturing function of the mother in healthy child development – an emphasis elaborated by such post-Freudians as Bowlby, Winnicott, Fairbairn, Guntrip and Balint in the United Kingdom, and Erik Erikson in the United States. Rank saw severe attacks of anxiety in later life as a re-enactment of the original birth trauma.

In therapy, he concentrated on the patient's *present* condition, aiming to resolve the primal fear of separation from the mother by offering short-term help. The resulting anticipation of 'losing' the therapist seemed to precipitate dreams about the patient's birth and an opportunity to overcome deeply imprinted 'separation-anxiety'. In time, Rank settled in the United States where he established a non-analytical therapy which sought to stimulate the patient to a self-assertion that aimed at freedom from a sense of guilt and a bid for 'health'.[1]

Arthur Janov (b 1924), based in Southern California, argues that his primal therapy is the only valid approach to treating neurosis and psychosis. Psychoanalysis is seen as 'invalid', the neo-Freudians as 'retrogressive', Reichian views as perhaps 'too body-orientated', reality therapy as 'simplistic', psychodrama as perpetuating make-believe.[2] Janov defends his universalistic methodology in these words: 'One might cavil and question about my intolerance of others. But I am not the one who is intolerant; it is the Primal hypothesis. The truth is highly intolerant of untruth.'[3]

Janov, trained in Freudianism and working for seventeen years 'as a psychologist and psychiatric social worker', stumbled across the first inklings of his 'Primal hypothesis' by chance. During a session of group therapy, he felt he should ask a 'withdrawn and sensitive' male student in his early twenties, who was showing signs of infantile need, to call out, 'Mummy! Daddy!'. Janov describes the young man's initial delay, his subsequent upset state, sudden squirming on the floor, rapid breathing, almost involuntary cries for his parents, and continues:

The writhing gave way to small convulsions, and finally, he released a piercing, death-like scream that rattled the walls of my office . . . All he could say afterwards was: 'I made it! I don't know what, but I can feel!'[4]

The *assumptions* of primal therapy have gradually grown out of the observation of such harrowing episodes as this one. Indeed, the whole methodology is a response to the gut-level experiences of patients expressing some deep and long-forgotten agony. This spine-chilling subjectivism has the last word. As Janov writes, 'There is no meaning to life, only meaning to experience, which is life in process', adding: 'To feel Pain . . . is to rediscover meaning.'[5]

Janov believes that it is when a baby's basic, or 'Primal', needs are not met for some time that there is a danger of neurosis. When a toddler, for example, falls over there may be a bruised knee but no psychic damage. When that same degree of physical injury arises because a child is pushed aside by an irritated parent then there may be psychological harm leading to Primal Pain.[6] Where such a child is repeatedly rejected the accumulation of Primal Pains (the Primal Pool) can lead to an inner conviction: 'There is no hope of being loved for what I am.' The boy or girl learns to repress genuine feeling, conforming to the sort of behaviour that the parents seem to expect. This shift from reality is a move into the neurotic process, wherein 'neurosis involves being what one is not in order to get what doesn't exist'. The resulting tension can, through the years, lead to a confused mind, poor memory, tight muscles and a host of psychosomatic symptoms.[7]

The aim of primal therapy is to reverse this impoverishing trend and, Janov argues, there is only one approach: Pain was the route into trouble, Pain must also be the way out. He writes: 'Primal therapy is the process of neurosis in reverse. Instead of blocking Pain, which leads to neurosis, it releases Pain so that a person can be free.' Whereas neurosis is an 'unconscious process', primal therapy is a 'conscious one' in that the critical episodes of earlier life are painfully re-experienced.[8] This 'way of Pain' is a journey towards an integration of body, feelings and intellect so that, with Janov's first primal patient, the client can cry 'I made it! I don't know what, but I can feel!'

After the patient's initial enquiry, preliminary medical check-up and production of a letter outlining the story, the *method* of primal therapy starts with an intensive three-week period, in which each individual is the only person treated by the therapist. The patient, instructed to take no medication, alcohol or other drugs for the duration of therapy, is isolated in a hotel room without television, reading matter and phone for the first twenty-four hours; sleep may also be advised against for that night. On arriving at the soundproof office where treatment is to take place he may be kept waiting deliberately. This seemingly sadistic exercise is to lessen the patient's defences and allow nervous tension to build up. Spreadeagled on a couch, he is encouraged to discuss his problems, while the therapist, in time, asks him to let his feelings of fear and tightness overtake him. If he panics, he is urged to call for his parents. Situations early in life are recalled and, when the patient is reliving some of the emotions thus aroused, he is told to breathe deeply and hard from the abdomen. Asked to open his mouth as wide as possible and 'pull' the feelings 'up from below', he may call out tearfully to a parent. Sometimes, with repetition of these grim procedures over a few days, the patient may scream out in a series of shudders such phrases as, 'Be nice to me, Mum!' or 'Daddy, help me!' This is Janov's 'Primal Scream', a cry which is 'pushed out by the force of years of suppressions and denials' of feeling. This dramatic breaking down of defences is seen, by the therapist at least, as a liberating experience. In time, it is argued, the patient agrees with this view as successive layers of resistance are peeled away and a flood of new emotions is experienced. Each successive Primal 'lessens the unreal self and broadens the real self'.

After these three weeks of individual and intensive attention, the patient joins a 'post-Primal' group, which meets twice weekly for three or more hours. Here, as in the initial treatment, there is very little interaction between one person and another. Each is absorbed in his or her own retrogressive journey, although several therapists may mingle within the group to help certain individuals 'get into' their painful feelings. The 'group room' is not a place for a casual visitor to stumble into. There may be five or six patients turning and twisting on the floor, undergoing their noisy Primals at one and the same time, while elsewhere in the room other individuals may be locked into childhood in one way or another – one cuddling a teddy bear, another playing with bricks, another laying into a punch-bag and a fourth rocking in a chair sucking at a nursing bottle. In ways like these, it is said, the patients work towards their own goals of self-discovery and integration. Regular group therapy may last for six months or so with the opportunity of continuing for longer, especially where childhoods have been most severely damaged.[9]

Janov claims a high success rate for those who persist in treatment although others, he admits, 'get impatient and decide to opt for the neurotic life'. Those who endure, the 'post-Primal' patients, have a simple lifestyle, are 'most content', 'rarely sick' and know how to 'feel'.[10] Janov also declares that a number of physiological measurements give evidence of improved biological function, including a decrease in body temperature, slower heart-rate, lower blood-pressure, less muscular tension, lighter and calmer breathing, and a better balance between the activity of the right and left sides of the brain.[11]

What are we to say to this absolutist system which offers psychological salvation to those who will follow its exhausting pathway to a 'defenceless' state? There can be no doubt that there are many who have spent a lifetime repressing authentic feeling and whose tense rigidity may be traceable to parental neglect or tight control in their earliest years. Such may find a deep emotional release as their defences are stripped away, but is a human condition without any barriers towards the outside world so desirable? Further, as with so many of our humanist theorists, the assumptions seem to be that all our evil is the result of what has been done to us – particularly by our parents – and that, if the right key can be found, we can enter again the lost innocence of our 'normality'. Just how utopian this scheme is we can see when Janov writes of the Primal Revolution that 'a society that fulfils needs will have no violence, no mental hospitals, prisons, or specialists in psychotherapy'.[12] This is indeed a worthy aim, but there is no substantial evidence that life after the Primal Scream ushers in the kingdom.

Having looked in outline at the thinking of Rank and Janov, let us turn now to some Christian perspectives on the voyage backwards in time.

Inner healing

Inner healing, healing of the memories, faith-imagination therapy and prayer counselling are approaches which, in one way or another, seek to bring the power of the risen Lord to heal and transform the hidden hurts of the past and their baleful influence on the present. Well known practitioners in these areas include Agnes Sanford, Anne White, Catherine Marshall, Ruth Carter Stapleton, Francis MacNutt, Michael Scanlan, Reg East and Roger Moss.

Ruth Stapleton describes *inner healing* as 'a process of emotional reconstruction experienced under the guidance of the Holy Spirit' and adds that there is no attempt 'to supplant psychiatry or to ignore the wisdom found in secular psychology'.[13] The assumption here is that our past is an open book to God, a book in which the pages can be turned back with a sense of Christ's companionship, revealing those blotted paragraphs we had forgotten about, the pictures of which we are ashamed, the leaves that have stuck together through life's spillages. Inner healing may involve our personal repentance as our hidden resentments and jealousies are exposed, our need to forgive another as we see anew that we have been victims and, overall, our Lord's healing of sad, disappointing and fearful memories. The book can be restored, its whole story know the refreshment of the Spirit and so become a clearer, less compromised tale to be told to the glory of its divine author.

A number of techniques are used to facilitate this inner renewal, including faith-imagination and prayer counselling. Whatever the precise approach, it is usually helpful for the person who seems trapped by, for example, persistent anxiety or recurring fear to talk initially about their difficulties with a perceptive counsellor. In exploring the past, vivid memories of hurtful experiences may be recalled. Where there seems to be some psychological 'block', the helper may pray to God for a clear revelation of the hidden area. Ruth Stapleton's method of *faith-imagination* incorporates the use of praying a prayer in which the Lord is pictured as standing with the oppressed person at the foot of a stairway, each step representing a year of life. From birth through to the present, Christ is seen ascending the stairs in close companionship, while at each stage his healing is sought and, in faith, accepted. Ruth Stapleton describes how, on one occasion, reaching the imaginary twelfth step, the woman she was counselling screamed out and began to recall the horror of, as a twelve-year-old, being raped by her father. In visualising the Lord's presence in the room of the original assault, his hand placed on the shoulder of the miscreant father, the daughter was enabled to voice words of forgiveness. In turn, she found a profound release in her relationships in the coming days.[14] Christopher Bryant, who at times finds this way of faith-imagination deeply healing of his own past, writes: 'This can be a symbolic and therefore powerful representation of two realities, that of a past experience partly active in the present and that of the living Christ.'[15]

Prayer counselling is similarly open to the Spirit's leading and incorporates a group of, say, two or three counsellors, with at least one of the same sex as the person in need, meeting with the counsellee for up to four or five hours. In a relaxed and informal atmosphere, a time of introductions is followed by prayer in which the 'presence and protection of God is claimed'. Those attending are invited to open their lives afresh to the Lord and to seek the Spirit's guidance, wisdom and discernment. This initial praying precedes a period of discussion in which the one being counselled is encouraged to share situations and relationships that are of particular concern. The counsellors aim to be caring and prayerful throughout, listening for God's leading as best how to help. Their ministry, it is argued, needs to be sensitive to the possibilities of meeting occultic involvement, physical disease and personal sin, as well as emotional scars that may require the journey of 'faith-imagination'. Such work necessitates men and women of high spiritual calibre, psychological maturity, wide experience and adequate training. In the United States Anne White has taught prayer counselling along these lines through a series of training schools under the general title of 'Victorious Ministry through Christ' (VM).[16] Her influence has led to the extension of this approach to the United Kingdom where a trust for VM was formed in 1975. This body arranges residential workshops at its 'Retreats of the Healing of the Whole Person' and 'Schools of Prayer Counselling'. Wherever it is propounded, this ministry of prayer counselling always seeks to be exercised with the support of the Christian community.

Primal integration

Frank Lake (1914–1982) was something of a Renaissance man in terms of his wide reading, fertile mind, ready imagination and innovative ideas. Like many of the leading lights of the four-teenth and fifteenth centuries, he was also a bit of a maverick, in the sense that his intensity of thinking and speaking gave the impression of a roving spirit that could not settle with a newly emerging theory for too long before cantering off into fresh pastures. Endowed with a somewhat restless variety of genius he was also a man who gave himself wholeheartedly to the cause in hand, inspiring both irritation and strong loyalty from those around him. One of his former colleagues writes: 'If Frank had espoused the theory that skipping for ten minutes a day was the answer, he would still have had success.'[17] Brian Lake, a consult-ant psychiatrist in Leeds and Frank's younger brother, describes him as 'an outstanding but enigmatic and complex figure' who 'excited growth but was unable at times to sustain and maintain it'.[18]

The brothers grew up in the family home in Aughton, Lancashire in an environment which Brian Lake calls 'a safe but rather anxious place to live' and where Anglicanism and church attendance were part of the fabric of life. Frank Lake qualified in medicine at Edinburgh and went to India in 1939 as a medical missionary. During the War he was seconded to the Army Medical Training Centre at Poona, while, in the post-war years, he worked as superintendent of the Christian Medical College of Vellore, South India. His main commitment through-out this time abroad was in parasitology although he found himself responding to 'dynamic psychiatry' while at Vellore. In 1950 he returned to Britain, with his wife, Sylvia and their small son, to retrain as a psychiatrist at the request of the Church Missionary Society. Looking back at this period of transition, from studying tropical parasites to a training in psychiatry which included some Kleinian influence, he used to say that he had exchanged 'exploring internalised physical for internalised psychological bad objects'.

1954, with the introduction of LSD into clinical psychiatric practice in England, was a significant year for the direction Frank Lake was to take. Using this hallucinogenic drug for the treat-ment of neuroses and personality disorders, he was astounded to find, as defences crumbled to expose the unconscious, how graphically the patient's actual birth experience was re-enacted. He recorded every detail of what was said, and observed that vivid accounts of, for example, a forceps delivery or of the cord being tight around the neck were later confirmed by the mothers. He felt that Otto Rank's insistence on the primacy of birth trauma in the production of anxiety began to make sense. From this point on Lake deliberately chose to allow his patients 'to continue (his) education'.

In the autumn of 1958, Frank Lake started a series of training seminars in order to teach his distinctive brand of therapy called 'clinical theology'. Thousands of clergy of all denominations, as well as smaller numbers of general practitioners, consultant physicians, psychiatrists, and other professionals, attended these courses of training. I remember the puzzlement and amusement on the face of a vicar I knew, who was attending such a course in the mid-1960s, as he quizzed me about the authenticity of the 'birth experience' and its relation to later life. The material for the first year of this two-year series, comprising twelve meetings of three hours duration a year, was collated for Lake's monumental *Clinical Theology*, published in 1966. This impressive tome includes a compendium of case-studies of those patients whom he tried to help by using LSD. The work's size and psychiatric language do not make it an easy read – as another clergyman friend discovered; however, he found that massive scholarship has its uses in that the two and a half inch depth of the book was perfect for supporting the broken leg of his bed! In all fairness, there are others whose ministries have been revolutionized by *Clinical Theology* and its publishers are at the moment preparing an abridged version in response to continuing demand.

In 1962 the Clinical Theology Association (CTA) was formed, based on Frank Lake's interdisciplinary seminars and fostering, in time, a network of clinical tutors to help disseminate training in 'human relations, pastoral care and counselling' throughout the country. This movement, centred for many years at 'Lingdale' in Nottingham, also sought 'to promote an understanding between the disciplines of psychiatry and theology'.

It was in the late 1960s that Frank Lake found that Reichian and bio-energetic theories of deep-breathing could lead to a recapitulation of the birth experience without exposing patients to the unwanted effects of LSD. The use of the drug was stopped and groups of people were invited to residential conferences at Lingdale, in order to work together 'at primal depth'. It was within the context of these 'primal integration workshops' that Frank

Lake's attention shifted from birth to the first three months of pregnancy as the time of greatest significance for the future well-being of the individual. Following his untimely death in May 1982 there was a reaction within the Council of CTA which favoured closing the association. However, further reflection has shown that a movement of value should not stand and fall with its founder. CTA is now based in Oxford and seeks to continue its commitment to training, a Christ-centred theology and to research. Dr Roger Moss, a consultant psychiatrist based in Exeter, has been given the task of assessing Frank Lake's work of primal integration with a view to publication.

Let us now attempt a closer evaluation of Lake's methodologies.

Assumptions

It is far from easy to be categorical about Frank Lake's assumptive basis because his approach to both psychology and theology is exploratory and largely open-ended. We have already seen his resolve, in the context of LSD therapy, to allow the patients 'to continue his education' into the depths of the human psyche. Similarly, in his Christian thinking, he seeks to be alert to the 'not-yet-searched-out' riches of Christ. Nonetheless, his essentially *inductive* stance also looks to a meeting between the secular psychologies and theological belief. His desire for a degree of *integration* is apparent when he writes that CTA began

> . . . as an attempt to bridge the river that ran between secular psychiatry and Christian theology, not so much at its intellectual headwaters as down towards the estuary where thousands come to one bank or the other, hopefully to drink some healing waters.[19]

His concern, to change the metaphor, is that psychiatry and theology should join forces, not necessarily at the base-camp of theoretical discussion but out on the front line where people perish. Let us examine his understanding of the 'two river banks' more fully.

Psychology

Brian Lake writes that his brother was 'deeply attached to' the Church, medicine and psychiatry, and yet 'deeply frustrated by their limitations'. We see the resulting individualism at every turn, especially in his psychiatric career. Frank Lake came into the profession comparatively late and was open to influences of an unusually dynamic nature for the state of psychiatry in Britain in the 1950s. His early interest in Kleinian 'object relations theory' was reinforced by his discovery of 'primal memories' through the use of LSD and, in time, he turned his back on the more organic 'medical model' of British psychiatry. His new conviction that therapy needed to rediscover a patient's primal roots meant that he looked to those analysts who saw the relevance of birth trauma, such as Otto Rank, Nandor Fodor, Francis Mott and Donald Winnicott. It is interesting to note that the start of Frank Lake's work with LSD preceded and has since paralleled the comparable studies by Stanislav Grof in the United States.[20] At the same time, we should point out that Lake's christocentric exploration of Primal therapy is quite independent of Arthur Janov's humanistic methodology.

It is in Frank Lake's warm response to the armamentarium of the 'newer therapies' that we see his wide-ranging *eclecticism*. Although he can be accused of assimilating humanistic methodologies too readily – 'baptising the therapies' – he is not indiscriminate in his assessments. For example, he follows Oden in criticising certain aspects of TA, such as its demotion of individual conscience.[21] Nevertheless, Lake hails many of the systems within the 'growth movement' because, amongst other things, their emphasis on 'being', personalism and discovery seems to echo the 'new' dimensions brought to the Church in recent years through the work of the Holy Spirit. CTA is said to be indebted 'in varying measure' to Gestalt therapy, TA, bioenergetics, behaviour therapy, encounter groups, family therapy and reality therapy.[22]

This may be the place to say something about *co-counselling*, and the closely allied *re-evaluation counselling*, one of the many components amongst the 'newer therapies' that Lake acknowledged. This method originated in Seattle, USA in the early 1950s through the work of Harvey Jackins, a man from 'the world of industrial labour'. Following an initial period of training, pairs of co-counsellors meet once a week taking the roles of counsellor and client in turns. It is this mutuality which enables the participants to grow in warmth of attention to another and in openness to their own inner conflicts and past hurts. Although this approach can be used in therapy, it is most recommended – at least it was in the UK in its earlier years in the mid-1970s – for the personal development of counsellors. The 'discharge' of buried emotional stress leads to a conscious 're-evaluation', where fresh insight can pave the way to wiser action in situations where formerly one was driven by ill-understood and negative feelings. In Britain, the names of John Heron, Rose Evison and Karen Howard are amongst those associated with co-counselling, while Colin Davison and Audrey Shilling have written about the method of 're-evaluation' and its potential for Christian growth.[23]

Amongst the 'pastoral' counsellors we have referred to, Frank Lake declares the influence on his thinking of Anton Boisen, Seward Hiltner, Wayne Oates,. Howard Clinebell, Edward Thornton, Tom Oden, Morton Kelsey, Jay Adams and Paul Tournier. His overall eclecticism is supported by a world view which looks, in effect, to both general and special revelation. He writes:

> The task of a Christian philosophy of science and knowledge in any generation is to press human reason to its proper limits and then to use the wisdom which God gives us by the Holy Spirit, expounding Christ to us, to bring insight and understanding to all those matters which the order of science cannot reach.[24]

Theology

Frank Lake describes his theology of pastoral counselling as 'para-modern' to distinguish it from Oden's categories of 'pre-modern' and 'post-modern' orthodoxies (see pp. 240–241). While 'post-modern' orthodoxy has journeyed through liberal theology and 'pre-modern' has not, the exponents of 'para-modernism', according to Lake, '. . . have responded to modernity but always with reservations, because alongside its flux we have been abiding in Christ, who is not just today but tomorrow, who links us to past, present and future'.[25]

With his sense of the ever-present Christ, Lake tackles theology inductively, taking up a situation in the front line of counselling, analysing it deeply, 'to see what is at stake', and then evaluating 'how Christian truth may be related to it'. In this enterprise he moves away from a purely propositional and deductive use of the scriptures, seeking rather to follow the Spirit's leading as to 'what particular word, or insight, or meaning, clinches the matter in hand and makes the task clear'.[26] He sees biblical perspectives as including a much neglected 'right side of the brain' component, where, in contrast to the intellectualisations of 'left-sided' thinking, revelation is 'enshrined in images, symbols, pictures, parables, ceremonies and liturgical actions'. Lake regards this comprehensive theology as more fully biblical than an over--dogmatic approach.[27]

Although Frank Lake's 'para-modern' theology is genuinely orthodox in its trinitarian stance, it is in his belief that the effectiveness of Christ's death ranges widely beyond the forgiveness of sins and entry into God's kingdom that he is at his most controversial – and most stimulating. He follows Pope John Paul II in seeing a profound identification between the passion of Christ and people's suffering. In 'sharing intimately' with the appalling array of individual and corporate affliction, the Lord 'justifies the ways of God' to those who suffer. Moreover, they 'can then forgive God, and his careless surrogates, their parents'. This theodicy, seeking to 'make sense' of the problem posed by the existence of both evil and a God of love, is the touchstone of Frank Lake's later methodology.[28]

Let us examine how his inductive theology of the cross and his psychological observations are brought together in the hypothesis of the 'Maternal-Foetal Distress Syndrome'.

Maternal-foetal distress syndrome

Frank Lake and a number of his colleagues, in carrying out 'fantasy journeys' with the members of the workshops at Lingdale, developed an 'intuition' that the 'origins of the main personality disorders and the main psychosomatic stress conditions' lie not primarily at birth, and the perinatal period, but *in the first three months of pregnancy*. By studying the experiences of those 'who have relived the intra-uterine journey' within these groups, a 'Maternal-Foetal Distress Syndrome' has been postulated. It is argued that once the umbilical circulation is established, by about five weeks, the foetus is susceptible to the emotional state of the mother. Whatever her ingrained feelings are about life, her awareness of the pregnancy will compound these emotions with joy, gratitude, relief, worry, disappointment, anger, fear or depression. Where the maternal feelings are mainly negative, their powerful effect on her own body will, according to Lake's theory, transfuse 'all kinds of persecutory and annihilatory anxiety' to the foetus. This 'negative umbilical affect' may be coped with, opposed or succumbed to by the organism.

Where the foetus is overwhelmed, the 'mirror images' of hysterical and schizoid reactions may arise and colour the rest of his or her life.[29] In the *hysterical personality* the response to intra-uterine rejection is one of movement towards other people in 'an attempt to gain and keep their attentive acceptance'.[30] For example, a young woman may bind herself resolutely to an over-dependent relationship with a boyfriend because of her 'separation' anxiety; typically, she is extraverted, spontaneous, fearful of being ignored and needs a full social life. The *schizoid personality*, in its extreme form, is one in which 'all desire for life through personal relationships' is 'extinguished'.[31] Here, we might visualise a man in his middle years who has a lifelong tendency to introversion and withdrawal from the world of people and things, due to his 'commitment' anxiety; he is probably unmarried, eccentric, intellectualising and covets solitude.[32]

Frank Lake tells an arresting story which seems to offer some confirmation of the maternal-foetal distress syndrome. He recalls the response of an American mother who had been puzzled by the behaviour of the middle of her three daughters and its striking resemblance to that of others in the girl's class. These young women would suddenly break down in tears, admitting to a deep distress 'with a cutting sense of shame and guilt that some terrible thing had happened'. The outbreaks were unlike mass hysteria and their origin had remained obscure. However, the mother, hearing Lake's theory, told him of her sudden realisation that this mystifying behaviour was explicable. She declared that the emotional pattern was identical to her own in 1963 when, during the early months of carrying her middle daughter, she had heard the news of John F. Kennedy's assassination. She remembered that her female contemporaries, including those at a similar stage of pregnancy, reacted similarly. Her daughter's peers would have been subject to the same distressed feelings in their own mothers. She concluded: 'The whole thing makes sense to me for the first time.'[33]

It is in the face of such unsolicited foetal suffering that Frank

Lake's theodicy applies. He argues a 'theology of correlation', in which there are 'close and significant correspondences' between the agonies of Christ in Gethsemane and on Golgotha and the afflictions of the foetus and newborn. The 'piercing' of the foetus by maternal distress, the asphyxiating experience of the birth process and the separation anxiety of the neglected neonate are paralleled by the 'crushing' horror of the Garden, the 'pinioning' of crucifixion and the dereliction in the hours of darkness.[34] It is in this divine identification with innocent suffering that the hope of primal integration lies.

Aims

The objectives of counselling within clinical theology can be described in both theological and psychological language. Overall, in contrast to the Jungian ambition of self-realisation, the goal is *Christ-realisation* in which the individual 'seems more often to be travelling towards the death of the self than to its realization'.[35] Lake writes concerning this aim:

> It clearly places Christ in the centre of the field of vision and points to His offer of a New Being through new relationships with God in Him, of sustenance by feeding on Him, of status within the Divine Family, of a daily achievement of such good works as God has for us to do, all bound up with an eternal destiny.[36]

Thus we see that 'Christ-realisation' means an 'absolute dependence of the self upon its true Self, Christ'. As an example, 'the neurotic's national anthem, of which every verse begins with the words "if only", is swept away in a strong affirmative "Thou only"'.[37]

In *primal integration*, the initial task is to form an alliance, in TA terms, with the client's 'Adult' so that he or she can 'descend into, identify with, and give recognition and acceptance to their own inner child of the past and foetus in the womb'. Ultimately, the aim is to bring together what primal pain has split: 'the cognition, the imagination, the sensation and the emotion' – the 'four essential aspects of experience'. It is the discovery of these 'in all their original uterine context' that can open the way to their reconnection and integration.[38]

Method

As we have already seen, Frank Lake's methodology has been in a state of flux throughout its history and so we find, in assessing his thirty or so years of developing a clinical theology, a considerable range of methods and techniques being used. These include the relaxation and assertion training of behavioural therapy, the guided imaginings and fantasy journeys of Gestalt therapy, the sensitivity to posture of bio-energetics and the intensive journal-keeping advocated by Ira Progoff in the United States. Similarly, amongst approaches put forward by Christians, prayer counselling and healing of the memories are important adjuncts.

Let us consider some of the more general aspects of Frank Lake's style of counselling before concentrating on the unique work of primal integration.

General aspects

Lake's overall fashion of therapy is a 'non-directive listening' which, with its emphasis on the counsellor-client relationship, has something in common with Tournier's 'dialogue' counselling – although it seems to lack the mutually confessional nature of the latter. Lake sees Christ not only as the proclaimer of the Good News but also as the 'great listener'; he therefore stresses the primacy of listening in his own counselling ministry, seeking to be open to the Spirit's restraining influence. This sensitivity does not preclude Lake's desire 'in some way' to declare his conviction 'about God's revelation of our true humanity through Christ' but, on balance, he believes that 'hurt people have a greater need to meet a God who hears and groans, who struggles for words, than a God who has much to say to them'.[39]

Within his openness to the Holy Spirit, Frank Lake stresses the fundamental importance of *Kairos*, a Greek word used in the New Testament to denote 'the right moment'. He points out how susceptible Jesus was to God's timing; we read, for instance, how, 'just before the Passover Feast', 'Jesus knew that the time had come for him to leave this world and go to the Father' (John 13:1). Frank Lake asks whether, as counsellors, we too can 'be endowed by the Spirit with his impeccable sense of the right time'; in which case, the Holy Spirit can use our 'spiritual senses' to show 'some change of direction, to halt, or to move forward at once, a voice behind saying, "This is the way, walk in it"'.[40]

In order to sharpen our understanding of the counsellor's awareness during therapy, Lake offers the analogy of a pair of glasses with trifocal lenses: the upper ones picking up 'known or presumed patterns' in the 'distant past'; the middle ones focusing on the client in the 'here-and-now'; and the lower ones reflecting on the counsellor's own 'intimate responses'. This attentiveness, with its background alertness to the Spirit's promptings, has its 'perilous' dimension since whatever is happening within the client can be mirrored within the counsellor. In this context, for the sufferer to find substantial help, there may have to be an off-loading of heavy burdens on to the shoulders of the man or woman who seeks to 'come alongside'. One example is that the client may present a stony silence to the well-intentioned counsellor. The helper will need to feel the pain of that silence, which may have its roots in a primal response to parental rejection. The explanation is that the infant met a rebuttal of his or her requests for understanding and is now inflicting that same cold taciturnity on the counsellor. Such a 'perilous' experience may provide the clue to the client's dilemma.[41]

Primal integration

The move towards primal integration takes place within a group process in which the members, after an initial meal and introductions, are encouraged to declare what they would like to work on. Guidelines are suggested, including the need to make 'I' statements rather than refer to third parties ('I feel angry' rather than 'Some people would feel angry'), to be honest with self and others, to allow an 'inner sense of spontaneity to lead the way' and to try to progress towards 'areas of new behaviour'. With a beginners' group, it may well be the second day of a residential workshop before anyone is ready for primal experience.[42]

Typically, a primal integration group works together for five or six days and comprises four self-selected members – the subject, a facilitator, a scribe to take verbatim notes and someone who may record the encounter on tape. Although there may be three other groups present in the same large room, each subject, once the re-experiencing of early life events is under way, is oblivious of any potential distraction. Following the taking of an accurate history, the subject, lying in the foetal position on a mattress on the floor, is encouraged to get in touch with primal emotions by taking an imaginative journey into some cave deep in the ocean. This uterine imagery is fostered by the womb-like security of the encircling small group of colleagues. Alternatively, the 'voyager' is invited to 'feel into' his or her mother's and father's feelings about themselves, each other and life generally on the night of the subject's conception. Lake writes that participants are 'often astonished at how vividly and movingly they can reconstruct the relationship within which they were conceived'.[43]

The person in need is then taken in imagination through the various stages of pregnancy, birth and emotional bonding with the mother, step by step. At four to five weeks, the facilitator places three fingers over the client's navel to signify the initiation of the foetal-placental circulation, from which point he or she may have been subject to maternal distress. The physiological background to the primal process is a Reichian form of deep breathing and it is at this stage that the person who is getting in touch with long-lost emotions is asked to give vent to whatever sound seems appropriate to these rediscovered feelings. One may shake with convulsive sobs, another may sigh contentedly, another tremble with fear, another scream out in anger and yet another be overwhelmed by a deep longing for recognition. These powerful emotions are understood to be within the full flood of the mother's anguish over, rejoicing at or rejection of her pregnancy. The subject's Adult reaches back to feel with, be with and comfort the frightened child in the womb, the painful journey being rendered safer by the loving support of the group. Thus 'the terrified child from which the adult had been in flight, feels itself calmed and cared for'.

As we have previously noted, all this 'innocent suffering' is taken up in the afflictions of the crucified Christ. The sacrament of the Lord's supper makes tangible his liberating sacrifice and at least one day in each conference begins with a service of Holy Communion. The cross of Christ is seen to make bearable the therapeutic journey back to the womb, for the pain and affliction are known and shared by a Companion who comforts in the presence of a handful of fellow-believers. Frank Lake says this of the recalled distress:

The suffering is the same, and more may follow, but the meaning of it, how it is perceived, is transformed by the new metaphor: 'He is with me; they are with me; I am not alone'. So much of the horror of

primal affliction lies in the solitariness of the suffering. With someone else there, in whose face I can see every familiar agony of my
own soul, the intensity and bearableness of the suffering are quite
changed.[44]

Healing the family tree

The most outlandish and controversial of the Christian
approaches to counselling considered in this book is, to my mind,
that of Dr Kenneth McAll. Born in China in 1910 and with a family
background of Congregational missionary work, McAll, like
Frank Lake, graduated in medicine at Edinburgh University.
Returning to China as a 'missionary-surgeon', he, his wife and
their child were interned by the Japanese for four years during the
1940s. After the war, the family returned to England where
Kenneth McAll worked as a general practitioner for the next ten
years. While in China he had become convinced 'that the spirit
world holds both good and evil influences' and, during his
medical work in the south of England, he concluded that 'mind-
sick, "devil-mad" people' can be found anywhere. Consequently, again like Lake, McAll decided in 1956 to re-train in
psychiatry – in order to find the best way to help those so
afflicted; his deep desire was that such should 'get in touch with
God and learn to live completely under his direction'.[45] As a
psychiatrist, seeking to use the full panoply of traditional care
and yet open to the therapeutic power of the Christian community, he gradually developed his idiosyncratic approach of 'healing
the family tree'.

His experiences of spiritual warfare in the Far East and his
observation of the 'possession syndrome' in Wessex have led him
to some powerful *assumptions* about the state of the dead and their
influence on the living. Those who suffer from this syndrome are
usually passive individuals who have relinquished virtually all
sense of identity and are 'taken over' by more dominant characters. Most of us would agree that such possessiveness, whether it
is a mother with a grown-up son or an egocentric and demanding
husband with a compliant wife, is invariably a source of potential
destructiveness. However, McAll concludes that such malignant
influence on the life of a 'possessed' person may emanate from
unknown others, be they living or dead. In the case of the latter,

the baleful effects of 'possession', including phobias, schizo-phrenia and a range of physical conditions, may derive from recent or remote ancestors, from still births, miscarriages or abortions amongst forbears, and from hauntings by the 'unquiet dead' in a place where the sufferer now lives. Victims of violent death, those who committed suicide and those who died 'unbles-sed' are, it is said, often the source of inexplicable malaise in their unfortunate descendants.[46]

In pursuing his *aim* of delivering the needy from such evil control through the power of Christ, he puts forward a *method* which centres on the Eucharist, or Lord's supper. Initially, the patient is helped as fully as possible by traditional psychiatric means. Where a diagnosis of ancestral 'possession' is suspected, a family tree is drawn up in order to identify those forbears who might be the origin of the patient's troubles. As well as the 'unquiet dead' already mentioned, McAll takes note of any familial behaviour disorder, such as destructive temper tan-trums, that seem to span the generations. He stresses the import-ance of locating the 'controlling spirit' and, where possible, the name of the ancestor. In the case of a stillbirth or miscarriage, an appropriate first name is offered by the family or sought in prayer, so making the search for deliverance 'more specific and personal'. Using a rite called 'The Eucharist of the Resurrection', McAll outlines four stages in the demonstration of God's healing power:[47]

1 *Prayer for deliverance.* Either with the person in need and his or her family present or, less suitably, in their absence, the service opens with the Lord's prayer, where special emphasis is made on the phrase, 'deliver us from evil'. In this and other prayers, the celebrant asks that the blood of Jesus 'cleanse the blood lines of the living and the dead of all that blocks healthy life, especially by breaking any hereditary seals or curses and by casting out evil spirits'.

2 *Prayer for forgiveness.* Here there is the idea of a 'double forgiveness' in which the patient willingly forgives dead relatives for their 'possessing' influence and, at the same time, asks forgiveness from them for any unloving attitudes. McAll sees Jesus Christ as the mediator of this two-way reconciliation.

3 *Drawing the dead to Christ.* Following prayers for deliverance and forgiveness, the family tree may be placed on the altar along with the bread and wine, all being offered to God and

consecrated. Prayer is made that as Christ's life 'comes into' the elements so 'it will come also into the families that are being offered' – both the living and the dead.

4 *Drawing the living to Christ.* During the final blessing, hands may be laid on the heads of those who have sought deliverance. McAll writes that this may be a time of dramatic physical healing as the assembled group looks to the power of the Lord over all the works of the Evil One.

In his accounts of such Eucharistic services, McAll describes many incidents in which long-lost ancestors are seen and their voices heard. He regards these visions and sounds as confirming the authenticity of the profound release many of his patients are said to experience. Indeed, the wife of a personal friend received considerable relief from a depressive illness through such a Eucharist.

McAll seeks to supplement his inductive reasoning by referring to pre-Reformation religious practice and a handful of unconvincing texts in the Bible and Apocrypha. He defends his position by saying that he advocates praying *for* the dead rather than *to* them, acknowledging that the latter is expressly forbidden in the scriptures. However, his practice of looking for forgiveness from departed spirits seems to me to come dangerously near to conversing with them. Moreover, McAll, in his belief in the 'unquiet dead', appears to be obliged to agree with the unbiblical doctrine of purgatory, the state of progressive purification between death and resurrection. He regards such restless spirits, still 'very much earth-bound', as the source of the possessions and hauntings with which he deals, and declares that they need our prayers if they are to reach the everlasting halls.[48]

I suggest the issue here is not so much whether supernatural spirits exist, as the scriptures clearly proclaim they do, as whether these same spirits at least include those for whom issues of repentance and forgiveness are relevant. There is no tangible biblical evidence for such a notion. Rather, the scriptures have little to say in the way of an elaborate demonology and, where they do point to the spirit world, they usually do so in the context of the Lord's victory over enemy forces. Kenneth McAll seems to move into forbidden territory, albeit in the name of Christ.

Discussion

In both the 'journey inwards' and the 'journey backwards' we are dealing primarily with inductive reasoning. In the former, a holy man here or a saintly woman there is rapt in some mystical experience and returns to the workaday world with shining face and a new humility. In the latter, a burdened Christian may be taken, step by step, on a pilgrimage of the imagination back to a childhood crisis, or a distressed believer, curled up like a foetus, may cry out in some long-lost anguish that seems to come from the pre-verbal world of the womb; both these voyagers return to home-base chastened and yet refreshed, proclaiming a sense of cleansing and integration. From experiences like these, multiplied many times over, the inductive thinker begins to draw conclusions and make explanations of a general nature. At a certain level, I suggest, the rest of us, fellow-mortals who have been too sceptical, afraid, busy or wise to venture on such perilous explorations, need to accept cautiously the testimony of the returning, happy-faced wanderers. Nonetheless, in doing so we should also apply our critical faculties.

Firstly, there is the difficulty of substantiating claims of life-changing experience. This is as much a problem for evaluating the story of a young man who goes forward after a Billy Graham mission as assessing the authenticity of a middle-aged woman's account that she has seen the 'beatific vision'. In either case, 'time will tell'. The evidence of transformed lives cannot be gainsaid. However, behind the glowing testimonies there lurks another question. Is the *explanation* offered for this or that seeming encounter with God reasonable, plausible, correct? In some ways the answer to this is much less pressing. If the young man was, in reality, on his way to the loo when waylaid by a mission counsellor, and meekly responded to all that was said in order to obey a less exalted call, or if the middle-aged woman's transportation into the heavenlies took place a week after taking some especially effective antidepressants, so what? If their lives are changed for the better, does the precise reason for that change matter? Surely it does. If we believe in the objective reality of a personal God, who made us and offers us new life in his Son, as well as in the subjective experience that can arise from this reconciliation, then the answer to the question 'What *really* happened?' is crucial. After all, apart from physical and psychological explanations for what befalls us, there is also a master of masquerade at large who can appear even as an 'angel of light'.

It is in responding to such queries that we experience increasing difficulty the further back in time we go on our journey of discovery. Proponents of 'inner healing' and 'healing of the memories' are on relatively safe ground when they use 'faith-imagination' to help open up areas of past hurt to the salve of the Lord's presence. This is a means of bringing repressed memories and feelings to consciousness and of facing up to their implications – and there is ample support in psychology for doing this. Further, the ability of Christ to forgive, heal, deal with negative emotions and change ingrained attitudes must be unquestioned. Although there is no doubt of our being fully accepted in Christ as we trust him, the Spirit may still need to work in the deep and hidden places of our lives to bring us towards conformity to the Son's image.

Even though the declaration of Hebrews 13:8 that 'Jesus Christ is the same yesterday and today and for ever', must have implication in our area of discussion, we still have the challenge of working out the relevance of this for the more long-distance expeditions back into the womb, to conception and beyond, marching back into history through the tangled branchings of the family tree. The venture to bring retrospective healing to troubled and troublesome ancestors, as we have seen, seems to fly in the face of Reformed Christianity. A methodology which proposes that remote ancestral sin can bind people centuries later seems dubious on many grounds, not least that such a pinpointing perspective does not appear to be part of the biblical record.

In Frank Lake's primal integration we can ask whether his theory of the maternal-foetal distress syndrome is valid and whether his resulting theodicy is compatible with God's revelation. He admits that the development of the hypothesis is largely on observational grounds – the outcome of painstaking note-taking and recording during hundreds of primal workshops. In one place he indicates a sense of divine calling, commenting on the way 'prayer counselling' and 'healing of the memories' in certain charismatic groups, exercising the gift of discernment, have pointed up the existence of 'deep distresses, beginning at or shortly after conception'. This information, he writes, gave him 'the impulse and "permission" to undertake . . . research into intra-uterine maternal-foetal exchanges'.[49]

At a more objective level, Lake refers to the work of Karl H. Pribram which demonstrates that long-term memory is based on the junctions between nerve-cells rather than in the cells themselves. These synapses multiply readily and contain the biochemical processes that make adaptation to new information and experience possible. Consequently, it is argued, memory can begin to be stored as soon as the synaptic junctions appear in the brain of the tiny foetus. However, a number of Lake's clients declare an experience of 'primal bliss' which is understood, within the framework of his theory, to pre-date the implantation of the embryo in the wall of the womb. Such speak of 'going back to an astonishing sense of being perfectly self-subsistent, of radiant wholeness and blessedness' and of 'having God and the universe within this perfect sphere which they feel themselves to be'. Those from a contemplative tradition identify the 'unitive experience' they seek with this primal state of the blastocyst, the cluster of cells that arise from the fertilised egg before implantation. Lake, in turn, looks to the embryologist, Richard Dryden who declares the possibility that the early cellular stages of a pregnancy may be able to store information in the cytoplasm – a discovery that may give some biological feasibility to Lake's views on 'pre-verbal memories'.[50]

Whatever further study and research reveals about these theories on primal pain, there also remain some important theological questions about Frank Lake's 'theology of correlation'. Once again we have some difficulty in assessment since the inductive nature of this thinking tends to invite us beyond the pages of scripture. He writes:

> We should expect to know more about the relevance of the Cross of Christ as we get to know more about man, since depth calls to depth . . . The Holy Spirit's work is to draw out truths about Christ which we have not recognized.[51]

Lake adds that Paul, who spoke of 'the unsearchable riches of Christ' (Ephesians 3:8 AV), would be astounded at our latter-day hesitancy to delve into such 'treasures of wisdom' – simply because we can see 'no precedent for them' in the apostle's writings. It is at this point that I would like once more to underline the blend of special and general revelation that seems to me to be the biblical perspective. As we seek to help those in anguish, may we not, at times, perceive aspects of, for example, the cross of Christ which we had not seen before in our reading of scripture? The important questions appear to be, 'Is this "new" understanding compatible with the biblical record?', 'Does it contradict plain scriptural words?' and 'Does it draw us into deeper commitment and greater love for Jesus, the word made flesh?'. Where the answers are 'Yes', 'no' and 'yes' respectively, I believe God may be applying some eternal truth to our previously blind hearts.

Where I am happiest with Frank Lake's understanding of the relevance of Christ's suffering to the afflictions of our early lives is in his allusion to those declarations in Hebrews which show that Jesus shared our humanity, was 'made like his brothers in every way' and tasted 'death for everyone' (see Hebrews 2:9–18). The Lord too had once been simply a fertilised egg, mysteriously conceived by a union of the Spirit and Mary, had survived whatever emotions his godly mother had in her pregnancy, had his own birth experience and had lived through those vulnerable neonatal days of being nursed at the breast and snuggled up to sleep in a feeding-trough. It is here, I believe, that the Lord is seen to identify most straightforwardly with his 'little brothers and sisters'. This is not to deny the conclusion, suggested by Lake, that Christ's sufferings at Gethsemane and in his brutal treatment at the hands of the Roman soldiers correlate in some measure with intrauterine and perinatal anguish. We can see all his multi-faceted affliction as covering and going beyond the bounds of human pain, including that of the defenceless foetus and infant.

I am less happy when Frank Lake writes that the passion of Christ, in identifying with primal distress, 'justifies the Father' and enables the innocent sufferer to forgive God.[52] What I think he means is that, as with 'healing the memories', many of us do suffer directly because of the sins of others and Christ can release us from a sense of outrage. We may, in our unhappiness, blame God for our misfortune but the Spirit will surely show us that the culpability is human rather than divine. Thus the Father can be justified, in the sense of exonerated, and those who need forgiveness can find their place in Christ.

Frank Lake was a man of ideas who wielded the English language with great panache, writing and speaking in a style that is vivid with analogy and illustration. I only met him once – when I attended a lecture he gave at the Bristol Psychotherapy

Association just over a year before his death. The hall was packed with men and women of great experience in the world of psychiatry, psychology, psychotherapy and counselling, many of them extremely sceptical of a Christian viewpoint. This small, dynamic man commanded our rapt attention, shifting eloquently in what he said from physiology to philosophy, psychology to theology and from intrauterine existence to life in the Spirit. It was stimulating, provocative, impressive and audacious. Even though Lake was a man who could get carried away by his rich use of the language and by his daring ideas, I am nonetheless grateful to him for his enterprise in seeking to show Christ's boundless love for the forgotten ones.

16

THE WONDERFUL COUNSELLOR

If Jesus Christ is not true God, how could he help us? If he is not true man, how could he help us?

Dietrich Bonhoeffer

He became what we are that he might make us what he is.

Athanasius

Let us then approach the throne of grace with confidence, so that we may receive mercy and find grace to help us in our time of need.

Hebrews 4:16

Throughout this book we have gradually built up a *theory* for evaluating counselling methodologies. A theory has been defined as 'a general principle formulated to explain a group of related phenomena'[1] – in our case, a principle to help us make sense of the bewildering array of therapeutic approaches. Our attempts to clarify a biblical anthropology will come to nothing unless they focus at some point or other on the person of Christ. It is here that our theory can be fleshed out by considering the encounters between the Son of man and needy people. His relating to those around him was of course undergirded by a God-given understanding of human nature. The Lord's theology and anthropology were impeccable! Thus we can add to our theory a *model* – where a model is 'a person, or work, that is proposed or adopted for imitation'[2] It is as we seek to imitate something of Christ's handling of others that our assumptions, aims and methods can be lifted out of the rut of rigid theorising and revitalised by his Spirit of counsel.

In Isaiah 9:6 we read that the promised Son will be called 'Wonderful Counsellor, Mighty God, Everlasting Father, Prince

of Peace' and it is in the first of these four names that we see that
'the wisdom which is necessary for a ruler will be his in an
extraordinary degree'.[3] This divine wisdom includes the perspectives of insight, knowledge, shrewdness and wise dealing[4] so
that we can be assured we have a Lord who can impart deep and
timely counsel to his subjects. Every facet of who Christ is – king,
son, saviour, deliverer, servant, anointed one, etc. – could be
studied with profit but I would like to concentrate on just four
aspects of his ministry to others: those of *prophet*, *pastor*, *priest* and
paraclete.[5] Having looked at these four dimensions of the Christ
'model', we will be better placed to complete our evaluation of
Christian methodologies of counselling.

The example of Christ

Prophet

Colin Brown writes that the Old Testament prophet is 'a proclaimer of the word, called by God to warn, exhort, comfort, teach
and counsel, bound to God and thus enjoying a freedom that is
unique'.[6] This prophetic activity comprised both warnings of
judgment and promises of restoration; in Jeremiah, for example,
the certainty of exile and the guarantee of a return were both
anticipated (Jeremiah 16:5–15). In Deuteronomy 18:14–22 we
read that a prophet 'like Moses' will be raised up, one of whom
the Lord God says, 'I will put my words in his mouth, and he will
tell them everything I command him'. This obedient proclaimer is
clearly seen to be Jesus Christ by Peter in his sermon following the
healing of the crippled beggar (Acts 3:22,23) and by Stephen in his
speech before the Sanhedrin (Acts 7:37,52). Although the Lord
never referred to himself as a prophet, the authority of his words
and miracles led to such exclamations from the people as 'A great
prophet has appeared among us' (Luke 7:16) and 'He is a
prophet, like one of the prophets of long ago' (Mark 6:15).[7]

The Jews regarded the possession of the Holy Spirit as *the* mark
of the prophet and it was Jesus' clear empowering that confirmed
his unique call. Here was the one on whom the Spirit descended
'like a dove', who was declared to be the Son by 'a voice . . . from
heaven', who, full of the Spirit, overcame the Enemy's wiles in
the desert and who, in the synagogue at Nazareth, proclaimed
the fulfilment of the messianic promise of Isaiah 61:1,2:

The Spirit of the Lord is on me, because he has anointed me to preach good news to the poor. He has sent me to proclaim freedom for the prisoners and recovery of sight for the blind, to release the oppressed, to proclaim the year of the Lord's favour.[8]

Here was one greater than the prophet Jonah (Matthew 12:41), for he not only stood in the prophetic tradition in heralding deliverance but he was also the deliverer.

Although Christ was more than a prophet, we observe, in his everyday encounters with others, a prophetic strain emerging as he teaches, declares, exhorts, challenges, confronts and calls to repentance. Even though he is at his most confrontational in the presence of the self-righteous and hypocritical, we also see that plain-speaking is a necessary element in his approach to the misguided, wayward and outcast. He rebukes, for example, Peter, when he baulks at the Lord's pending rejection and crucifixion, and James and John, when they seek immediate judgment on an unwelcoming village (Mark 8:33; Luke 9:55). Within the delicate fabric of his dialogue with the Samaritan woman at Jacob's well, Jesus, although misunderstood at first, tests her out repeatedly (John 4:4–42). Taking his offer of 'living water' as an invitation to slake her physical thirst once and for all, she responds to his exhortation, 'Go, call your husband and come back' with the evasive, 'I have no husband.' Jesus then, in true prophetic manner, says, 'You are right when you say you have no husband. The fact is, you have had five husbands, and the man you now have is not your husband. What you have just said is quite true.' And so we find here a style of caring which is confrontational and yet, in this case, is couched in words that are tender and affirming. Her bald statement 'I have no husband' is not attacked; rather, it is taken at face value and, at the same time, the full truth behind it is gently but firmly exposed. It is Christ's prophetic insight that leads to her exclamations, 'He told me everything I ever did' and, thereby, to the conversion of many of her fellow-Samaritans.

Pastor

Within the pastoral community of the late patriarchal period, Yahweh is seen as the one true Shepherd of his people. In blessing Joseph the favourite, Jacob speaks of 'the God who has been my Shepherd all my life to this day' (Genesis 48:15; 49:24). This picture of nurturing and protection is most clearly presented in the psalter and in the exilic 'prophets of comfort'.[9] It reaches its zenith of poetic imagery in Psalm 23 and Isaiah 40:11, where we read this of the sovereign and faithful Lord:

> He tends his flock like a shepherd:
> He gathers the lambs in his arms
> and carries them close to his heart;
> he gently leads those that have young.

In contrast to this portrayal of divine tenderness, the kings of Israel and Judah, and other 'under-shepherds' of the Lord's people, are castigated for their faithlessness and self-centredness. Their neglect is condemned, for example, in Ezekiel 34 where the true shepherd declares that he will rescue the flock from the mouths of the false ones (verse 10). Here, as well as in Jeremiah and Zechariah, promise is made of a Messiah-shepherd in the Davidic line:

> I will place over them one shepherd, my servant David, and he will tend them; he will tend them and be their shepherd. I the Lord will be their God, and my servant David will be prince among them. I the Lord have spoken (Ezekiel 34:23,24).

Most of us have a somewhat romantic view of the shepherd as a rugged but gentle figure, striding the hills with a lamb under one arm, a faithful sheepdog at his heels and a versatile crook held to steady him in the steeper places. However, during post-exilic times, whatever loftier opinions had been held, religious leaders tended to see shepherds as rogues who responded dishonestly to their conditions of low pay. The Jewish Midrash on Psalm 23 declared, 'No position in the world is as despised as that of the shepherd.'[10] It is perhaps surprising that this negative view of the pastoral life is not taken over into the New Testament, where Jesus is openly set forth as the messianic Shepherd who has compassion on the crowds, 'because they were harassed and helpless, like sheep without a shepherd' (Matthew 9:36). Here was a faithful and loving shepherd who fulfilled the words of Zechariah 13:7, 'Strike the shepherd, and the sheep will be scattered', as he faced betrayal and desertion on the eve of his death (Matthew 26:3; Mark 14:27).

This smiting of the good shepherd was to be endured voluntarily. In John 10, the phrase 'I lay down my life for the sheep' runs like a refrain through Jesus' discourse with the Jews. It is in this chapter that we receive the full impact of the intimate, trustworthy, self-sacrificing, personal, guiding, keeping and nurturing qualities of our Lord's relating to his own. His protection of the disciples by calming the storm (Luke 8:24), his feeding of the five thousand and, later, of the four thousand (Mark 6:30–44; 8:1–9a) and his prayer for Simon Peter (Luke 22:32) all spring from his shepherding concern for the needy. In his encounter with the woman at the well, his pastoral instinct to give her sustenance and companionship is expressed in the offer of 'living water'.

Priest

In the letter to the Hebrews, the levitical priesthood of the Old Testament is contrasted with the infinitely superior, high priestly function of Christ. As representative of men and women before a holy God, an effective high priest needed both to be at one with humankind and to have a clearcut divine calling.[11] These requirements were met perfectly by Jesus. On the one hand, he was 'made like his brothers in every way' and was 'tempted in every way, just as we are' and, on the other hand, he 'was designated by God to be high priest' (Hebrews 2:17; 4:15; 5:10). Here was one who, unlike the priests and Levites of old with all their fallibility, was 'without sin'. Further, this unique high priest was not only the sacrificer, he was also the sacrificed. Here, at last, was the all-sufficient intermediary who had 'appeared once for all at the end of the ages to do away with sin by the sacrifice of himself' (9:26). Thus, Jesus Christ, fully human and fully divine, joined hands, as it were, with fallen humanity and a righteous God, making reconciliation possible through his perfect self-giving.

During his earthly days we witness the Lord's priestly role as he reaches out to those in distress – mediating healing, forgiveness and new life. The paralytic at Capernaum, the woman at the house of Simon the Pharisee, and Zacchaeus the tax-collector are a few of the countless people who experienced peace, joy and new beginnings through the restoring touch of Christ (Mark 2:1f; Luke 7:36f; 19:1f). In his interchange with the Samaritan woman,

we see Jesus not only as prophet and shepherd but as priest too as
she takes of the water that will become in her 'a spring of water
welling up to eternal life'.

Paraclete

In secular Greek from the fourth century BC onwards the noun
parakletos referred to a 'person called in to help, summoned to
give assistance'. It could be seen as denoting a 'helper in court',
paralleling the Latin word *advocatus*.[12] In the Old Testament, the
notion of 'an advocacy of the divine Spirit for man in the here and
now of his earthly life' is clearest in the book of Job (Job 5:1; 16:19;
19:25–27). In the New Testament, this idea of a 'Go-Between God'
is seen, for example, in the way both the Holy Spirit and the
ascended Lord intercede for us 'at the bar of heaven' (Romans
8:26,27,34).

However, it is in the word *parakletos*, used exclusively in the
New Testament by John, that we find the richest range of
meaning concerning the God who comes alongside the needy.
The term is used of both Jesus and the Spirit and refers variously
to the Son's advocacy before the Father on behalf of sinners (1
John 2:1), to the Spirit's convicting work in the everyday world
(John 16:8–11) and to the way the Spirit, living within God's
people, continues the teaching and revealing work of Jesus, the
first Paraclete (John 14:26; 15:26; 16: 13–15). J. Behm writes that the
two Paracletes of John are 'Jesus and the Spirit, of whom the latter
follows the former, is linked to Him, represents Him, and is
dependent on Him.'[13]

Translations of *parakletos* include 'comforter', 'counsellor',
'helper', 'supporter' and 'advocate' and it is perhaps within these
nuances of meaning that we have the most comprehensive
picture of our Lord's relating to others. We can argue that the
teaching and convicting as prophet, the fellowship and leading as
shepherd and the reconciling work as priest are all subsumed in
Christ's paracletic presence. Certainly, the woman at the well
eventually responded to the one who came to give assistance, as
did the two on the Emmaus road whose hearts 'burned within
them' at the divine encounter. The 'other' paraclete, the Spirit of
truth, continues God's gracious activity of coming alongside
those in distress, not least, it seems to me, within the context of
compassionate counselling.

Towards a Christian methodology

General considerations

In chapter eleven we attempted to spell out the main assumptions of a biblical anthropology, showing that men and women have supreme value, are living unities, have broken relationships and yet are restorable in Christ. From this basis, together with an acknowledgment that God speaks through both his word and the created order, we have evaluated the mainstream secular psychologies and a series of Christian responses to the needs of humankind. All these responses purport to be truly Christian – and many claim to be fully biblical. This multiplicity of Christian positions should not surprise us in the face of differing views held on the relationship between the authority of the scriptures, tradition and reason, as well as the varying emphases given to general and special revelation, inductive and deductive argument, and the value of the secular psychologies. Even where thinking upholds the primacy of the Bible we still find a medley of approaches. Apart from variations in interpreting theological truth, this variety of methodologies relates, I suggest, to an assortment of psychological factors:

1 The personality, experience and training of the *counsellor*, which result, inevitably, in certain trends in both the interpretation of and selectivity towards the scriptures. One Christian, whose experience and training have confirmed a dogmatic, 'black-and-white' approach to life, will tend to favour a rigid assumptive basis and a confrontational and directive style of counselling. Whereas another, who is more 'intuitive' and sees living as a complex affair, may lean towards more open presuppositions and a more consoling and identifying approach.

2 A similar range of characteristics in the *client*. For example, a certain man may, because of a passive and submissive personality, influence the counsellor towards being doctrinaire and directional. Conversely, a woman, say, of an independent and decisive frame of mind, may stimulate a form of counselling which allows her the greatest freedom for choice and action.

3 The *relationship* between the counsellor and client, which may demonstrate great variety depending on what each party brings

to the encounter. This may range from a virtual 'non-relationship' in an extremely dogmatic and managing type of counselling ('This is what you must do. Go and do it and I will see you again next week') to a long-term and open-ended therapeutic commitment ('Let us see, during the coming months, how our relationship can be mutually helpful').

4 The *situation* that has brought the client. Someone who comes because she is finding difficulty in being rejected by family and friends may need a different quality of counselling to someone who is living unashamedly in continuing adultery.

I believe that we should be grateful that this range of variables is mirrored in the realism of the biblical record, where we find a wide spectrum of encounters between a variety of people within a host of different contexts. Further, as we study the scriptures, we find, to quote Donald Capps, that there is 'no single biblical perspective that applies to all pastoral counselling situations'.[14] The Bible is not simplistic; although it is clear in its setting forth of the fundamentals for our faith, it also recognises the complexity of the human condition and offers us a rich mosaic of ways of helping. As Capps continues, 'This diversity frustrates efforts to formulate *the* biblical approach to pastoral counselling'.

We have already put forward what I trust are valid *assumptions* for any biblically-based methodology to consider. Although we have surveyed a multiplicity of legitimate objectives within Christian approaches, let us now summarise some of the *aims* warranted by scriptural perspectives before we examine, finally, some aspects of *method*, gleaned from the Bible.

Aims

As we look at the ways Jesus reached out to the needy and study, in the New Testament, the clarification of all he had to offer the sinful and distressed, we find a wealth of concepts that should never be far from our thoughts as we counsel. The Bible speaks of the call to repentance, restitution, faith, obedience, love, fruit-bearing, walking in the Spirit, conforming to the image of Christ as the 'response' side to God's work of conviction, justification, redemption, reconciliation, restoration, regeneration, sanctification and glorification. Here we have a formidable galaxy of theological words whose wondrous meanings have a great deal of overlap and interplay. The list is not exhaustive. Let us, in our limited space, select a few of the cardinal perspectives that fit with our model of Christ's prophetic, shepherding, priestly and paracletic work, keeping in mind our examination of objectives in counselling: *repentance, restoration, redemption* and *regeneration*.

Repentance

The Greek word *metanoia*, paralleling one of the meanings of the Hebrew *shub* in the Old Testament, indicates the 'turning round' of the whole person. The call by the prophets of Israel and Judah for the people to change direction, or repent, involved both their renewed commitment to the Lord God and responsive lives lived out in trust and obedience. We see, for example in Jonah's message to Nineveh, and Amos's castigation of other pagan nations, that God wills that all people turn their backs on injustice, oppression and other forms of wickedness. John the Baptist preached in the same tradition when he called men and women to 'a baptism of repentance for the forgiveness of sins'. In reply to the crowd's question, 'What should we do then?', he gave straightforward, practical advice about sharing both food and clothing with the more needy, avoiding exploiting others and being content with one's lot (Luke 3:10–14). John prepared the way for Jesus, the Spirit-baptiser, who, in turn, began to preach, 'Repent, for the kingdom of heaven is near' (Matthew 4:17). Here was the promised one, the 'Prophet greater than Moses', who proclaimed the dawning of a new age by his words and actions, calling the nation of Israel (Matthew 15:24), whole cities (Matthew 11:20–24) and individuals to repentance.

Certainly, one of our prime goals in counselling must be that our clients will hear God's call to a radical change of direction. As counsellors we may have the joy of witnessing the Holy Spirit's convicting work in the life of a non-Christian and the resulting switch in orientation; we may, in fact, be privy to a conversion experience, a true turning from self-centredness to God-centredness through faith in Christ. More frequently, you and I will see the achievement of less exalted, but nonetheless important, goals. These will be, generally, within the orbit of God's common grace for all humankind and, more specifically, within the activity of the Spirit in bringing men and women gradually to Christ. Where the counselling process enables an unjust employer to be more fair, an employee to be more conscientious, a selfish husband to be more considerate, a spendthrift mother to be more careful with money or an unsociable flat-mate to be more friendly then we should feel that valid progress has been made. Christian clients, too, need to be open to the call to repentance – as did the lukewarm believers at Laodicea who, because they were loved by the risen Lord, were commanded to 'be earnest, and repent' (Revelation 3:19). In all these instances, we should urge our clients to find practical expressions of their alleged change of hearts. As Martin Luther said, 'To do so no more is the truest repentance.'

Restoration

Our God-given repentance opens the door to many blessings including 'restoration' and 'reconciliation'. These privileges and responsibilities remind us of our Lord's pastoral ministry towards his people. David declares in Psalm 23 how his Shepherd-God nurtures and leads him, restoring (or 'turning back') his soul; and his plaintive prayer in Psalm 51:12, 'Restore to me the joy of your salvation' is the cry of a penitent sinner who longs to recover the peace and security of the fold. In the New Testament, the theme of restoration, promised earlier to the homesick Israelites in exile, is taken up by the word *apokatastasis*. In Acts 3:19–21 (RSV), for example, Peter addresses the astonished crowd, following the healing of the man lame from birth, with these words:

> Repent therefore, and turn again, that your sins may be blotted out, that times of refreshing may come from the presence of the Lord, and that he may send the Christ appointed for you, Jesus, whom heaven must receive until the time for establishing (*apokatastaseos*) all that God spoke by the mouth of his holy prophets from of old.

These 'times of refreshing' and the time for 'establishing', or restoration, may be seen as the fulfilment of the messianic hope when there will be the removal of all disorder resulting from sin.[15]

However we understand the compass of God's restoring work in Christ, the perspective of *reconciliation* is a crucial one in clarifying the aims of counselling. First and foremost, the 'ministry of reconciliation' is one in which God takes the initiative, 'reconciling the world to himself in Christ, not counting men's

sins against them' (2 Corinthians 5:17–21). This transformation of
the condition of enmity between God and people is effected
through the obedient Son who, although sinless, was made 'to be
sin for us' so that, in our relationship with him, 'we might become
the righteousness of God'. Again, at certain high points in
counselling, we may be privileged enough to see the wonder of
this most radical of transferences dawn on the person we try to
help.

Whether the 'message of reconciliation', which is committed to
you and me, strikes home to our clients or not, we are still called
to function in the wider context of our Lord's summary of the
commandments that we are to love the Lord our God with our
entire being and to love our neighbours as ourselves. Although
complete obedience to these lofty commands is impossible without the Spirit's help, it is clear from the gospels that these
injunctions are laid before all people. In reply to the legal expert's
question, 'And who is my neighbour?', Jesus tells the parable of
the good Samaritan – the story of the man who, even though
outside the ranks of the 'covenant people', nonetheless demonstrated the practical care between one human being and another
that our God commends (Luke 10:25–37). 'Go and do likewise',
says Jesus to his questioner. We see in this tale that neighbourli-
ness should be for all and from all. There are to be no exceptions
to both the giving and receiving of love. Jesus underlined the
point on another occasion when he urged us to love even our
enemies (Matthew 5:43f).

And so, in our counselling, besides witnessing reconciliation
between God and our clients, and between our Christian counsellees and those with whom they have been out of fellowship, we
also work in the broader realm of neighbourly love. Wherever
we see an element of restoration, reconciliation or new harmony,
we can praise God. We will rejoice where a husband and wife are
reconciled, an anxious teenager begins to find her own identity in
a bewildering world, a young man with homosexual tendencies is
able to turn aside from genital involvement and yet foster a wide
range of valuable friendships, a bereaved woman learns to look
back on her husband's life with gratitude and to live in the
present creatively once more.

Redemption

Within the concept of redemption we have the idea of being freed from bondage through the action of a third party. An example that is all too familiar to us as we hear or see the daily news is that of paying a ransom in order to effect the release of a loved one from the hands of a gang of terrorists. As we have seen in Luke 4:17–21 (see page 388), Jesus is the foreordained, supreme deliverer, anointed by the Spirit and fulfilling Isaiah's messianic prophecy. He brings the good news of freedom, recovery and release for those imprisoned by poverty, disability and oppression. The Lord's power over every work of the Enemy is manifested as he reaches out to the needy – healing, forgiving, casting out evil spirits and raising from the dead. The most widely used word in the New Testament for this saving activity is *sozo* and, in certain contexts, this has the meaning of bringing healing to the whole person.[16] Blind Bartimaeus (Mark 10:52), the woman with menorrhagia (Luke 8:48), the grateful leper (Luke 17:19) and the woman at the house of Simon the Pharisee (Luke 7:50) all received Christ's assurance of a new wholeness, knowing forgiveness and peace of mind as well as healing of past hurts and physical affliction.

As we listen, advise and pray, within the counselling process, we will also seek to be open to the redemptive power of Christ and his Spirit – releasing, rescuing and saving those in bondage. Thus, we may discern that the objectives of this or that counselling encounter may include physical healing, 'healing of the memories', 'primal integration', the beginnings of victory over some besetting sin, release from an obsessive habit or deliverance from an evil influence.[17]

Regeneration

In the New Testament, the word *palingenesia* (*palin*, again and *genesis*, birth or origin) can be translated as regeneration, or rebirth. The link between this radical new beginning and both baptism and the gift of the Holy Spirit is indicated in Titus 3:5, where we read that 'God our Saviour' has saved us 'through the washing of rebirth and renewal by the Holy Spirit'. Although *palingenesia* is an unusual scriptural word, the ideas of 'new birth', being 'in Christ' and 'putting on Christ' have similar connotations of a profoundly new and life-changing state.[18]

This regenerative work of the Spirit is shown in both the state and process of *sanctification*, whereby the believer is both set apart for God and gradually changed towards Christlikeness. This lifelong growth of an increasing conformity to the image of the Son (Romans 8:29) is marked by spiritual conflict (8:12f), the gifts of the Spirit (12:6–8) and the Spirit's fruit (Galatians 5:22,23). These changes are no individualistic affair; they are to take place within the Church's 'body-life'. Such transformation displays a Christ-centred unity and a maturity (*teleios*) that attains 'to the whole measure of the fulness of Christ'. This goal of 'adulthood' is distinguished by stability in the face of fads and fashions in teaching and the scheming of the deceitful, as well as by 'speaking the truth in love' (Ephesians 4:11–16).

In counselling our fellow-Christians we seek to encourage their openness to the paracletic activity of Christ and the Spirit. Our wish for them is that some new facet of Christlikeness will be allowed to develop. This may mean a willingness to make a difficult decision for God, an admission of weakness and a new response to the Lord's strengthening, a giving up of a selfish habit and a fresh determination to use the resulting time well, an acknowledgment of an isolating lifestyle and a resolve to be more open to brothers and sisters in Christ, or a new commitment to the underprivileged and oppressed.

Methods

We have argued throughout this book the need to test out assumptions, aims and methods by scriptural norms. Since the Bible is a revealer of God's nature and his ways with humanity rather than a 'how-to-do-it' manual for the counsellor, it is perhaps a more precise guide in the establishing of assumptions and aims than in clarifying methods. However, as we have already seen, we can learn a great deal from how Jesus handled those he encountered. Further, we can trace prophetic, pastoral and priestly elements in the styles of helping others to which the Lord's followers are called. With Donald Capps we can admit that there is no *one* biblical approach – rather a range of ways of reaching out that depends on the circumstances already enumerated (pages 393–394). Let us examine then the *prophetic, pastoral* and *priestly* modes as important ingredients in a biblical form of counselling.

Prophetic

It is probably the Greek verb *noutheteo* and the noun *nouthesia* that best express the prophetic function in counselling. These are exclusively Pauline words and have the sense of warning, advising, admonishing and instructing. As we examine the contexts of *noutheteo* we find that it refers primarily to a response that warns fellow-believers who are either tempted to wrong ways or are already a prey to sinful living. We read of the admonition of the idle (1 Thessalonians 5:14), the disobedient (2 Thessalonians 3:14) and the divisive (Titus 3:10). This nouthetic ministry is to be carried out by the good and knowledgeable (Romans 15:14), in a spirit of wisdom (Colossians 3:16) and with the goal of Christian maturity (Colossians 1:28). Other Greek words (such as *chrematizo*, to warn, and *epitimao*, to rebuke) carry a prophetic challenge to believer and non-believer alike.[19]

It seems that for admonition to be appropriate, there needs to be an appreciation of the issues involved on the part of the person being warned. Further, as we noted in our Lord's dealings with the woman at the well, it is desirable for a level of trust to be established before a word of warning can be effective. It is for such reasons, reinforced by research into the therapeutic relationship, that the nouthetic component, if needed, should emerge comparatively late in the counselling process. It is when the story has been well understood and a measure of confidence in the counsellor attained, that words of rebuke or instruction are less likely to fall on deaf ears. Scriptural contexts emphasise the need for an approach of wisdom and a desire for the well-being of the person at fault. Once again, the counsellor's self-knowledge and awareness of his or her own frailty are prerequisites – lest the would-be admonisher should be blind to a personal plank while pointing out the client's splinter. Where such preconditions are followed, then you or I may be required to say, for instance, 'Now come on, Mary. You *know* it's wrong to steal. How are you going to make amends?' or, 'John, we have discussed your adultery many, many times. I warn you, if you go on burying your head in the sand, you'll not only lose Jane but your relationship with the Lord will be jeopardised too.'

Pastoral

The verb *parakaleo* and the noun *paraklesis* are much more widely distributed in the New Testament than *noutheteo* and *nouthesia* and also cover a broader spectrum of meaning (see page 288). *Parakaleo*, occurring 109 times, is used in three main senses: to *ask*, to *exhort* and to *comfort*.[20]

To ask. In the synoptic gospels, *parakaleo* is used primarily where the needy ask or implore Jesus for help. These straightforward requests for aid in times of distress have a great significance for both the counsellor and client. Like Tournier, I seek to bring the counsellee's situation to the Lord in prayer by way of preparation. During a counselling session I will frequently send up 'arrow' prayers while I listen to the client and seek discernment, wisdom and enabling. This is a case of responding to the Danish proverb: 'Pray to God in the storm – but keep on rowing'! The counselling relationship is enhanced rather than distracted by such silent prayer. Further, when the client is also open to God's provision, then a time of shared thanksgiving and petition towards the end of an appointment is often right.

To exhort. G. Braumann writes that to exhort means 'to exert influence upon the will and decisions of another with the object of guiding him into a generally accepted code of behaviour or of encouraging him to observe certain instructions'. It is here that *parakaleo* is nearest to the more urgent and pressing tones of *noutheteo*. Paul, in particular, uses the word a great deal in this sense as he exhorts the churches 'in' or 'through' the Lord to lives of obedience. We see this refrain at its clearest towards the ends of his letters: 'Therefore, I *urge* you, brothers, in view of God's mercy, to offer your bodies . . .' (Romans 12:1); 'By the meekness and gentleness of Christ, I *appeal* to you . . .' (2 Corinthians 10:1); 'I *plead* with Euodia and I *plead* with Syntyche to agree with each other in the Lord' (Philippians 4:2); and 'Now we ask you and *urge* you in the Lord Jesus . . .' (1 Thessalonians 4:1).

Often in counselling we will find ourselves exhorting and encouraging others to be true to what they know is right. Where we appeal to Christian clients to follow the path of obedience we are at our most cogent and effective when we do so in the name of the Lord. There is no higher appeal, and so we need to be sensitive to the Spirit on the timing and the strength of our plea. It may be relevant to our point that the Pauline exhortations come mostly *after* he has established rapport with his readers and spelt out his main, Christ-centred message. In counselling, too, there should be a building up of relationship first, so that there can then be an element of 'Since all this has happened to you and since God is still a God of love who calls you to discipleship, *therefore* I appeal to you . . .'. Our exhortation will not necessarily be couched in 'God-talk', although we should speak in such a way where it seems right to do so. More generally, when we say, for example, 'Remember, Jack, what promises you have already made to Jill. I urge you to be true to them' we are using a 'parakaleo' style of exhortation.

To comfort. The third aspect of our 'shepherding' mode in counselling is to comfort, console, strengthen, encourage or help. Such consolation takes place in the face of suffering and is a strengthening that we receive both from God and others. In 2 Corinthians 7:6,7 Paul writes of the God who 'comforts the downcast' as well as of a relay of comforting that is passed from the Corinthian Christians to Titus and so to Paul and his companions. God comforted Paul 'by the coming of Titus', who had returned to the apostle in Macedonia presumably with the good news that the Corinthians were, after all, responsive to Paul's 'severe letter' (see 2 Corinthians 2:1–4). In 2 Corinthians 1:3,4, we see that such God-given encouragement is ours 'so that we can comfort those in any trouble with the comfort we ourselves have received from God'. I have written elsewhere of the strengthening I experienced when visiting a married woman friend in her early thirties who was dying of a particularly virulent form of cancer of the lymphatic system.[21] My visits were made during a period when I was blind, due to a complication of diabetes, and, although my intention was to console my friend, I found her honesty and fortitude a great source of personal comfort. She was to me a true 'missionary of comfort'.

Even though theologians disagree about the significance of the connection between the words *parakaleo* and the Johannine word *parakletos* for Christ and the Holy Spirit, there is clearly an overlap in meaning with respect to coming alongside to aid another in need.[22] In the former the help is mediated by the Christian, in the latter by the Lord directly. Both words are used, in fact, in the Septuagint, the Greek Old Testament, with the sense of to comfort or console. It is perhaps in our comforting and encouraging roles as counsellors that we are most readily reminded of the other Paraclete whom Jesus promised. As we seek to reach out to the anxious, distressed, depressed or otherwise afflicted, we should be aware that the Spirit also 'comes alongside' to strengthen both counsellor and client. Once more, we should realise that the helper wants help too. The counsellor needs to receive encouragement from God and others in order to console those who suffer. Then, in the counselling situation, we will have the resources to comfort, to exercise a paracletic ministry. At times this will be through our words of empathetic understanding, such as, 'I can see how distraught you are. Do be assured that I am with you in this situation.' At times it will be in a sensitive and caring silence that we are the most helpful. We may not match the vigil of Ezekiel who sat among the exiles 'for seven days – overwhelmed' before speaking God's words (Ezekiel 3:15), but the principle of compassionate identification is the same. At other times, as when Paul received comfort from the reassuring presence of Titus, it may be that the warmth of our welcome will be sufficient to put heart into a lonely and misunderstood client.

Priestly

On Mount Sinai God declared to the Israelites through Moses: 'you will be for me a kingdom of priests and a holy nation' (Exodus 19:6) and we see the fulfilment of that promise in the 'priesthood of believers' in the new age. The old priestly system, offering up endless animal sacrifices and tied primarily to the tribe of Levi and, in time, to an earthly building, the Temple, is superseded within the new covenant. Here the 'once for all' sacrifice of Jesus Christ, our great High Priest, releases all his people to offer themselves in praise and service to 'the Lord God Almighty and the Lamb' who are the new Temple (Revelation 21:22). As a 'holy' and 'royal priesthood' our 'spiritual sacrifices' are made 'through Jesus' and, having offered ourselves to God as our 'spiritual worship', we show forth his praise through renewed minds, confessing lips and good and selfless action (see Romans 12:1,2; Hebrews 13:15,16; 1 Peter 2:4,5,9). With this perspective we can appreciate the force of our Lord's challenging words in his picture of the sheep and the goats (Matthew 25:31–46). On the judgment day, he will say to the righteous who met the needs of the hungry, thirsty, estranged, naked, sick and imprisoned, 'I tell you the truth, whatever you did for one of the least of these brothers of mine, you did for me' (verse 40).

In our encounters with those who are broken in spirit and sick at heart we can exercise a priestly function as we mediate God's tangible and practical love. If we dare use Bob Lambourne's bold phrase, we are 'mini-Christs' in that we make real to others something of the compassion and faithfulness of our loving Father.[23] Like that of the righteous in Christ's portrayal of his kingly judgment, our intermediary role should not be a self-conscious affair. We are not to look over our shoulders, as it were, to the day of reckoning. Through his grace, we hope to bring solace to our clients to alleviate their pains and not to chalk up merit. Here we have no doctrine of salvation by 'good works' but the down-to-earth living out of the love that has caught hold of us. In this sense, for much of the time our priestly concern will be covert, although at other times, as we have seen, our mediatory role will be explicit as we share with the client our understanding of God's ways through conversation, prayer or reflection on words from the Bible.

Conclusion

And so we have traced the origins and growth of the tree of pastoral care, along with the rise of the secular psychologies and their derivative methodologies of psychotherapy and counselling. In turn, we have studied some of the main Christian responses to this secularisation, observing a range of outgrowths from the 'pastoral care' tree, from isolationism to hybridisation. We have sought to map out the forest of concern for human need using a compass which gives us our bearings in relation to this or that methodology. Arguing from a biblical theology and anthropology, including a comprehensive view of general and special revelation and the permissibility of both inductive and deductive reasoning where they accord with scriptural insight, we have sought to lay out an assumptive basis for Christian methodologies of therapy. In turn, albeit briefly, we have examined the model of Christ with respect to the aims and methods of counselling, declaring that there can be no *one* biblical approach but rather a spectrum of styles that vary with counsellor, client and the precise counselling situation. In other words, God is not to be tied to any one methodology. It is we who categorise and, in our enthusiasm, threaten to narrow the field of divine activity. Fortunately for us, God is infinitely greater than our capacity for pigeon-holing and, when we believe we have worked out *the* method, is ready to break down the walls of our pet theories and watertight techniques.

Moreover, we have noted that Christian methodologies draw from the same repository of wisdom and knowledge within the created order as do the secular systems. The 'biblical' approaches tend to emphasise those aspects of life that we see more widely in the behavioural and cognitive therapies; the 'relationship' styles are essentially personalistic; the more mystical components of the 'inner journey' look to transpersonalism; and the many forms of 'inner healing' and 'primal integration' have some kinship with the analytic therapies. This observation is not to demote the ways Christians counsel so much as to remind ourselves that God is at work in his world and that both believer and non-believer handle the same raw material of human psychology. Nonetheless – and we have argued the point throughout – the Christian counsellor *does* have a distinctive calling and the wherewithal in Christ to respond to that call. Behind this vocation of bringing something of God's love and remedy to needy men and women is the prerequisite to think carefully about our assumptions, aims and methods in the light of a biblical anthropology. This is no easy task, but I trust this book will help many to test out the claims of both secular and Christian methodologies – as well as to establish personal thought and practice in the sphere of counselling and psychotherapy.

We have used the analogy of a forest as we have considered the rise of the main systems of secular psychology surrounding the tree of pastoral care. The Bible often looks to the imagery of vegetative growth to symbolise the vitality and influence of God's people – both as the old Israel and as the new kingdom spreading out its branches in Christ. We see, too, the biblical picture of the forest extended to other nations outside the covenant, as when Ezekiel 17:24, in the context of Babylon and Egypt, declares the Lord's sovereignty over 'all the trees of the field'. Let us then, in conclusion, be reminded of two things: first, that in our attempts to bring counsel to others we can only be fruitful as we allow Christ's life to flow through us; and, finally, that we reach out alongside friends and colleagues who, even though they may not share our faith, are recipients of common grace and members of our common humanity. Our prayer is that they too may enter the kingdom, partaking through Christ of the tree of life, whose leaves 'are for the healing of the nations' (Revelation 22:2).

NOTES

Chapter 1

1 See, for example: John T. McNeill *A History of the Cure of Souls* (Harper & Brothers 1951); H. R. Niebuhr and Daniel D. Williams (eds.) *The Ministry in Historical Perspectives* (Harper & Brothers 1956); and William A. Clebsch and Charles R. Jaekle *Pastoral Care in Historical Perspective* (Jason Aronson 1975).

2 Clebsch and Jaekle, p. 4. Here the authors acknowledge some debt to Seward Hiltner *Preface to Pastoral Theology* (Abingdon Press 1958) pp. 89–172.

3 Thomas C. Oden 'Recovering Lost Identity' *The Journal of Pastoral Care* 34 (1980) pp. 4–18, *Pastoral Theology: essentials of ministry* (Harper & Row 1983) and *Care of Souls in the Classic Tradition* (Fortress 1984). See Chapter 10 for an assessment of some of Oden's thought-provoking views.

4 Clebsch and Jaekle, p. 69.

5 Clebsch and Jaekle cite the *Letter to a Young Widow* by John Chrysostom (*c.*347–407) as typical of the Imperial Church's guidance – with its strong flavour of contemporary Stoic psychology. In this example, the grieving young woman is urged to see her lot as better than that of other women whose husbands had died while away at war. See Philip Schaff (ed.) *The Nicene and Post-Nicene Fathers* (Eerdmans 1975) First Series vol. IX 'St Chrysostom' p. 121.

6 The philosophy of Thomas Aquinas (1226–1274) – the 'Common Doctor' of the Catholic Church – was strongly influenced by Aristotle's thinking that people can only acquire knowledge through sense experience and reason. See Colin Brown *Philosophy and the Christian Faith* (Tyndale Press 1962) pp. 24–36 and Morton Kelsey *Encounter with God* (Hodder and Stoughton 1974) pp. 64ff.

7 John Keble (1792–1866), the Oxford Tractarian, is given by Clebsch and Jaekle as an example of a pastor whose guidance emphasised the adequacy of human faculties to extricate the needy from trouble. See, for instance, his letter to William Copeland (Spring, 1846), urging him to refrain from emulating Newman's move from Anglicanism to Rome, in Georgina Battiscombe *John Keble: a study in limitations* (Constable 1963) p. 277.

8 Important names in the furtherance of medical science during this period include William Harvey (1578–1657), Thomas Sydenham (1624–1689) and van Leeuwenhoek (1632–1723). Before the establishment of psychiatry as a medical discipline in Germany in the middle of the nineteenth century, the following were amongst those influential in the care of the mentally sick: George Cheyne (1671–1743), William Tuke (1732–1822) and John Haslam (1764–1844) in England, and Philippe Pinel (1745–1826) and Jean Esquirol (1772–1840) in France.
9 Clebsch and Jaekle, p. 29.
10 William James *The Varieties of Religious Experience* (Fount 1981) p. 103.
11 ibid., pp. 172ff.
12 ibid., pp. 496–7.
13 ibid., p. 499.
14 Clebsch and Jaekle, p. 69

Chapter 2

1 For a discussion on pastoral counselling, see chapter ten, pp. 221–222.
2 See also Allen E. Ivey and Lynn Simek-Downing *Counseling and Psychotherapy: skills, theories, and practice* (Prentice Hall 1980).
3 Thomas Szasz *The Myth of Psychotherapy: mental healing as religion, rhetoric, and repression* (1979) p. 9.
4 See particularly: Michael Balint *The Doctor, His Patient and The Illness* (Pitman 1957) and Michael Balint and Enid Balint *Psychotherapeutic Techniques in Medicine* (Tavistock 1961).
5 On the diversity of meanings of the word 'psychotherapy', see Michael S. Aronoff and Stanley Lesse in Benjamin B. Wolman (ed.) *The Therapist's Handbook: treatment methods of mental disorders* (van Nostrand 1976) pp. 46–60.
6 See the Introduction to Eliot Slater and Martin Roth *Clinical Psychiatry* (Baillière, Tindall and Cassell 1969) where the authors argue the case for a 'scientific approach' to psychiatry. For a clear approach to the 'medical model' in psychiatry, see Sidney Crown *Essential Principles of Psychiatry* (Pitman 1970) pp. 70–75. For a more detailed discussion of 'models', see Arnold H. Buss *Psychopathology* (John Wiley and Sons 1966) pp. 18–30. For the issue of classifying mental illness in the setting of general practice, see Anthony W. Clare and Malcolm Lader (eds.) *Psychiatry and General Practice* (Academic Press 1981) pp. 15–25.
7 E. W. Anderson and W. H. Trethowan *Psychiatry* (Baillière, Tindall and Cassell 1967) p. 1.
8 Slater and Roth pp. 1–7.
9 For a clear comparison of 'neurosis' and 'psychosis', see Ivor R. C.

Batchelor (revis.) *Henderson and Gillespie's Textbook of Psychiatry: for students and practitioners* (Oxford University Press 1969) pp. 131–135.

10 For a helpful outline and bibliography on the classification, diagnosis and management of schizophrenia, see John E. Cooper 'Schizophrenia and allied conditions' *Medicine International* 33 (1983) pp. 1546–1550. For a comprehensive and scholarly work on the psychoses, see J. K. Wing and Lorna Wing (eds.) *Handbook of Psychiatry, Vol. 3: Psychoses of Uncertain Aetiology* (CUP 1983).

11 R. H. Cawley 'The Teaching of Psychotherapy' *Association of University Teachers of Psychiatry Newsletter* (Jan. 1977) pp. 19–36, referred to in Dennis Brown and Jonathan Pedder *Introduction to Psychotherapy: an outline of psychodynamic principles and practice* (Tavistock 1979) pp. 91ff.

12 Brown and Pedder, pp. 97–99.

13 ibid., p. 95.

14 Charles B. Truax and Robert R. Carkhuff *Towards Effective Counseling and Psychotherapy: training and practice* (Aldine 1967) p. 4.

15 Anthony Storr *The Art of Psychotherapy* (Heinemann 1979) p. vii. For a useful discussion of and bibliography on 'professionalism', see Alastair V. Campbell *Paid to Care? the limits of professionalism in pastoral care* (SPCK 1985).

16 Jerome D. Frank 'What is Psychiatry?' in Sidney Bloch (ed.) *An Introduction to the Psychotherapies* (OUP 1979) p. 1.

17 Lawrence J. Crabb Jr. *Effective Biblical Counseling* (Zondervan 1977) pp. 164ff.

18 Ranald Macaulay and Jerram Barrs *Christianity with a Human Face* (IVP 1979) p. 76.

19 There are innumerable books on the 'how to' of counselling. At an introductory level, see Roger F. Hurding *Restoring the Image: an introduction to Christian caring and counselling* (Paternoster 1980), Evelyn Peterson *Who Cares? a handbook of Christian Counselling* (Paternoster 1980) and Myra Chave-Jones *The Gift of Helping* (IVP 1982). For good 'intermediate' books, see Eugene Kennedy *On Becoming a Counselor: a basic guide for non-professional counselors* (Gill and Macmillan 1977) and Gary R. Collins *Christian Counseling: a complete guide* (Word Books 1980). Amongst more technical books, see Gerard Egan *The Skilled Helper: model, skills, and methods for effective helping* (Brooks/Cole 1982), Laurence M. Brammer *The Helping Relationship: process and skills* (Prentice Hall 1979) and Part 2 of Richard Nelson-Jones *The Theory and Practice of Counselling Psychology* (Holt, Rinehart and Winston 1982).

20 Carole Sutton *Psychology for Social Workers and Counsellors* (Routledge and Kegan Paul 1979) pp. 20, 30ff.

21 H. J. Eysenck (ed.) *Behaviour Therapy and the Neuroses* (Pergamon Press 1960), quoted by Truax and Carkhuff, p. 5.

22 The debate on the efficacy of psychotherapy has flared up once more in the 1980s. See, for example: Jerome D. Frank 'The placebo is psychotherapy' *Behavioural and Brain Sciences* 6 (1983) pp. 291–292; Mark Aveline 'What price psychiatry without psychotherapy?' *Lancet* 2 (1984) pp. 856–859; Michael Shepherd 'What price psychotherapy?' *British Medical Journal* 288 (1984) pp. 809–810; Sidney Bloch and Michael J. Lambert 'What price psychotherapy? A rejoinder' *British Journal of Psychiatry* 146 (1985) pp. 96–98; Michael Shepherd, and H. J. Eysenck in correspondence in *British Journal of Psychiatry* 146 (1985) pp. 555–557.

23 Truax and Carkhuff, p. 34.

24 Sutton, p. 38.

25 Truax and Carkhuff, p. 36.

26 See, for example: Matthew 5:43ff.; 7:1–5; Luke 18:9ff.

27 Truax and Carkhuff, p. 42.

28 2 Corinthians 1:3,4 (RSV).

29 Truax and Carkhuff, p. 46.

30 ibid.

31 Quoted by Paul Halmos *The Faith of the Counsellors* (Constable 1965) p. 49. Halmos, a sociologist, traces how the need for a level of warm caring towards the client has become integral to the counselling process. He uses a religious analogy, seeing the counsellor's 'prevailing love for his charges' as a 'modern refinement' of the 'ancient paradigm of "forgiveness"' p. 89.

32 Jerome D. Frank *Persuasion and Healing: a comparative study of psychotherapy* (Johns Hopkins Press 1973) p. 167.

33 Truax and Carkhuff, pp. 175–176.

34 J. Schofield *Psychotherapy: the purchase of friendship* (Prentice Hall 1964), referred to in Sutton, p. 34.

35 Many counsellors and psychotherapists in the West work primarily in white, middle-class contexts and are slow to think through approaches to the socially disadvantaged. The greatest advances in care for the underprivileged have probably been made by social workers, general practitioners, community nurses, health visitors and voluntary workers. The work of Eugene Heimler, a Hungarian who survived Nazi concentration camps and came to England in 1947, is important here. He devised a Scale of Social Functioning which encouraged clients towards a self-evaluation with respect to a range of issues, including work, money, friendship, family life, values, meaning, etc. See his *Survival in Society* (Weidenfeld and Nicolson 1975) and the interview in Brigid Brophy *Counselling Shop* (Burnett Books 1978). For an approach to the range of cultures in the United States, see Derald Wing Sue *Counseling the Culturally Different: theory and practice* (John Wiley and Sons 1981).

36 See, for example, Isaiah 1:17; 42:1–9; 58:6,7: Amos 1,2; Matthew 25:31–46; Luke 3:10–14.

37 Richard F. Lovelace *Dynamics of Spiritual Life: an evangelical theology of renewal* (Paternoster 1979) p. 108.

38 For good overviews of the different concepts behind the main approaches to psychology and psychotherapy, see John Medcof and John Roth (eds.) *Approaches to Psychology* (Open University 1979) and Part 1 of Nelson-Jones *The Theory and Practice of Counselling Psychology*, op. cit.

Chapter 3

1 For much of the framework of this and the next few chapters I am indebted to Benjamin B. Wolman (in collaboration with Susan Knapp) *Contemporary Theories and Systems in Psychology* (Plenum Press 1981). For this section, see pp. 1–16.

2 For a masterly overview of the history of psychology and psychiatry (with particular emphasis on American psychiatry), see George Mora in Harold I. Kaplan, Alfred M. Freedman and Benjamin J. Sadock (eds.) *Comprehensive Textbook of Psychiatry* (Williams and Williams 1980) Vol. 1 pp. 4–98. See also Gregory Zilboorg *A History of Medical Psychology* (Norton 1967).

3 Wolman, p. 13.

4 ibid., pp. 16ff.

5 ibid., p. 22.

6 William James *Principles of Psychology* (Holt 1890) Vol. II, p. 309, quoted in Wolman, p. 23.

7 Wolman, p. 42.

8 Robert S. Woodworth *Contemporary Schools of Psychology* (Methuen and Co. 1951) p. 52.

9 ibid., p. 70.

10 John B. Watson *Behaviourism* (Kegan Paul 1925) p. 82, quoted in Wolman, pp. 77–78. Watson's bold claim echoes the words of Francis Xavier, the sixteenth-century Jesuit missionary, who declared, 'Give me a child for the first seven years, and you may do what you like with him afterwards.'

11 Woodworth, p. 75.

12 B. F. Skinner *Particulars of My Life* (Jonathan Cape 1976) p. 108.

13 ibid., p. 219.

14 ibid., p. 291.

15 Skinner *Beyond Freedom and Dignity* (Penguin 1973) pp. 31–32.

16 ibid.

17 ibid., p. 46.

18 ibid., p. 104.

19 ibid., p. 115.

20 ibid., p. 172.

21 ibid., p. 178.
22 ibid., p. 186.
23 ibid.
24 ibid., pp. 187–188.
25 ibid., p. 195.
26 ibid., p. 196.
27 ibid., p. 197.
28 ibid., p. 200.
29 ibid., p. 203.
30 ibid., pp. 178–179.
31 ibid., p. 210.
32 C. Stephen Evans *Preserving the Person: a look at the human sciences* (IVP 1977) p. 88.
33 Joel Kovel *A Complete Guide to Therapy: from psychoanalysis to behaviour modification* (Penguin 1978) p. 284.
34 See, for example, Gary R. Collins *The Rebuilding of Psychology: an integration of psychology and Christianity* (Tyndale House 1977) pp. 21–30; Mark P. Cosgrove *Psychology Gone Awry: four psychological world views* (IVP 1982) pp. 37–38, 42–43, 77–78; Evans, pp. 45–57; Malcolm A. Jeeves *Psychology and Christianity: the view both ways* (IVP 1976) pp. 60–62, 92–99.
35 Jeeves, pp. 61–62.
36 Wolman, p. 136.
37 H. J. Eysenck *The Structure of Human Personality* (Methuen and Co. 1970) p. 2.
38 ibid., p. xi.
39 Arthur Koestler *The Ghost in the Machine* (Hutchinson 1976) p. 17.
40 V. Meyer and Edward S. Chesser *Behaviour Therapy in Clinical Psychiatry* (Penguin 1970) p. 25.
41 ibid., p. 121.
42 Kovel, p. 279.

Chapter 4

1 See, for example: Frank J. Sulloway *Freud, Biologist of the Mind: beyond the psychoanalytic legend* (Fontana 1980) p. 67; Wolman *Contemporary Theories*, p. 6; Woodworth *Contemporary Schools*, pp. 46–47.
2 Sulloway, p. 276.
3 For a stimulating and accessible book on Freud for both general reader and specialist, see J. N. Isbister *Freud: an introduction to his life and work* (Polity Press 1985).
4 Ernest Jones *The Life and Work of Sigmund Freud* (Penguin 1964), see pp. 31–43.
5 ibid., p. 47.

6 ibid., p. 48.
7 ibid., p. 53.
8 ibid., pp. 62–64.
9 Sulloway, pp. 279–315.
10 For this section on Freud's theories I am especially indebted to Wolman, pp. 203–282.
11 ibid., p. 204.
12 ibid., p. 209.
13 For an introduction to Freud's theories, see David Stafford-Clark *What Freud Really Said* (Penguin 1967).
14 Sigmund Freud *An Autobiographical Study*, in Standard Edition, Vol. 20 (1925) p. 1, quoted in Sulloway, p. 32.
15 Freud *Beyond the Pleasure Principle*, 1920 (The Hogarth Press and the Institute of Psychoanalysis 1971) p. 28.
16 See Charles Rycroft *A Critical Dictionary of Psychoanalysis* (Penguin 1972) pp. 121, 138.
17 Freud *An Outline of Psychoanalysis*, 1938 (Norton 1949) p. 20, quoted in Wolman, p. 231.
18 Freud *Pleasure Principle*, p. 34.
19 Freud *New Introductory Lectures on Psychoanalysis*, 1933 (Norton) pp. 87–88, quoted in Wolman, p. 261.
20 Wolman, pp. 248ff. Freud used the imagery of riding a horse to illustrate the ego's mastery of the id; see Freud *New Introductory Lectures* in The Pelican Freud Library, Vol. 2 (Penguin 1973) pp. 109–110.
21 The Freud-Fleiss letters show that Freud's ideas on religious questions were forming as early as the 1890s. See, for example, Freud's letter of 12 December 1897 in *Complete Letters to Wilhelm Fleiss* (Harvard University Press 1985) – reference from J. N. Isbister.
22 Freud *The Future of an Illusion*, 1927 (Hogarth Press 1962) p. 13.
23 ibid., p. 27.
24 ibid., p. 39.
25 ibid., p. 40.
26 Wolman, p. 274.
27 ibid., pp. 273–274. See also Freud *New Introductory Lectures* p. 93. For a scholarly assessment of the relationship between Freud and religion, and discussion of a 'psychology of religious experience', by a Catholic writer, see W. W. Meissner *Psychoanalysis and Religious Experience* (Yale University Press 1984). For an earlier work, by someone with a Russian Orthodox background, see Gregory Zilboorg *Psychoanalysis and Religion* (George Allen and Unwin 1967).
28 Freud *Introductory Lectures on Psychoanalysis*, 1916–1917 in Pelican Freud Library (Penguin 1973) p. 136.
29 See Kovel *Complete Guide*, pp. 111–114.

30 See Freud *New Introductory Lectures* p. 112, where he declares the aim of psychoanalysis in terms of the 'dynamics of the mind':

Its intention is . . . to strengthen the ego, to make it more independent of the super-ego, to widen its field of perception and enlarge its organization, so that it can appropriate fresh positions of the id. Where id was, there ego shall be.

31 D. H. Malan *A Study of Brief Psychotherapy* (Tavistock 1967) p. 274.
32 ibid.
33 Freud did not see the super-ego and the conscience as the same thing. Unlike as in the normal use of the word 'conscience', the super-ego includes *unconscious* elements. Further, the super-ego's functions comprise both conscience and self-observation. The gentleness or severity of the super-ego derives, in part, from the subject's childhood feelings towards parental figures. See, Freud *New Introductory Lectures* pp. 91, 96, 199 and Rycroft *Dictionary* pp. 22, 160–161.
34 Freud *Introductory Lectures* pp. 374–375.
35 Harold W. Darling *Man in his Right Mind: an integration of psychology and biblical faith* (Paternoster 1969) p. 33.
36 See also, for example: John 3:19; Romans 1:18–2:1; 3:9–20,23; 5:12–14; 1 Corinthians 15:22; Ephesians 4:17–19.
37 Freud *Illusion* p. 23.
38 See, for example: Genesis 12:1–3; Exodus 3:13–15; Jeremiah 1:1–3; Luke 1:1–4; Acts 1:1–3; Hebrews 1:1–4; 1 John 1:1–3.
39 Wolman, p. 403.

Chapter 5

1 J. A. C. Brown *Freud and the Post-Freudians* (Penguin 1961) pp. 11–13.
2 ibid.
3 Alfred Adler *Religion and Individual Psychology* (1935) p. 61, quoted in Lewis Way *Alfred Adler: an introduction to his psychology* (Penguin 1956) p. 53.
4 See chapter fourteen for a further consideration of Jung's interest in the occult. See, also J. A. Emerson Vermaat 'Jung and the supernatural' in *Third Way* 4/6 (1980) pp. 15–18.
5 For further insight on Jung's rift with Freud, see C. G. Jung *Memories, Dreams, Reflections*, 1963 (Collins 1977) pp. 172, 174. Here Jung sees Freud's views on sexuality as a new dogma, constructed to replace a 'jealous God'.
6 Jung *The Practice of Psychotherapy* in Collected Works, Vol. 16 (RKP 1954) p. 30.
7 Jung *Two Essays in Analytical Psychology* (1928) p. 78, quoted in Wolman *Contemporary Theories* p. 300.

8 Frieda Fordham *An Introduction to Jung's Psychology* (Penguin 1966) p. 51.

9 Jung *Modern Man in Search of a Soul*, 1933 (RKP 1961) p. 70.

10 ibid., pp. 71–72.

11 Morton Kelsey *Encounter with God* (Hodder and Stoughton 1972) p. 160.

12 ibid., p. 119.

13 Christopher Bryant *Jung and the Christian Way* (DLT 1982) p. 2.

14 Jung *Modern Man* p. 273.

15 Brown, p. 64.

16 ibid., pp. 66–67. See Ian D. Suttie *The Origins of Love and Hate* (Penguin 1960).

17 Hanna Segal *Klein* (Fontana 1979) pp. 27ff.

18 ibid., pp. 32–33.

19 Anna Freud was one of the earliest and most influential of the psychoanalysts to stress the capacity of the ego to defend itself. In *The Ego and the Mechanisms of Defence* (1937), which she presented to her father on his eightieth birthday, she put forward a systematisation of psychological 'defences' (techniques which the ego uses to protect itself from anxiety, shame or guilt). She listed ten defences: repression, regression, reaction-formation, undoing, isolation, projection, introjection, turning against the self, reversal and sublimation. Sublimation, in which unacceptable social behaviour is redirected into more acceptable channels, is generally not now seen as a defence. For further reading on Anna Freud's 'ego psychology', see Paul Roazen *Freud and His Followers* (Allen Lane 1976) pp. 447–452 and Brown, pp. 68–71.

20 Segal, p. 42.

21 Melanie Klein *Envy and Gratitude and Other Works 1946–1963* (The Hogarth Press and The Institute of Psychoanalysis 1975) p. 137.

22 Segal, p. 91.

23 ibid., p. 95. I am grateful to Segal, pp. 91ff. for this section. See also Brown, pp. 77ff. for a helpful summary of the views of Anna Freud and Melanie Klein.

24 Segal, p. 171.

25 Harry Guntrip is another very important British writer in the psychoanalytic tradition; his thinking owes a great deal to Fairbairn and Winnicott. See his *Personality Structure and Human Interaction* (Hogarth 1961), *Schizoid Phenomena, Object-Relations and the Self* (Hogarth 1968) and *Psychoanalytic Theory, Therapy, and the Self* (Hogarth 1971), in which he looks at the theories of Freud, Klein, Fairbairn, Winnicott, Erikson and others.

26 Brown, pp. 83–84.

27 See, for example, D. W. Winnicott *Playing and Reality* (Penguin 1974) pp. 11–12.

28 Winnicott 'Paediatrics and Psychology' *Br. J. Med. Psychol.* 21 (1948) pp. 229–240, quoted in John Bowlby *Attachment and Loss, Vol. 1 Attachment* (The Hogarth Press and The Institute of Psychoanalysis 1969) p. 372.

29 Wolman, p. 324.

30 See Chapter 2, note 3. For an outline of Michael Balint's life, see his obituary in *International Journal of Psycho-Analysis* 52 (1971) 331ff. On Balint's thought, see Masud Khan's paper in *Int. J. Psycho-Anal.* 50 (1969) pp. 237–248.

31 Bowlby, p. 17.

32 ibid., pp. 228–229.

33 Wolman, p. 333.

34 Kovel *Complete Guide* pp. 175ff.

35 Brown, p. 103.

36 Robert Coles *Erik H. Erikson: the growth of his work* (Souvenir Press 1973) pp. 21–22.

37 Erikson *Young Man Luther* (Norton 1958) p. 18, quoted in Coles, p. 63.

38 For a most interesting use of Erikson's developmental theory to clarify the objectives of pastoral care, see Donald Capps *Life Cycle Theory and Pastoral Care* (Fortress Press 1983).

39 Erikson *Identity: youth and crisis* (Faber and Faber 1968) p. 92.

40 Modified from Erikson *Identity* p. 94. See also his *Childhood and Society* (Penguin 1965) pp. 239–266.

41 Coles, p. 82.

42 ibid.

43 ibid., p. 165. For a valuable book giving a Christian understanding of 'identity', see Dick Keyes *Beyond Identity: finding your self in the image and character of God* (Servant Books 1984).

44 Coles, p. 154.

45 Erikson *Insight and Responsibility* (Norton 1964) 'The Golden Rule in the Light of New Insight' p. 233, quoted in Coles, p. 281.

46 Erikson *Gandhi's Truth* (Norton 1969) p. 20, quoted in Coles, p. 297.

47 Jack L. Rubins *Karen Horney: gentle rebel of psychoanalysis* (Weidenfeld and Nicolson 1979) pp. 18–19.

48 ibid., p. 23.

49 Karen Horney *New Ways in Psychoanalysis* (Kegan Paul, Trench, Trubner and Co. 1939) p. 51.

50 Wolman, p. 373.

51 ibid., p. 376.

52 ibid., pp. 383–384.

53 Erich Fromm *Psychoanalysis and Religion* (Victor Gollancz 1951) pp. 79–80.

54 ibid., p. 82.

55 ibid., p. 93.

56 ibid., p. 120.
57 James W. Sire *The Universe Next Door: a guide to world views* (IVP 1976) p. 17.
58 Klein, p. 231.
59 ibid., p. 232.
60 Thomas S. Szasz *The Ethics of Psychoanalysis: the theory and method of autonomous psychotherapy* (RKP 1974) pp. 52–53.
61 ibid., p. 18.
62 ibid., p. 24.
63 ibid., p. 28.
64 ibid., pp. 22–23.
65 Kovel, p. 180.
66 Horney, p. 282.
67 Kovel, p. 128.
68 ibid., p. 351. See also Wolman, pp. 325ff.
69 B. A. Farrell *The Standing of Psychoanalysis* (OUP 1981) p. 194. Also see Adolf Grünbaum *The Foundation of Psychoanalysis: a philosophical critique* (University of California Press 1985).
70 Farrell, pp. 30ff.
71 ibid., pp. 48ff.
72 ibid., p. 89.
73 ibid., pp. 89–90.
74 ibid., pp. 126–127.
75 ibid., p. 146.
76 ibid., pp. 179ff., where Farrell gives a fuller critique of the difficulties in assessing psychotherapeutic method.
77 ibid., pp. 181ff.
78 ibid., p. 187.
79 ibid., p. 218.

Chapter 6

1 Wilhelm Dilthey, who had an historical approach to psychology, was described by Husserl as 'without doubt one of the very great socio-cultural scientists of the nineteenth century' in Edmund Husserl *Phenomenological Psychology: lectures, summer semester; 1925* (Martinus Nijhoff 1977).
2 Wolman *Contemporary Theories* p. 423.
3 Theories about personality types have abounded since very early times. Ancient Chinese medicine postulated that the body was composed of the five elements of earth, water, fire, wood and metal. Hippocrates held that imbalance between the body's four 'humours' (blood, phlegm, yellow bile and black bile) was the cause of disease. This 'humoral theory' was espoused by Galen and became a key

418 ROOTS AND SHOOTS

teaching in medicine for centuries. It was the basis of the idea that people primarily displayed one of four main temperaments: sanguine (stable and expressing feelings), phlegmatic (stable but passive), choleric (unstable and excitable) and melancholic (unstable and paralysed by fear). In this century, Ernst Kretschmer and W. H. Sheldon have put forward theories relating physique and character, while Jung's typology of personality has had a wide influence (and will be considered in chapter fourteen). Much of this categorisation has been heavily criticised in recent years. For a major work on the range of approaches to personality, see Calvin S. Hall and Gardner Lindzey *Theories of Personality* (John Wiley and Sons 1970).

4 Julian Huxley (ed.) *The Humanist Frame* (George Allen and Unwin 1961) p. 19.

5 ibid., p. 26.

6 For biographical details of this section, see: Carl R. Rogers *On Becoming a Person* (Constable 1967) pp. 5ff.; *A Way of Being* (Houghton Mifflin 1980) pp. 27ff.; Harry A. Van Belle *Basic Intent and Therapeutic Approach of Carl R. Rogers* (Wedge 1980) pp. 8ff.

7 Rogers, *Being* pp. 27–28.

8 ibid., p. 30.

9 Van Belle, p. 13.

10 For Dewey's influence on Rogers, see Van Belle, pp. 15–23.

11 ibid., p. 30.

12 Rogers *Becoming* p. 91.

13 Noël Coward *Bitter Sweet* Act 1, scene ii.

14 Rogers *Becoming* p. 23.

15 ibid., p. 174.

16 Van Belle, p. 49.

17 ibid., p. 98.

18 ibid., p. 71.

19 Rogers *Being* p. 133.

20 Van Belle, p. 36.

21 Rogers *Becoming* p. 32.

22 ibid., p. 61.

23 ibid., p. 33.

24 ibid., p. 37. See also Carl R. Rogers and David Ryback 'The Alternative to Nuclear Planetary Suicide' *Journal of the British Association for Counselling* 52 (1985) pp. 1–17, where the principles of person-centredness are applied to efforts for world peace.

25 Rogers *Encounter Groups* (Penguin 1969) p. 16.

26 Van Belle, pp. 127–129.

27 Rogers *Being* p. 129.

28 See, for example, Jay Adams *Competent to Counsel* (Baker 1970) pp. 78–104; Mark P. Cosgrove *Psychology Gone Awry* pp. 64ff.;

O. Hobart Moreer *The Crisis in Psychiatry and Religion* (Van Nostrand 1961) p. 164; Paul C. Vitz *Psychology as Religion: the cult of self worship* (Lion 1979) pp. 40–49, 75–77, 121.

29 For example: Gerard Egan *The Skilled Helper* (Brooks/Cole 1982) pp. 87, 103, 127; Carole Sutton *Psychology for Social Workers and Counsellors* pp. 40–44, 154–155.

30 Van Belle, p. 145.

31 Rogers *Becoming* pp. 26, 194.

32 ibid., p. 27.

33 ibid., p. 74.

34 ibid., p. 171.

35 Vitz, p. 78.

36 Van Belle, pp. 112, 120.

37 For a classic survey of our Lord's emotions, see 'On the Emotional Life of Our Lord' in B. B. Warfield *The Person and Work of Christ* (Presbyterian & Reformed 1950) pp. 93–145.

Chapter 7

1 Walter Kaufmann *Existentialism from Dostoevsky to Sartre* (World Publishing 1956) p. 11. This book gives a useful introduction to the lives and works of a representative range of existentialist thinkers.

2 Jean-Paul Sartre 'Existentialism is a Humanism' in Kaufmann, p. 289.

3 ibid., pp. 290–291.

4 Karl Jaspers' *General Psychopathology* (1913) has been of special significance in Western European psychiatry. See, for example, Anderson and Trethowan *Psychiatry* pp. 9–41.

5 Ludwig Binswanger (1881–1966), who had been one of Freud's friends, was another important proponent of an existential approach within psychiatry. See Binswanger *Being-in-the-World: selected papers* (Basic Books 1963) where Jacob Needleman, the translator, gives a critical introduction to Binswanger's existential psychoanalysis. For a general critique of existential psychology, see Igor A. Caruso *Existential Psychology: from analysis to synthesis* (DLT 1964).

6 On Rollo May, see Kovel *Complete Guide* p. 145. For a sample of May's approach to psychotherapy, see his *Love and Will* (Collins 1972) pp. 246–272.

7 Donald F. Tweedie Jr. *Logotherapy: an evaluation of Frankl's existential approach to psychotherapy* (Baker 1961) p. 35.

8 ibid., pp. 29–30.

9 Viktor Frankl *The Unconscious God: psychotherapy and theology* (Hodder and Stoughton 1977) p. 59. See also his *Man's Search for Meaning: an introduction to logotherapy* (Beacon Press 1959) and *The Doctor and the Soul: from psychotherapy to logotherapy* (Souvenir Press 1969).

10 Frankl *Unconscious God* p. 84.
11 ibid., pp. 91–92.
12 ibid., p. 77.
13 ibid., p. 89.
14 Tweedie, p. 55.
15 ibid.
16 Frankl *Unconscious God* pp. 60–61.
17 ibid., pp. 62–63.
18 ibid., p. 68.
19 ibid., p. 143.
20 ibid., p. 84.
21 ibid., pp. 126–127.
22 Tweedie, p. 142.
23 Frankl *Unconscious God* p. 51.
24 ibid., p. 35.
25 ibid., p. 128.
26 ibid., p. 96.
27 Tweedie, pp. 112–116.
28 ibid., pp. 117–118.
29 Frankl *Unconscious God* p. 37.
30 Research by S. Kratochvil and I. Planova of the Department of Psychology at the University of Brno, Czechoslovakia, mentioned in Frankl *Unconscious God* p. 79.
31 Frankl *Unconscious God* p. 77.
32 Tweedie, p. 146.
33 See, for example: the book of Job; Romans 5:3–5; 2 Corinthians 1:3–11; 4:16–5:5; Hebrews 12:1–13; James 1:2–8; Revelation 21:4. On the question of suffering, see also: C. S. Lewis *The Problem of Pain* (Geoffrey Bles 1940) and *A Grief Observed* (Faber and Faber 1966); John Job *Where is my Father? Studies in the book of Job* (Epworth Press 1977); Edith Schaeffer *Affliction* (Hodder and Stoughton 1979); Roger F. Hurding *As Trees Walking* (Paternoster 1982); and B. Gärtner in Colin Brown (ed.) *The New International Dictionary of New Testament Theology* (NIDNTT) Vol. 3 (Paternoster 1978) pp. 719–725.
34 On our freedom in Christ, see: Isaiah 61:1; Luke 4:16–21; John 8:31–36; Romans 6:17; 8:21; 2 Corinthians 3:17; Galatians 5:1; James 1:25; 2:12; etc.
35 Tweedie, p. 175.
36 ibid.
37 Andrew Collier *R. D. Laing: the philosophy and politics of psychotherapy* (The Harvester Press 1977); M. Howarth-Williams *R. D. Laing: his work and its relevance for sociology* (RKP 1977); and J. N. Isbister 'Are the Mind-Benders Straight?' *Third Way* 1/18 (1977) pp. 3–6, 'Anti-Psychiatry: Christian roots in the thought of R. D. Laing' *Faith and Thought* 106 (1979) pp. 23–49.

38 Howarth-Williams, p. 94, quoted by Isbister in 'Anti-Psychiatry' p. 34.
39 R. D. Laing *The Facts of Life* (Penguin 1977) p. 16, quoted by Isbister in 'Anti-Psychiatry' p. 34.
40 For further biographical details, see Laing *Wisdom, Madness and Folly: the making of a psychiatrist* (Macmillan 1985); on his early Christian involvement, see pp. 58–63; on his meeting with Tillich, see pp. 143–144 (references supplied by J. N. Isbister).
41 The term *schizophrenia* was first introduced in 1911 by Eugen Bleuler (1857–1939), whom Jung worked under in Zurich, and is regarded by many as a generic term that covers a wide range of mental illness in which the personality is disintegrated and detached from its surroundings. Bleuler emphasised that the schizophrenic, to quote Anderson and Trethowan, experienced a 'basic disconnectedness in the association of ideas, inappropriate expressions of emotion and detachment from reality' (*Psychiatry* p. 107). Symptoms may include: the hearing of thoughts as if spoken aloud; a form of hallucination in which voices are heard that give a running commentary on actions; 'passivity', in which the body feels influenced from outside; and delusions, in which everyday observations and incidents take on bizarre and inexplicable significance. Although Laing would probably accept Anderson and Trethowan's generalities, quoted above, he would reject the validity of using such words as 'inappropriate' and 'detached from reality' in this context. He might ask, 'Inappropriate to whom?' and 'Who defines the reality from which the schizophrenic is said to be detached?' For some refutation of Laing's views on schizophrenia, see John K. Wing *Reasoning about Madness* (OUP 1978).
42 Laing *Divided Self* (Penguin 1965) p. 26.
43 ibid., p. 38.
44 Quoted by Isbister 'Anti-Psychiatry' p. 41.
45 Peter Sedgwick 'R. D. Laing: self, symptom and society' in Robert Boyers (ed.) *Laing and Anti-Psychiatry* (Penguin 1972) pp. 33–34.
46 Laing *The Politics of Experience and The Bird of Paradise* (Penguin 1967) p. 104.
47 ibid., p. 108.
48 ibid., p. 136, footnote.
49 Mary Barnes in Boyers (ed.) *Laing and Anti-Psychiatry* p. 218.
50 ibid., p. 222.
51 David Reed *'Anna'* (Penguin 1977); here 'Anna's' husband raises many questions about Laing's approach to psychosis.
52 Laing *Divided Self* p. 117.
53 Laing *The Voice of Experience* (Penguin 1982) pp. 11–12.
54 ibid., pp. 35–62.

55 ibid., p. 43. Also see chapter 2, note 5 on the 'medical model' in psychiatry.
56 Collier, pp. 191–192.
57 Laing 'An Examination of Tillich's Theory of Anxiety and Neurosis' *Br. J. of Med. Psychol*, 30 (1957) pp. 88–91, referred to in Isbister 'Anti-Psychiatry' p. 37.
58 Laing *Divided Self* p. 25.
59 Laing *Politics* p. 45.
60 Laing *Divided Self* p. 34.
61 Laing *Politics* p. 45.

Chapter 8

1 Abraham H. Maslow (ed.) *New Knowledge in Human Values* (Harper and Row 1959) p. 134.
2 Maslow *Toward a Psychology of Being* (Van Nostrand 1968) pp. iii–iv.
3 ibid., p. viii.
4 ibid., p. 167.
5 ibid.; see Maslow's argument on pp. 3–4.
6 ibid., pp. 165–167.
7 See Maslow *Motivation and Personality* (Harper and Row 1970) pp. 35–51 and *Toward a Psychology of Being* p. 153.
8 Maslow *Psychology of Being* p. 25.
9 ibid., pp. 26–27.
10 Maslow *Motivation and Personality* (Harper and Bros. 1954) pp. 199–224, referred to in Darling *Man in his Right Mind* p. 88.
11 Maslow *Psychology of Being* pp. 41–43. For further reading on human 'need', see Michael Ignatieff *The Needs of Strangers* (Chatto and Windus 1984) and Tony Walter *All You Love is Need* (SPCK 1985); the latter looks at Maslow's thinking.
12 Maslow *Psychology of Being* p. 96.
13 ibid., p. 24.
14 ibid., pp. 44–48.
15 ibid., p. 55.
16 ibid., p. 39.
17 ibid., p. 212.
18 ibid., p. 206.
19 *NIDNTT* Vol. 3 p. 212.
20 See, for example: Matthew 11:2–5, 14:13–21, 25:31–46; Mark 1:32–34; Luke 4:16–21.
21 W. Somerset Maugham *The Moon and Sixpence* (Pan 1974) p. 64.
22 E. W. Sinnott *Matter, Mind and Man* (1957), quoted by Maslow *Psychology of Being* p. 35.
23 Robert Assagioli *Psychosynthesis: a manual of principles and techniques*

(Turnstone Books 1975) p. 16. See pp. 16–20 for his 'pluridimensional' view of human nature.

24 ibid., p. 20.
25 ibid., p. 193.
26 ibid.
27 ibid., p. 9.
28 ibid., pp. 21–27.
29 ibid., p. 30.
30 ibid., pp. 5–8, 22ff.
31 ibid., pp. 199ff.
32 1 Samuel 16:23.
33 Assagioli, pp. 239ff.
34 Aleks Pontrik *Fundamental Thoughts on the Psychic Healing Effect of Music* (1948) p. 30, quoted in Assagioli, p. 251.
35 Assagioli, pp. 6–7.
36 ibid., p. 206.
37 Another representative figure of transpersonalism is Alan Watts, a former Anglican counsellor who became 'the foremost spokesman for the East in America'; see Os Guinness *The Dust of Death* (IVP 1973). Also see Alan W. Watts *Psychotherapy East and West* (Jonathan Cape 1960).
38 Ken Wilber *No Boundary: Eastern and Western approaches to personal growth* (Shambhala 1981) p. 15.
39 ibid., p. 19.
40 ibid., pp. 31ff.
41 ibid., p. 31.
42 ibid., pp. 39–40.
43 ibid., pp. 45ff.
44 ibid., pp. 9ff.
45 ibid., p. 95. See, generally, pp. 89ff.
46 ibid., p. 80.
47 ibid., p. 105.
48 ibid., pp. 109ff.
49 For more on Lowen's 'bioenergetic therapy', see Alexander Lowen *The Betrayal of the Body* (Collier-Macmillan 1969); Kovel *Complete Guide* p. 184; and Geoffrey Whitfield in *Contact* 58 (1978) pp. 28–32.
50 Wilber, p. 128.
51 ibid., p. 129.
52 ibid., p. 141.
53 ibid., pp. 144–146.
54 ibid., p. 152.
55 ibid., p. 76.
56 ibid., p. 64.
57 ibid., p. 43.
58 ibid., p. 64.

59 James W. Sire *The Universe Next Door: a guide to world views* p. 132.
60 Wilber, p. 74.
61 ibid., p. 58.
62 ibid., p. 124.
63 See, for example, Dom Robert Petitpierre (ed.) *Bishop of Exeter's Commission, 1964 Exorcism* (SPCK 1972). Also, John Richards *Exorcism, Deliverance and Healing: some pastoral guidelines* (Grove Booklet on Ministry and Worship no. 44 1979) p. 3 for further references.
64 Jung *Memories, Dreams, Reflections* pp. 215–216.
65 For a fuller account of 'psychic diagnosis', see Stephen Annett (ed.) *The Many Ways of Being* (Abacus 1976) pp. 205ff.
66 Unlike many other Eastern techniques, Rajneesh meditation involves vigorous physical activity. To start with, the method is one of 'chaotic breathing', in which the whole body is used, in order to 'break tension spots and emotional blocks'. Secondly, catharsis is encouraged with the often dramatic release of pent-up emotion, leading to laughing, screaming, dancing, etc. Thirdly, a Sufi mantra is shouted repetitively over about ten minutes 'to raise the energy level still further'. Finally, meditation is carried out in total silence and stillness. Meditation in groups is an important part of a continuing commitment. See Annett, pp. 60–62.
67 See accounts in Annett, pp. 121ff. and pp. 220ff., and Charles T. Tart (ed.) *Transpersonal Psychologies* (Harper and Row 1975) pp. 281ff. and pp. 329ff.
68 Tart *Transpersonal Psychologies* p. 238.
69 Quoted in Richard Hollings *Transcendental Meditation: an introduction to the practice and aims of TM* (The Aquarian Press 1982) pp. 11–12; see also pp. 7–28.
70 Ronald L. Carlson *Transcendental Meditation: relaxation or religion?* (Moody Press 1979) p. 85; Carlson gives a valuable bibliography on the subject. For other Christian criticisms of TM, see: James Bjornstad *The Transcendental Mirage* (Bethany Fellowship 1976) and John Allan *TM: a cosmic confidence trick* (IVP 1980).
71 Carlson, pp. 110–125.
72 See, for example Carlson, pp. 129–145 and Richard J. Foster *Celebration of Discipline: the path to spiritual growth* (Hodder and Stoughton 1980) pp. 13–29.
73 A recent extension of twentieth-century transpersonalism has been to look back to Anglo-Saxon sorcery. Brian Bates, a psychologist at Sussex University, in *The Way of Wyrd* (Century 1983) sees this early tradition as a Western equivalent of the transcendental views of Zen and Tao; see article in *Guardian* (Nov. 9 1983) p. 13. For a book which demonstrates links between transpersonal psychology (for example, that of Assagioli) and occultism, see A. D. Duncan *The Christ, Psychotherapy and Magic: a Christian appreciation of occultism* (George Allen and Unwin 1969).

74 For a helpful critique of Eastern monism, see Os Guinness *Dust of Death* pp. 211–231.
75 See, for example: Hollings, pp. 69–71; Sanders G. Laurie and Melvin J. Tucker *Centering: the power of meditation* (Excalibur Books 1982) pp. 20–23; and Peter Russell *The TM Technique* (Routledge and Kegan Paul 1978) pp. 52–66. For a wider assessment of the paranormal, see J. D. Pearce-Higgins and G. Stanley Whitby (eds.) *Life, Death and Psychical Research: studies on behalf of The Churches' Fellowship for Psychical and Spiritual Studies* (Rider and Company 1973).
76 For a comprehensive study on Christian care for those oppressed by occultism, see Kurt E. Koch *Christian Counseling and Occultism* (Kregel Publications 1968).

Chapter 9

1 For comprehensive treatments of today's therapies, see: C. H. Patterson *Theories of Counseling and Psychotherapy* (Harper and Row 1980), which includes assessments of Rogers, Frankl, Berne and Gestalt therapy; and Raymond J. Corsini (ed.) *Handbook of Innovative Psychotherapies* (John Wiley and Sons 1981), which examines many of the 'new therapies'.
2 Family therapy has become an extremely important aspect of psychotherapy amongst social workers, psychologists and psychiatrists. Beginning tentatively in the United States in the early 1950s, it grew out of a post-war emphasis on social groups and the emerging science of systems analysis. As a result, the family is seen as a whole unit of function and therapy concentrates on the overall behaviour of that unit. For helpful introductions to the 'general systems theory' behind family therapy, see: Sue Walrond-Skinner *Family Therapy: the treatment of natural systems* (RKP 1976) pp. 10–22; and A. C. Robin Skynner *One Flesh: Separate Persons: principles of family and marital psychotherapy* (Constable 1976) pp. 3–25. These books contain extensive references and bibliographies. Amongst more recent works, see: Walrond-Skinner (ed.) *Family and Marital Psychotherapy: a critical approach* (RKP 1979); John K. Pearce and Leonard J. Friedman (eds.) *Family Therapy: combining psychodynamic and family systems approaches* (Grune and Stratton 1980); Andy Treacher and John Carpenter (eds.) *Using Family Therapy: a guide for practitioners in different professional settings* (Basil Blackwell 1984).
3 Feminism has brought corrective dimensions to psychology and psychotherapy. Literature relating to this important field includes: Karen Horney *Feminine Psychology* (R KP 1967), which looks at such issues as 'inhibited femininity' and 'distrust between the sexes'; Jean Baker Miller *Psychoanalysis and Women* (Penguin 1973) and

Toward a New Psychology of Women (Penguin 1978); Irene Claremont de Castillejo *Knowing Women: a feminine psychology* (Harper and Row 1974); Juliet Mitchell *Psychoanalysis and Feminism* (Penguin 1975); Robert A. Johnson *She: understanding feminine psychology* (Harper and Row 1977); Joanna Ryan *Feminism and Therapy* (Dept. of Applied Social Sciences, The Polytechnic of North London 1983); Luise Eichenbaum and Susie Orback *Understanding Women* (Penguin 1985).

4 The introduction of psychodrama by J. L. Moreno (1892–1974) has been an influential addition to ideas of group therapy. Arriving in the United States from Vienna in 1927, he pioneered *sociometry* – 'the study of interpersonal relationships in the light of individuals choosing or rejecting relations with members of their own group'. He regarded acting as a better vehicle for catharsis than the 'talking cure' of Freud. His major works include *Who Shall Survive?* (1934) and three volumes of *Psychodrama* (first Vol. 1946). See sympathetic view in William S. Sahakiean *History and Systems of Psychology* (John Wiley and Sons 1975) pp. 279–280. Moreno's introduction of *role-play*, in which participants re-create everyday interactions with one another in a supervised setting, has wide implications for learning in many fields other than therapy. See critiques on Moreno in Kovel, pp. 230–232 and Anthony W. Clare (with S. Thompson) *Let's Talk About Me: a critical examination of the new psychotherapies* (BBC Publications 1981), where there are assessments of Rogers, Berne, Reich, Janov and Erhard, as well as Moreno.

5 Albert Ellis *Reason and Emotion in Psychotherapy* (The Citadel Press 1979) pp. 4–21.

6 ibid., p. 38.

7 ibid., p. 36.

8 ibid., p. 134.

9 ibid., pp. 130ff.

10 ibid., p. 142.

11 ibid., p. 147.

12 ibid., pp. 36–41.

13 ibid., p. 109.

14 ibid., p. 54.

15 ibid., p. 133.

16 ibid., p. 146.

17 ibid., p. 95.

18 ibid., p. 105.

19 ibid., pp. 52–59.

20 ibid., pp. 159, 324.

21 ibid., p. 134, also p. 159.

22 ibid., pp. 107–109.

23 ibid., p. 322.

24 ibid., Chapter 3.
25 ibid., p. 325.
26 ibid., p. 95.
27 ibid., p. 188.
28 ibid., p. 365.
29 See Derek Kidner *Proverbs* (IVP 1964) p. 41.
30 Ellis, p. 158.
31 ibid., p. 138.
32 See, for example, Psalm 103:8–14; Luke 7:47; 15:11–24.
33 Ellis, pp. 92–94.
34 See, for example, T. Sorg in *NIDNTT* Vol. 2 pp. 180–184.
35 Ellis, p. 365.
36 ibid., pp. 200ff.
37 ibid., p. 119.
38 For the idea of prescribing the drug 'doctor', see, for example, Michael Balint *The Doctor, His Patient and The Illness* (Pitman 1957) p. 5.
39 For example, see Jon Tal Murphee *When God Says You're OK* (IVP 1975).
40 Eric Berne *Transactional Analysis in Psychotherapy: a systematic individual and social psychiatry* (Souvenir Press 1975) pp. 11–20 and Paul Roazen *Freud and His Followers* (Allen Lane 1976) pp. 310–315. Berne explains how Weiss systematised Federn's ego psychology and described an ego state as 'the actually experienced reality of one's mental and bodily ego with the contents of the lived-through period'.
41 Berne *What Do You Say After You Say Hello? the psychology of human destiny* (Corgi Books 1975) p. 21.
42 See Berne *Transactional Analysis* p. 17 and Thomas A. Harris *I'm OK – you're OK* (Pan Books 1973) pp. 5–11.
43 Berne *Transactional Analysis* pp. 75ff.
44 Berne *Games People Play: the psychology of human relationships* (Penguin 1968) p. 27.
45 Berne *Transactional Analysis* p. 31.
46 Harris, pp. 36–50.
47 Berne *Games* pp. 28ff.
48 ibid., pp. 33–58.
49 Harris, p. 50.
50 Berne *Transactional Analysis* pp. 125–126.
51 Harris, p. 56.
52 Berne *Games* pp. 158ff.
53 Berne *Transactional Analysis* p. 21.
54 Berne *Hello* pp. 376–377.
55 This book concentrates mainly on the one-to-one aspects of counselling and psychotherapy without denying the great efficacy and

importance of group work. Some key books on this dimension within the therapies include: W. R. Bion *Experiences in Groups* (Tavistock 1961); I. D. Yalom *The Theory and Practice of Group Psychotherapy* (Basic Books 1970); and S. H. Foulkes and E. J. Anthony *Group Psychotherapy: the psychoanalytic approach* (Penguin 1973). For an assessment of the main approaches in group therapy, see James C. Hanson, Richard W. Warner and Elsie M. Smith *Group Counseling: theory and process* (Rand McNally College 1976).

56 Berne *Transactional Analysis* p. 159.
57 ibid., pp. 68ff., p. 166.
58 Berne *Hello* pp. 315–377.
59 ibid., p. 370.
60 Harris, pp. xiv–xv.
61 Thomas C. Oden *Game Free: a guide to the meaning of intimacy* (Harper and Row 1974) p. 86.
62 Harris, pp. 219ff.
63 See, for example, Romans 3:23, 24; 5:12–21.
64 Oden, p. 93.
65 Frederick S. Perls, Ralph F. Hefferline and Paul Goodman *Gestalt Therapy: excitement and growth in the human personality* (Souvenir Press 1972) pp. 25–26.
66 Vernon Van De Riet, Margaret P. Korb and John Jeffrey Gorrell *Gestalt Therapy: an introduction* (Pergamon Press 1980) preface.
67 Perls *et al.*, p. 117.
68 ibid., p. ix.
69 ibid.
70 Van De Riet *et al.*, pp. 6–7.
71 ibid., p. 10.
72 ibid., p. 21.
73 Perls *et al.*, p. viii.
74 ibid., pp. 118–122.
75 ibid., pp. 85–87.
76 ibid., p. 284.
77 ibid., p. 73.
78 ibid., p. viii.
79 ibid., p. 232.
80 Van De Riet *et al.*, p. 8.
81 Perls *The Gestalt Approach and Eye Witness to Therapy* (Bantam Books 1976) pp. 100–101.
82 ibid., p. 115.
83 ibid., p. 16.
84 For a helpful section on the helping process in Gestalt therapy, see Van De Riet *et al.*, pp. 75ff.
85 ibid., p. 86.
86 Perls *Gestalt Approach* pp. 65–66.

87 Perls *et al.*, p. 177.
88 Perls *Gestalt Approach* p. 79.
89 Perls *et al.*, p. vii.
90 E. W. L. Smith (1976), quoted in Van De Riet *et al.*, p. 15.
91 Perls *et al.*, p. 33.
92 See Romans 12:3 and Philippians 2:4.
93 Perls *Gestalt Approach* p. xiii.
94 Perls *et al.*, pp. 278–279.
95 Van De Riet *et al.*, p. 24.
96 Perls *et al.*, p. 101.
97 ibid., pp. 376–377.
98 Van De Riet *et al.*, p. 26.
99 ibid., p. 29;
100 For critiques of the 'new therapies', see Clare *Let's Talk* and Vitz *Psychology as Religion*.

Chapter 10

1 Wayne E. Oates (ed.) *An Introduction to Pastoral Counseling* (Broadman Press 1959) p. 13.
2 See, for example: Charles W. Gusmer *The Ministry of Healing in the Church of England* (Mayhew-McCrimmon 1974) pp. 12ff.; Morton T. Kelsey *Healing and Christianity: in ancient thought and modern times* (SCM 1973) pp. 240ff.; and Morris Maddocks *The Christian Healing Ministry* (SPCK 1981) pp. 99–111.
3 See Anton T. Boisen *Out of the Depths: an autobiographical study of mental disorder and religious experience* (Harper and Bros. 1960) for biographical details.
4 ibid., p. 47.
5 ibid., p. 151.
6 ibid., p. 186.
7 See Kingsley Weatherhead *Leslie Weatherhead: a personal portrait* (Hodder and Stoughton 1975) for biographical details.
8 ibid., p. 41.
9 ibid., pp. 66–67.
10 ibid., p. 93.
11 Leslie D. Weatherhead *Psychology, Religion and Healing* (Hodder and Stoughton 1955) (*PRH*) p. 483.
12 ibid., pp. 269–279.
13 ibid., p. 270.
14 ibid., pp. 466, 484.
15 K. Weatherhead, p. 61.
16 Weatherhead *PRH* p. 290.
17 ibid., p. 466.

18 ibid., p. 467.
19 ibid., pp. 486–491.
20 ibid., pp. 482–484.
21 ibid., see pp. 301ff.
22 Leslie Weatherhead *Psychology in Service of the Soul* (The Epworth Press 1958) p. 52.
23 Weatherhead *PRH* p. 490.
24 For Weatherhead's encounters with spiritualism, see: K. Weatherhead, pp. 128ff.; and Weatherhead *PRH* pp. 105ff.
25 K. Weatherhead, pp. 212–216.
26 Quoted in Kenneth Leech *Soul Friend: a study of spirituality* (Sheldon Press 1977) p. 94.
27 Wayne Oates, p. 325.
28 Seward Hiltner *Preface to Pastoral Theology* (Abingdon Press 1958) p. 15.
29 ibid., pp. 18ff. and Leech, p. 91.
30 Leech, pp. 100ff.
31 Halmos *The Faith of the Counsellors* pp. 43–47.
32 ibid., pp. 108–109, quoted in Leech, p. 95.
33 See Donald Capps *Biblical Approaches to Pastoral Counseling* (The Westminster Press 1981) pp. 28ff. for an excellent overview of contributions from European pastoral counselling.
34 The Marriage Guidance Council in Britain was set up in London in 1943 and the first general secretary of the National Council was Dr David Mace, who was then a Methodist minister and later began work with his wife in the United States.
35 William H. Kyle (ed.) *Healing Through Counselling: a Christian counselling centre* (The Epworth Press 1964) pp. 72–86.
36 ibid., p. 85.
37 John Maes 'An intimate sketch of the early years: recollections of Bill Kyle' *Westminster Pastoral Foundation Quarterly* (1980) 14, pp. 12–13.
38 Edward E. Thornton 'Citizen of Two Worlds' *WPF Quarterly* 14 (1980) p. 11.
39 David Porter 'The Purpose of Counselling: does religion come into it?' *WPF Quarterly* 18 (1982) pp. 4–6. Canon Derek Blows, the Director of the Westminster Pastoral Foundation and a psychotherapist at University College Hospital, London, is the general editor of the 'New Library of Pastoral Care', an excellent series which is doing a great deal to clarify today's thinking on pastoral counseling. See, for example Michael Jacobs *Still Small Voice: a practical introduction to counselling for pastors and other helpers* (SPCK 1982) and Alastair V. Campbell *Paid to Care? The limits of professionalism in pastoral care* (SPCK 1985).
40 Peter G. Liddell *A Handbook of Pastoral Counselling* (Mowbray 1983) p. 10.

41 Mowrer *The Crisis in Psychiatry and Religion* p. 70.
42 ibid., pp. 115–116.
43 ibid., pp. 26–27, 48, 82, 236–237.
44 ibid., p. 107.
45 ibid., p. 199.
46 ibid., pp. 109, 159, 186–189, 199.
47 ibid., pp. 159–160.
48 ibid., pp. 182–184.
49 Thomas Szasz *The Myth of Psychotherapy* (OUP 1979) p. 40.
50 Vitz *Psychology as Religion* pp. 9–12.
51 Quoted in Colin Brown *Philosophy and the Christian Faith* (Tyndale Press 1969) p. 134.
52 Vitz, pp. 64–67.
53 ibid., p. 71.
54 ibid., pp. 89–103.
55 ibid., p. 110.
56 ibid., pp. 113–120.
57 ibid., pp. 115–116.
58 ibid., p. 122.
59 See, for example: Matthew 18:3,4; Mark 10:42–45; John 10:1–18, 25–30.
60 Vitz, p. 124.
61 William Kirk Kilpatrick *Psychological Seduction: the failure of modern psychology* (Thomas Nelson 1983) p. 23.
62 ibid., pp. 43ff.
63 ibid., pp. 152ff.
64 ibid., pp. 161ff.
65 ibid., p. 235.
66 John Foskett 'Pilgrimage to Poland' *Contact* 75/2 (1982) p. 7.
67 Malcolm A. Jeeves *Psychology and Christianity: the view both ways* p. 11.
68 ibid., pp. 145ff.
69 ibid., p. 151.
70 ibid., p. 83. See also, for example: Gary R. Collins *The Rebuilding of Psychology* p. 85 and his reference to Donald M. MacKay *The Clockwork Image*.
71 Jeeves, p. 171.
72 C. Stephen Evans *Preserving the Person* pp. 101ff.
73 ibid., p. 116.
74 Collins, pp. 77ff.
75 ibid., p. 90.
76 ibid., pp. 106–110.
77 ibid., pp. 120–132.
78 ibid., pp. 146ff.
79 ibid., pp. 170–177.
80 Oden *Kerygma and Counseling* (Harper and Row 1978) pp. 9, 146.

81 ibid., p. 24.
82 ibid., p. 17.
83 ibid., pp. 38–46.
84 ibid., p. 115.
85 ibid., p. 117.
86 ibid., p. 16.
87 ibid., pp. 49ff.
88 ibid., pp. 55–56.
89 ibid., pp. 3–4.
90 Oden 'Recovering Lost Identity' *The Journal of Pastoral Care* 34/1 (1980) pp. 4–18.
91 ibid., p. 15.
92 Oden *Agenda for Theology: recovering Christian roots* (Harper and Row 1979) p. 25.
93 ibid., pp. 36–43.
94 ibid., pp. 49–52.
95 ibid., pp. 56–60.
96 ibid., p. 59. Oden is aware that the term 'fundamentalist' can raise evangelical hackles. He uses the word in its strict historical sense as descriptive of one who adheres to the five 'fundamentals' of faith agreed at the Bible Conference at Niagara in 1895: the inspiration and infallibility of the scriptures; the deity of Jesus Christ; the virgin birth and miracles; Christ's substitutionary death; and his bodily resurrection and personal return. Oden does not so much quibble with the orthodox nature of these 'fundamentals' as with their *selectivity* and the pietism that has marred the 'fundamentalist' movement.
97 ibid., p. 103.
98 ibid., pp. 112–127.
99 ibid., p. 164.

Chapter 11

1 Albert Ellis *Reason and Emotion in Psychotherapy* p. 365.
2 P. G. Wodehouse *The Code of the Woosters* (Penguin 1953) p. 63.
3 H. D. McDonald *The Christian View of Man* (Marshall Morgan and Scott).
4 See the apparent interchangeability of *tselem* and *demuth* in Genesis 1:26,27, 5:1 and 9:6 as pointed out in G. C. Berkouwer *Man: The Image of God* (Grand Rapids: Eerdmans 1962) pp. 68–69.
5 Berkouwer *Man* p. 67.
6 McDonald, pp. 37–39.
7 Berkouwer *Man* pp. 72–73.
8 Paul K. Jewett *Man as Male and Female: a study in sexual relationships from a theological point of view* (Eerdmans 1975) p. 49.

9 Berkouwer *Man* p. 100.
10 David Clines 'A Biblical Doctrine of Man' *The Journal of the Christian Brethren Research Fellowship* 28 (1976) p. 24.
11 Derek Kidner *Genesis: an introduction and commentary* (Tyndale Press 1967) p. 51.
12 McDonald, pp. 39–41.
13 ibid., p. 77.
14 Quoted in Clines, p. 10.
15 McDonald, p. 42.
16 See, for example, Romans 8:11,29,30; 1 Corinthians 15:20–58; 2 Corinthians 5:1–5; 1 John 3:2.
17 McDonald, p. 78.
18 Karl Barth *Church Dogmatics* III, 2, pp. 471–472, referred to in Berkouwer *Man* p. 94.
19 Berkouwer *Man* pp. 140–141.
20 See, for example: Deuteronomy 32:6; Job 10:8–12; Psalm 139:14–16; Isaiah 44:28; 45:11–13; also see Berkouwer *Man* p. 133.
21 See also Henri Blocher *In the Beginning: the opening chapters of Genesis* (IVP 1984) p. 94, where he writes, 'Mankind remains the image of God, inviolable and responsible, but has become a contradictory image, one might say a caricature, a witness against himself'. Blocher pp. 79–94 give an excellent overview on the theme, 'The Image of God'. See also C. Westermann *Creation* (SPCK 1971).
22 Kidner, p. 71.
23 John V. Taylor *The Go-Between God* (SCM 1972) p. 48.
24 Berkouwer *Man* p. 182.
25 Opening verse of George Herbert 'Giddiness' in John N. Wall Jr. (ed.) *George Herbert/The Country Parson, The Temple* (SPCK 1981) p. 249.
26 McDonald, p. 40.
27 See, for example: John 15:8; Romans 8:29; 12:1,2; 15:7–9; 1 Corinthians 6:20; 2 Corinthians 5:17; 1 Peter 2:4,5.
28 See John 8:50; 17:1–5; 21:19; Colossians 1:15; Hebrews 1:3.
29 See Galatians 3:23–29; 4:4,5; Ephesians 2:13–22; 4:11–16; Colossians 3:11; 1 John 1:3.
30 For a brief discussion of philosophical thought on 'truth', see: A. C. Thiselton in *NIDNTT* 3, pp. 894–901. Also, for a helpful description of the scientific approach to 'truth', see Donald M. MacKay *The Clockwork Image* pp. 22–32.
31 Bernard Ramm *Special Revelation and the Word of God* (Eerdmans 1961) p. 17.
32 Calvin *Institutes* I.v.1.
33 Berkouwer *General Revelation* (Eerdmans 1955) p. 162.
34 Ramm, p. 18.
35 ibid., p. 19.
36 ibid., p. 20.

37 See, for example: John 12:45; 14:9; 16:13–15; 17:26.
38 See: 2 Corinthians 3:12–18; Ephesians 6:17; 2 Timothy 3:16,17; 1 Peter 1:10–12.
39 Colin Brown *Philosophy and the Christian Faith* p. 33.
40 Berkouwer *General Revelation* pp. 22ff.
41 Calvin *Institutes* I.vi.1.
42 Berkouwer *General Revelation* p. 134.
43 ibid., p. 331.
44 Thomas F. Torrance *The Ground and Grammar of Theology* (Christian Journals Ltd. 1980) p. 6.
45 Philip Brian Bell and Phillip James Staines *Reasoning and Argument in Psychology* (RKP 1981) p. 23.
46 ibid., p. 28.
47 ibid.
48 Charles H. Kraft *Christianity in Culture* (Orbis Books 1979) pp. 108–115.
49 Quoted in H. Richard Niebuhr *Christ and Culture* (Harper and Bros. 1951) p. 54.
50 See Niebuhr, pp. 45ff. and Kraft, pp. 105–106.
51 Kraft, p. 105.
52 Niebuhr, pp. 76–82.
53 See chapter ten; also William Kirk Kilpatrick *Psychological Seduction* p. 9.
54 Niebuhr, p. 101.
55 John D. Carter and Bruce Narramore *The Integration of Psychology and Theology: an introduction* (Zondervan 1979) p. 85.
56 As we noted in chapter ten, there are other Christians who have assimilated certain aspects of the more atheistic methodologies. R. S. Lee, an Australian who worked at St Martins-in-the-Fields in London and later became a college chaplain in Oxford, looks to Freudianism. He writes that he has found 'the concepts of the Freudian school . . . the most convincing in explaining human behaviour in general and therefore the particular field of religion'. In his 'Ego-religion', with its stress on the powerful influences of both the id and the super-ego, the perspectives of human culpability seem to be watered down. See his *Freud and Christianity* (Penguin 1967) pp. 155–160 and *Principles of Pastoral Counselling* (SPCK 1968) pp. 96–100.
57 In Gary R. Collins (ed.) *Helping People Grow: practical approaches to Christian counseling* (Vision House 1980) p. 111.
58 See the account in Joel Kovel *Complete Guide* pp. 227–230.
59 In *Shorter Oxford English Dictionary*.
60 See Carole Sutton *Psychology for Social Workers and Counsellors* pp. 33–34.
61 Niebuhr, pp. 120ff.
62 Kraft, p. 111.

63 Carter and Narramore, p. 95.
64 Pal Meehl *et al. What, Then, Is Man? a symposium of theology, psychology, and psychiatry* (Concordia 1971) p. 169.
65 See R. V. G. Tasker *Matthew: an introduction and commentary* (The Tyndale Press 1961) p. 210.
66 Niebuhr, p. 129.
67 ibid., p. 141.
68 ibid., pp. 191–196.
69 Carter and Narramore, pp. 103–104.
70 ibid.
71 ibid., pp. 106–113.
72 Niebuhr, p. 145.
73 Carter and Narramore, pp. 118–119.
74 For a valuable paper that explores the integration of theology and psychology, see David Atkinson 'Covenant and Counselling: some counselling implications of a Covenant Theology' *Anvil* 1/2 (1984) pp. 121–138.

Chapter 12

1 See, for example: Paul D. Morris *Love Therapy* (Tyndale House 1974) pp. 19–23, 43, 154; O. Quentin Hyder *The Christian's Handbook of Psychiatry* (Fleming H. Revell 1971) Chapter 14; and Roger F. Hurding *Restoring the Image* pp. 22–30.
2 William Glasser *Reality Therapy: a new approach to psychiatry* (Harper and Row 1965) p. 57; see also Martin and Deirdre Bobgan *The Psychological Way/The Spiritual Way* (Bethany Fellowship 1979) pp. 124–132, where they argue that 'self, not God, is at the centre of Reality Therapy'.
3 James Dobson, a Christian psychologist, looks to E. L. Thorndike and B. F. Skinner and the 'law of reinforcement' in granting 'rewards', achieving 'extinction' of undesirable behaviour. See, for example, his *Dare to Discipline* (Coverdale House 1975) pp. 59ff. His books and videos are a valuable contribution to teaching on relationships internationally.
4 Gary R. Collins (ed.) *Helping People Grow* pp. 154–155.
5 Jay E. Adams *Competent to Counsel* (Baker 1970) pp. xvii–xviii.
6 Adams *The Christian Counselor's Manual* (Presbyterian and Reformed 1973) p. 72.
7 Adams *More than Redemption: a theology of Christian counseling* (Baker 1979) p. 4.
8 Adams *Competent* p. xxi; it was my privilege to be part of a small group who met Jay Adams at Hildenborough Hall in May 1982 to discuss his views.

9 Cornelius Van Til *The Defense of the Faith* (Presbyterian and Reformed 1955) p. 286.
10 ibid., pp. 288–299.
11 ibid., p. 306.
12 Adams 'Nouthetic Counseling' in Collins *Helping People Grow* p. 155.
13 Adams *Manual* p. 9.
14 Adams *Competent* p. 70.
15 Adams *Redemption* p. 326.
16 See, for example: Adams *Competent* pp. 73–76; *Manual* pp. 28, 172; *Redemption* pp. 103–105, 120, 250.
17 Adams *Competent* pp. 54–55, 239.
18 ibid., p. 57.
19 Adams *Manual* p. 29.
20 ibid., p. 28.
21 Adams *Competent* p. 23.
22 Adams 'Nouthetic Counseling' p. 158.
23 Adams *Manual* p. 99.
24 Adams *Competent* pp. 44–50.
25 Adams *Manual* p. 94.
26 Adams *Competent* p. 51.
27 Adams *Manual* p. 13; see also *Competent* pp. 59ff.
28 Adams *Competent* p. 60.
29 Adams *Manual* pp. 12–13.
30 Ibid., pp. 16–17.
31 ibid., p. 225.
32 Adams *Competent* p. 193.
33 Adams 'Nouthetic Counseling' pp. 156–157.
34 Adams *Redemption* pp. 324–325.
35 Adams *Manual* p. 182.
36 See *Competent* pp. 177ff., 193ff.; *Manual* pp. 228ff., 301ff.
37 *Competent* pp. 148–151.
38 ibid., p. 201.
39 *Manual* p. 234.
40 See, for example: Donald Capps *Biblical Approaches to Pastoral Counseling* pp. 33ff., 101ff., 114ff.; John D. Carter 'Adams' Theory of Nouthetic Counseling' *Journal of Psychology and Theology* 3/3 (1975) pp. 143–155; Richard L. Ganz 'Nouthetic Counseling Defended' *Journal of Psychology and Theology* 4/3 (1976) pp. 193–205; Richard D. Winter 'Jay Adams – is he really biblical enough?' *Third Way* 5/4 (1982) pp. 9–12; Raju Abraham 'Yes, Jay Adams is biblical enough' *Third Way* 5/7 (1982) pp. 15–16.
41 Private discussion, along with Rev Dr David J. Atkinson and Dr Richard D. Winter, with Jay Adams at Hildenborough Hall in May 1982. See also *Competent* pp. 72–73 and *Manual* pp. 76, 92–93.
42 See *Competent* pp. 72–73 and *Manual* pp. 76, 92–93.

43 *Redemption* p. 141, footnote.
44 ibid., pp. 139–140.
45 ibid., pp. 110ff.
46 ibid., pp. 140ff.
47 *Competent* pp. 108–109 and *Redemption* p. 140.
48 *Redemption* pp. 141–142.
49 ibid.
50 See *Competent* pp. xx, 269; *Manual* pp. 33, 82, 92–93.
51 See Luke 10:18, 19; John 12:31; 16:11.
52 *Redemption* p. 120.
53 *Competent* p. 51.
54 Adams *Ready to Restore: the layman's guide to Christian counseling* (Presbyterian and Reformed 1981) p. 9.
55 Capps, p. 101.
56 ibid., pp. 114ff.
57 *Manual* pp. 109–110; see also *Competent* p. 93.
58 *Manual* p. 113.
59 Lawrence J. Crabb Jr. *Basic Principles of Biblical Counseling* (Zondervan 1975) p. 17.
60 Bobgans, pp. 10–12.
61 ibid., pp. 193–197.
62 ibid., pp. 161–163.
63 ibid., p. 161.
64 ibid., p. 166.
65 ibid., pp. 168ff.
66 ibid., p. 176.
67 Information from personal discussions with Jim Craddock and his colleague, Tom Paige, in November 1984, from 'Scope' publicity material and from unedited writing by Craddock: *Counselor's Desk Reference Manual*, Vol. 1 (1981) and the *CDR Counselor's Training Course* (1983) – quoted with permission.
68 Crabb, pp. 9–12.
69 ibid., p. 18.
70 Crabb *Effective Biblical Counseling* (Zondervan 1977) pp. 47–52.
71 ibid., p. 191.
72 ibid., p. 61.
73 Crabb *Basic Principles* p. 81.
74 Crabb *Effective* pp. 126–135.
75 ibid., pp. 22–27.
76 ibid., p. 139.
77 ibid., pp. 165–191.
78 ibid., pp. 147–148; Carter 'Adams' Theory' p. 152.
79 Crabb *Effective* pp. 149ff.
80 ibid., pp. 104–105.
81 Crabb *Basic Principles* p. 68.

82 The material for this section has been gleaned from a personal discussion with Selwyn Hughes in November 1982, supplemented by his writings and the literature of CWR and the Institute of Christian Counselling.

83 Selwyn Hughes *A Friend in Need* (Kingsway 1982) p. 100.

84 ibid., p. 26.

85 Hughes *The Christian Counsellor's Pocket Guide* (Kingsway 1982) pp. 8 –9.

86 The information on Gary Sweeten comes from a personal meeting with him in November 1983, from literature supplied by his 'Counseling With Power' ministry and from his *Discipleship Counseling* manual.

87 Richard Lovelace *Dynamics of Spiritual Life* p. 219.

Chapter 13

1 Richard Nelson-Jones *The Theory and Practice of Counselling Psychology* pp. 210–211.

2 See Mose J. Glyn and Gary R. Collins 'Catholic Approaches to Counseling' in Collins (ed.) *Helping People Grow* pp. 279ff. Works by Gerard Egan and Eugene Kennedy have already been mentioned and Henri Nouwen, a priest from the Netherlands whose writings give invaluable insights in the field of spirituality, will be referred to again in chapter fourteen. John Powell, of the Society of Jesus, is a popular American writer and has a widely eclectic approach. For example, in his *Why Am I Afraid to Tell You Who I Am?* (Fontana 1975) he looks to Adler, the ego psychologists, Stack Sullivan, Fromm, Berne, Rogers and Maslow. Amongst Catholic writers in the United Kingdom, Jack Dominian, a psychiatrist, is particularly important in the field of marital therapy. See, for instance: Jack Dominian *Marital Breakdown* (Penguin 1968), *Cycles of Affirmation* (DLT 1975), *Marital Pathology* (British Medical Association and DLT 1980) and *Marriage, Faith and Love* (DLT 1981).

3 Howard Clinebell *Basic Types of Pastoral Care and Counselling* (SCM 1984) *(BT)* p. 30.

4 ibid., pp. 38, 133, 153.

5 Clinebell 'Growth Counseling' in Collins (ed.) *Helping People Grow* p. 88; also Clinebell *BT* p. 56.

6 Clinebell in *Helping People Grow (HPG)* p. 91.

7 *HPG* p. 93; *BT* pp. 30, 57–58, 89.

8 *HPG* pp. 85–87; *BT* pp. 109–110.

9 *BT* pp. 37–38, 64.

10 *BT* pp. 96–97.

11 *HPG* p. 89; *BT* pp. 28–29.

12 H. Beck and C. Brown write that *shalom* 'has a social dimension, being bound up with the political aspirations of Israel, and has a public significance far beyond the purely personal', *NIDNTT* 2, p. 777.

13 *BT* pp. 31–34.

14 ibid., p. 26.

15 ibid., pp. 42–43.

16 *HPG* p. 87.

17 *BT* pp. 36, 98.

18 ibid., p. 171.

19 ibid., p. 133.

20 ibid., pp. 100–101.

21 ibid., p. 17.

22 *Shorter Oxford English Dictionary*

23 *BT* p. 94.

24 ibid., p. 56; see also *HPG* p. 84.

25 *BT* p. 103.

26 ibid., pp. 121–127.

27 *HPG* p. 84.

28 *BT* pp. 141–146.

29 Throughout this section, I am indebted to Gary Collins' biography of Paul Tournier, as well as Tournier's own writings. Collins' *The Christian Psychology of Paul Tournier* (Baker 1973) was the outcome of a sabbatical year, with six months based in Geneva. See pp. 25ff. for Tournier's family details. There is an adaptation of Chapter Five of this book in *HPG* pp. 56ff.

30 Paul Tournier *Creative Suffering*, 1981 (SCM 1982) p. 24.

31 Tournier *The Violence Inside*, 1977 (SCM 1978) p. 108.

32 Tournier *The Gift of Feeling*, 1979 (SCM 1981) pp. 2–7.

33 *Creative Suffering* (CS) p. 13.

34 Tournier *A Doctor's Casebook in the Light of the Bible*, 1951 (SCM 1954) pp. 189–190.

35 Collins *Paul Tournier* p. 33.

36 Tournier *Doctor's Casebook* (DC) pp. 20–21 and *A Place for You* (SCM 1968) pp. 86–87; Collins *Tournier* pp. 38–39.

37 *CS* p. 36.

38 Collins *Tournier* p. 130.

39 Tournier *The Strong and the Weak*, 1948 (SCM 1963) p. 179; *The Meaning of Persons*, 1955 (SCM 1957) p. 58.

40 *The Violence Inside* (VI) p. 65.

41 *A Place for You* (APY) p. 87.

42 Collins *Tournier* p. 119.

43 *CS* pp. 35–36.

44 *DC* p. 42.

45 *The Meaning of Persons* (MP) pp. 162–163.

46 *APY* pp. 92, 210–216.

47 Collins *Tournier* p. 81; see also pp. 79–104.
48 ibid., p. 100.
49 *DC* pp. 18–32; *VI* p. 160.
50 Collins *Tournier* p. 83.
51 *VI* p. 145.
52 Tournier *Guilt and Grace*, 1958 (Hodder and Stoughton 1962) p. 212.
53 ibid., p. 187.
54 *VI* p. 56; see also p. 193 and *CS* pp. 89–90.
55 *VI* p. 129; *The Gift of Feeling* (*GF*) p. 10.
56 *MP* pp. 79–81.
57 ibid., pp. 165–172.
58 *GF* pp. 13–14.
59 ibid., pp. 19ff.
60 ibid., p. 23.
61 ibid., pp. 79–83.
62 ibid., pp. 122–123.
63 ibid., pp. 130–131.
64 Collins *Tournier* pp. 122–134.
65 *APY* p. 204.
66 *DC* p. 135.
67 *MP* pp. 202–206; *APY* pp. 163–164.
68 *CS* pp. 73–74.
69 *The Strong and the Weak* (*SW*) p. 241.
70 *APY* pp. 141–142.
71 *Guilt and Grace* (*GG*) p. 142.
72 *DC* p. 235.
73 *MP* pp. 191–195.
74 Tournier *The Adventure of Living*, 1965 (Edward England 1983) p. 68.
75 *MP* pp. 159–169.
76 *DC* pp. 73–74.
77 *APY* p. 34.
78 See Tournier *Escape from Loneliness*, 1943 (Edward England 1983) pp. 166–167; *MP* p. 145; *GG* pp. 73, 103; *The Adventure of Living* (*AL*) p. 219; *APY* pp. 85, 151.
79 *DC* pp. 209–214.
80 *GG* p. 112.
81 ibid., p. 202.
82 *MP* pp. 35–36.
83 *AL* pp. 212–215.
84 *AL* pp. 217–219.
85 *SW* p. 150; *DC* pp. 184–185; *MP* p. 166; Collins *Tournier* pp. 125–127.
86 *AL* p. 69.
87 Donald Capps *Biblical Approaches to Pastoral Counseling* pp. 30–32; Collins *Tournier* pp. 81, 93, 101.
88 Collins *Tournier* pp. 102, 198.

NOTES **441**

Chapter 14

1 Morton T. Kelsey *The Other Side of Silence: a guide to Christian Meditation* (SPCK 1977) pp. 136ff.

2 Books by these writers include: Victor White *God and the Unconscious* (The Harvill Press 1952); Thomas Merton *Contemplation in a World of Action* (Allen and Unwin 1971); H. A. Williams *Poverty, Chastity and Obedience: the true virtues* (Mitchell Beazley 1975); Henri J. M. Nouwen *Reaching Out: the three movements of the spiritual life* (Collins 1976); Catherine de Hueck Doherty *Poustinia: Christian spirituality of the East for Western man* (Collins 1977); and Martin Israel *The Spirit of Counsel: spiritual perspectives in the counselling process* (Hodder and Stoughton 1983).

3 Kenneth Leech *Soul Friend* pp. 100–121. See also Ian G. Williams 'Counselling and Spiritual Direction' in *Anvil* 1/3 (1984) pp. 219–230.

4 Introductions to Christopher Bryant *The River Within: the search for God in depth* (Darton, Longman and Todd 1973) and *Jung and the Christian Way* (DLT 1983); see also his *Depth Psychology and Religious Belief* (Mirfield Publications 1972) based on lectures given in 1968.

5 William Johnston *The Mirror Mind: spirituality and transformation* (Collins 1983) pp. 2–5.

6 See Kelsey *Silence* pp. 48, 85 and Kelsey *Christo-Psychology* (DLT 1983) Introduction and pp. 1–8, 146.

7 Evelyn Underhill *Mysticism* (Methuen and Co. 1926) p. x.

8 ibid., p. 86.

9 Kelsey *Silence* pp. 127–142.

10 Kelsey *Encounter with God: a theology of Christian experience* (Hodder and Stoughton 1974) pp. 51–60.

11 ibid., pp. 64ff.

12 Kelsey *Silence* p. 147.

13 ibid., p. 190.

14 Bryant *River* pp. 7–9.

15 Kelsey *Silence* pp. 11–12.

16 ibid., pp. 57–59.

17 Bryant *Jung* pp. 93–94.

18 Kelsey *Silence* p. 77.

19 Kelsey *Christo-Psychology* (CP) p. 57.

20 Bryant *River* pp. 74–75.

21 ibid., pp. 20–23.

22 Kelsey *CP* p. 53.

23 Kelsey *Silence* p. 40.

24 Bryant *Jung* p. vii; Kelsey *CP* p. 7.

25 Bryant *Jung* pp. 3–9.

26 Kelsey *CP* p. 121.

27 Bryant *River* pp. 12–13.

28 ibid., pp. 24–27.
29 Charles Rycroft *A Critical Dictionary of Psychoanalysis* (Penguin 1972) p. 9.
30 Kelsey *CP* pp. 131–136.
31 Kelsey *Silence* pp. 23–26; Barbara Kelsey in Kelsey *CP* pp. 68–90.
32 Johnston *Mirror Mind* p. 149; see, for example: C. G. Jung *Modern Man in Search of a Soul* (Routledge and Kegan Paul 1961) pp. 249–251.
33 Johnston, p. 5; see, more generally, pp. 2–23.
34 ibid., pp. 13–14.
35 ibid., pp. 20–22.
36 Bryant *Jung* p. 89.
37 Bryant *River* p. 29; and p. 43 where he quotes Galatians 2:20.
38 ibid., p. 112.
39 Kelsey *Silence* pp. 97–98.
40 Bryant *River* pp. 121, 143–144.
41 Kelsey *CP* pp. 137–138.
42 Bryant *River* p. 16.
43 Bryant *Jung* p. 44.
44 Bryant *River* pp. 43–44.
45 Bryant *Jung* pp. 94–95.
46 Johnston, pp. 31–37.
47 ibid., p. 37.
48 Kelsey *CP* pp. 58–64.
49 ibid., pp. 65–66.
50 William H. Shannon *Thomas Merton's Dark Path: the inner experience of a contemplative* (Farrar, Straus and Giroux 1981) p. 20.
51 Bryant *River* pp. 108–109.
52 ibid., pp. 88, 108–111.
53 ibid., pp. 112–114.
54 Johnston, pp. 50–53.
55 Kelsey *Silence* p. 56.
56 ibid., pp. 76–78.
57 Kelsey *CP* pp. 92–98.
58 ibid., pp. 99–106.
59 Kelsey *Silence* pp. 82–92.
60 ibid., pp. 93–108.
61 Kelsey *CP* p. 127; generally, pp. 120–130.
62 ibid., pp. 130–138.
63 Bryant *River* p. 87.
64 Kelsey *Silence* p. 225.
65 Jung *Memories, Dreams, Reflections* pp. 200–201.
66 Kelsey *CP* pp. 136–137.
67 Underhill *Mysticism* p. 84.
68 Christmas Humphreys *Buddhism* (Penguin 1962) p. 170.
69 Kelsey *Silence* p. 1.

Chapter 15

1 J. A. C. Brown *Freud and the Post-Freudians* pp. 52ff. and Paul Roazen *Freud and His Followers* pp. 389ff.
2 Arthur Janov *The Primal Scream* (Sphere 1973) pp. 221–248.
3 Janov *The Primal Revolution* (Sphere 1975) p. 24.
4 Janov *Scream* p. 9.
5 Janov *Revolution* p. 152.
6 Janov *Prisoners of Pain* (London: Sphere 1982) p. 9.
7 Janov *Scream* pp. 25–38.
8 Janov *Prisoners* p. 36.
9 Janov *Scream* pp. 83–95; *Revolution* pp. 214–225.
10 ibid., p. 226.
11 Janov *Prisoners* pp. 140–163.
12 Janov *Revolution* p. 239.
13 Ruth Carter Stapleton *The Experience of Inner Healing* (Hodder and Stoughton 1978) Introduction.
14 Stapleton *The Gift of Inner Healing* (Hodder and Stoughton 1977) pp. 78–82.
15 Christopher Bryant *The River Within* p. 39.
16 Ian Davidson 'Prayer Counselling' in *Contact* 1 (1978) pp. 38–40.
17 Louis Marteau 'Remembering Lake' in *Contact* 4 (1983) p. 11.
18 Brian Lake in *Contact* 4 (1983) p. 3; more generally, pp. 3–6; also Frank Lake *Clinical Theology: a theological and psychiatric basis to clinical pastoral care* (Darton, Longman and Todd 1966) pp. xvff.; Frank Lake *Tight Corners in Pastoral Counselling* (DLT 1981) pp. viiiff.
19 Frank Lake 'The Newer Therapies' in *Contact* 1 (1978) p. 6.
20 See Stanislav Grof *Realms of the Human Unconscious* (Dutton 1976).
21 Frank Lake 'Newer Therapies' pp. 14–20.
22 ibid., pp. 2, 11–13.
23 Colin Davison 'Re-evaluation Counselling' in *Contact* 1 (1978) pp. 33–37; private correspondence with Audrey Shilling; and Alexander A. J. Wedderburn 'Co-Counselling in a University Setting' in *The Proceedings of the British Student Health Association* July 1984 pp. 87–90.
24 Frank Lake *Tight Corners* p. 60.
25 Frank Lake 'The Theology of Pastoral Counselling' in *Contact* 3 (1980) p. 41.
26 *Tight Corners* p. 52.
27 'Theology' pp. 29ff.
28 'Theology' p. 1; also *Tight Corners* pp. 47–50.
29 'Theology' p. 11; *Tight Corners* pp. ix–x.
30 *Clinical Theology* p. 380.
31 ibid., p. 69.
32 ibid., pp. 766–772.
33 *Tight Corners* p. 41.

ROOTS AND SHOOTS

34 ibid., pp. 51–52.
35 *Clinical Theology* p. xvi.
36 ibid., p. 422.
37 ibid.
38 *Tight Corners* pp. 24–27.
39 *Clinical Theology* pp. 8–14; *Tight Corners* pp. 55–59.
40 ibid., pp. 93–97.
41 ibid., pp. 75–79.
42 'Newer Therapies' pp. 24–25.
43 *Tight Corners* pp. 26–28.
44 ibid., p. 175.
45 Kenneth McAll *Healing the Family Tree* (Sheldon Press 1982) pp. 2–4.
46 ibid., pp. 6–7, 53–58.
47 ibid., pp. 22–34.
48 ibid., pp. 88–97, 106.
49 Lake *Tight Corners* pp. 12–13.
50 ibid., pp. xv–xvi; 62–66.
51 ibid., p. 53.
52 See, for example, Lake 'Theology' p. 1.

Chapter 16

1 J. P. Chaplin *Dictionary of Psychology* (Dell Publishing 1975) p. 538.
2 *The Shorter Oxford English Dictionary*.
3 Edward J. Kissane *The Book of Isaiah* Vol. 1 (The Richview Press 1960) p. 106.
4 See Derek Kidner *Proverbs* pp. 36–37 and *NIDNTT* 3, p. 1027.
5 See David Carlson 'Relationship Counseling' in Gary R. Collins (ed.) *Helping People Grow* pp. 31ff. for an outline of his views on the roles of Jesus in relating to others. I am indebted to his seminal ideas. For an inspirational study of the Christ 'model' in counselling, particularly emphasising his 'Abba' relationship with the Father, see Duncan Buchanan *The Counselling of Jesus* (Hodder and Stoughton 1985).
6 Brown *NIDNTT* 3, p. 79; see also pp. 74–75.
7 On Jesus as prophet, see David Hill *New Testament Prophecy* (Marshall, Morgan and Scott 1979) pp. 48–69.
8 Luke 4:18,19; see also 3:21,22; 4:1–15.
9 *NIDNTT* 3, pp. 564ff.
10 ibid., p. 566.
11 ibid., pp. 37ff.
12 G. Kittel (ed.) *Theological Dictionary of the New Testament* (Eerdmans 1967) 5, pp. 800ff.
13 Kittel, p. 804.
14 Donald Capps *Biblical Approaches to Pastoral Counseling* p. 206.

15 H. G. Link on Origen in *NIDNTT* 3, p. 148.

16 *NIDNTT* 3, p. 212.

17 It is here that we will recall that both counsellor and client need the 'full armour of God' to withstand 'the devil's schemes' (Ephesians 6:11). We should pray for the Lord's discernment, particularly where a person seems bound by some intractable bad habit or attitude in spite of a longing for change. Such a situation *may* indicate the need for prayer for deliverance but such a ministry, to quote Francis MacNutt, should be exercised 'with great caution', since it is especially open to exhibitionism in the counsellor and to a damaging preoccupation with evil on the part of the client. See Francis MacNutt *Healing* (New York: Bantam Books 1977) pp. 189ff. and Richard F. Lovelace *Dynamics of Spiritual Life* pp. 140–144 for thoughtful accounts of this controversial ministry. Also see the series of articles on aspects of mental health and exorcism, including Montagu G. Barker 'Possession and the Occult: a psychiatrist's view', in *The Churchman* 94/3 (1980).

18 *NIDNTT* 1, pp. 185–187.

19 The 'prophetic' element in counselling has wider concepts than those of *noutheteo*, *chrematizo* and *epitimao*. The word *propheteuo*, to make prophetic revelations, to prophesy, is used in a number of contexts in the New Testament. Its function in the Corinthian church was to include exhorting, comforting, edifying and revealing what had been formerly hidden (see 1 Corinthians 14:3–5,19,22–25) – and, as such, may play a part in the counselling process; see C. H. Peisker in *NIDNTT* 3, pp. 81–84. As well as the gift of prophecy, the gifts of 'knowledge', 'wisdom' and 'discernment' may have relevance for counselling. Michael Green describes the gift of knowledge as a 'God-given disclosure of knowledge that could not normally be available to the recipient' – as we have seen in Christ's awareness that the woman at the well had five husbands. For further discussion on the gifts of prophecy, knowledge, wisdom and discernment, see Michael Green *I Believe in the Holy Spirit* (Hodder and Stoughton 1975) pp. 168–174, 181–192. For an important recent review of New Testament concepts of prophecy, see Max Turner 'Spiritual Gifts Then and Now' *Vox Evangelica* 15 (1985) pp. 7–64, especially pp. 11–16.

20 See Kittel 5, pp. 773ff. and *NIDNTT* 1, pp. 570–571.

21 Roger F. Hurding *As Trees Walking* pp. 228–229.

22 See Behm in Kittel 5, p. 804 and Braumann in *NIDNTT* 1, pp. 88, 91.

23 R. A. Lambourne *Community, Church and Healing* (DLT 1963) pp. 110–111.

INDEX OF BIBLICAL REFERENCES

GENERAL INDEX

Names of people are shown in bold print.